D0884475

AESTHETICS OF OPERA IN THE ANCIEN RÉGIME, 1647–1785

This is the first study to recognize the broad impact of opera in early-modern French culture. Downing A. Thomas considers the use of operatic spectacle and music by Louis XIV as a vehicle for absolutism, the resistance of music to the aesthetic and political agendas of the time, and the long-term development of opera in eighteenth-century humanist culture. He argues that French opera moved away from the politics of the absolute monarchy in which it originated to address Enlightenment concerns with sensibility and feeling. The book combines close readings of significant seventeenth-century and eighteenth-century operatic works, and circumstantial writings and theoretical works on theater and opera, together with a measure of reception history. Thomas examines key works by Lully, Rameau, and Charpentier, among others, and extends his reach from the late seventeenth century to the end of the eighteenth.

Downing A. Thomas is Associate Professor and Chair of the Department of French and Italian at the University of Iowa. He is the author of *Music and the Origins of Language: Theories from the French Enlightenment* (Cambridge, 1995), and co-editor of *Empire and Occupation in France and the Francophone Worlds*, a special issue of *Studies in Twentieth-Century Literature* (1999). He has also published numerous articles.

CAMBRIDGE STUDIES IN OPERA
Series editor: Arthur Groos

Volumes for *Cambridge Studies in Opera* explore the cultural, political
and social influences of the genre. As a cultural art form, opera is not
produced in a vacuum. Rather, it is influenced, whether directly or
in more subtle ways, by its social and political environment. In turn,
opera leaves its mark on society and contributes to shaping the cultural
climate. Studies to be included in the series will look at these various
relationships including the politics and economics of opera, the operatic
representation of women or the singers who portrayed them, the history
of opera as theater, and the evolution of the opera house.

Editorial Board
Tim Carter, *University of North Carolina, Chapel Hill*
John Deathridge, *King's College, University of London*
James Hepokoski, *University of Minnesota*
Paul Robinson, *Stanford University*
Ellen Rosand, *Yale University*

Already published

Opera Buffa in Mozart's Vienna
Edited by Mary Hunter and James Webster

Johann Strauss and Vienna: Operetta and the Politics of Popular Culture
Camille Crittenden

German Opera: From the Beginnings to Wagner
John Warrack

Opera and Drama in Eighteenth-Century London: The King's Theatre,
Garrick and the Business of Performance
Ian Woodfield

Opera, Liberalism, and Antisemitism in Nineteenth-Century France:
The Politics of Halévy's *La Juive*
Diana R. Hallman

Aesthetics of Opera in the Ancien Régime: 1647–1785
Downing A. Thomas

Aesthetics of Opera in the Ancien Régime, 1647–1785

Downing A. Thomas

CAMBRIDGE
UNIVERSITY PRESS

PUBLISHED BY THE PRESS SYNDICATE OF THE UNIVERSITY OF CAMBRIDGE
The Pitt Building, Trumpington Street, Cambridge, United Kingdom

CAMBRIDGE UNIVERSITY PRESS
The Edinburgh Building, Cambridge CB2 2RU, UK
40 West 20th Street, New York, NY 10011-4211, USA
477 Williamstown Road, Port Melbourne, VIC 3207, Australia
Ruiz de Alarcón 13, 28014 Madrid, Spain
Dock House, The Waterfront, Cape Town 8001, South Africa

http://www.cambridge.org

© Downing A. Thomas 2002

This book is in copyright. Subject to statutory exception
and to the provisions of relevant collective licensing agreements,
no reproduction of any part may take place without
the written permission of Cambridge University Press.

First published 2002

Printed in the United Kingdom at the University Press, Cambridge

Typeface Dante MT 10.75/14 pt   *System* LATEX 2$_\varepsilon$ [TB]

A catalogue record for this book is available from the British Library

Library of Congress Cataloguing in Publication data

Thomas, Downing A.
Aesthetics of opera in the Ancien Régime, 1647–1785 / Downing A. Thomas.
      p.   cm. – (Cambridge studies in opera)
Includes bibliographical references and index.
ISBN 0-521-80188-5
1. Opera – France – 17th century.   2. Opera – France – 18th century.
3. Music and state – France – History.   4. Enlightenment – France.
5. Music – France – Philosophy and aesthetics.   I. Title.   II. Series.
ML3858 .T46   2002
782.1′0944′09032–dc21   2002067211

ISBN 0 521 80188 5 hardback

WITHDRAWN
UTSA LIBRARIES

CONTENTS

ILLUSTRATIONS

Introduction

"Thus true philosophers go about their lives trying not to be taken in by what they see and attempting to guess at that which they cannot see . . . On this topic, I always imagine nature as a grand spectacle which resembles the opera. From where you are seated at the opera you do not see the stage exactly as it is: the decor and the machinery have been set up in order to produce a nice effect when seen from afar; and the pulleys and counterweights that produce all the scene changes have been shielded from view . . . But what complicates things for philosophers is that the cogs of the machines that nature presents to us are perfectly hidden."

Bernard le Bovier de Fontenelle[1]

Fontenelle's image of opera as a world and the world as opera serves as an inviting and appropriate opening to this study, given the culture in which early-modern French opera developed and flourished. First of all, there is the flirtatious setting, not unlike that of the eighteenth-century opera house, in which the marquise and her male interlocutor stroll beneath the evening sky as they discuss the universe which spreads out before them. The image aestheticizes the natural world, transforming it into a grand spectacle which is available for our contemplation and admiration, though not always for our close scrutiny. At the same time it urges us to consider the opera as a form of spectacle resulting from mechanisms existing behind or beyond that stage – a figure for the natural forces that ebb and flow beyond human control and even sometimes beyond perception, and of the possible connections between that world and the realm of the spectator's thoughts, desires, and passions. Within the context of the dialogues that make up the *Entretiens sur la pluralité des mondes*, opera serves as an apt metaphor for nature and for the power it wields across the boundaries that separate (and join) the natural and the human worlds.

The thematics of loss and recovery that shaped the very first operas derive their impact from the foundational quality, within early-modern culture, of these boundaries and connections. Loss and recovery figure prominently in the plots of many early operas; and, as a meta-narrative, they reflect the widespread conviction at the time that opera had reclaimed from antiquity a lost mode of representation. Alessandro Striggio's and Claudio Monteverdi's *Orfeo*, for example, places the story of Orpheus and Euridice within a self-reflexive frame, staging the renaissance and apotheosis of *la musica* as part and parcel of the presentation of their *favola in musica* and, by extension, of the emergence of the form itself around 1600. Euridice, bitten by a snake, is first lost to Hades, then brought back by Orpheus, whose voice has the power to move Proserpine to solicit her release. No sooner has she been liberated then Euridice disappears once more when Orpheus attempts to catch a glimpse of her as they return to the world of the living. With Apollo's intervention, however, Euridice does return, but only as a figure – a substitute for the original – in the sky. In the end, Orpheus can once again sing to Euridice who has been transfigured, transported to the heavens. *Orfeo* thus reflects upon its own coming-into-being as marking a dramatic and musical renaissance through the story of Euridice's passage from the underworld and of her transformation: like opera itself, Euridice is lost, then reborn. Moreover, music is presented as a form of mourning and as a "magical" commemoration, since it brings about the rebirth of this story and by extension that of a particular kind of dramatic representation, previously known only to ancient Greece. Music is shown to exert a special force over inanimate objects, and over mortal and immortal beings; and Striggio's story and Monteverdi's music have the power to evoke Euridice's presence once again just as they re-animate a lost form. If Fontenelle set nature in relation to the human through the image of a grand spectacle, similarly *Orfeo* articulated a connection between the human realm and the world beyond that realm through the powers of *favola in musica*. The issues of loss and of power and powerlessness, and the musico-dramatic articulation of human feeling and cosmic forces, structure not only those operas based on the Orpheus myth such as Francesco Buti's and Luigi Rossi's *Orfeo* (1647) – among the first operas performed in France, to be discussed in chapter 1 – but also Jean-Baptiste Lully's foundational *tragédies en musique*, many of the stage works that took Lully's creations as models, and the eighteenth-century operatic works that otherwise self-consciously set themselves apart from that tradition.

Complex links between opera and power, or powerlessness, were discerned by early-modern spectators and commentators, and represented or enacted on stage in performance. Early opera depicted natural, political, and human forces on stage; it was understood to exert a powerful influence on the listener-spectator; and its musical, textual, and theatrical dimensions represented and enacted relationships between gods and mortals, kings and subjects, and individuals and social groups. Much of opera's identity in this respect can be un derstood to derive from the particular virtues that were associated with the singing voice. The *seconda pratica* of the opera composers and their predecessors was intended to foreground the words uttered by the voice and to restore ancient Greek forms and the values associated with them. Though late Renaissance theorists such as Girolamo Mei and Vicenzo Galilei argued that the music of ancient tragedy was exclusively monodic, and based their sense of the power of ancient music on this assumption, the emphasis placed on the singular line of the voice carried over into discussions of opera. Furthermore, the Florentine Camarata's formal innovations, and in particular the notion of *recitar cantando*, were understood to constitute in some measure a resuscitation of ancient practices. For the very reason that the first operas adopted loss and recovery as the basis for the stories they told, they also gave the impression that they constituted a revival of ancient drama and therefore possessed a certain power over loss. Renaissance theorists had recreated or recovered a lost form; and they hoped to regain the magical power of this lost form. Later, in the very different cultural context of the French eighteenth century, the fascination with aboriginal speech as undifferentiated voice tended to frame opera as a phantasmatic version of an original human lyricism. In both instances, opera was associated with the origins of humanity and of human expression. Because early opera is in this sense about the invention or recovery of an imaginary object, its performance is also touched by this recovery and by its presumed fundamental or primordial calling.

If opera deals with the loss of objects and the phantasmatic erasure of that loss, it also necessarily invokes at some level a loss on the part of the spectator, notably a loss of self – a moment in which the spectator is made to lose his or her usual bearings, is moved, troubled, estranged, or exposed.[2] At once derived from its Italian predecessors and native to French soil, the *tragédie en musique* carried with it many of these meanings and functions as it evolved in the particular cultural climate of late seventeenth-century and eighteenth-century France. By taking early French opera as my focus, I hope to elucidate the historical and cultural specificity of these circumstances at a time when a unified "Europe" did not truly exist as such and when individual national traditions were being defined in relation to and against each other.

My study, a cultural history of French opera up to the Revolution, rests on two basic assumptions. First, that individual operas not only display traces of the aesthetic and ideological circumstances of their creation, but that they also engage productively in those circumstances. Second, that opera came to serve as a touchstone in the eighteenth century for understanding the mechanisms behind human feeling and for reflecting upon how emotion impacts social relations. Because opera found itself out of sync within the aesthetic discourses of early-modern France, a number of incongruities resulted, both ideological and aesthetic. At its inception, *tragédie en musique* served to showcase the glory of the monarch; yet at the same time, as individual operas, it often tends to undermine the supposed self-sufficiency and integrity of the hero and of his theatrical genre (tragedy). In so doing, opera reveals problems inherent in the representation of the king on the lyric stage. Another disparity involves the relationship of music to words. Though libretti clearly must remain central to any consideration of opera, music nonetheless comes to be foregrounded to an unprecedented degree in a genre that was initially centered on the absolute primacy of the word. One could say that *tragédie en musique*, as tragedy in music, was reshaped in profound ways through the very process in which it emerged and developed in France through the eighteenth century. Opera in general and individual works in particular functioned as lightning rods for the heated debate on music and shaped that debate in important ways. Insofar as opera gave increasing attention to feeling, it prompted discussion and reconsideration of French culture's foremost values, insofar as they were embodied in the theater.

If I had to identify the fault line or epicenter of this project, it would be the abbé Jean Terrasson's prescient claim, made in 1715, that the dramatic elements of opera functioned as backdrop for the presentation of music. Terrasson asserted, contrary to all accepted views of opera at the time, that the music, which was understood at the time as entirely secondary to the moral framework of the art, was its central feature. This remarkable assertion signals a significant change. In proposing to examine French opera and reflections on opera from 1647 to 1785, I will give attention to the ways in which individual works can be understood to participate in a shift in the status of opera within French culture, from an uneasy absolutist vehicle and foil to spoken tragedy in the late seventeenth century, to a spectacle that had turned away from the moral aims of tragedy to embrace new concerns with sensibility and feeling. Whereas recent scholarship has examined the larger cultural and political significance of later opera in France, these dimensions of the earlier periods remain underexplored.[3] In a rich, exceptionally useful and well-documented study, Catherine Kintzler has reconstructed the literary foundations – the "poetics" – that sustained early French opera.[4] Kintzler's study is based on the hypothesis that opera in France from the 1670s through the mid-eighteenth century is a product of the neoclassical aesthetic (*"l'esthétique classique"*) which shaped the works of dramatists such as Pierre Corneille; and her arguments are admirably and exhaustively made.[5] However, in part because the object of her study is to reconstruct with full historical hindsight a poetics of opera which was never fully articulated at the time, Kintzler does not sufficiently address the many ways in which the operatic works themselves take their distance from the values that are embedded in those literary foundations.

Other scholars have sought to link opera to the rise of aesthetics in the eighteenth century. Peter Kivy, for example, has argued that eighteenth-century opera was shaped by a conflict between purely musical concerns and the contemporaneous urge to understand theater as a representation, as mimetic.[6] Up to a certain point, my argument runs parallel to that of Kivy; for I see the emergent aesthetics of the eighteenth century as a rich ground for understanding the contemporaneous musical culture. In ways similar to Kivy, taking a certain distance from Kintzler's approach, I argue that opera is non-coincident with the poetic models with which contemporary commentators sought to explain it; yet, differing in this respect from Kivy, I do not claim that music is entirely incompatible with them. Instead of looking at the rise of instrumental music as evidence of a radical shift to a non-mimetic theory of the arts, I propose to examine the development of opera as coincidental with, even implicated in, the development of an aesthetic discourse that is, on the contrary, thoroughly invested in a certain understanding of mimesis. My larger claim, then, is that the urge to see opera as upholding literary and moral values was increasingly undermined by the fact that these meanings were often framed as secondary (as Terrasson argued), or bypassed, ignored, or consumed by the music. It is not that music somehow moves "beyond" narrative, linguistic, or moral frames, or is always in opposition to them; but rather that in opera music puts a particular spin on those structures and values, alters, or transforms them. By examining a handful of significant seventeenth- and eighteenth-century operatic works, in tandem with the theoretical, political, cultural, and aesthetic contexts of their creation, I propose a brief cultural history of opera in early-modern France constructed through specific flashpoints and issues explored in detail rather than through a comprehensive survey. My study therefore combines close readings of specific operas, circumstantial writings and theoretical works on theater and opera, together with a measure of reception history. Where the documentation was available, and where they were pertinent to my arguments, I have also discussed variants in order to be able to understand the ways in which works were adapted to new circumstances and how audiences reacted to the changes. Given that complete recordings of many operas of this period have only recently become available, it is an apt time to consider in more depth the ways in which they fit into their historical and cultural contexts.

The first part examines French opera in the shadow of seventeenth-century spoken tragedy – identified at the time as unparalleled, the pinnacle of theatrical history – and of the dramatic theory that underlay tragedy. I trace the development of opera from its earliest days in France to 1733 in order to reveal the ways in which the new genre transformed conceptions of tragedy and of its effects on the spectator. The first chapter outlines the emergence of opera in seventeenth-century France and the issues that it raised for spectators and commentators. From its beginnings in the early 1670s with the works of Jean-Baptiste Lully and Philippe Quinault, French opera (termed *tragédie en musique*) was modeled on contemporary spoken tragedy. The literary credentials that this model provided, however, worked both in favor of *tragédie en musique* and against it. Some sensed the mythical presence of ancient Greek theater in opera; yet, because it incorporated the supposedly vacuous pleasures of music and spectacle, opera was also attacked as a moral danger and as having precipitated the demise of tragedy. In chapter 1, through an analysis of Buti's and Rossi's *Orfeo*, I return to the inaugural moment of opera in France to examine the ways in which the Italian import tested the limits of contemporary aesthetic assumptions from its very first appearance on French soil. I analyze the ways in which *Orfeo* frames song as performance not only by examining the important difference between speech and song, but also by revealing how the opera problematizes the distinction between story and performance – a distinction that was crucial to seventeenth-century views of tragedy, such as those of the influential abbé d'Aubignac, and which was designed to erect a firewall between the moral values conveyed by the story and the questionable pleasures of the spectacle. At a time when music was understood to be secondary to the mimetic and moral concerns of theater, opera tended to dismantle the distinction between music as diegetic (story-telling) and music as extradiegetic (decoration, arabesque). The first theorist to recognize and embrace this tendency in opera was the abbé Terrasson. Pointing away from the usual concerns with opera as a form of tragedy, Terrasson questioned the traditional hierarchy of genres, thereby revealing their ultimate relativity, and drew attention to the music and the spectacle that provided enjoyment for all kinds of spectators.

Chapter 2 explores the political dimensions of early French opera by examining the strategies developed by Louis XIV's ministers to represent the king through allegory. After reviewing the various ways in which the king was represented allegorically (as Apollo, for example, or as a Roman hero), I examine the opera prologue as a representation of the king. Given the difficulties that Louis XIV's advisors saw in other forms of representation (architectural monuments, painting, history, epic), the explicit references to and praise of the king in the opera prologue can be understood as fulfilling a political need by portraying him to the court and to the nation. The mythical relationship between opera and the Greek models it supposedly embodied, and the political image of the monarch as consummate ruler, go hand in hand. Yet, when one moves beyond the prologue into the body of the opera, a noticeable gap appears between the unsurpassed hero depicted in the prologue and the dubious heroic figures represented in the opera. This gap, I argue, is indicative of the precarious position that opera occupied in early-modern French culture.

Each of the three subsequent chapters of this section focuses on individual operas in order to explore the ways in which particular composers and librettists engaged, through their works, the cultural meanings and aesthetic debates surrounding opera. Early French opera placed more emphasis on spectacle than any other dramatic idiom of the time. This emphasis was criticized as appealing exclusively to the senses, drawing spectators away from the attention spoken theater gave to catharsis and moral redemption. In Quinault's and Lully's *Armide* (1686), the focus of chapter 3, we witness an effort to define early French *tragédie en musique* as a viable alternative to its spoken counterpart. A detailed reading suggests that by directing attention away from the hero, Renaud, and toward the music and its ability to evoke Armide's passion, librettist and composer sought to carve out a distinct space for opera within the literary culture of late seventeenth-century France.

By focusing attention on the sublime effects of music and the voice, *Armide* put into question the critical standards by which opera was judged at the same time that it suggested how opera might live up to its name as tragedy.

If *Armide* can be understood as an attempt to reinstate opera as a viable parallel to spoken theater, Thomas Corneille's and Marc-Antoine Charpentier's *Médée* (1693) blatantly embodied the foreignness of the lyric theater in relation to seventeenth-century tragedy. Chapter 4 centers on this work which highlights the gap separating tragedy and *tragédie en musique* while at the same time framing the conflictual relationship between French *tragédie en musique* in the Lullian model and Italian musical influences, whether real or perceived. Charpentier emphasized this second conflict by making the music Medea sings alien to the French vocal tradition. By producing a discrepancy within the musical fabric itself through his use of dissonance and by opposing the French and Italian styles, Charpentier's compositional practice rehearses an aesthetic departure in which opera would no longer be merely tragedy set to music. Charpentier frames the musical voice of Medea as excessive, even for opera, as a series of utterances that undermine any possible reconciliation between opera and spoken tragedy. I argue that *Médée* presents and embodies this conflict through the way in which Medea's voice is treated in a field of other incongruous and irreconcilable musical utterances.

Chapter 5, the final chapter of the first part, focuses on *Hippolyte et Aricie* (1733) by the abbé Simon Joseph Pellegrin and Jean-Philippe Rameau. Seen as an audacious rewriting of Jean Racine's by-then canonical tragedy, *Phèdre* (1677), *Hippolyte et Aricie* pushes opera's relation to so-called "regular" tragedy even further than the two previously examined works. As Rameau's first opera, *Hippolyte et Aricie* can be read as a response to Racine and a commentary on the situation of the lyric theater after Racine, framing opera as the ruin or reincarnation of a moribund genre. I argue that Rameau's work could only succeed by simultaneously embodying and erasing *Phèdre*. In his commentaries on *Hippolyte et Aricie*, Rameau described the effects he sought to provoke in the listener-spectator by using particularly unusual musical resources (such as the enharmonic genre). By proposing "horror" instead of "terror" – two highly coded words in early-modern poetic theory – Rameau forced the issue of the spectator's physical presence in a way music had never explicitly done before in opera, moving away from the Aristotelian framework of catharsis that defined the purpose of tragedy. In this way, *Hippolyte et Aricie* can be seen as fulfilling Terrasson's visionary remarks. Opera, it turned out, was not tragedy in music at all, but rather a new genre based on a new aesthetic whose foundation was music.

As the cultural issues surrounding opera shifted during the course of the eighteenth century, the question of opera's relationship to the spoken genres came to be seen in a substantially different light, illuminated by questions that were central to the *philosophes* and their contemporaries. In contrast with the first part of this book, though it does include analyses of individual operas, the second part explores the operatic work often indirectly through writings as diverse as theories of musical affect, architectural projects, and the operatic fantasies of a naturalist. Here, I will examine opera as a barometer of Enlightenment by exploring the interface between the culture of opera in the eighteenth century and the then burning question of the existence of a common moral fabric of humanity. If music was at the center of operatic experience (as many argued, following Terrasson's lead), and if music had at best questionable mimetic capabilities (one of the key objections of opera's detractors all along, mimesis being the traditional moral measure of artistic value), on what moral compass could opera rely? Taking enduring notions of music's relationship to forms of passion and ecstasy as points of departure, chapter 6 reinterprets the question of mimesis by arguing that longstanding beliefs in the magical powers of music were transformed in the early eighteenth century by a newly formed sensationist discourse. In the view of many commentators of the period, the common ground of operatic representation was not merely the *muthos*, or story, that it conveyed; more importantly, what was shared in the lyric theater was the experience of being touched or "transported" by music, which, as I argue, may be understood as a form of mimesis. Whereas Renaissance theoreticians believed that music had occult properties which endowed it with an ability to affect the body and soul in certain ways, eighteenth-century writers saw in music a form of therapy and a catalyst for sympathy – a trigger for a deep-seated intersubjectivity. This latter view was based on new directions in eighteenth-century philosophy and medicine. Recent scholarship has established close parallels between medical theory and experimentation in the area of sensation, on the one hand, and the literary and dramatic focus on sensibility, on the other.[7] The tapping of sensation was thought to lead, ultimately, to a truer, deeper understanding of the moral and physical character of humanity. Medical treatises written by doctors associated with the Montpellier school of medicine, such as Claude-Nicolas Le Cat and Joseph-Louis Roger, privileged musical sound in their models of human sensibility. By charting a course through early-modern speculations on music, and its relation to the listener's body and mind, I propose a more ample understanding of the ways in which eighteenth-century writers and composers attributed to music in general, and to opera in particular, the power to create sympathetic responses in the listener-spectator.

Chapter 7 pursues the importance of sympathy and identification through the development of the new *opéra comique*, exploring what Gary Tomlinson has described as a naturalization of musical magic.[8] Framing the question through the contemporary lenses of moral philosophy and dramatic theory, I argue that sympathy – as a theme, certainly, but more importantly as an integral aspect of the cultural meaning and function of the lyric theater – was integral to the new genre because it was perceived to cement each spectator's participation in values and beliefs that were central to Enlightenment culture. Composers and librettists such as Michel-Jean Sedaine, François-André Danican Philidor, Jean-François Marmontel, and André-Ernest-Modeste Grétry wrote *opéras comiques* in which the function and value of music were brought to the fore, giving shape to the stories these works told, and accentuating the affective dimension of spectatorship and, by extension, that of the social bond itself. By juxtaposing the links between opera and the medical models of sensibility explored in the previous chapter through an examination of scenes of sympathy in several *opéras comiques*, we can gauge the degree to which consideration of the power of music remained a constant source of fascination and of anxiety within the specific cultural framework of eighteenth-century France.

In chapter 8, I argue that the institution founded by Lully – the Académie Royale de Musique – was not immune from the changes that were taking place at a much more rapid pace in the more marginal theaters where eighteenth-century spectators flocked to see *opéras comiques*. By examining Charles-Nicolas Cochin's *Lettres sur l'opéra* (1781) in relation to other proposals for a new opera house following the fires that destroyed two earlier structures, I assess the ways in which architects and planners sought to highlight a self-reflexive public space by inviting spectator feeling and facilitating identification. The projects of Cochin in particular elicit intervisibility and intercommunication among spectators by shaping the ways in which they approached the opera house, entered, and were placed in relation to the stage and to each other. Unlike Louis-Étienne Boullée's proposal, for example, Cochin's design articulates the stage with the building to optimize the spectator's affective experiences while at the same time demonstrating a concern for ease of movement and safety. I see the *Lettres sur l'opéra* as crystallizing Enlightenment ideals about the affective connections that brought groups of spectators together and about the articulation of different public spaces.

The final chapter centers on Bernard Germain de Lacépède's authoritative *Poétique de la musique* (1785) and its account of several operas or operatic texts: Pietro Metastasio's *Ciro riconosciuto*, two versions of *Iphigénie en Tauride*, and *Alcyone* by Houdar de la Motte and Marin Marais. Lacépède highlights the identificatory power of song through operas that focus on sympathy. Following in the footsteps of writers such as Étienne Bonnot de Condillac and Jean-Jacques Rousseau, Lacépède's first chapter tells the story of the origin of humanity, focusing on the emergence of intersubjectivity through a narrative in which the first man and the first woman engage in their world through song and emotion. For Lacépède, these primeval moments are ones that we perpetually re-enact; and the act of listening to music in the opera house is inextricably linked to them. Lacépède supports his claims through analyses of specific operas. By resuscitating the presumably hidden foundation of humanity, opera accomplishes something other cultural forms cannot, according to Lacépède, recalling and commemorating foundational human moments to which we no longer otherwise have access. Opera has the ability to evoke the origins of human feeling through the experience of the listener-spectator. The model of spectatorship advanced by his *Poétique de la musique* therefore returns us to the question of a common humanity with which this section of the book began. For, in the ideal terms of Lacépède's treatise, the experience of the opera spectator verifies the ultimate exchangeability or translatability of human feeling on which Enlightenment epistemology and, to an even greater degree, aesthetics were based.

I have incurred many debts during the writing of this book. Warm thanks go to all those who took the time to read and comment on early drafts, encouraged me along the way, or lent their expertise to answering questions and resolving problems: Antonia Banducci, Gregory Barnett, Geoffrey Burgess, Thomas Christensen, Charles Dill, Sarah Farmer, David Gompper, Jeffrey Ravel, Sophie Rosenfeld, Pierre Saint-Amand, Harriet Stone, and Guenter Zoeller. I would like to recognize support received from the National Endowment for the Humanities which provided time for sustained work in the archives during summer, 1997. The American Society for Eighteenth-Century Studies/McMaster University Library Fellowship I received in 1998 greatly advanced work on the manuscript, as did Charlotte Stewart, Carl Spadoni, Eden McLean, and the expert archivists and gracious staff of the William Ready Division of Archives and Research Collections at McMaster University. The University of Iowa provided support in 1997 and again in 2000, allowing me to travel to Paris to tie up bibliographic loose ends and giving me the computing power to bring the manuscript to completion. I am grateful to the staff of the Music Library at the University of California, Berkeley, for very liberal access to scores, and to Ruthann McTyre, Music Librarian, and Susan Malecki for their assistance with the small but key store of French materials in the Rita Benton Music Library at the University of Iowa.

Capable research assistants Steven Hartlaub, Sophie Watt and Janet Leavens helped at many stages; and Janet Leavens deserves additional accolades for working through the arcane details of music notation software. I am also grateful to the anonymous readers who helped me revise the book with their expert criticism, and to Victoria Cooper for her encouragement and skillful editorship. Dina Blanc and Kevin Kopelson accompanied the writing of this book from beginning to end.

I would like to thank the following libraries or collections for their permission to use the images reproduced in this book: the Biblio-thèque-Musée de la Comédie-Française; the Bibliothèque nationale de France; the Réunion des Musées Nationaux; Special Collections Department, University of Iowa Libraries, Iowa City, Iowa; and the Special Collections Library, University of Michigan.

Earlier versions of chapters 3, 5, and 8 were published, respectively, in *Theatre Journal* (vol. 49, no. 2), *L'Esprit Créateur* (vol. 38, no. 2), and *Representations* (no. 52). I acknowledge The Johns Hopkins University Press, the University of Kentucky, and The Regents of the University of California (by permission of the University of California Press) for kindly granting authorization to reproduce that material here. All translations are my own unless otherwise noted.

Part I | French opera in the shadow of tragedy

1 | Song as performance and the emergence of French opera

Though French opera utterly transformed its remote Italian cousin to suit indigenous cultural and aesthetic exigencies, Italian opera continued to loom over the newly minted French genre. Aesthetic conflict melded with political tensions to make French opera highly contested in its infancy. In Italy, opera emerged as the imaginary restoration of ancient tragedy, and at the same time as a strong bid for the superiority of modern music through its *stile rappresentativo* and the text-centered compositional usages of the *seconda pratica* on which it was based. It offered sovereigns grand spectacles with which they could celebrate important marriages and victories, and stage their power and influence as permanent and timeless. Brought to France, opera continued to benefit from its Greek pedigree and from the lure of the modern; and it continued to be used as a form of political display to further the aims of the sovereign. Ever since the days of Catarina de' Medici, however, though Italian actors and singers were welcome at court they were treated as pariahs by the French public. As one can see from the many disparaging references to opera in the *Mazarinades*, the barrage of writings against Cardinal Mazarin emanating from the civil war known as the Fronde, in its early days in France opera retained a degree of association with things Italian and with the memory of aristocratic recrimination against the monarchy.[1] The development of *tragédie en musique* generated intense discord within the aesthetic discourse generally referred to as neoclassicism because French opera was seen as a bastardized or corrupt form of tragedy. As such, it became an instrumental force in the skirmishes that finally erupted as the Quarrel of the Ancients and the Moderns in 1687. When the first French opera, Pierre Perrin's *Pomone*, opened on March 3, 1671, at the Guénégaud theatre – a modified tennis court known as La Bouteille in the rue des Fossés de Nesle (now rue Mazarine) – opera was already implicated in a series of interlocked cultural problems and conflicts, at once aesthetic and political.[2]

Jules Cardinal Mazarin, first minister under the regency of Anne of Austria, brought Italian opera to Paris in the mid-1640s, importing or commissioning works by Venetian and Roman composers. Francesco Sacrati's *La Finta pazza* was given at the Petit Bourbon in December, 1645; Francesco Cavalli's *Egisteo* came to the Paris stage in 1646, his *Xerse* in 1660, and his *Ercole amante* was performed at the Tuileries in 1662, the year following Mazarin's death; Carlo Caproli's *Le Nozze di Peleo e di Teti* premiered in 1654; Luigi Rossi's *Orfeo* opened at the Palais Royal in 1647 with the eight-year-old Louis XIV and the young Charles II of England in attendance.[3] Giacomo Torelli's machines and stage effects entranced the French courtiers. Torelli, according to Prunières, was referred to as "le grand sorcier."[4] Parisian accounts of Sacrati's *La Finta pazza*, a Venetian opera on a libretto by Giulio Strozzi which Ellen Rosand characterizes as "the first operatic hit," are particularly striking in their insistence on the effects of Torelli's machines: "the entire audience was no less enthralled by the poetry and the music than it was by the stage decoration, the ingeniousness of the machines and of the admirable scene changes, until now unknown in France and which captivate the eyes of the mind no less than those of the body through imperceptible movements."[5] The poet François Maynard dedicated to Mazarin a sonnet on these special effects:

> Jule, nos curieux ne peuvent conçevoir
> Les subits changemens de la nouvelle scene.
> Sans effort, & sans temps, l'art qui l'a fait mouvoir,
> D'un bois fait une ville, & d'un mont une plene.
>
> Il change un antre obscur en un palais doré;
> Où les poissons nageoient, il fait naistre les rozes!
> Quel siecle fabuleux a jamais admiré,
> En si peu de momens tant de metamorphozes?
>
> Ces diverses beautés sont les charmes des yeux.
> Elles ont puissâment touché nos demy-Dieux,
> Et le peuple surpris s'en est fait idolâtre.

Mais si par tes conseils tu r'amenes la paix
Et que cette Deesse honore le Theâtre,
Fay qu'il demeure ferme, & ne change jamais.

Jules, the curious cannot conceive
The sudden [scene] changes of the new theater.
Effortlessly and in an instant, the art that moves it
From a wood makes a city, and from a mountain a plain.

It changes a dark cavern into a golden palace;
Where fish once swam it produces roses!
What fabulous century has ever admired
In so few moments so many metamorphoses?

These diverse beauties charm the eyes.
They have powerfully touched our demi-Gods,
And the amazed public worships them.

But if by your counsel you restore peace
And this Goddess honors the theater,
Pray that it remains firm and never changes.[6]

Written near the end of the Thirty Years' War, when conflict with Spain remained a constant backdrop, Maynard's sonnet skillfully praises Mazarin along with the marvelous theatrical transformations made possible by Torelli's engineering. The spectators – both of royal blood ("nos demy-Dieux") and of less dignified extraction – admired and were transfixed by the effects they witnessed. Similarly, the larger public which could not have actually attended the opera ("le peuple") is said to have delighted in what they heard of these effects. The final stanza abruptly shifts perspective, mimicking the swift transformations of Torelli's machines ("Où les poissons nageoient, il fait naistre les rozes!"), to foreground the ongoing European conflicts of the 1640s. The magic of the stage suddenly vanishes to reveal the potential effects of Mazarin's resourceful diplomacy. In the imagination of the poet, the stunning instability of the stage gives way to an even more impressive, and more lasting, peace.

However different they were in formal and aesthetic terms, the Italian operas imported or commissioned by Mazarin were important precursors for the genre that emerged in France during the early 1670s.

Responses to them likewise prefigured aspects of the reaction to *tragédie en musique*. I want to consider in this light *L'Orfeo*, termed a *tragicomedia per musica*, that Francesco Buti and Luigi Rossi created for Mazarin in 1647. In a sonnet to Rossi ("Monsieur de Luiggy"), Charles Coypeau d'Assoucy writes above all of the sensuality of the opera:

> Ange qui nous ravis Dieu de la Simphonie,
> Pere des doux accords dont les inventions,
> Font gouster à nos sens tendres aux passions,
> Des delices du Ciel la douceur infinie.

> Angel who ravishes us, God of music,
> Father of the gentle chords whose inventions
> Give our senses, susceptible to passions, a taste
> of the infinite sweetness of heavenly delights.[7]

Coypeau's sonnet goes so far as to make of Rossi's music a foretaste of heavenly delights. In its praise, however, Renaudot's *Gazette* revealed the potential ambivalence that lay behind this sensuality. The *Gazette* commented on the "perpetual ravishment of the spectators," and "the grace and harmonious voices" of the singers and "the magnificence of their costumes," while attempting nonetheless to shore up the questionable morality of the spectacle, affirming that "virtue always wins out over vice."[8] The Parfaict brothers later noted the mixed reception *Orfeo* received: "this dramatic poem, which was even more well attended than the precedent [*La Finta pazza*] for the beauty of the voices, the variety of the airs, the scene changes, and the magnificence of the costumes, was nonetheless criticized *for the bizarre storyline, the useless proliferation of events, and the singular character of its music*."[9] Taken together, these comments point to issues – the sensual deluge, the questionable poetic construction – that return later in the quarrels surrounding French opera. *Orfeo* also figured prominently in the many political recriminations against Mazarin. Rossi had to bring a veritable army to Paris for the performance, and the expense of the opera was a recurrent source of hostility against Italian opera generally and against Mazarin, hostility which focused at times on the Cardinal's extravagance and at other times on the opera's perceived shortcomings (such as its inclusion of castrati, who were constantly reviled by the French public) and its immorality.[10]

Orfeo's focus on song as performance – song that is explicitly or implicitly identified as such by the operatic characters – can be said to resonate in particularly important ways with aspects of the future *tragédie en musique*. This self-reflexivity relates less to specific musical structures or forms per se, than it does to a way of framing music within opera, of determining where and how music belongs. The use of song as performance is not the only link to *tragédie en musique*; nor is this aspect of early Italian opera unique to *Orfeo*. There are a number of other connections between *Orfeo* and later French opera: notably, the sleep scene in act 2, scene 9, which returns as a virtually required element in the Lullian *tragédie en musique*, and the astounding music of the Chorus of Graces ("Dormite, begl'occhi, dormite" [Sleep, beautiful

Example 1: "Dormite begli occhi"

Example 1: *(cont.)*

eyes, sleep]) which lulls Euridice into slumber, prefiguring the way in which Lully used the sleep scene to lavish attention on the music and produce impressive ensemble numbers, as he did, for example, in *Atys* and *Armide* (see example 1). The specific argument I advance here, however, is that song as performance in *Orfeo* points to uncertainties that opera provoked in theorists and commentators in France over the

Example 1: *(cont.)*

next several decades regarding the aesthetic and moral foundations of the genre.

Ellen Rosand has argued that songs in *dramma per musica* tested the limits of verisimilitude, requiring composers to frame them within "situations in which singing was either natural or purposely unnatural," such as musical scenes, moments of madness, or other extraordinary situations.[11] This usage holds, Rosand points out, even after the formal aria had been fully accepted after mid-century. She summarizes the situation by noting that songs therefore "acquired a special significance within the context of opera as a kind of test of the basic premise of the genre: the distinction between speech and song."[12] Rossi's *Orfeo*, too, repeatedly probes this distinction. Before presenting Euridice with an ominous vision of her future marriage to Orfeo, a vision in which she sees two turtledoves carried off by black vultures, an Augur introduces a chorus of fellow fortune-tellers, suggesting that they can summon the turtledoves only by imitating their songs: "Ma sol da questa parte / invitiamo con canti / i più miti volanti" [But only from this region shall we invite with songs the gentlest birds].[13] Here, the song of the chorus becomes plausible as a form of solicitation, one which must deviate from ordinary speech in order to elicit the cooperation of creatures who communicate in another "language." Later in the act, Euridice suggests that she, her father, and her nurse sing the song whose title is "Al fulgor" [In the brightness] while they make their way to the wedding (1:27). In this case, song is naturalized as a way to pass the time: the actors sing because the characters would be expected to sing in this circumstance (see example 2). In scene 3, Aristeo – Orfeo's rival – and a Satyr exchange opposing views on jealousy by quoting lyrics that are said to come from popular songs. Aristeo says, "Non rammenti quei carmi?" [Do you not remember those verses?], before launching into a canzonetta on the torments of jealousy. The Satyr counters with another song, "Mi piaccion più quegli altri" [These other verses are more to my liking], in order to take an opposing position in the argument: "Che m'importa?" [What's it to me?], he sings, why should I be unhappy about another man's happiness (1:40)? Here the song's verses are cited by the characters who are therefore permitted to sing them. In act 2, song becomes a cover for Aristeo and Venere who, disguised as an old woman, has promised to help him in his bid for Euridice's hand in marriage. When Euridice and her Nurse appear, the "Old Woman" whispers to Aristeo: "Fingerò d'insegnarti / quella bella canzon sopra la speme" [I shall pretend to be teaching you that lovely song about Hope] (II:74). As for Orfeo himself, because he must "sing his way into Hades," as Ellen Rosand has remarked, his songs are integrated into the drama as its very premise.[14] Song in

Example 2: "Al fugor"

Orfeo becomes increasingly naturalized as the plot moves into the netherworld where gods and goddesses can speak in otherworldly tones, and particularly at the conclusion where a heavenly chorus sings and the harmonies of Orfeo's lyre overtake the world, thereby making the difference between song and speech, in a sense, irrelevant.

Another wrinkle within the question of verisimilitude in song as performance – one which Rosand does not consider and which moves beyond the strict concern with the seamlessness of appearances on stage – involves larger questions of musical and dramatic rhetoric and truth. There are several reasons, of course, that make Ottavio Rinuccini's and Jacopo Peri's opera on the subject of Orpheus's descent, or that of Alessandro Striggio and Claudio Monteverdi, the epitome of opera: the identification of music with grief, the attempted resurrection of a lost loved one (in part, at least, as the figure of ancient tragedy), and, in the case of the latter opera, the apotheosis of music as Orpheus ascends to the heavens.[15] In the *Orfeo* of Buti and Rossi, however, when operatic characters make statements such as "now let's sing," or "listen to this song," they specifically draw attention to the musical rhetoric that is at the heart of the Orpheus myth as the original operatic fiction. In other words, they emphasize the fact that the story hinges on Orpheus's ability to persuade and seduce listeners through his art. This focus on the performance of song allowed Rossi to frame Orfeo as a convincing and successful performer and Aristeo as an unconvincing and therefore unsuccessful one. Because song is so often staged as song – in other words, as a performance – it elicits a particular form of attention on the part of the audience. Song may indeed be naturalized as the expression of pastoral idleness, or as celebration; yet it is also framed as an extraordinary and expressive moment, as a moment of transcendence in which the acts of singing and listening stand out (see example 3). As such, it draws attention to such moments as either authentic or inauthentic, furthermore highlighting them as specifically musical. Song may be introduced with careful consideration for the verisimilitude of musical interventions within drama, yet Rossi presents singing in such as way as to make the truth of expression itself an issue in the relationship between singer and listener. Because

Example 3: "O tu non sai"

song is so often staged as performance in *Orfeo*, Orfeo's and Euridice's act 1 duets, which are not marked in this way, are made all the more salient as signs of transcendence and truth – not performances, but rather moments of "pure expression." This situation can, of course, easily be reversed, so that song reverts to "mere" performance, as in act 2 when Aristeo's bid for Euridice is staged as a naked stratagem. As a result, Aristeo, whose songs are constantly full of repetitive, empty rhetoric, is never taken seriously. It is in this way that Rossi uses the performativity of song to frame ideal versions of virtue and truth. On the one hand, song can easily become mere pretense, as in the example of Venere (as the old woman) and Aristeo noted above; on the other hand, Orfeo is told that he cannot be virtuous – he cannot be himself – if he is silent.

A decade after the performance of *Orfeo* at the Palais Royal, the dramatic theorist d'Aubignac made a point of distinguishing between *représentation* [performance] and *vérité de l'action* [truth of the action] in his *Pratique du théâtre* (1657): "I therefore call truth of theatrical action the story of the dramatic poem, insomuch as it is considered veracious, and as all the things that occur in it are considered as having actually happened or having had to have happened. But I call Representation the bringing together of all the things that can serve to represent a dramatic poem."[16] The truth of dramatic action concerns the story itself; *représentation*, or performance, pertains to the presence of spectators, musical instruments, costumes, actors, and the like. D'Aubignac emphasized the proper separation of these two spheres, and condemned the practices of ancient comedy, such as that of Aristophanes, in which no such distinction was maintained. In Aristophanes, he noted, an actor on stage might gesture to a man in the audience whose character he represented.[17] Indeed, by abandoning the chorus of ancient tragedy, seventeenth-century spoken tragedy had eliminated a significant "relay" between audience and stage.[18] D'Aubignac shunned any such element of theater that might blur the boundaries between story and its performance: "one would not approve of it if [the actor] Floridor, representing Cinna, saw fit to confuse the city of Rome with that of Paris, such distant actions with our current affairs, and the day of that conspiracy with a public entertainment taking place sixteen hundred years afterward."[19]

By framing song as performance, *Orfeo* drew attention to the fact that opera often explicitly violated the distinction d'Aubignac later stressed. Sometimes accoutrement, sometimes central to the dramatic action, song obscures the boundary between *représentation* and *vérité de l'action*. Saint-Évremond pointed directly to this "problem" when he wrote that "the composer comes to mind before the operatic hero does; it is Rossi, Cavalli, Cesti whom we imagine . . . and one cannot deny that in the performances at the Palais Royal everyone is thinking a hundred times more of Lully than of Thésée or of Cadmus."[20] In *Orfeo*, Buti and Rossi underscored this oscillation between story and performance when they framed Aristeo's songs as counterfeit or unconvincing performances to onstage audiences, and Orfeo's performances as genuine expressions of the truth and as integral to the progression of the drama. With the exception of Mercurio's concluding speech

("Mortali, udite" [Mortals, listen]), there is no straightforward address to the spectator (III:202). However, because Buti and Rossi staged song as performance – not merely naturalized within the plot – they made a distinct bid for the spectator's attention to the undifferentiated presence of the two facets of theater that d'Aubignac sought to distinguish. Opera ultimately attempts to dismantle the opposition between music as diegetic (part of the plot) on the one hand or extradiegetic (external to the plot) on the other by engaging song in a theatrical mode distinct from that of poetics or diegesis, and by rendering it transcendent when it reaches out as a speech act, or rather as a song act, to the audience.[21] The question of the deceptiveness or illusionality of song as it was raised in *Orfeo*, and by extension that of opera's truth or integrity and of the value of music itself, returned later in critical reactions against French opera, and in what I see as its programmatic response to these accusations.

Even before the final performance of imported Italian opera that Mazarin was to organize before his death, with *Ercole amante* in 1662, a number of French genres – the *pastorale*, the *ballet de cour*, the *comédie-ballet*, and the *tragédie à machines* – had begun to appear, anticipating or preparing the development of French opera. Through-sung pastorals were produced in the 1650s, such as *Le Triomphe de l'Amour* (1655) by Charles de Bey and Michel de La Guerre, and the so-called *Pastorale d'Issy* and *Ariane* (both 1659) by Pierre Perrin and Robert Cambert. Defining this genre, d'Aubignac remarked that pastorals were composed of "several episodes and entertaining circumstances, everything deriving from country life. The characters are but shepherds, hunters, fishermen, and similar kinds of folk; thus we have taken in its entirety the stuff of the ancients' idylls and eclogues, and we have applied to it the economy of satyric tragedy."[22] Unfortunately, the music to these French pastorals has been lost. Dances, elaborate machinery, and music were also present in the *ballets de cour* created by Isaac Benserade during the same period, such as the *Ballet de la nuit* in which both Louis XIV and Lully danced. These creations joined a series of *entrées* into a loose narrative whose verse texts were printed and distributed to the spectators.[23] Molière's *comédies-ballets* with music by Lully, and later by Marc-Antoine Charpentier, burgeoned in the 1660s. This genre was without question a crucial aspect of Molière's creative output: twelve of his twenty-nine plays are *comédies-ballets*, "a dramatic hybrid designed to enliven and enhance celebrations at the French court, and composed of alternating segments in which a spoken comedy [*actes*] is punctuated by episodes of music and dance [*intermèdes*]."[24] Finally, there were the spectacular machine plays, staged beginning in 1650 with Pierre Corneille's *Andromède* which recycled Torelli's machines and sets from *Orfeo*. The *tragédie à machines* adopted the elaborate machinery and décors of Italian opera to create a mixture of spoken text, music, and ballet.[25] With the founding of the Académie Royale de Musique in 1672, the French court officially created an opera of its own, and *tragédie en musique* emerged from the ruins of these genres which were larged subsumed by it.

Two interrelated views of opera in late seventeenth-century France had a particularly determinant influence on its creation and reception well into the eighteenth century. First of all, as its name indicates, *tragédie en musique* was understood to be tragedy set to music. Tragedy was the matter at hand; music was a mode of delivery or was supposed to be an added *agrément*, or charm. The pleasure of spoken tragedy was understood by its theorists to be an intellectual and moral one. For the père René Rapin, tragedy used *terreur* and *pitié* to produce pleasure and ultimately, through this pleasure, moral lessons:

> This pleasure, which properly speaking belongs to the mind, consists in the agitation of the soul when moved by the passions. Tragedy becomes pleasurable to the spectator only because he himself is affected by everything that is represented to him, because he enters into the various emotions of the actors, because he becomes involved in their experiences, because he fears, hopes, grieves, and rejoices with them.[26]

Music could conceivably contribute to the moral workings of tragedy by enhancing these effects. Le Cerf de la Viéville succinctly articulated the basic tenet of the poetics of opera as it was understood in the late seventeenth century. Music was obliged to adhere in all ways to the centrality of the poetic text: "music is there only in order to express the discourses and emotions of tragedy."[27] Similarly, for Antoine-Louis LeBrun, "sometimes music enhances the beauty of the words; but sometimes, when it strays from its model only in order to follow its whims, it diminishes their enjoyment."[28] The poetry provides a model with which the music must always coincide. When it does, as if transparent, it enhances the text; when it does not, it erupts in unwelcome and unpleasantly conspicuous display. Furetière expounded a similar understanding of the relationship between music and text when he discussed Philippe Quinault's lyric texts, "which are very pleasant when they are set to music, just as drugget is striking when it is covered in embroidery."[29]

The second view of opera focused on the strong affective force of its music, and often led theorists and commentators to degrade the operatic spectacle to the low status of mere sensual pleasure. If opera was only for the senses, if it had lost its "true" identity as tragedy, it could not be an intellectual or moral vehicle. Whatever the Greeks may have believed about the moral power of music, many early-modern theorists argued that the effects described by the ancient historians were the result of circumstances particular to those peoples and that they no longer applied in early-modern Europe. The abbé Dubos, for example, speculated that "perhaps the war sounds from *Thésée*, the muted passage [*les sourdines*] from *Armide*, and several other instrumental passages from the same composer would have produced these [moral] effects, which seem incredible [*fabuleux*] to us in the texts of the ancients, if we had played them to men of such a spirited nature as the Athenians."[30] Ideally, the effects of music would still demonstrate a link to morality; however, for late seventeenth-century theorists, opera always risked falling into pure sensation. The music and spectacle of opera stretched the limits of an aesthetics based on mimesis (where tragedy was understood as the imitation of certain kinds of actions) and therefore also threatened to annul the moral basis for such an art. Art without a proper object would be mere display. *Tragédie en musique* was thus for many commentators a misnomer or a contradiction in terms.

While perhaps some may have believed that the affective force of the music reached beyond the senses, before the eighteenth-century rehabilitation of musical sensibility, in part through forms of medical discourse – a topic that will be explored in subsequent chapters – there was no compelling and theoretically sophisticated defense of opera. Some may have agreed with the abbé Pierre Bourdelot and Jacques Bonnet in their *Histoire de la musique et de ses effets*, that music was not "for the pleasure of the senses, but rather serves as a guidepost for the governing of men and can correct the tumult of their passions."[31] At the turn of the eighteenth century, however, few were able to articulate strong arguments in this direction. Some commentators, however, were forthright in their assertion that sensual saturation constituted the dominant pleasure of opera. Antoine-Louis LeBrun made distraction central to the spectator's enjoyment: "for fear that the sight of a wood becomes tiresome, you are led into a magnificent palace; and from this palace you are brought to the seaside; from this seaside you are ushered to a glorious temple. The spectator, whose senses are charmed, is thus led every which way . . ."[32] Because opera was properly "a poetic monster," because it had neither the constraints of tragedy nor the freedom of epic, "one does not risk breaking the rules since there are none, and since the slightest constraint is incompatible with the supernatural which is its principal character . . . the spectator must be almost constantly spellbound."[33] For LeBrun, opera was an aesthetic free-for-all, a world of pleasure with few or no rules – and so much the better. Yet for many there was a decided emptiness to this pleasure. Samuel Chappuzeau, a defender of spoken theater against the religious *dévots*, bore witness to the fact that Lully "has charmed the entire court, the whole of Paris, and all foreign nations that come there. Yet these beautiful spectacles are only for the eyes and ears. They do not reach to the bottom of the soul; and afterwards one can say that one has seen and heard all, but not that one has learned anything."[34] For Chappuzeau, opera took pleasure too far: whereas the potentially objectionable pleasures of spoken theater were offset by its function as a moral vehicle, opera had no such redeeming feature. The abbé François de Châteauneuf argued similarly that opera was for the eyes and ears only, and had no positive impact upon the soul. Discounting the stories of the power of music found in ancient texts, he argued that the ancients had "souls cast in a different mold from ours, and far more susceptible to good or bad impressions. For how could one ascribe to music the *exemplary power* [*la vertu instructive*] that was formerly attributed to it? What power does it exert over us to make us better?"[35]

For Saint-Évremond, music and spectacle had a decidedly negative effect on the intellectual value of tragedy: "it is in vain that the ears are delighted and the eyes enchanted if the mind is not satisfied."[36] André Dacier was careful to exclude music altogether from the essential components of tragedy by making it fall entirely within the realm of what he called "sentiment," by which he means the perception of physical sensation: "I call 'sentiment' the impression that the animal spirits make on the soul." Dacier argued that the purpose of tragedy was instruction – if the Bible were accessible to everyone, we would not need tragedy at all.[37] The addition of music takes tragedy beyond its purpose of instruction, even reversing its desired effects: "if there is anything in the world that seems foreign and even contrary to tragic action, it is music . . . For operas are, if I may say so, the *grotesques* of poetry, and grotesques that are all the more unbearable that they are made to pass for works created according to the rules of art."[38] Music was in no way essential to Greek tragedy, Dacier argued, though it might seem so from a cursory examination of Aristotle; it was, rather, a cultural accident.[39] By qualifying music as pure arabesque, thereby separating it from the central concerns of a poetics of tragedy, even apologists for theater such as Dacier could use arguments against opera that were virtually identical to those employed by pious theorists and clergymen against all theatrical spectacle.[40]

The condemnation of opera spearheaded by the partisans of the ancients during the various skirmishes that defined the Quarrel of the Ancients and the Moderns took the sensual arousal associated with opera as a serious problem by arguing that it served as a conduit and catalyst for the lax morality of lyric poetry. Boileau's condemnation of opera in his "Satire X" (1692), entitled "Les Femmes," is surely the most well-known example. He railed against opera's sensual distraction as an outright sinister, malevolent force. Writers like Antoine Arnauld, who noted that Boileau is "among my best friends," reiterated these attacks against opera and, in particular, against Lully's airs as "effeminate":[41]

> But what is specific about the author of the Satire [Boileau], and where he is most praiseworthy, is in having represented with so much wit and force the devastation that opera verses can wreak upon good morals, verses which are all centered on love and sung to airs which he is perfectly correct in calling *licentious*, since songs can hardly be imagined that would be more likely to ignite the passions and to convey into the hearts of spectators *the lewd morals* of the verses. And what is worse is that the poison of these lascivious songs is not confined to the place where these performances are held but spread throughout France, where an infinite number of people try to learn them by heart and amuse themselves by singing them wherever they go.[42]

Adrien Baillet remarked that because of this focus on pleasure, "if it were permitted to name all those who have been perverted at the opera, whether actors or spectators, their numbers would be infinite."[43] Saint-Évremond repeated many of the same remarks in his comedy, *Les Opéra*, about a young girl who has been damaged from overexposure to fiction and who, having read too many libretti, now believes that she is an operatic heroine: "the *Astrées* had given her the fantasy of being a shepherdess; novels had inspired in her a desire for adventures; and what we see today is the work of operas."[44] In the end, the only way to cure this madness is show her the true face of opera by sending her off to attend one:

> Only opera can detach her from the foolishness of her belief. When she sees that the most marvelous machines are but painted cloth, and that the Gods and Goddesses who descend to the stage are but opera singers, when she touches the ropes which make possible the most amazing flights, goodbye Jupiter and Apollo, goodbye Minerva and Venus. She will shed all those illusions.[45]

For Saint-Évremond, theatrical illusion disappears and the object of drama is lost amidst the visual and auditory profusion and confusion. We are faced with the here-and-now of performance which cannot be separated from the objects being represented because it merges with them. After a few moments at the opera, he argued, "the music is no longer but a muddled noise from which nothing can be distinguished . . . the mind, which has exerted itself vainly trying to sort out these impressions, lets itself wander into reverie or is dissatisfied in its uselessness."[46] Though the abbé Pierre de Villiers does not reject music per se when it is used outside of opera, "operas," he writes, "are but a monstrous jumble"; and he refers to their "poison" and to their "lascivious songs."[47] Promising instruction through terror and pity, opera arouses only sensation:

> Juger donc, si je puis, judicieux & sage,
> Coûter sur le papier cette espece d'ouvrage,
> Qui loin de l'embellir estropie un sujet,
> Et n'ayant que la danse & le chant pour objet,
> Nous fait voir des Heros, des amants sur la Scene,
> Qui viennent, transportez ou d'amour ou de haine,
> Sans jamais exciter ny pitié ny terreur,
> Au goût seul de l'oreille ajuster leur fureur.

> Judge therefore, if I may, judicious and wise,
> Put down on paper this kind of work,
> Which far from embellishing mutilates its subject,
> And having only song and dance for objects,
> Shows us heroes, lovers on the stage
> Who appear, swept away by love or hate,
> Exciting neither pity nor fear,
> To the ear's taste alone directing their furor.[48]

For many, opera's appeal to the senses signaled a decline in taste. Villiers argued that the *amateur*, "Ainsi l'esprit nourri de spectacles frivoles, / Rebute tout bon Livre, & court aux fables folles" [Whose mind is thus nourished on frivolous spectacles, / Turns away from all good books, and rushes over to absurd fictions].[49] As tragedy's monstrous other, opera was destined to destroy its spoken counterpart: "what angers me the most about this opera mania is that it will ruin tragedy, which is the most beautiful thing we have, the most appropriate for lifting the soul and the most effective in shaping the minds of spectators."[50] The supposedly inherent softness of *tragédie en musique* put tragedy itself in danger. Villiers criticized the devastating influence he believed that opera had on tragedy:

> La fiere Tragedie en auroit moins souffert,
> On n'eût point sous son nom impunément offert
> Les lubriques chansons, & la danse effrontée;
> Peut-être dans sa force elle seroit restée.

> Proud tragedy would have suffered less
> Had we not with impunity under its name presented
> Lewd songs and shameless dance
> It might have kept its forceful stance.[51]

Having dared to steal the name of tragedy, as *tragédie en musique* opera was the harbinger of a general decline in taste. Villiers argued that if opera could be eliminated, good taste would return again to France.[52]

Saint-Évremond's and Villiers's remarks were not isolated ones, nor were their views short-lived. One can see traces of the conviction that opera was to blame for the decline of tragedy in France in reactions to the works of Quinault, Lully's principal librettist, from the 1690s through the mid-twentieth century. Although later critics sought to distance themselves from certain positions taken by Boileau, his judgments on opera were echoed and elaborated by generations of critics from Saint-Évremond to La Harpe, and from Gustave Lanson to Antoine Adam, and were intentionally used by these critics to generate an image of a golden age of seventeenth-century stage works which suffered from the influence of opera but eventually overcame it to become classics. Quinault and the dramatic characters he created, in both his spoken works and in those written for the lyric stage, were belittled as "unmanly" [*damerets*].[53] True works of art – in contrast to opera, it was understood – should be masculine and virile. Adrien Baillet noted of Quinault: "It is said that sentimentality [*la tendresse*] is the principal quality of this author's plays."[54]

For nineteenth-century literary history, opera posed a real threat to the future of literature as long as opera remained a part of *belles-lettres*. Promoting Racine above the other minor writers of the seventeenth and eighteenth centuries, pedagogues such as Gustave Lanson were able to tell the story of the ultimate triumph of great literature over opera. The opposition between "real" literature and opera is clear in the preface to Lanson's 1896 edition of selected works of Racine. Alluding to the plotting of envious, minor writers, Lanson describes the final apotheosis of the great Racine: "it was not long before those who had been seduced by Quinault's sentimentality came to prefer the forceful elegance of Racine to his vapidity."[55] For Lanson, Quinault was bland and artificial. Even if great writers eventually overcame opera, *tragédie en musique* nevertheless took its toll on literature: "until the end of the eighteenth century, opera belonged at least as much and perhaps more to literature than it did to music. We will see that opera, through its glitter and seductions, exercised a real and sometimes regrettable influence on literature."[56] The decline of theater through the eighteenth century, the origin of which many critics saw in Racine's "silence" after *Phèdre*, was imagined to be the direct result of the emergence of opera. Paul Brunetière's *Manual of the History of French Literature* claimed that "the success of opera made tragedy veer off its evolutionary course."[57] *Tragédie en musique* had diluted the tragic style and weakened its conception of drama.[58] *Phèdre* was the turning point for Brunetière, cited here by Étienne Gros:

> Enraged by the way Quinault had distorted the truth, with *Phèdre*, Racine wanted "to put Quinault in his place, to reconcile the public with the truth, and to set antiquity in its proper light." The sad fact is that in order to succeed in this task he was obliged "to borrow some of the more than artificial means that Quinault had overused . . . the décor, her love, Phèdre and all the mythology, fused together uniformly by the harmony of the verse, we all recognize this, it's grand opera emerging from tragedy, while tragedy . . . searching for a new pathos and new resources with Crébillon and Voltaire, would slowly but surely, with Diderot, Beaumarchais and Mercier, move towards melodrama."[59]

Brunetière adds: "If one were to study closely the unraveling of French tragedy in the seventeenth century, one would have to devote a large space to the influence of opera."[60] Another critic, one Doumic, writing the same year as Lanson (1896), repeated similar arguments, seeing in Racine's religious tragedies, *Esther* and *Athalie*, the unfortunate influence of opera.[61] Gros, Quinault's often sympathetic biographer, also agreed with Doumic's conclusion.[62] Referring to Voltaire's *Sémiramis*, whose third act is said to be a true opera scene, Gros argued that "no one more than Voltaire suffered from the fascination of lyric tragedy. Voltaire's tragedy leads straight to [bourgeois] drama, and drama sounds the death knell for tragedy."[63]

Antoine Adam, one of the most influential French literary historians of the twentieth century, compared the great Racine to the lesser dramatic poet, Quinault. Whereas Racine sought "to reveal true Greek tragedy to his century," Adam wrote in his massive 1954 *Histoire de la littérature française au XVIIe siècle*, the opera librettists Quinault and Thomas Corneille were only "mediocre rhymesters," more concerned with crowd pleasing and bending to passing fashions than with the lasting forms and values of classical tragedy.[64] Adam complained that "all the characters in his plays are interested only in love. They sacrifice their duty, their interests, the grandeur of their rank, to love."[65] On style, Adam condemned Quinault's language, speaking of "the mediocrity of these facile works, the paucity of the invention, the monotony of the effects, the flabbiness and imprecision of the language."[66] This characterization fit perfectly with Adam's notion of Quinault as a salon poet and, not incidentally, with Arnauld's portrayal of Lully's airs as effeminate. For women were supposedly the key to Quinault's success: "women made Quinault a success; they were delighted with the praise Charles Perrault bestowed on their wit and taste. It was they who ensured the vogue of operas and novels, and the success of gallant literature, to the detriment of great poetry."[67]

Adam's position clearly reveals gender issues that lie behind his rejection of opera. The characterization of opera as effeminate was supported, in the minds of the critics, by the fact that Quinault was always labeled by his contemporaries as a disciple of the *précieuses*, as a product of women and of women's literature. As Joan DeJean has pointed out, women's literature was associated on the one hand with the passing fads of the salons and, on the other, with political engagement – two qualities that nineteenth-century literary history found both unpalatable and counter to their notion of the timeless values of the classic.[68] For Étienne Gros, "Quinault was, by his very nature, a fashionable author. If he did not only count among his admirers the *précieuses* and their supporters, he was above all the poet of an era and a milieu."[69] As a *précieux* product, Quinault could never aspire to the universality of a classic writer, but would remain a historical curiosity, a passing trend. Similar deprecations of Quinault can be found in the margins of literary histories throughout the nineteenth and twentieth centuries, and hostility towards Quinault can produce agreement in very unlikely camps. Both the standard-bearers of Great French Literature and more recent critics adopting a feminist perspective concur in their aversion to Quinault, though for very different reasons. Patricia Howard, for example, contrasts Molière's enlightened advocacy for "the right of a girl to marry the man of her own choice" with that of Quinault, whose libretti "constitute nothing less than a school for royal mistresses."[70]

From the perspective of these literary historians, by the end of the eighteenth century the separation between literature and opera was fortunately complete. La Harpe was categorical about the matter: "Where did you get the idea that opera is or could ever be tragedy for us?"; "Let us not seek to join that which must be separated. At the Théâtre-Français, tragedy is in its place; and music is in its place at the Opéra."[71] Opera was no longer considered a form of tragedy; and with opera out of the way, the world was safe for serious literature. At the same time, though, literary historians sensed that something had been forever compromised or lost in the world of letters after the new genre's appearance in France in the late seventeenth century. The burgeoning theatrical world of the late seventeenth century was of course quite different from the image we are given of it by later literary histories. As Roger W. Herzel reminds us, this was "a time when everything related to stage practice was in question, not settled by some calm, pervasive doctrine."[72] Yet the rivalry between tragedy and *tragédie en musique* in the seventeenth century, and particularly the voices of opera's strongest and most influential critics like Boileau, were recuperated in the nostalgic and reverent attitude of nineteenth- and twentieth-century literary historians towards neoclassical tragedy.

From the perspective of literary history, opera brought tragedy into relief as its rival – its "other" – and eventually effaced it. As La Harpe suggested, referring to the operatic audience, "it is not the hero they are watching; they are listening to the soprano."[73]

Ironically, the abbé Jean Terrasson, a *moderne* whose *Dissertation critique sur l'Iliade d'Homere* (1715) presented a staunch defense of opera against Boileau and André Dacier, may have done much to set the stage for the future extradition of opera from *belles-lettres*. Whereas commentators such as Charles Perrault and Antoine-Louis LeBrun had defended opera in various ways against the attacks of Boileau, Bossuet, Saint-Évremond, Dacier and others, Terrasson provided the first positively compelling case against the position of the *anciens* on opera, arguing that opera was not tragedy set to music.[74] The most turbulent vortex of the *Querelle d'Homère* revolved around Anne Dacier and her 1711 translation of the *Iliad*. Terrasson entered the Quarrel only later, in 1715. In his discussion of opera Terrasson engaged remarks made by André Dacier, Anne's husband and secrétaire perpetuel de l'Académie, in his translation of Aristotle's *Poetics*. Terrasson's case was built upon three major arguments. First, he attacked the position of the *anciens* by undercutting their valorization of ancient music. Secondly, he established the inconsistencies of Boileau's argumentation, arguing that the famous writer and critic had adopted the same grounds to reject the sensuality of opera that he had used to justify poetry and theater. Finally, Terrasson provided a definition of opera that went beyond the usual nomenclature and conceptual apparatus that subsumed opera to regular tragedy. Surprisingly, given its insights and innovations with regard to the early debates on opera, the *Dissertation* has been largely ignored by scholars.

For seventeenth-century critics of opera, the music of Greek tragedy was a phantasmic object – fascinating precisely because it remained unknown. For many, it was an inescapable point of reference for modern music and its lingering presence could be felt in opera. The abbé Dubos, for example, imagines that he hears something like the music of the ancients in an arresting instrumental number from act 5 of the opera *Roland* by Quinault and Lully: "this beautiful music even evokes those which Cicero and Quintilian say that the pythagorians used to ease the tumultuous thoughts that the day leaves in the imagination before putting one's head down to rest."[75] For Le Cerf de la Viéville, the simplicity of ancient music was captured by Lully, a "simplicity that he has better imitated here in France than anyone has anywhere for 1600 years, which is what I believe to be the source and character of his merit."[76] *Armide*, in particular, is judged to be "the most beautiful piece of music which has been written for fifteen or sixteen centuries, of this I am utterly convinced."[77] Despite the tendency to account for the reported miraculous effects of Greek music with natural or anthropological explanations, and in part because of the Quarrel of the Ancients and Moderns, the impact of an image of Greek music continued to be felt in discussions of opera.[78]

In contrast to Le Cerf de la Viéville, Terrasson built his argument squarely on "the superiority of modern music over the ancient variety."[79] Indeed, for Terrasson, opera was not ancient at all, but rather a purely modern invention (II:229–30). Ancient music "seems to have been only a kind of plainchant without any set harmony [*contre-partie*]"; and when the Greeks used more than one voice, "it was in order to sing the same thing at the octave or at another set interval" (II:219). In support of the inferiority of ancient music, he refers the reader to Gioseffo Zarlino's great theoretical treatise, *Istituzioni harmoniche* (1558), and to Charles Perrault's annotated translation of Vitruvius (II:220).[80] Dacier contended that the poets were responsible for both the verse and the music of their plays and that this situation contributed to the unity of purpose that makes Greek poetry superior to modern French works – an oft repeated argument in support of the ancients. Terrasson rejected Dacier's argument, replying that this supposed advantage was in reality a liability and citing contemporary practice:

> The spirit of method proper to the modern age has made the art of music extremely easy . . . yet our composers [*musiciens*], ordinarily free of all other occupation from childhood, manage only with great difficulty to arrive at pleasing the public. How, therefore, at a time when the basic

principles of music appear to have been very difficult could poets compose music comparable to ours – poets [moreover] who must have had to cultivate so many other areas of knowledge and exerted their imagination and taste on so many other objects (II:217–18)?

Terrasson considered the simplicity of ancient Greek music unworthy of modern composers and audiences. The highly prized unity of poet and composer in antiquity was, in reality, indicative only of the ancients' lack of modern method and division of labor. How could composers who were deprived of clear and simple pedagogical methods for acquiring a musical education, and who further extended themselves with the burden of composing the poetry, produce anything comparable to the works of Lully and Quinault?

On a second front, Terrasson attacked the inconsistencies of the case of the supporters of the ancients. Here, Terrasson focused particularly on Boileau. He began by conceding that many recent operas were merely "love idylls empty of all other interest and all other example" (II:242). His aim extended only as far as to defend Quinault's operas, "or those that resemble them," precisely the ones Boileau and others had attacked (II:242). Terrasson carefully skirted around the objections of the religious *dévots*: "I do not direct this justification at those authors who through their pious Christian principles have written against theater [*les spectacles*] and novels; I leave their arguments untouched" (II:242). His argument was leveled not at the true *dévots* but only at those who wrote "secular works" on worldly topics in their capacities as secular critics, and who nonetheless "avail themselves of the arms of moral theology to attack modern works which are infinitely more modest than the ancient works that they recommend ad infinitum" (II:242). The accusation was directed specifically against Boileau who had decided to include as an appendix to the 1701 edition of his works Arnauld's previously cited letter praising Boileau's satire and censure of opera. Arnauld, however, was a Jansenist theologian who "had always condemned theater and novels" (II:242–43); and yet, Terrasson continued, Boileau had adopted Arnauld's conviction to further his own repudiation of opera despite the fact that he was "a secular

author who had only ever criticized opera and novels on secular principles" (II:244). It is one thing to have objections to opera (and novels and
theater) that are based on consistently held religious beliefs. It is quite
another, Terrasson contended, to use these arguments against opera,
on the one hand, and to forget them conveniently when considering
other forms of spectacle or fiction.

Boileau's arguments against *tragédie en musique* relied primarily on
his assertion that it revolved solely around love interests and that it
fired the passions. However, in making those claims, Terrasson asserted, Boileau contradicted his own praise of the elegy and the ode
in his *Art poétique*. Terrasson cited an excerpt from its second "Chant":
"La plaintive Elegie, en longs habits de deüil, / Sçait, les cheveux épars,
gémir sur un cercuëil; / Elle peint des amans la joye & la tristesse, / Flate,
menace, irite, appaise une Maîtresse; / Mais pour bien exprimer ces
caprices heureux, / C'est peu d'être Poëte, il faut être amoureux"
[The plaintive Elegy, in long mourning clothes, / Knows how, hair di-
sheveled, to sob on a casket; / It paints the joy and sadness of lovers, /
Flatters, threatens, arouses, calms a mistress; / But to express well these
felicitous fancies, / It is not enough to be a poet, one must be in love]
(II:244–45). In Boileau's treatment of tragedy in the third "Chant," and in
other arguments from the fourth "Chant" of the *Art poétique*, Terrasson
noted further, Boileau set down as a rule of good fiction precisely those
love interests that Arnauld had condemned in the letter Boileau had
nonetheless seen fit to include in the 1701 edition of his works:

> Je ne suis pas pourtant de ces tristes esprits,
> Qui, bannissant l'amour de tous chastes écrits,
> D'un si riche ornement veulent priver la Scene,
> Traitent d'empoisonneurs & Rodrigue & Chimene:
> L'amour le moins honnête exprimé chastement,
> N'excite point en nous de honteux mouvemens;
> Didon a beau gémir, & m'étaler ses charmes,
> Je condamne sa faute en partageant ses larmes.
> Un Auteur vertueux, dans ses vers innocens,
> Ne corrompt point le coeur, en châtoüillant les sens;
> Son feu n'allume point de criminelle flâme (II:246–47).

Yet I am not one of those sad spirits
Who, banishing love from all chaste writings,
Wish to deprive the stage of such a rich ornament,
Accusing Rodrigue and Chimène of corruption.
The least honest love chastely expressed
Excites not in us shameful feelings.
Let Dido sob and display her charms to me:
I condemn her error as I share her tears.
A virtuous author through innocent verses
Corrupts not the heart by exciting the senses;
His passion lights no criminal flame.[81]

By appropriating Arnauld's letter, Boileau had borrowed a form of discourse – the pious condemnation of spectacle – to which he himself did not subscribe in his *Art poétique*.

Given that Boileau's satire put into question public conduct and decency, Terrasson saw fit to remark that Paris had never been better policed than it was at that time: "the wise piety of the King, seconded by the intelligence and the attention of the illustrious magistrates who are charged with maintaining public order, keep the streets of a city as immense and sumptuous as Paris so lawful that the centuries to come will hardly believe it" (II:248). He noted "the care that is taken to suppress anything that could bring and spread the appearance of, and the taste for, licentiousness in society," above all in "theaters" [*les lieux de spectacle*] (II:248). Whereas the Spartans allowed young women to spar "naked amongst themselves, and sometimes even with men," in Paris not only did the magistrates keep public order, they encouraged spectacles "as an amusement for countless and at the same time lively and impetuous youth, who are diverted in this way from an infinite number of criminal actions" (II:248–49). Terrasson suggested that "all the fine arts, which temper the manners according to one ancient author, seem to converge in opera so as to develop the mind of the spectator" (II:249). The theater tempers and refines the moral sensibility of the spectator: "I need no other proof," he wrote, "than the mere difference between the French of our century, beginning with the renewal of the theater, and those of all preceding centuries"

(II:250). The real object of Boileau's animosity, Terrasson argued, was much closer to home: he was simply "angry to see that the public condemned, through their approbation of the operas of Quinault, the censure he had imposed on them for intellectual reasons [*du côté de l'esprit*]" (II:247). Reacting to the public acclaim of opera, like so many older writers, "[he] had thrown himself, toward the end of his days, into morality, as one can see in his satire against women, and as is known from his private conversations" (II:247). In the end, Terrasson saw in Boileau a poet who, "in order to take his revenge on the public which, despite his own personal decision, had a great taste for opera," had turned toward a sanctimonious piety: "Mr. Despreaux, full of a piety in keeping with his temperament and his genius, griped and maligned in penance" (II:247).

The truly momentous contribution of the *Dissertation critique sur l'Iliade d'Homere* to the debates on opera can be found in the distinction it established between opera and other forms of theatrical spectacle. Terrasson maintained that opera differed from tragedy in three ways: first, it necessarily involved machines; second, it presented "to the eyes of the spectators those intermediary actions which in other tragedies are only recounted"; and third, it was thoroughly "in music," from beginning to end – "tout en musique" (II:207). The use of machines was justified, Terrasson argued, because opera was based on the interaction of gods and men; and an important aspect of the interest of opera derived from the confusion of the celestial and worldly realms when human beings become the object of supernatural desire or wrath, "and [thus] subject to miraculous and supernatural incidents that the Gods produce themselves or through those whom they have endowed with their powers" (II:207–08). The contribution of the moderns was to have invented a spectacle specifically devoted to these interactions: "the creation of a spectacle specifically for this combination is so fitting that all the divine characters who produce such a great effect in our operas appear as so many flaws in the ancient tragedies," something for which Dacier had in fact chided Sophocles and Euripides (II:208). The supernatural or miraculous elements of opera authorized scene changes and eliminated the need for a strict unity of place, "since machines can transport the actors in an instant from one end of the earth to the other, and from the tip of the heavens to the deepest corner of the underworld" (II:208). The critics of opera assumed that *tragédie en musique* violated the unities to which it ought to be subject as tragedy. Terrasson, however, eliminated for opera "the exact unity of place, from which I would not want to exempt natural [as opposed to supernatural] tragedy" (II:209).

With regard to those actions which were visually withheld in regular tragedy because they were consigned to narration in conformity with the rules of theatrical decorum, opera delivered them to the spectator in all their visual luster: "any fair judge will praise the moderns for having imagined a spectacle that represents, as it were, epic itself, and which gives the merits of both works to tragedy alone" (II:209). Through its use of machines and dance, opera perfected and appropriated the old genres of tragedy and epic. One of the most important ways in which opera represented that which had previously been relegated to narration was through its use of dance. Terrasson divided dance into *danse simple* and *danse figurée*, or naturalized dance and allegorical dance. The first type was incorporated in situations, such as religious ceremonies or public celebrations, when the dance could be said to form a part of the plot and when the characters would be expected to dance on stage. The second occurred during situations such as dream sequences when the spectators might witness "combats or even natural or supernatural effects transformed into allegorical characters, such as the winds and all kinds of spirits" (II:209). Opera made a virtue out of the faults of ancient tragedy through its use of machines during the intervention of gods or supernatural beings; moreover, using these machines and the visual splendor of dance, opera placed before the spectator's eyes that which remained devoid of movement and life in the epic.

Terrasson's argument was particularly innovative in its treatment of the music of opera. Alluding to the discontinuity of the music of Greek tragedy, he asserted that "it was their intermittent music which truly revealed the absurdity of using music for tragic actions," whereas the fully musical nature of opera makes it far superior: "in opera, which is always filled with supernatural characters, music is like a continuous spell that one enters at the beginning of the spectacle, leaving it only at the end" (ii:225). Whereas spoken language fit ordinary tragedy, it was a musical language that best suited the fully supernatural quality of the operatic plot and its characters; and because the supernatural suffused opera, so should music be its uninterrupted form of discourse. Terrasson rested his case against the superiority of ancient tragedy by underscoring the fact that the ancients could not have had an opera, since "their music was not capable of supporting an autonomous spectacle," again basing his argument on the specificity of the operatic spectacle and the forms of representation it deployed (ii:230). Precisely because "it is music which supports these kinds of representations, and which covers that which could be licentious, it is the use of music above all that one must examine when speaking of opera" (ii:210).

Terrasson cited Dacier's condemnation of the alliance of music and tragedy and his praise of the "skillful" and "delicate" Athenians who nonetheless, and inexplicably for Dacier, combined music, dance, and tragic actions in their theatrical performances (ii:211). Terrasson pointed out that the effect of Dacier's erudite argument about tragedy and opera, and of his remarks about the ancient Greeks, was above all to belittle the discernment of the contemporary French spectator: "Mr. Dacier inserts a condemnation of the opera which is very belittling to the public in the very Dissertation in which he says that the Athenians, of whom he speaks only with respect, lose touch with verisimilitude and with the spirit of tragedy by introducing music into it" (ii:211–12). Terrasson suggested that the discrepancy between Dacier's favorable treatment of the ancient Greek people and his rejection of their use of music and dance in the theater was glaring: "thus it seems to me that it is the Athenians who merit the insults that Mr. D. keeps for his own country" (ii:211). One of the most intriguing aspects of Terrasson's defense of opera against Dacier's attacks is that it relied on a strikingly modern conception of the public as a judge of cultural productions. He noted both Dacier's and Boileau's disregard for the overwhelming public approbation of opera and the former's overly highminded and academic discussion of ancient practices. Terrasson took exception to Dacier's scorn for the public, and to Boileau's act of vengeance against a public that disagreed with his presumptions, and referred to the public interest in having available to it "all genres from the sublime to the lowest, provided that they are well treated" (II:231). Terrasson's understanding of the public anticipated by a few years the true "democratization of taste" that Joan DeJean sees in the work of the abbé Jean-Baptiste Dubos.[82]

Terrasson sidestepped Dacier's view of the problem – how could the otherwise keen Athenians include music and dance in their tragedy? – to consider opera as an entirely separate genre. Greek tragedy "had originally been nothing but the unbroken song of Tabarins [jesters] which later were interspersed with scenes drawn from some more noble and broader subject" (II:212). Music had not been inserted into tragedy out of superstition or a particular taste for music, as Dacier argued, but rather because tragedy had been added to these musical practices and was left to develop there out of custom (II:213). Terrasson argued that opera – an exclusively modern genre – had an entirely different origin. Opera derived less from tragedy, which is in the most important ways an entirely distinct form of spectacle, but rather from the extraordinary resources of music itself. Music's "prodigious scope" and "perfection," instrumental airs, songs for solo voice and ensembles – opera brought together "in a single spectacle all these advantages" (II:213). Song mixed with declamation produced an unprecedented spectacle and "a new type of beauty very worthy of being preserved" (II:214). Simply put, opera was not tragedy in music at all, but rather a genre based on a new aesthetic whose foundation was music: "one must not consider operas as simple tragedies that we have decided to set to music; but one must consider them as subjects created in order to support and to connect all kind of music" (II:214). We have come a long way from Charles Perrault's defense of Quinault, the bulk of which focused on the advantages and disadvantages of poetic and narrative choices that Quinault made in relation to Euripides.[83] Whereas critics and supporters of opera alike had understood opera only as a form of tragedy that was set to music, where tragedy was the substance at hand and the music added piquancy, Terrasson came surprisingly close to asserting that the tragedy in opera was a supplement to the music.

It must be acknowledged that Terrasson clearly assumed that the object of opera must ultimately have a moral dimension, just as was the case for tragedy; and he devoted a substantial article to a discussion of the question, "of what morality *tragédie en musique* is capable" (II:234): "is it not admirable that from a [secondary] supporting and bonding element we have created a subject that is both ethical and interesting; and Mr. Quinault, is he not by virtue of this not only an excellent author but also unique [*un excéllent original*]?" (II:214). What is remarkable in Terrasson's defense of opera is that he argued throughout for the specificity of the operatic spectacle which was not to be judged according to rules and assumptions that applied to another genre. Poetry and music and spectacle were joined in opera "in order to offer a different kind of pleasure to which the soul easily lends itself; and they even gain a great deal from it, provided that their creators [*les auteurs*] know how to temper those sorts of embellishments and to take *from within these very arts*, which appear to deviate from the natural, all the imitation of which they are capable" (II:215–16; my emphasis). Music and dance were assumed to be something more than a pleasant supplement to tragedy, because they too contained the raw materials necessary for representation. For Terrasson, music gained a measure of autonomy from poetics, not because music had an "absolute" aesthetic value or was disconnected from morality, but rather because it achieved a status commensurate with that of the other imitative arts. What is more, Terrasson asserted, music did not *always* have to produce representational meaning. Noting that music could produce imitations, he wrote:

> I say that it could be imitative, for it is not necessarily so . . . Music also
> continues to exist, and is even very pleasant, without imitation, not only
> in its chords but also in the mere arrangement of tones, which neither
> imitate nor signify anything in moderato passages [*les mouvements moyens*]
> and in the natural keys. On the other hand, however, since it contains
> very fast and very slow passages and transposed keys, it is well adapted
> for imitation whenever one wishes, not only the sound of the wind or the
> murmur of water, but also joy, sadness and all the passions that are
> distinguished by accents or characteristic vocal expressions. One opera –
> a single opera – brings together all these uses of music: one hears in it

tunes or airs that are only for the ear, and others which speak to the mind and the heart. Music is thus reconciled with tragic subjects as with all others (II:223–24).

When music does represent, Terrasson argued, it can represent not only the sounds of physical objects but also the inner, moral life of men and women. However, it does not have to follow painting and sculpture as an imitative art. Though music can represent, there is no necessary reason to require it to do so. One should be able to enjoy its non-imitative pleasures as well. For the *anciens*, the power of ancient music to move the passions attested to its superiority. Dacier had complained about the claims Greek writers made for these effects, noting his exasperation at Aristotle for having left the presence of music in tragedy unexplained: Dacier wrote that Aristotle "would have truly obliged us by indicating how music could have been judged necessary to tragedy. Instead of that, he was content with saying that the extent of its power is well known" (II:211). After laying out his new understanding of opera, Terrasson reasserted Aristotle's claim: "Thus, to justify the music of opera in its entirety, we could well confine ourselves to the reason that Aristotle puts forward in order to justify the music of the ancient choruses, by saying that the extent of its power is well known" (II:216–17). Whereas Dacier felt that he had to rely on the authority of Aristotle when he established the superiority of ancient practice, but could not in the case of opera, Terrasson simply pointed to the music that the public could hear for themselves in the opera house.

Terrasson's perspective on opera was exceptionally modern. Like Dacier, he cited the ancients to support his position. The considerable difference in Terrasson's reference to the ancients is that he did not consider ancient Greece and Rome as absolute, fixed points of perfection. He referred to them as cultural examples, as cultures that are in all respects at least potentially comparable to others. His perspective was essentially pluralistic; and his *Dissertation critique* compared the merits of various cultures as relative, not as absolutes. Arguing that all genres were worthy in their own right, according to the lights of ordinary people, Terrasson wrote: "Even the performances of acrobats, in their own right, can be made into something excellent by a clever man; did the ancients not have their own *Sylles* [Greek satires], their Satires, their Farces [*Atellanes*], all plays of a different and specific character?" (II:232). Whereas for the *anciens'* camp, the Greeks were a fixed point of excellence (however much their arguments clearly played into a cultural politics of the present), for Terrasson they represented only one set of cultural choices. Similarly, within early eighteenth-century France, different cultural choices and circumstances allowed for the variety of spectacles, from acrobatics to tragedy, and their various publics.

Returning to the writings of the early critics of opera, nineteenth- and twentieth-century literary historians made their case for the distinction between opera and tragedy, a distinction that may not have made much sense to some late seventeenth-century theorists and commentators, and with which, in any event, they had not yet wholly come to terms. Literary historians used this distinction in order to highlight the "classicism" of spoken tragedy, and to provide it with an adversary that would eventually cause its fall. In making a hard distinction between tragedy and opera, they essentially reiterated d'Aubignac's demand for separation between the represented action as an intellectual object and the apparatus or circumstances of performance. Similarly, around the turn of the eighteenth century, the partisans of the ancients had used this same distinction to condemn opera's sensuality and lack of positive moral content, rejecting opera as pure display and sheltering the moral core of tragedy as worthy of preservation from the onslaught of vacuous operatic spectacle. Terrasson boldly reconfigured the parameters of the debate by transforming the opposition between opera and spoken tragedy into a virtue. His efforts opened the door to new forms of operatic meaning that specific *tragédies en musique* had in fact already begun to explore.

Though tragedy per se was not at issue in *Orfeo*, questions about the value of song, which would later erupt into full-fledged debates and quarrels, were already manifest in the attention given to song as performance in Rossi's work. In *Orfeo*, as I argued at the beginning of this chapter, particular attention is given to moments in which characters sing; and the truth-value or effectiveness of these performances is frequently emphasized or put into question by those onstage characters who, just like spectators, bear witness to them. Bernard Williams has insightfully remarked on the spectator's self-consciousness in opera: "a theatrical device is made to work, not by concealing it, but by securing the audience's complicity in it. This technique is not peculiar to opera, but it is specially important to it."[84] Subsequent chapters will take up the issue of the performativity of song discussed in connection with Rossi's *Orfeo* as well as Terrasson's insights about the function of music in opera. For it was not only the statements of theoreticians but also the operatic works themselves that demonstrated an awareness of opera's singular and often awkward situation within the cultural politics of late seventeenth- and early eighteenth-century France. If Terrasson's carefully crafted response to André Dacier decisively challenged the *anciens'* assumptions about opera, a number of the great operatic works of the period can be understood as testing the limits of the aesthetic premises that surrounded *tragédie en musique* through the innovative ways in which they constructed the relationship between the poetic text, the music, the visual spectacle, the spectator, and the cultural assumptions that governed these complex interrelations.

In his splendid study, *Portrait of the King*, Louis Marin examined the conflation of representation and power in the many cultural and artistic manifestations of the reign of Louis XIV: historical writing, the *fêtes* at Versailles, medallions and coins, and poetic forms from encomium to fable. Marin argued that the king comes into being as monarch only in the written and visual "portraits" that create him as sovereign: "the king is only truly king, that is, monarch, in images." The king's "portrait" is simultaneously story and icon: "to tell the king's history in a narrative is to show it (*faire voir*). To show the king's history in his icon is to tell it (*faire raconter*)."[1] The "iconic effect" of narrative texts and the narrative effect of contemporary painting, Marin argued, produced a unified portrait of the king. What interested Marin was the effective power of representation: the ability of image and narrative to legitimate and actuate royal power.

The prologues to the first French operatic spectacles – the *tragédies en musique* of Philippe Quinault and Jean-Baptiste Lully, written from 1673 to 1686 – functioned as spectacular and explicit celebrations of the king, distinct from, yet framing, the narratives of the operas themselves. However, Marin never discussed *tragédie en musique*, a form neither merely textual nor exclusively visual, nor even a simple combination of these two elements. How might the particular complexity of early French opera – with its vocal and instrumental music, its spectacle, and its dramatic representation of a text – be understood from Marin's perspective as contributing to the representation of the king? In addition to, and perhaps because of, the explicit and ritualistic celebration of the monarch and his military exploits in the operatic prologues, the court also "saw" Louis XIV hidden in the mythology and in the fanciful historical narratives of the operas themselves, which were adapted from works by Ovid, Euripides, Tasso, Ariosto, and others.

Jupiter's pursuit of the nymph Io and Juno's ultimate revenge in the opera *Isis* (1677), for example, led the court to identify Io with Marie-Élisabeth de Ludres whose liaison with Louis was broken off when Madame de Montespan had her rival exiled from court. Half veiling an observation about the rivalry between Mademoiselle de Ludres and the marquise de Montespan, the marquise de Sévigné wrote on June 30, 1677, that *"Io* roams free in the prairies and is observed by no Argus; Juno is thundering and triumphant."[2] Invoking Marin's bipartite notion of the portrait, one could certainly consider the prologue and its explicit evocation of the king as emblematic or iconic, and the body of the opera as producing a narrative portrait of the king. Yet I wonder how Marin's notion of "portrait" (of textual image and visual narrative) might be modified or challenged by the unique complexity of the operatic form, if one considered, for example, the relationship between the prologue and the body of the opera or the presence of music and singing voices in a genre that was largely based, at least ostensibly, on literary precedents.

Incorporating these questions of form within the topic of royal representation that commands Marin's study, I will examine the relationship between the new genre of *tragédie en musique* and the policies and initiatives surrounding the representation of the king from the early 1660s to the 1680s. The presupposition that guides my study is that a comprehensive understanding of the emergent *tragédie en musique* must necessarily include a consideration of the state's ambitions to produce representations of the king. I will suggest that the opportunities and difficulties opera presented in this regard were part and parcel of the intricacy of the form and, ultimately, of its particular status within neoclassical aesthetics. In the final analysis, I will argue, the exaltation of the monarch in the prologue produced an awkward and equivocal gap in relation to the shortcomings of the operatic hero to whom he was implicitly compared – men whose fragility revealed a cowardice and duplicity unknown to the ironclad heroes in Corneille's tragedies and also quite distinct from the fated or tenacious corruption and relentless depravity found in Racine's characters. I begin by examining the larger political and speculative issues surrounding the

use of allegory in the representation of the king, moving on to introduce at length some of the principal modes of representation chosen
by Louis XIV and his advisors, and finally to examine the panegyrics
of the operatic prologue in order to determine how *tragédie en musique*
might fit alongside, and yet be distinguished from, the vast array of
paintings, coins, tapestries, and histories that make up Marin's portrait
of the king.

On June 10, 1664, when Louis XIV was only beginning to rule on his
own, Jean Chapelain wrote to Jean-Baptiste Colbert to confirm an
agreement on the use of allegory in the paintings and tapestries for the
projected history of the king, *l'Histoire du Roi*. Colbert's reponses to
Chapelain appear to have been lost. In his letter, Chapelain notes that
the king, via Colbert, had approved their project: "Sir, I have received
with respect the response that it pleased you to make to my letter
touching upon the use of allegory in the paintings and tapestries that
you have ordered made for the history of the King, and I felt highly
honored that neither His Majesty nor you have disapproved of it."[3]
Chapelain insists repeatedly that the future "first painter," Charles
Le Brun, be made to conform to their views on the matter, adding
finally that he hopes that "this rare painter, being as judicious as he
is, will not stray from them; above all if we were allowed to insinuate
that in adopting them he would not displease His Majesty nor do
anything with which you might find fault."[4] Le Brun must have been
persuaded by their reasons since he was given the title of *Premier Peintre*
twenty days later. Unfortunately, Chapelain's letter reveals nothing
substantive about their agreement concerning allegory, for he says
nothing about the precise terms of their agreement. We can only know
for certain, therefore, that allegory was an important consideration in
their discussions about the project that would later be objectified as
l'Histoire du Roi.

We may speculate that allegory in the visual arts was considered
as a possible remedy to the delicate problem of political allusion. It
would veil what otherwise might be overly manifest references to specific events which could be extremely sensitive to the eyes of foreign

sovereigns, ambassadors, and other visitors. Since allegory substitutes one thing for another, it could be seen as an implicit solution to the problem of representing hidden motives and secret truths, as well as veiling references to contemporary political events that might otherwise have been too offensive to important foreign dignitaries. One of the functions of allegory, in addition to conveying a message with a specifically moral intent, is indeed to displace or hide meaning by creating a gap between what is manifest and what is hidden.[5] Allegorical representation does double duty, concealing and revealing at the same time. As Walter Benjamin argued, allegory is more than "a playful illustrative technique": rather, it constitutes a distinct form of expression, producing specific kinds of meaning.[6] In addition to concealing sensitive aspects of the historical record, by fusing the image of Louis XIV with figurative depictions, allegory also allows "the connection between representation and reality to seem natural, seamless," introducing Louis into the larger-than-life world of mythology.[7]

At the same time that he was named first painter, Le Brun also assumed the directorship of the Manufacture Royale des Meubles de la Couronne at the Gobelins in 1663, a position he had already held for all intents and purposes since the preceding year.[8] Le Brun was responsible, at least in part, for two particularly important projects beginning in the 1660s: the series of colossal paintings of epic scenes from the military campaigns of Alexander the Great, executed throughout the 1660s, and the tapestry series that issued from the Gobelins workshop and which Le Brun directed beginning in 1665.[9] The two projects differ insofar as in the first Alexander was present as a transparent figure for Louis XIV, whereas the latter represented the king with no allegorical enhancement. Yet the projects remain comparable in that they both depict specific actions and historical moments – the first in antiquity, the second in the historical present of Louis XIV.

The fourteen tapestries for *l'Histoire du Roi* that were produced during the reign of Louis XIV, executed in three series of different quality, depict momentous occasions or show the king in significant places at significant times: among these are the *sacre*, his marriage, his visit to the Gobelins workshop, and several important battles.[10] The

Fig. 1. *Siege of Douai* (1667) by Charles Le Brun and François-Adam Van der Meulen, after cartoon by Baudoin Yvart. Châteaux de Versailles et de Trianon, Versailles. Réunion des Musées Nationaux/Art Resource, N.Y.

scenes create an impression of realism and contain no mythological or allegorical figures. François-Adam Van der Meulen, *Peintre Ordinaire de l'Histoire du Roi*, and certainly Le Brun's most important collaborator for the series, accompanied the king on his campaigns in an effort to capture the character of the landscapes on location.[11] One example depicting a victory during the campaign in Flanders in 1667 – the Siege of Douai – provides an idea of the way in which the tapestries represented the king (fig. 1).[12] The caption reads: "Siege of Douai in the year 1667 where the King Louis XIV is leaving the trenches when the city's cannon kills the horse of a bodyguard near His Majesty." The king, imperious and unflinching, stands just right of center next to the Vicomte de Turenne and the Maréchal de Duras, observing the commotion of battle which surrounds him and apparently unconcerned for his personal safety as cannons blast away at Douai from the trenches where he stands. Branches are being gathered nearby and everyone is actively involved in the industry of making war. The horse carrying the bodyguard mentioned in the caption has been hit and has fallen to the ground, a gaping wound opening its flank near the center of the composition. The bodyguard who had been riding the horse, caught unawares, has lost his hat, which lies in the foreground, and may also be partially trapped by his horse.

An official moment of capitulation or victory was not chosen for representation, but rather, the king's visits to the trenches when Tournay was taken a month before. "The tapestry of *l'Histoire du Roi* devoted to the taking of Douai," Daniel Meyer remarks, "does not represent the entry of the souverain into the city. A scene taken during the day of the fourth of July was preferred when, yet again, Louis XIV personally took part in the operations."[13] Four days later French troops entered the town and Douai surrendered. In the tapestry, the king's presence – the conceptual and visual focus of the representation – is overwhelming. The composition brings our attention to bear on his presence, his body, in the midst of battle, alongside his advisors and troops, on July 4, 1667, just outside of Douai. The tapestries represent the monarch making history in battle at a specific time and at a specific place. He is there, in *that* landscape, engulfed but untouched by *that* smoke, both the subject and object of *l'Histoire du Roi*. As one of the most important acts of God's representative on earth, Joël Cornette has argued, war partook of destiny: "war is truly consubstantial with the royal State: not only is it closely linked to the authority of public power incarnated by the prince, but furthermore it makes it possible to make the supreme judge 'speak.'"[14] From a more secular perspective, as the Prussian military theoretician and general Carl von Clausewitz would later argue, the king's bodily presence on the battlefield was a way of uniting deft politics and astute military tactics.[15] Miraculously untouched by the shot that brought down a horse only a few feet away, his real, singular body – his heroic presence on the battlefield – opens and closes the meaning of the scene.

In contrast to the absence of allegory in the tapestries, the Alexander series, now on permanent display at the Louvre, projects a heroic past onto the present through the figure of Alexander the Great. Despite the presence of allegorical representation in one and its absence in the other, both the Alexander paintings and the tapestries create their effect by focusing on the significance of a historical moment and the larger-than-life heroic presence that dominates it. The père Étienne Carneau praised Le Brun for precisely this effect: "On pourroit te nommer le dieu de la peinture. / Puisque tu rends divin ce qui n'estoit qu'humain" [One could name you the god of painting. / Since you make divine that which was only human].[16] Alexander is represented at specific moments in the past, accomplishing unprecedented actions of victory and mercy, just as Louis is represented at significant turning points in the tapestries that contribute to *l'Histoire du Roi*, demonstrating his real, yet untouchable, presence on the battlefield, accompanied by his officers and men. In the series of tapestries woven for *l'Histoire du Roi*, the king is shown at a specific place and time, though this specificity was designed in the end to inflate that presence beyond the proportions of the moment and to produce an effect of awe in the spectator. Likewise, in the Alexander series, though the painting was ultimately intended to produce a singular and uncanny parallel between Alexander and Louis, Le Brun accomplished this effect by depicting a particular moment in time. The commentary offered in Charles Perrault's *Parallèle des anciens et des modernes* emphasizes the unity and singularity of effect created in Le Brun's *The Queens of Persia at the Feet of Alexander*: "the unity of action is Alexander who enters Darius's tent. The unity of place is the tent where are found only those persons who should be there. The unity of time is the moment in which Alexander [speaks]."[17]

Another project executed by Le Brun and his assistants, the decoration of the series of seven rooms at Versailles known as the Grand Appartement, took up allegory as its principal mode of representation. As in the Alexander paintings, Louis was represented *in absentia*, under the cover of allegory. Brimming with allegorical figures, these rooms were realized between 1671 and 1681 and dedicated, following Italian models, to Diana, Mars, Mercury, Apollo, Jupiter, Saturn, and Venus. One of Perrault's interlocutors, strolling through these rooms, admires their use of allegory:

> The God of each planet is represented in the center of the ceiling in a
> chariot drawn by appropriate animals and is surrounded by the proper
> attributes, influences, and spirits. In the paintings on each of the four
> sides [of the room] the actions of the greatest men of Antiquity are
> shown, connected to the planet that accompanies them; [these actions]
> are also so similar to those of His Majesty that one sees in them in a way
> the whole history of his reign although his person is nowhere depicted.[18]

Jean-François Félibien's description confirms the account of Perrault's
fictional abbot. For Félibien, the paintings lead the spectator from the
mythological realm of the gods into the histories of Alexander and
Augustus, leaving the spectator to make the final but obvious leap to
the present and to Louis. Louis XIV was figured as the implicit endpoint
of the entire trajectory. As Paul Duro remarks, however, the meaning
driving these paintings is potentially lost in the ingenious and confusing
design. Though the king is the ultimate destination of these myriad
chains of signifiers, "Louis himself has literally been allegorized out
of the picture, as he is nowhere represented."[19] From this perspective,
one could say that the presence Le Brun sought to capture had been
muted, even lost.

The Escalier des Ambassadeurs, built under Le Brun's supervision
between 1674 and 1678 and designed as a breathtaking approach to the
public apartments on the first floor of Versailles, reveals a somewhat
different strategy with respect to allegory in the representation of the
king. Here, Louis XIV is represented as himself along with various allegorical figures. The grand staircase was used by foreign envoys on their
way to the king's audience and was demolished in 1752 by Louis XV to
make way for new construction. Louis Le Vau drew up the plans which
were realized after his death in 1672 by François d'Orbay, though it appears certain that Le Brun participated extensively in the conception
of the project as it unfolded.[20] The staircase was illuminated by a large
glass roof and surrounded by a vaulted ceiling painted with scenes from
the king's most recent military victories.[21] In each of the four corners
of the ceiling, the prow of a ship was depicted, accompanied by figures
representing one of the four corners of the world. These vessels may
have been intended to recall the naval combat near Messina against the

Spanish and Dutch forces where the admiral Ruyter was killed.[22] On the first floor, real and *trompe l'oeil* openings were separated by marble pilasters. Four false, painted tapestries by Van der Meulen appeared to hang along the two longer walls near the doors depicting recent battle scenes. Near these, Le Brun had colonnade galleries painted where foreign envoys from the four continents were depicted admiring the magnificence of the palace behind heavily draped balustrades in the foreground.[23] The entire composition was grounded in a bust of Louis XIV placed in the center of the lower landing.

Allegory appears throughout this scheme. Le Brun's contemporary biographer, Claude Nivelon, remarked that "the entire Attic side is composed of paintings from *l'Histoire du Roi*, allegorized and simulated in lapis lazuli with a gold background."[24] In one painting, *Louis XIV Reforming Justice*, with one hand the seated king offers a book to a group of venerable old men, and with the other he hands a sword and scales to a woman. The description of this painting given by the *Mercure galant* explains that the old men are jurisconsults and that the viewer easily recognizes the woman as Justice accompanied by Equity.[25] A recent analysis provides still more explanation, noting that the painting actually represents the judicial reform of April, 1667, known as the "Code Louis."[26] L. C. Le Fèvre, who wrote a commentary in 1725 to accompany a collection of engravings of the decoration, remarked on the allegorical strategy of Le Brun's design:

> It was necessary to represent the king as a conqueror, as a supporter of virtue and as protector of the sciences and the arts. It was very difficult to express such a vast idea without employing allegorical symbols, and without a particular arrangement [of the scenes], as one could show only a small number of the heroic actions of the king. However it was necessary to show all the greatness of this Prince and to show it in its best light: allegorical symbols appeared more than equal to the task, but they lose their force and degenerate into pure poetic imaginings if they are not supported by sufficient evidence, I mean if they are not accompanied by known and widely approved facts. M. Le Brun therefore decided to intermix poetic references with the History of the king in such a way that each lends the other support.[27]

Since the king was depicted in some scenes, the use of allegory in the Escalier des Ambassadeurs provided him with a double image: he could claim simultaneously to be "a giant among men," as Paul Duro remarks, and "the equal of the gods."[28] The fusion of "poetry" and history accomplished in the Escalier may be said to set the tone for future developments.

Around 1678, a deliberate and official shift in the politics of representation took place. By August and September, when the treatises of Nijmegen were concluded, marking a major victory for France over Spain, the latter forced to give up the Franche-Comté, Le Brun had already made extensive plans for the paintings that were to adorn the ceiling of the Grande Galerie at Versailles, now known as the Galerie des Glaces, built the same year by Jules Hardouin-Mansart. Le Brun's original designs for the Galerie, based on liberal borrowings from earlier work in the Louvre and from designs by Pietro da Cortona for the Pitti Palace, were mythological and revolved around schemes representing Hercules and Apollo.[29] The ceiling's central compartment was to represent the apotheosis of Hercules, welcomed among the gods on Olympus. After Nijmegen, Louis XIV met with Colbert and others in his secret counsel where he abruptly decided to replace Le Brun's original design with one in which he would appear himself in scenes depicting the military accomplishments of his reign, tracing the king's heroic history from 1661 when he personally took control of government to the capping victory of 1678. The latter is the design that was executed. The ceiling constructs a vast narrative, moving from the start of the conflict (the 1672 coalition uniting Germany, Spain, and Holland) at the end of the gallery that leads to the Salon de la Guerre, to the 1678 treatises at the other end above the entrance to the Salon de la Paix. After submitting his revised plans which adopted the new program decided upon in the secret counsel, Le Brun was advised to move forward, according to Nivelon, "with the prudent restriction on the part of Mr. Colbert that nothing should be allowed to enter into it that was not in keeping with the truth nor that would be too onerous to the foreign powers that it might concern."[30]

Louis XIV had taken the place of Hercules and Apollo, albeit in Roman dress; the historical had upstaged the mythological. The Escalier had blended representations of a fictional, timeless present, in which ambassadors stood in awe of the king, his court, and the palace at Versailles, with historical representations of past events during Louis's reign, and allegorical representations of Louis conducting business with the gods.[31] In contrast to this scheme, the Grande Galerie used allegory to fuse these disparate temporalities into a single sequence of historical events, taken out of time. Le Brun's strategy here took into account the simultaneous existence of the king's two bodies – "his immaterial and immortal body politic and his material and mortal body natural" – articulating the present moment with the past and with eternity.[32] As Thomas Kavanagh has argued with respect to one example found in the Grande Galerie, *The Franche-Comté Conquered a Second Time in 1674*, "the painting certainly refers to a military conquest drawn from history . . . [yet] the unstable eventualities of the moment are replaced by a series of visual tautologies that are forever fixed outside of time and change."[33] In this painting, which is just beyond the central composition towards the Salon de la Paix, Louis XIV is dressed *à l'antique*, in full military regalia, looking down on a soldier representing terror and on weeping women representing the conquered towns whose number and identity are shown in escutcheons linked together by a chain (fig. 2). Each town surrenders its crown to the throne and therefore its keys to the king. To the left, Mars, carrying a shield with the fleur-de-lys, represents the French army. In the middle, Hercules (heroic valour) attacks and is assisted by Minerva (protection). A rock, to which the Spanish lion clings, represents the fortress of Besançon. The fortress is defended by a soldier, but also by the harshness of the season (a grizzled old man), accompanied by winds and the signs of Pisces, Aries, and Taurus, indicating the time of year that the conquest took place. Victory gestures toward the king from above with a laurel wreath. Also present are glory (with her obelisk and golden diadem), renown (with trumpets), and peace (holding olive branches and the horn of plenty). To the right we see the menacing Imperial Eagle,

Fig. 2. *The Franche-Comté Conquered a Second Time in 1674*, drawing by Jean-Baptiste Massé after Charles Le Brun. Louvre, Paris. Réunion des Musées Nationaux / Art Resource, N.Y.

unable to intervene.[34] As in the tapestries, the king is represented immobile, untouched by the fray; yet here, unlike the monarch shown in the trenches outside Douai in the tapestry for *l'Histoire du Roi*, Louis does not appear to be at risk or even really present at all. He is there abstractly, only *to represent* himself. His immobility is in contrast to the bustling activity of the gods and allegorical figures who strain and struggle in combat, doing the bidding of the king.

Louis XIV's decision to suspend Le Brun's original plans for the Grande Galerie led the painter to use allegory in a new way, representing the history of the monarch through the figure of the king in Roman attire, while using allegory freely in the rest of the composition. The tapestries for *l'Histoire du Roi* presented Louis XIV in scenes that were entirely devoid of mythological or allegorical characters.[35] In the decorations for the Grand Appartement, Louis appeared only in the guise of Apollo or Hercules, or as a projected heir of the gods. On the ceiling of the Grande Galerie, however, the representation of the king was fully integrated with allegory and orchestrated around historical events. This is not to say that the history presented in the Grande Galerie is in any way realistic or direct. To grasp this fact, one only has to glance at *The Franche-Comté Conquered a Second Time in 1674* or at the image, near the entrance to the Salon de la Guerre, of Louis sailing across the Rhine in a Roman chariot surrounded by winged allegorical figures. The history of the king as it is presented on the ceiling of the Grande Galerie – what Jean-Marie Apostolidès has called "la mythistoire" – is manifestly just as imaginary as the images depicting Apollo in the Grand Appartement even though Louis is painted into the image.[36] Yet it nonetheless marks an important re-configuration of the king's image. No longer modeling himself after the gods, Louis XIV has enlisted *their* services as he is placed above the fray. Given Colbert's concerns with discretion, Le Brun's paintings engaged historical events through a mass of allegory, thus abstracting the king's history from the myriad of particular circumstances and dif-ficulties that accompanied each battle while preserving, in its largest sense, the supposed historical "truth" – a term that, in the eyes of these cultural politicians of the reign of Louis XIV, perhaps referred simply to the all-encompassing *gloire* of the king – that was so important for Colbert. Paradoxically, then, representing the "true" Louis XIV, rather than Apollo, meant abstracting the king from actual circumstances. By using historical painting to produce an impression of timelessness, the ceiling of the Grande Galerie comes close to the effect, as I will describe it below, of the operatic prologue.

Le Brun's historical paintings and tapestries, however, were not the only means of self-representation chosen by the monarchy. Years before Le Brun completed the new designs for the Grande Galerie, the various advantages and drawbacks of painting, sculpture, and medallions for the celebration of the king were discussed by the members of the Petite Académie, an association founded in 1663 to regulate the glorification of Louis XIV through the arts and letters. This group was concerned with the theoretical as well as the strategic difficulties in establishing an effective poetics and politics of encomium. Among other responsibilities, the Petite Académie reviewed, corrected, and even revised the verse for the *tragédies en musique* proposed by Quinault, Lully's librettist and also a member of the organization as early as 1674. Colbert's founding group included Jean Chapelain, Charles Perrault, the abbé de Bourzeis, the abbé de Cassagne, and, later, François Charpentier. Narrowing the scope of its influence in 1701, the Petite Académie became the Académie Royale des Inscriptions et Médailles.[37] From its inception, the Petite Académie debated strategies and problems concerning the representation of Louis XIV. In a letter to Colbert dated November 18, 1662, Chapelain outlined the various merits of medallions, historical narratives, poems and other visual and textual means for the glorification of the king, and summarized some of the questions that the Petite Académie must have debated from the very beginning. Chapelain's main concern throughout the letter appears not to have been with a politics of the present but with the effects of time – that is, with a search for the means to extend indefinitely the memory of the king through various forms of representation. The glorification of the king was aimed almost exclusively at posterity; and Chapelain clearly imagined aesthetic objects and texts as if projected into the distant future, being contemplated and read by future populations. For these men and women, Louis XIV would be as a Roman emperor whose miraculous achievements had been preserved in cultural artifacts through the counsel of a few wise men.

In his letter, Chapelain noted that medallions, historical narratives, and poems all have the prestige of Greek and Roman precedent. If the goal is to "eternalize" or "perpetuate" the memory of the king, gold and silver medallions have the advantage of resisting the effects of time.[38] Poetry, however, is the form of memory that appears to have been the most successful in defeating time, above painting, sculpture, and even architectural objects: "all tombs, all portraits, all the most renowned statues have run aground on its shores [time's]; even the most exquisite works of prose have come down to us but mutilated and maimed, and only poetic works, beginning with Homer – the excellent ones at least – have passed down to us."[39] Poetry was seen as the most resistant to the effects of time – an infallible way of conferring immortality on the king and his actions. However, the difficulty with narrative poetry, Chapelain remarked, is that since it necessarily relies heavily on fiction, there is always the risk of losing credibility. What was at stake was the ability of readers to distinguish "the marvels that His Majesty has already accomplished in such great number, and that he will accomplish in still greater number in the future," from the exaggerations and fabulations of the epic poet.[40] Epic poetry ran the risk of encouraging readers to see the the king himself and his heroic actions as mere fictions. Though the epic was in principle at the summit of all genres, and thus perhaps the obvious medium for royal commemoration, there was a certain hostility toward epic poetry on the part of French theorists. In his 1674 poetic treatise, René Rapin condemned Ariosto and Tasso for what epic poets did best, for their abuse of *le merveilleux*: "this hippogriff or Roger's winged horse, these giants, these monsters, this magic ring belonging to Angelica which makes her invisible, these combats of Marfise, Bradamante, Olympia . . . these visions, these enchantments and all these prodigious events are like the empty illusions of a madman, and they are pitiful to all those who have any sense because they have no hint of verisimilitude."[41] Epic was contemptible, in Rapin's eyes, as soon as it strayed from the central poetic criterion of verisimilitude.

Though it may appear to be the ideal solution to the vagaries of epic, historical writing presented other complications for Chapelain. He was convinced, however, that it must be at least "one of the principal means for preserving the splendor of the undertakings of the King and the detailed account of his miracles."[42] In his "Projet de l'Histoire de Louis XIV," Pellisson observed that the history of the king should be "neither in the form of a journal, nor of a report, nor simple memoirs, nor eulogies, nor panegyrics . . . It should rather be like a great history in the manner of Livy, Polybius, and other ancients."[43] Similarly, Chapelain remarked that history must not be a simple narrative of events, "a pure recounting," like a "gazette," but must be well documented and prudently speculative so as to explain "the reasons behind things."[44] Yet there lies the rub; for to explain the meaning of events fully during the reign of the king is to risk exposing state secrets and to betray the king's alliances with other powers, "which survive only through secrecy and in the shadow of a profound silence."[45] Even if one could keep the king's written history secret during his lifetime, Chapelain considered, the many qualities needed to be a good historiographer are almost impossible to find in one man, not the least of which is what Chapelain understood to be the innate "genius of this profession":

> For, to be a good historian, one should be a very trustworthy man, know perfectly the objective of the projects and of the conduct of the Prince who initiates them, be informed of the interests of his friends and his adversaries, master political theory, understand the conduct of war, not be unacquainted with chronology or geography, not be inexperienced in the manners and customs of nations, have seen and transcribed the originals of dispatches and treatises, all of which is not terribly common.[46]

Given the near insurmountable problems of the demands imposed on the historian and the implausibility of the epic poet's creations, Chapelain fell back on the panegyric as a temporary solution to the problem of glorifying the king. This alternative may seem to be a strange one. Reflecting on historical writing in the margins of a text by Lucian that he had copied out, Racine wrote that "panegyrics and history are as distant as the heavens are from the earth"; he added that "the poet needs all the Gods to paint his Agamemnon."[47] Racine's odd ellipsis leaves us in suspense. If history and panegyric are antithetical, and if the poet needs the full assortment of gods to tell his story, what is it that the historian needs to render *his* Agamemnon? Perhaps he meant us to understand that the late seventeenth-century historian needs only Louis le Grand. In 1662, however, Chapelain was in a position to suggest that embellishment has its merits. In panegyric verse or prose, like that of Pliny for the Roman emperor Trajan, he remarked, historical personages and events are able to tolerate embellishment more easily than they can in forms such as history or epic poetry. Panegyric can even reach out to the sublime and is not burdened by the titanic requirements of history.[48] Though he did not claim to have found the ideal solution to the problems of representing the king, Chapelain advocated panegyric texts so that the king would not lack some form of tribute in the present.[49] Chapelain's central concern was to find a way to represent the king to contemporaries and, simultaneously, to posterity: as the sovereign of France in the present and as part of a larger historical scheme. Despite the exaggeration of the panegyric, which might be seen as being at odds with historical accuracy, for Chapelain it nonetheless reconciled a present need for encomium with the goal of recording Louis XIV's deeds for posterity.[50] Indeed, Chapelain appears to have been at least partially right about the need for an immediate solution to the Petite Académie's charge. For the formidable project of constructing the history of the king in narrative form, though it escaped the jurisdiction of the Petite Académie in the end, would never amount to anything other than a collection of fragments.[51]

As for painting, the strategies Le Brun retained in the representations of the king at Versailles may also have been seen as problematic. Chapelain observed that painting had not demonstrated the longevity of poetry. Yet, in addition to material considerations, difficulties can be discerned in the very modes of representation chosen by Le Brun. Paul Duro writes that the length of the description of the Escalier des Ambassadeurs given by Le Fèvre testifies not only to the complexity of the scheme but also to the fact that "the ideological message is here at war with the limits of painting."[52] As painting strained to provide the ideal representation of the king and his history, accompanying narratives proliferated to control the meaning of these complex objects. In their recent commentary on the Escalier, Lydia Beauvais and Jean-François Méajanès feel the need to provide explanatory remarks not only on the decoration of the staircase itself, but also on the supplementary narrative provided by Nivelon which was intended to clarify the meaning of Le Brun's work in the first place.[53] Le Brun's work is certainly not transparent to us; but it may not have been immediately obvious to contemporaries either, despite their familiarity with mythology or the events of the king's campaigns. The fact that handbooks were printed at the time to reveal the meanings of the allegories attests to their inscrutability.[54] In December 1684, for example, the *Mercure galant* published a description and explanation of the ceiling of the Grande Galerie, attributed to "Mr Lorne peintre." The writer noted the distinguished pedigree of allegory – "the most ancient way of expressing thoughts in characters" – and that Le Brun has been so careful to make his allegories clear that, even if the observer knows little of the Greek and Roman poets, his paintings are easy to understand.[55] Tellingly, however, the writer remarked that the many explanations he nonetheless felt obliged to offer (as in his comment on *The King Governs by Himself*, explaining that the king "holds a rudder to indicate that he has begun to govern his State") have left no room for the discussion of the material and aesthetic qualities.[56] As Paul Duro has suggested, this statement reveals "the gap between allegory and intelligibility" which is bridged only by narrative explanation. Duro concludes: "By overdetermining the potential for painting to be framed by discourse, to find its truth in one reading, Le Brun forced painting to act in a totalitarian way; and it hardly needs saying that a closed reading is not one that may be expected to bear the full weight of analysis without revealing inconsistencies and contradictions."[57]

The prologues to *tragédies en musique* may have been initially seen as better suited than painting to the representational aims of the Petite Académie. They were built on the poetic core that, for Chapelain, assured longevity, and avoided the mythological dispersion found in the scheme for the Grand Appartement. In its strategies of representation, the prologue can be seen to emerge from Le Brun's work in the Grande Galerie, with which it is largely contemporary. Taking these representations of Louis XIV one step further, I will argue, early French opera withdrew the person of the king from the stage while nonetheless retaining his overwhelming presence.

Louis XIV did appear in person in one of opera's forerunners, the court ballet. The young king excelled at dancing and played many different roles in the ballets written by Isaac Benserade beginning in 1651. As Sarah R. Cohen has argued, Louis XIV's appearance in court ballet, beginning in the early 1650s when he "had just reached his majority and the French monarchy was on the defensive against the agitation of the Fronde," had strong political overtones.[58] He appeared onstage not only as Apollo, but also, over the years, as Spring, a Bohemian, a Moor, a village girl, a European, Rinaldo, Alexander, and Cyrus.[59] Louis danced alone and with other members of the royal family and the court. As the Morning Star, for example, Monsieur, the king's brother, preceded Louis's appearance in *Le Ballet de la Nuit*.[60] *Le Ballet de la Nuit*, permeated with allegory, was given several days after Carnival in 1653, shortly after the victory of the monarchy in the Fronde and the return of Mazarin from exile. The king danced six roles. He shone as the most brilliant of the Hours of the day; as a *"Curieux,"* he was keen (*curieux*) on seeing his people live in peace; he took a fierce attitude toward Spanish pride as a *"Furieux."* Finally, as these verses written for Monsieur indicate, Louis appeared as a figure for the rising sun in the final *entrée*:

Depuis que j'ouvre l'Orient,
Jamais si pompeuse et si fière,
Et jamais d'un air si riant,
Je n'ai brillé dans ma carrière,
Ni précédé tant de lumière.
Quels yeux en la voyant n'en seraient éblouis?
Le Soleil qui me suit, c'est le jeune LOUIS

From the moment I open the Orient,
Never so splendid nor so proud,
And never with such a joyful air,
Have I shone in my course,
Nor preceded so much light.
What eyes would not be dazzled upon seeing it?
The sun which follows me is the young LOUIS.[61]

In the 1654 ballet, *Les Noces de Pélée et de Thétis*, to give another example, the king again danced the role of Apollo, this time opening the spectacle surrounded by the nine muses. Making reference both to the role being played and to the player of that role, the verses of *Les Noces de Pélée et de Thétis* refer to his ability to successfully elude destructive passions ("Je cours sans cesse après la Gloire, / Et ne cours point après Daphné" [I run forever after Glory / But never run after Daphne]) and to defeat his enemies ("J'ai vaincu ce Python qui désolait le monde, / Ce terrible serpent que l'Enfer et la Fronde / D'un venin dangereux avaient assaisonné" [I vanquished the Python which was ravaging the world, / That terrible serpent which Hades and the Fronde / Had seasoned with a dangerous venom]).[62] In somewhat different circumstances, the king took the role of Roger in the "Plaisirs de l'isle enchantée," the massive court festivities of 1664 that were freely based on Ariosto's *Orlando furioso*.[63] In these loosely woven stories, pleasure, seduction, and the hero's ultimate resistence to seduction were the most prominent themes. On the subject of seduction, as Cohen has remarked, "the king's outstanding capacity to love and to be loved by women [emerged] as a major theme in the spectacles surrounding his marriage to Maria Teresa of Spain in 1660 . . . although the queen herself rarely performed [in the court ballets of the 1660s], both Louise de la Vallière and Madame de Montespan performed alongside other court ladies and received flattering verses of their own."[64] Discussing the "Plaisirs de l'isle enchantée," Cohen suggests that although "traditional wisdom has it that the king used the *Plaisirs* to celebrate his own love for his first *maîtresse en titre*, Louise de la Vallière," the political uses of a series of spectacles designed to entertain six hundred courtiers over several days were vastly more significant.[65]

Louis XIV made his last appearance on stage in a court ballet in the *Ballet de Flore*, which was first performed on February 13, 1669.[66] About a year later, Molière's *Les Amants magnifiques* began its run on February 4, 1670. The king had chosen the subject for the play and was scheduled to appear as Neptune and Apollo. His abrupt decision to have the comte d'Armagnac and the marquis de Villeroy replace him has been the subject of much speculation.[67] Louis's definitive withdrawal from the stage has been linked to a passage from act 4, scene 4, of Racine's *Britannicus*, represented about seven weeks earlier on December 13, 1669, in which Narcissus warns Nero that in order to be emperor he must not appear to be "staged" by others, that he must not appear to be acting a part or reciting lines.[68] In a letter to Losme de Monchenai from September 1701, Boileau noted that "having seen a performance of Racine's *Britannicus*, where Néron's passion for being on stage is so thoroughly condemned, [the king] never danced again in any Ballet, not even during Carnival."[69] The playwright's son, Louis Racine, wrote in his *Mémoires* that "these verses struck the young monarch, who had sometimes danced in ballets; and although he danced with much majesty, he refused to appear again in any ballet, recognizing that a king must never offer himself as a spectacle."[70]

Jean-Pierre Néraudau locates an earlier warning to Louis XIV in Molière's *L'Impromptu de Versailles*, first performed for the king on October 14, 1663. In the self-reflexive plot of *L'Impromptu de Versailles*, Molière's players are rehearsing a new work with no time to spare. The king's merciful reprieve comes at the final moment to save Molière's unprepared and bickering actors – played by themselves – from sure humiliation. Instead of the new play they are rehearsing, the king (in the words of his messenger) allows them to put on something from their repertoire. Néraudau remarks:

> But as he is offering [the king] this tribute, Molière makes a *Deus ex machina* of him . . . It is up to the King to understand that he must not be taken in by the illusion of his own play. The future shows that the King did not understand the wisdom of the playwright. On the contrary, he left the stage where he had danced to become lost in the illusion that he truly was the Sun King.

Néraudau surmises that by 1670, Louis XIV had decided to leave the stage, believing that, since he had become the image he constantly borrowed in performance, he no longer needed to "play" king.[71]

In a divergent analysis of the king's decision, Abby E. Zanger points out that in *Britannicus*, Narcissus, the evil advisor, does not offer Nero a condemnation of theater *tout court*; rather, he astutely points out the risks of playing when one might always appear to be a pawn in someone else's game – in this case, that of Nero's powerful mother, Agrippina. Zanger goes on to suggest that in *Les Amants magnifiques*, Molière does not caution Louis against theater, as Néraudau considered he had in *L'Impromptu de Versailles*. Rather, Molière offered the king an alternative role. Zanger suggests that the king's "abdication of the stage was not simply a reaction to Racine's evil advisor who urged his monarch toward violence, and away from theatrical pacification, but also an imitation of Molière's Clitidas," a character who comically climbs a tree at one point in *Les Amants magnifiques* in order to withdraw from the events below, but also to be able to survey the action from above and to draw attention to his unusual action.[72] Unlike Néraudau, who assumes that the king stopped dancing because he had begun to take himself for the characters he was playing, Zanger argues that Louis may have simply chosen another model for his strategy of self-representation. Louis's personal withdrawal from the stage implies neither that he had retreated into fantasy, as Néraudau suggests, nor that he had vanished altogether from the scene. Even as the *ballet de cour* disappeared, even as Louis stepped off the stage – whatever his personal and/or political reasons for doing so may have been – *tragédie en musique* continued to invoke his presence in ways that the earlier form could not, in part precisely because of his presence onstage. The prologue and its relation to the body of the opera would be central to the representation of the king in his *tragédies en musique*.

In antiquity, the prologue functioned to focus the attention of the spectators and to introduce the plot. Much later, writers used the prologue as a forum for the discussion of genre or their own innovations, as in Niccolò da Correggio's *Cefalo* (1486).[73] Tragedy speaks in Ottavio Rinuccini's prologue to *L'Euridice*, to argue that tragedy *in musica* is not about innocent blood or insane tyrants, but rather about mournful and tearful scenes.[74] Rinuccini's prologue goes on to praise the new queen, Maria de' Medici, whose wedding is being celebrated, and whose renown will surpass that of Athens and Rome, and to introduce the story of Orpheus. Though prologues had long disappeared from spoken tragedy in France, they were maintained in *tragédies à machines*, in *comédie-ballet*, and in *tragédies en musique*. The use of the operatic prologue to praise the king had precedents in the Italian operas imported by Mazarin in the 1640s and '50s, the court ballets, and the machine plays, all of which included elements of panegyric. Louis

XIV is praised, for example, in the French prologue to *Ercole amante* by Cavalli and Buti, which premiered on February 7, 1662, in the Tuileries palace to celebrate, belatedly, the 1659 peace treaty with Spain and the marriage of the king to the Spanish infante: "Et tout comme Hercule, / Après tant d'honneurs guerriers, / Finit par épouser la Beauté, / Ainsi, après mille lauriers / Et dans le plein soleil / De son âge éclatant, le roi des Gaulois / Sur cette scène, devant les Français heureux, / Reprend aujourd'hui les cothurnes d'Hercule amoureux" [And just as Hercules, / After so many battle honors, / Finally married Beauty, / Thus, after a thousand laurels / And at the zenith / Of his brightest age, the king of the Gauls / On this stage, in front of the happy French, / Takes up today the cothurni of Hercules in love].[75]

The action of the prologues to Lully's and Quinault's *tragédies en musique* is always distinct from that of the opera itself, even though characters who appear in the prologue may occasionally reappear in the opera, as is the case in *Amadis* (1684). These introductory pieces function as celebrations of the king and his military exploits through allegorical and mythological characters, expanding the traditional poetic domain of the panegyric to spectacular extremes. Considering the opera prologue in light of the initiatives of the Petite Académie, and in light of the difficulties that Chapelain had outlined in his 1662 letter to Colbert, we may be able to see in opera a temporary replacement – a stop-gap measure – to fill the need for encomium in the absence of viable epic or historical alternatives. It is interesting to note, as Siegbert Himmelsbach does, that the epic is eclipsed between 1670 and 1750, the years that mark the inception and rise of opera in France: "opera often seems to be the 'heir' of the epic supernatural at a time when this element was already more or less supressed in epic poetry."[76] L'abbé Terrasson, in his *Dissertation critique sur l'Iliade d'Homere*, remarked that in its use of *le merveilleux*, opera went beyond the other "high" genres – tragedy and epic – by staging actions that were only represented in words in the epic poem. *Tragédie en musique* rendered visually the fantastic splendor of epic writing.[77] The opera prologue might therefore be seen as the culmination and apotheosis of the encomiastic alternative to history and to epic poetry proposed by Chapelain.

The prologue continued to function as panegyric beyond the death of Lully in 1687, though this practice declined early in the eighteenth century. By the time of Jean-Philippe Rameau's *Zoroastre* (1749), the prologue was normally omitted.

Manuel Couvreur has even suggested a close relationship between medals and emblems – which became the sole purview of the Petite Académie – and opera. Regarding medals and emblems, Couvreur notes, one finds "on one side, the allegorical representation of a prominent event of the reign, on the other side the realistic portrait of the king." He finds a parallel structure in the bipartite *tragédie en musique*: "the libretti definitely propose a double image of the king. Realistic and nominative in the prologue, it is transfigured into the world of symbols by the tragedy."[78] Though we might take issue with Couvreur's use of the term "realistic" to describe the highly allegorical and mythological prologue, his sense that the two forms of representation have a parallel function is certainly correct. The king was both subject and object of the relatively short prologue; the opera that followed presented stories drawn from various sources – mythology, epic, and ancient tragedy. In part because the king chose these subjects, contemporary audiences looked for allegories relating to the king and the court in each opera, as keys to understanding their meaning. Néraudau has hunted down many of these keys in contemporary circumstances and events:

> The character of Hercules in *Alceste* cannot help but evoke the king, continuing a process of assimilation which, the same year, sees him placed in sculptural relief on the [arch at the] Porte Saint-Martin under the guise of Hercules treading upon Geryon, the emblem of the triple Alliance. The encounters between Theseus and the magician Medea, like the battle between Bellerophon and the Chimera, or that of Perseus and the monster who menaced Andromeda can be interpreted allegorically when we begin to think about the *affaire des poisons* and the fact that the king was combatting monstrous enemies. Less clear and more frivolous, a relationship can nonetheless be established between the plot of *Isis* and the passing inclination of the king for Mademoiselle de Ludres.[79]

Jean Duron, too, has attempted to piece together the meanings lurking behind the plot of *Atys* (1676). He writes:

> If one accepts the tempting principle of a relationship of character between Atys and the Louis XIV of late 1675, one will admit without further difficulty that Cybèle has many traits in common with the queen Marie-Thérèse: her boundless love for Atys, her total abnegation (Cybèle renounces, for him, her position as goddess, just as the queen loses her standing by accepting the most ignominious affronts, by lowering herself to console the king's mistresses), and above all the admirable energy she expends to try to protect her love.[80]

Contemporary audiences were clearly interested in the possibility of such correspondences between the operatic stories of superhuman beings and gods on the one hand, and the heroic and amorous exploits of the king on the other. Because the prologue made both implicit and explicit connections between Louis and the narrative of the opera, an indeterminate, yet appreciable, relation may be said to have existed between the king and the hero. The prologues' characters refer to the king, singing his praises as a "hero", a "conqueror," "the greatest king," "a new Mars," or, in the prologue to *Thésée* (1675), which is set at Versailles, as "the Master of the grounds." However, for the reasons outlined below, attempts such as those of Duron and Néraudau to identify specific correspondences as keys to the meaning of these operas are inevitably based on unconvincing and overly facile formulae.

In contrast to Louis XIV's bodily presence in the court ballet, and in contrast to his decision to appear painted onto the ceiling of the Grande Galerie in 1678, the *tragédies en musique* that Lully and Quinault produced for the Académie Royale de Musique from 1673 on concealed the king from direct view. Louis was never manifestly represented by any specific character in the *tragédies en musique*, with the exception of Lully's and Quinault's first work, *Cadmus et Hermione* (1673), where the sun appeared onstage in the prologue, satisfied after having saved the world from the serpent Python (fig. 3). Though tragedy by definition places kings and heroes onstage, this fact in and of itself does not imply that the operatic Theseus or Hercules represented Louis XIV. Buford

Fig. 3. Illustration of the prologue of *Cadmus et Hermione* (1673), engraving after Jean Berain. Photo courtesy of the Bibliothèque Nationale de France, Cabinet des Estampes, Paris.

Norman has remarked that attempts to identify the king with particular operatic kings or heroes eventually succumb to incoherence. Whereas one might compare Louis to Cadmus, for example, Norman notes that because of his dependency on Amour and Pallas, Cadmus is closer to Condé under Louis XIII, "or, in 1673, to Turenne, capable of great achievements but always needed divine / royal backing."[81] Norman concludes that it is impossible to find a precise image of Louis XIV or a coherent political lesson in these operas.[82] The juxtaposition and implicit comparison with the often weak and deceitful hero of the operas may also be seen to blemish the shimmering image of the monarch presented in the prologue. Norman has written of the powerlessness of the operatic king, noting that "the presence of a glorious hero who was in love allowed Quinault to flatter the King, but the juxtaposition of other heroes (Alcide, Theseus) to a weak king (Admetus, Aegeus) would also please a noble audience which had not forgotten the feudal ideal of the first part of the century."[83] William Brooks, too, has noted that the hero is often inglorious, and he has described the oversimplification of claiming that these operas were mere celebrations of Louis's heroism:

> For, in as much as the expected identification of Louis is with the hero of the tale, the reverse is often true. Jupiter's pursuit of the reticent Io is a disgraceful hole-and-corner affair, in which Mercure acts as his procurer . . . and then Jupiter abandons Io to her fate . . . There are numerous bad and ineffective heroes, and obviously so, so that wherever else the explanation for the persistent success of these works may lie, it is not in the omnipresent glorious and triumphant hero.[84]

If *tragédie en musique* can be considered a "school for heroes," it is at the very least a highly contradictory one.[85] Indeed, Quinault's biographer, Étienne Gros, made precisely the opposite claim, that opera encouraged the licentious behavior of the king: "opera, with its lax and indulgent morality, aimed, at each favorable occasion, to flatter the passions of the king and to shower praise on Louis XIV even in his least acceptable weaknesses."[86] If the triumph of rational self-control was ideally to be consummated in the deeds of the operatic hero, who is presumed to be "master of his love and of himself," as Charles Perrault remarked of Hercules in Quinault's and Lully's *Alceste* (1674), glory and love are not often so effortlessly compatible.[87] Since the hero often cannot control himself, as Perry Gethner notes, the only choice he is left with is to flee: "true love is an emotion which absorbs all the energy and all the thoughts of the lover; the physical presence of the other dazzles him, and a confession on his part causes a frenetic desire for consummation [*jouissance*]."[88] Paradoxically, in the very genre in which Louis's person disappeared so that his image could reappear triumphant in the prologue, the heroism of the central male character was shown up as precarious and insubstantial.

The question I want to ask is not so much that of Louis's concealed presence in a series of half-hidden meanings in which stories of court intrigue are prominent, or his explicit identification with the hero. Generally speaking, these were fleeting associations made by courtiers and intended to have only momentary and partial consistency and relevance. If Juno's actions in *Isis* may have underscored the jealousy of Mme de Maintenon, the story of Io was nevertheless chosen at a later date for a series of nine paintings commissioned from François Verdier for the Trianon. Hélène Himelfarb wonders about the lasting implications of these hidden meanings:

> If the connection, as was said, between the persecutions inflicted on Io by the jealous Juno and the triangular drama which had been played out between the King, Mme de Montespan and the beautiful Mlle de Ludres was truly behind it, would Louis XIV and his new wife have allowed a commission of such importance to eternalize them, ten years later, under their noses and at their expense?[89]

Similarly, as Buford Norman has argued, the spectator may also see many facets of the king in *Alceste*: "monarch, hero, lover, dancer, a general who is fond of sieges, builder of monuments and triumphal arches, organizer of entertainments, and more." Norman points out that one could always "extend this game of infinite reflections."[90] These connections were undoubtedly a source of pleasure for contemporaries who could exploit and vary them in social situations and in epistolary exchanges. What interests me here is not so much the specific identification of a given character with the life and times of the monarch; it is rather the more general effect of the degradation of the tragic hero on the image of the monarch constructed in the prologue. The relation in question is not that of the opera to the life of Louis XIV, but rather that of the prologue to the body of the *tragédie* and vice versa. At stake is the ability of opera to generate a coherent image of the king.

The *tragédies en musique* of Lully and Quinault, and the festivities of which they were sometimes a part, were always presented as moments of repose from battle. The prologues constantly reiterate the claim that the many wars in which Louis XIV (who, for his bellicosity, was later ironically baptized *Mars Christianissimus*) was engaged, from the 1674 conquests in the Franche-Comté to the "cold war" of the early 1680s, were undertaken to preserve peace for the French.[91] If the operatic prologue referred to the pastoral in part to commemorate its origins as a genre, bucolic love and peace were also precisely those pastoral values created or restored by the king for the pleasure of his subjects.[92] The pastoral setting and atmosphere are implicitly presented as the creation of Louis, and in turn reflect back upon him, shaping his image. In *Thésée*, music has a hand in this game when pastoral instruments appear in the gardens of Versailles in place of the (musical) instruments of war: "Que les hautbois, que les musettes / L'emportent sur les trompettes / Et sur les tambours. / Que rien ne trouble ici Vénus & les Amours" [Let the oboes and the musettes / Win out over the trumpets / And the drums. / Let nothing here trouble Venus and the Cupids]. The prologue concludes when the chorus joins Mars and Venus to sing: "Au milieu de la guerre / Goûtons les plaisirs de la paix" [In the middle of war / Let us taste the pleasures of peace].[93] Similarly, in *Proserpine* (1680), even if Peace is kept in chains by War at the opening, Victory arrives and calls Peace to her side: "Ah! qu'il est beau de rendre / La paix à l'Univers / Après avoir vaincu mille peuples divers, / Quand on ne voit plus rien qui puisse se défendre" [Ah! how beautiful it is to give / Peace to the Universe / After having conquered a thousand different nations, / When there is nothing in sight that can defend itself].[94] Démogorgon, "King of the Fairies, and the first of the Genies of the Earth," in *Roland* (1685), claims that "Le vainqueur a contraint la Guerre / D'éteindre son flambeau: / Il rend le repos à la terre; / Quel triomphe est plus beau!" [The conqueror forced War / To extinguish its flame: / He returns rest to the earth; / What triumph is greater!"[95] Astrée – the pastoral figure par excellence – has fled the earth because of war in the prologue to *Phaéton*. The stunning victories of a certain "Hero" have disarmed the earth and restored peace so that Astrée can now return it and its inhabitants to the golden age. Discussing the political theories of the period, Cornette has argued that, "for numerous legal experts and theoreticians of the royal State, the ruler was considered more than ever as the necessary guarantor of order, the manager of legitimate violence, the creator and the preserver of a space of peace . . . war was in a way consubstantial to his function, to his legitimacy, to the exercise of his power."[96] In the panegyric language of the prologue, as for numerous political theorists, war abroad creates peace at home.

A closer examination of *Atys*, termed "the opera of the king" by Le Cerf de la Viéville and by all accounts one of Quinault's and Lully's best works, will provide a more complex and nuanced picture of the workings of panegyric in these operas.[97] The prologue is set in the palace of Time, who appears surrounded by twenty-four singers representing the twelve hours of the day and the twelve hours of the night. In an appropriately formidable bass voice, Time announces the arrival of a new hero whose unprecedented excellence has eclipsed all previous examples of valor:

> En vain j'ay respecté la celebre memoire
> Des heros des siècles passez;
> C'est en vain que leurs noms si fameux dans l'Histoire,
> Du sort des noms communs ont esté dispensez:
> Nous voyons un heros dont la brillante gloire
> Les a presque tous effacez.

> In vain have I honored the celebrated memory
> Of the heroes of centuries past;
> In vain their names, so famed in history,
> Have been spared the fate of common names.
> We here behold a hero whose dazzling glory
> Has effaced nearly all of them.[98]

Because the function of the operatic prologue is to announce the resuscitation of an ancient and tragic story, it conventionally revolves around the topos of memory; and memory, as Perry Gethner has remarked, "becomes the center of a curious dialectic between past and present, and between memory and forgetting."[99] In the prologue to *Atys*, Time finds himself out of work. His age-old occupation has suddenly been outmoded; his efforts to celebrate past heroes are for naught because of the arrival of a new hero. History has been altered forever. By rendering history obsolete, the prologue to *Atys* adopts the same rhetorical strategy as Claude-Charles Guyonnet de Vertron in his panegyric *Parallèle de Louis le Grand avec les princes qui ont esté surnommez Grands*: "why, therefore, seek in fiction the deeds of a Hercules and in history those of an Alexander if Louis le Grand offers examples of all virtues?"[100] The famous heroes whose glorious deeds have been recorded in the annals of History, distinguished in this from common mortals, have all been eclipsed by a new hero – not a hero of the moment, but rather a hero for all eternity. If the Alexander paintings implicitly compared Louis to Alexander, the prologue to *Atys* eliminates the predecessor altogether. There are no longer any other models, any predecessors or successors. When Racine remarked that "panegyrics and history are as distant as the heavens are from the earth," he may have been thinking of this particular relation between panegyric and memory.[101] Indeed, to a great extent, panegyric effaces history. Though it may be able to realize similar objectives and at times draw from the same resources, the panegyric mode nonetheless flattens history into an apotheosis of the present moment as eternity in its praise of the monarch. If Le Brun's work on the ceiling of the Grande Galerie placed the gods at the service of an apotheosis of the king, they nonetheless remained on the same painted surface as he. In the operatic prologue, mythological and allegorical characters appear onstage to praise a king who seems no longer to exist on the same plane. In attendance offstage in flesh and blood, certainly, in the Salle des Ballets at Saint-Germain-en-Laye on January 10, 1676, his image as monarch can only truly emerge when redoubled in spectacular praise.

After his declaration, the single bass voice of Time is supplanted by the many voices of the Chorus of Hours which, together, sing the praises of the new hero:

> Ses justes loix,
> Ses grands exploits,
> Rendent sa memoire éternelle:
> Chaque jour, chaque instant
> Adjouste encor à son nom esclattant
> Une gloire nouvelle.

> His just laws,
> His great exploits,
> Render his memory eternal:
> Every day, every instant
> Adds yet more glory
> To his resplendent name. (55)

Time has come to a halt in an eternal present ("each day, each moment"), at once forever repeated and continually accrued in the individual accomplishments of the new hero. The twenty-four voices of the Chorus of Hours performatively realize Chapelain's concern with making the king's memory eternal. As echoed by the chorus of voices, praise of the king requires the forgetting of historical time. There is no room for details; the specifics are almost entirely suppressed by the panegyric mode. As panegyric, the opera prologue is at odds with history, indeed also to some extent with narrative; and yet it fulfills a portion of the aesthetic and political mission of the Petite Académie by having Time announce his "defeat" by the presence of a new hero. Louis Marin argued that "the desire for the absolute of power, for the *incomparable* glory of the monarch, will take the form of time" – an eternal present.[102] As panegyric, the prologue works to make immortality and perfection the two essential attributes of Louis XIV.

Interrupting the vocal celebration of the Chorus of Hours, the goddess Flore advances with Zephyrs and flower-bearing Nymphs. Time, now thoroughly bewildered, wonders why Flore has appeared in the middle of winter:

La Saison des frimats peut-elle nous offrir
Les fleurs que nous voyons paraistre?
Quel Dieu les fait renaistre
Lorsque l'Hyver les fait mourir?
Le froid cruel regne encore;
Tout est glacé dans les champs.
D'où vient que Flore
Devance le Printemps?

Can the winter season bring us
The flowers that we see appearing?
What God brings them back to life
When Winter has killed them?
The cruel cold reigns still;
All is frozen in the fields.
Why is it that Flore
Arrives before Spring? (56)

In response, Flore explains that she always arrives too late. Because the hero whom she seeks to please is away at war during the mild season, she must now do the impossible: she returns in January in order to find him willing to indulge in pastoral pleasures and rest, rather than off in the battlefield with Bellone in search of Glory. One of her Zephyrs echoes the complaint: "Le Printemps quelquefois est moins doux qu'il ne semble, / Il fait trop payer ses beaux jours" [Spring is sometimes less gentle than it seems; / It makes us pay too dearly for its fine days] (57).

In Flore's action, we see a gesture that is repeated in one form or another in all of Quinault's and Lully's prologues: the gods, goddesses, and other deities that populate the universe will do anything in their power to serve and please the new hero, sometimes, as here, rearranging the ordinary course of events in the cosmos. Thoughout Quinault's and Lully's prologues, gods and allegorized divinities appear only to await Louis's arrival, serve him, and sing his praises: in *Alceste*, la Gloire, with various Nayades, Dieux des Bois, and Nymphes, celebrates "sa Valeur triomphante" [his triumphant Valor] and awaits his imminent return from battle; in *Phaéton* (1683), Saturn has been ordered by "un Héros, qui mérite une gloire immortelle" [a Hero, who deserves immortal glory] to restore the golden age; "publiez des exploits nouveaux" [spread the news of his latest exploits], Neptune calls out in *Isis* (1677). Instead of following the example of the gods, the king has become their model and they his servants. In some cases, the king even appears to replace the gods altogether: in *Thésée* (1675), Mars multiplies his enemies only so "un nouveau Mars" [a new Mars] can bring even greater glory to France; in *Armide* (1686), la Sagesse sings that "Tout doit céder dans l'univers / A l'auguste Héros que j'aime" [All in the universe must cede / To the august Hero that I love].[103] In *Atys*, Time itself, dislocated, goes awry to accommodate the king's calendar, turning the month of January into May. The very order of the world is reconfigured in the service of the monarch. Flore insists that "Dans l'ardeur de luy plaire, on a bien-tost apris / A ne rien trouver d'impossible" [In our eagerness to please him, we quickly learned / Not to find anything impossible] (56).

Just as Flore's followers begin to make themselves at home onstage, dancing about and singing, the pastoral interlude is brought to a halt by the arrival of the tragic muse, Melpomène. The pomp of her arrival is conveyed by a French-style overture with majestic dotted rhythms interrupting the brisk gavotte of Flore's followers. Melpomène announces in imperious recitative that the Goddess Cybèle has summoned her to honor Atys in a stately spectacle. She reveals the scope of her art by bringing forth the heroes of antiquity – Hercules and Antaeus, Castor and Pollux, Lynceus and Idas, Eteocles and Polyneices – precisely those who have been surpassed and whom Time can no longer honor as he was accustomed to do before the reign of Louis. Once on stage, the heroes begin to reenact their ancient quarrels. Melpomène announces on behalf of Cybèle that the goddess has decided to revive the memory of her love for Atys in this illustrious court for the pleasure of the king and his courtiers. Whereas the king has been busy offstage making history, capturing the present for eternity, the mythological figures and gods of opera are trapped in their age-old stories which are presented as momentary diversions for a busy king.

At the end of the prologue, Iris arrives, sent by Cybèle to accord Flore and Melpomène:

Cybele veut que Flore aujourd'huy vous seconde,
Il faut que les Plaisirs viennent de toutes parts,
Dans l'empire puissant, où regne un nouveau Mars,
Ils n'ont plus d'autre asile au monde.
Rendez-vous, s'il se peut, dignes de ses regards,
Joignez la beaute vive & pure
Dont brille la Nature,
Aux ornements des plus beaux arts.

Cybele requests that Flore lend her help today,
Pleasures must come from all directions,
In the mighty empire where a new Mars reigns,
They no longer have any other home in this world.
Make yourselves, if you can, worthy of his glances,
Join the ardent and pure beauty,
With which Nature shines,
With the ornaments of the fairest arts. (58)

The peace and harmony created for France by the monarch and his war machine are reproduced in the prologue when the arrival of Isis settles the conflict created by the simultaneous presence of the pastoral goddess, Flore, and the tragic muse, Melpomène. At another level of meaning, the prologue's resolution of differences sets the stage for the harmonious hybridity of *tragédie en musique*, blending the amorous focus of the pastoral and the high concerns of the tragic. Not wanting to waste another second, ("Profitons du loisir du plus grand des heros" [Let us take advantage of the leisure of the greatest of heroes]), Time and the Chorus of Hours interrupt the light, triple-time air of reconciliation sung by Melpomène and Flore with a faster-moving air in double-time: "Preparons de nouvelles festes" [Let us prepare new festivities]. Musically and thematically, the prologue rapidly telescopes into a finale: all join in, inciting each other to serve and please the king and his court. All together, they reaffirm the harmonious accord that exists between the pleasures of pastoral affairs and the duties of glory and war: "Le temps des jeux et du repos, / Lui sert à mediter de nouvelles conquestes" [This time of sport and rest, / Allows him to meditate on new conquests] (59).

Musically, the prologue to *Atys* presents itself in bits and pieces, each miniature number doing its part for the glory of the king. The static quality of the praise, and the sense that time has come to a halt, creates short, disarticulated musical moments that do not lead to any larger structure. As Jean Duron has noted, Lully used the brightness of choral and dance music in the prologue, and a lack of large-scale direction, to allow Atys to enter the "half-light" of act 1 and to solicit the listener beyond the prologue by rapid and highly directive music.[104] It is also true that the music of the prologue – the musical praise of the monarch – derives meaning from Louis's bodily absence from the stage. In other words, the presence of the operatic voices and of the music they sing in some measure take the place of the king's visible presence on stage and of his power, standing in as the "image" of the king's two bodies. Opera was an obvious choice for acts of praise because song was, and still is, a traditional figure for entreaty and prayer. Yet, voices take on a particularly powerful performative role in the prologue. In *Alceste*, the impending return of the king resounds when the full chorus sings, with instrumental and vocal echoes: "Que tout retentisse. / Que tout réponde à nos voix. / Que le chant des Oyseaux s'unisse / Avec le doux son des hautbois" [Let all resound. / Let everything echo our voices. / May the song of the birds unite / With the sweet sound of the oboes].[105] In the prologue to *Roland*, Démogorgon notes the effect of the voice of the conqueror: "La Paix fuyoit au bruit des terribles combats, / Mais la voix du Vainqueur la rappelle ici-bas" [Peace fled at the sound of the dreadful battles, / But the voice of the Victor calls it back here to earth].[106] In this sense, filling in for the voice of the conqueror, music acts as a performative supplement for the absence of the king.

Other kinds of panegyric such as the ode were common during the reign of Louis XIV, celebrating everything from victories to royal births and in which the king was perpetually superlative, sublime, unmatched, divine: "Louis sur le Trône d'Astrée / Brillant comme le Dieu du jour" [Louis on the Throne of Astraea / Radiant like the God of day].[107] Because of the particular status of opera in seventeenth-century European culture, however, the prologues discussed above brought encomium to a new pitch. By creating *tragédie en musique*, the Académie Royale de Musique put at the king's disposal a genre that, while utterly without precedent for many writers, also benefited from the prestige of opera's perceived connection, however fanciful or remote, to Greek tragedy. At the same time, as a "native" French product, it asserted its superiority over the Italian imports of the 1640s and '50s. The prologues of the *tragédies en musique* "produced" the king in the genre's own image: spectacular, at once original and primordial, *nec plus ultra, sans pareil*. If the series of canvases painted by Le Brun in the 1660s adopted Alexander's greatness in order to fashion an image of the young king, *tragédie en musique* went further, resurrecting ancient tragedy within itself, as it were, to create something absolutely unprecedented. Which is to say that the aesthetic image of opera (recapturing the greatness of Greek models in a form that was utterly modern) and the political image of the monarch go hand in hand. That *le merveilleux* was often considered the soul of French opera, furthermore, as Grimm would later claim in his *Encyclopédie* article "Poëme lyrique," surely did not escape Louis XIV's cultural advisors.[108] To see the image of the king in these operas is to see Louis XIV's own *merveilleux* – his miraculous success in battle, his extraordinary feats of bravery – in the supernatural effects of the spectacle.

It is in this sense that opera fulfilled the temporary need for encomium articulated by Chapelain. As preeminent spectator (generally in attendance at the premiere), as "creator" of the spectacle (having chosen the subjects elaborated by Quinault), and as subject and object of the prologue, Louis XIV was omnipresent. This particular confluence could occur only when the king withdrew from the stage. In the case of *Atys*, the limitlessness of the king's presence was produced through his absence from the stage, and through the thematicization of time in which the present moment came into being as outside, or on the other side, of history. The "épître au roi" that prefaced the score of *Persée* (1682) articulated the relationship of the king to these operas: "Yourself, SIRE, You have deigned to choose the subject, and as soon as I had glanced at it, I discovered there the image of YOUR MAJESTY."[109] This praise was clearly meant to equate or assimilate the exploits of the operatic hero with those of the king; yet it also indicates that the opera itself was somehow to be identified with the monarch, that the spectacle *was* the king in his sublime absence. If, in the prologue to *Atys*, the spectacle of history in its entirety – its heroes and their exploits – was at once elicited and made obsolete by the unprecedented power of the king, Louis himself disappeared from the stage because he was "encor plus glorieux" [more glorious still] (*Amadis*), because "sa gloire [est] encor plus éclatante." [his glory is even more radiant] (*Thésée*).[110] This status was guaranteed only by his absence from the stage.

Two productions of seventeenth-century *tragédies en musique* that emerged from the renewed interest in this repertory during the final decades of the last century – both collaborations of director Jean-Marie Villégier and conductor William Christie – ingeniously underscored many of these effects. In both productions, Villégier played upon the absence of the king on stage, acknowledging him as the implicit spectator and subject of the spectacle. Both operas were notably staged with generous governmental subsidies during the presidency of François Mittérand, who was popularly termed "Dieu" for the many self-aggrandizing architectural projects which he hoped would mark his "reign." In the 1987 production of *Atys*, Time appeared center-stage, imposing and wizened in fabulous, mythological attire. The spectator soon realized that Time was central, not because he was in command, but because he was being rehearsed by others, for the pleasure of courtly spectators and ultimately in the service of the king. Surrounding the stage from a balcony were seventeenth-century courtiers, gossiping and looking down on the events below. A character who played a kind of "stage manager" directed Time to the appropriate spot and handed him his traditional scythe. Time had been summoned there, onstage, for the king. Shortly afterwards, the stage manager confiscated Time's scythe, using it as a baton to direct the courtiers above, who, it turned out, were none other than the Chorus of Hours, singing "Ses

justes loix, / Ses grands exploits" [His just laws, / His great exploits].
The stage manager, one discovered at the conclusion, was in fact Iris
who, after reconciling Flore and Melpomène, placed everyone sym-
metrically facing the audience and the implicit "first" spectator for the
final chorus in praise of the monarch.

Villégier's 1993 production of *Médée* by Thomas Corneille and
Marc-Antoine Charpentier went even further in its evocation of the
king, just as *Médée*'s prologue itself went further than those of
Quinault and Lully, actually naming the king: "Louis est triomphant,
tout cède à sa puissance, / La victoire en tous lieux, fait reverer ses
Lois [Louis is triumphant, everything yields to his power, / Victory
on all sides, causes his laws to be revered].[111] Transforming the encomiastic prologue into a tongue-in-cheek *sacre*, the ceremony of coro-
nation and anointment that inaugurated the reign of kings, Villégier
concluded the prologue with an extremely well-conceived gesture,
given the context of praise examined in this chapter. As the chorus
repeated its praise of Louis, giving thanks for the pastoral life made
possible by his wars ("le repos qu'il veut donner au monde" [the peace
that he seeks to give the world]), a procession of priests, nuns, and
other clerics advanced toward the audience.[112] As the chorus approached the final cadence, the leading ecclesiastical figure suddenly
knelt with the rest of the cast, brandishing a sizable cross and holding it out toward the audience as the prologue's final tribute. Villégier
truly captured the strategy of the prologue in this final gesture. Having
focused the spectator's attention unremittingly on "Louis," "this
Hero," "[this] great King," the final chorus delivered, not the king
himself, but instead presented yet another symbol, yet another
image of (an absent) divinity. Villégier's intuition revealed the performativity of the opera prologue as an imaginary *sacre* consecrating the
peace that Louis had engineered and at the same time ushering in
the spectacle that was about to unfold. Opera's double relation to
origins – its imaginary return to a founding moment of Western culture in Greek drama and its status as an inaugural form of aesthetic
modernity – coincides with the performative image of the monarch splendidly evoked in Villégier's *sacre*.

The operas that follow these prologues, however, do not entirely confirm their idealized meanings. Consider, returning again to *Atys*, the marked contrast of the body of the opera to the prologue. The subject, taken from Ovid's *Fasti*, centers on Attis, the "remarkably handsome Phrygian boy" who had attracted the notice of the goddess, Cybele, who made him keeper of her temple. When Attis fell in love with the nymph Sagaritis (Sangaride), Cybele took her vengeance by killing her. Furious, Attis went mad, climbing to "the heights of Dindymus." There, he hacked at himself with sharp stones and dragged his long hair in the dust. Finally, he cried, "I wish that these parts which harmed me were done for . . . and suddenly there wasn't a trace of his manhood left."[113] Having drawn his subject from an isolated handful of verses from Ovid with no dramatic precedent, Quinault avoided the problem of fidelity to ancient theatrical models, a charge he had endured two years earlier following the modifications he had made to Euripides's *Alcestis*. He could therefore shape the plot without regard to precedent. To reinforce the tragic dimension, Sangaride would die by Atys's own hand during wild hallucinations induced by the jealous goddess. To enhance amorous conflict and to compound the scenario of betrayal, Quinault invented Atys's rival and Sangaride's fiancé, the character Célénus. Finally, and most importantly for seventeenth-century proprieties, death is substituted for Atys's emasculation.

Atys is a far cry from Corneille's Horaces and Curiaces of 1640. Though it may be said that the tenor of *Atys* in some ways resembles Racine's fallen universe, the principal character is still quite distinct from the hard-wired cruelty and depravity of Racinian characters such as Pyrrhus, Néron, Phèdre, or Athalie. Anticipating Jason in *Médée*, Atys is duplicitous and false, though not from ambition or calculation. He has no larger vision at all, but betrays Cybèle and his own friend, Célénus, simply out of an overwhelming weakness of character. In act 1, Atys reveals his love to Sangaride, who is engaged to be married to Célénus: "Je meurs d'amour pour vous, je n'en sçaurois guerir" [I am dying of love for you, and I shall not recover] (1.6.72). At the end of the scene, complicitous, they agree to hide their love from the others. Sangaride interrupts Atys, "On vient: feignez encor, craignez d'estre écouté" ["Someone approaches: feign again, beware of being overheard] (1.6.74). In act 2, Atys barely hesitates when it comes to deceiving his friend and rival, Célénus, even when the latter confides in him that he suspects that Sangaride's marriage to him is driven more by duty than by love. Atys allows himself to be convinced by the confidants Idas and Doris in act 3. They argue that the only solution to his predicament is to betray Célénus by interceding, as Cybèle's chosen sacrificer, to stop the marriage, claiming to act on behalf of the goddess. Doris believes, as do all the other characters, that "L'amour dispence les rivaux / D'estre genereux" [Love exempts rivals / From being noble] (3.2.88). Atys hesitates only momentarily to act on their advice: "Je souhaite, je crains, je veux, je me repens" [I hope, I fear, I desire, I repent] (3.2.88). Six lines later, he gives in to his passion. As one critic remarks, "his hesitation to betray the king lasts only the space . . . of a line, he slides around on the tides of his passion."[114] After Cybèle reveals her passion to Atys through dreams she conjures up during his sleep, he again dissimulates, preventing Sangaride from revealing their secret to the goddess. As Atys interrupts the marriage ceremony, Célénus wonders in amazement: "Atys peut s'engager luy-mesme à me trahir? / Atys contre moy s'interesse?" [Can Atys take it upon himself to betray me? / Atys sides against me?]. At his most deceitful, Atys replies: "Seigneur, je suis à la Deesse, / Dès qu'elle a commandé, je ne puis qu'obeïr" [My Lord, I am beholden to the Goddess, / When she commands, I can only obey] (4.6.111). Zephyrs follow his orders; and he and Sangaride are whisked away on a cloud, safe from the recriminations of Célénus and the entire wedding party. In act 5, Cybèle and Célénus quickly catch up with the couple in their idyllic, pastoral retreat. Prey to hallucinations Cybèle has conjured up, Atys kills Sangaride with the sacrificial knife, believing that he has saved her by killing the goddess. When Sangaride's body is brought back on stage (Cybèle says to Atys, "Tu peux la voir, regarde" [You may see her, behold] [5.4.119]), he realizes his error and flees to turn the knife against himself offstage.

Finally, just as Euridice is resurrected in the stars at the close of Striggio's and Monteverdi's *Orfeo*, Atys forever takes the form of Cybèle's beloved pine tree.

In the critical introduction to his edition of the libretto, Stéphane Bassinet remarks: "Powerless to throw off the yoke of duty, or the yoke of passion, unable to reconcile them with the heroic moral code which has lost its very meaning, Atys comes after Suréna (1674), the hero in Quinault's play is utterly dead."[115] The values of glory and duty, preeminent in the early works of Pierre Corneille, are still embedded in *Atys*; yet, they are now merely empty tokens. When Atys attempts to reassure Célénus, who is worried that Sangaride does not truly return his love, or perhaps that she has another lover, Atys replies: "Son coeur suit avec soin le Devoir et la Gloire, / Et vous avez pour vous la Gloire et le Devoir" [Her heart eagerly follows Duty and Glory, / And you have both Glory and Duty] (2.1.79). The flat interchangeability of the two terms palpably echoes their fundamental lack of meaning, mere placeholders for a bygone or exhausted set of ethical protocols. As Bassinet argues, the opera is "a lucid and coherent vision of a decaying world."[116] No longer able to dispute its claims on him, the hero succumbs to fatal passion, which destroys all lives in its wake. Idas foreshadows this ultimate defeat in the first act: "Tost ou tard l'Amour est vainqueur, / En vain les plus fiers s'en deffendent, / On ne peut refuser son coeur / A de beaux yeux qui le demandent" [Sooner or later Love is victorious, / The most haughty defy him in vain. / One cannot refuse one's heart / To fair eyes that solicit it] (1.2.64). Love's antithesis, indifference, is seen as a utopian dream of freedom and tranquility – the balmy, pastoral fiction all the characters imagine beyond the tragedy of their own ethical indigence. "Qu'un indifferent est heureux! / Il jouit d'un destin paisible" [How happy the indifferent man is! / He enjoys a peaceful lot], Atys fantasizes (2.1.80). In the end, for Atys, the only escape is suicide. La Rochefoucauld wrote, as if describing Atys's deceitfulness and *le merveilleux* that made possible his flight with Sangaride: "Those great and striking actions which dazzle the eyes are represented by politicians as the effects of great plans, whereas they are usually the effects of temper and emotion."[117]

Bassinet contrasts *Atys* to *Phaéton*, *Persée*, and even *Armide*, noting that these other works "retain the values that had been those of Corneillian tragedy by viewing them through the lens of love; the love of grandeur, valor in battle, a concern for glory, in a word heroism, all remain present."[118] It is nonetheless true that the value system of *tragédie en musique* always tends to abrogate that of heroic tragedy, just as its poetics reverses that of neoclassical theater.[119] Alone among the *tragédies en musique* cited by Bassinet, *Persée* might be said to persist in the ethics of heroism. However, because Persée's *gloire* is inseparable from his love for Andromède (since he has been promised her if he can kill Méduse), the distinction between the two has been abolished. Given all the supernatural assistance he has received to destroy Méduse (a sword and wings from Vulcain, a magic helmet from Pluton and shield from Pallas), it is as if Persée needs only to love in order to win glory. Indeed, in the celebrations that conclude act 4, glory effectively disappears: "L'Amour n'a plus de traits terribles / Pour un coeur qui cède à ses coups" [Love's arrows are no longer frightening / For a heart that surrenders to its blows].[120] If the essential quality of the hero is a certain "greatness of soul," as Pierre Corneille argued, "which has something about it that is so elevated that, while one detests its actions, one admires the source from which they come," Quinault's heroes present only a faded, unconvincing, or fossilized grandeur.[121] Phaëton's desire for grandeur ("Je brûle de monter dans un rang glorieux" [I long to ascend to a glorious rank]; "Je veux me faire un nom d'éternelle mémoire" [I seek to make an eternal name for myself]), for example, is nothing other than naked ambition; and it is shown to be such when this ambition is replicated in an equally meaningless and triangulated amorous attachment.[122] "Plus mon rival est jaloux" [The more my rival is jealous], he admits in act 3, scene 3, "Et plus mon bonheur est doux" [The sweeter my happiness].[123] Far from being a legitimate property of his being, his grandeur is only a phantasm, emanating from the image he sees of himself in the eyes of others. Phaëton's wildly ambitious claims to an everlasting *gloire* cannot but reflect back upon the royal hero of the moment in the prologue, whose ambition for eternity receives praise from Saturne

("Son auguste Sang s'éternise" [His august Blood is eternal]).[124] In *Armide*, if Renaud finally escapes the "charms" of the sorceress with the help of two fellow warriors, the indolent pleasures he enjoyed in her pastoral paradise are not entirely effaced. In any event, as I will argue in the following chapter, Renaud's heroism is not the subject of the opera, and, in the final analysis, is of considerably less interest to the spectator who is riveted, instead, by Armide. A significant gap, therefore, remains between opera's function as a representation of the king and its subversion of the image of the hero.

Even within many of Quinault's and Lully's prologues, the message of *gloire* is far from unequivocal. The pastoral space made possible by the king's victories fuels love and amorous intrigues; and passions, amorous or otherwise, were considered to be threats within the dominant ethical system of seventeenth-century France, jeopardizing the glory that was the subject of the prologue in the first place.[125] In the prologue to *Cadmus et Hermione*, for example, the sun arrives to rid the world of the serpent Python which was threatening its safety, spitting flames from its mouth and eyes. After its demise, Palès, Mélisse and Pan sing in praise of love, pointing to the pastoral realm restored by the sun's victory over Python. The forest god, Arcas, sings: "Dans les beaux jours de notre vie / Les plaisirs sont dans leur saison, / Et quelque peu d'amoureuse folie / Vaux souvent mieux que trop de raison" [In the best days of our lives / Pleasure is in season; / And a bit of amorous folly / Is often better than too much reason].[126] In a similar conclusion to the prologue to *Amadis*, once the Hero they celebrate has made peace out of war, one of Cupid's followers sings: "Suivons l'Amour, c'est lui qui nous mène, / Tout doit sentir son aimable ardeur" [Let us follow Love; it is he who leads us. / Everyone must feel his pleasant ardor].[127] The prologue to *Cadmus et Hermione* depicts "[l']amoureuse folie" [the folly of love] as the spice of life, a drop of which corrects the excesses of reason. The prologue to *Amadis*, however, goes further: no one escapes love's ardor.

Reflecting on his gallant conduct as monarch, Louis XIV considered that he had been able to reduce the consequences of his amorous wanderings ("égarements"). The problem, he wrote in his *Mémoires*, is to ensure that political exigencies are not jeopardized in any way: "our first objective must always be to maintain our glory and our authority." Yet this is precisely what is placed in jeopardy by love, as he notes himself. At the heart of the matter, he wrote, lies a problematic self-control based on the divided allegiances of head and heart: the difficulty "is that while abandoning our heart, we remain master of our mind; we must separate the tendernesses of the lover from the resolutions of the monarch . . . the two things must be absolutely separate."[128] In *Atys*, Quinault and Lully staged the hero's inability to emerge from this predicament unscathed.

Writing on theater and politics at the court of Louis XIV, Jean-Marie Apostolidès has suggested that the coming of opera marks the exhaustion of cultural and artistic forms developed during the early part of the reign, the end of the "performative" phase of the monarchy, and the petrification of the image of the king:

> In the place of a universe without mediation, it presents a conciliatory, unifying myth, from which the very notion of conflict has been removed. Already in the prologue, the figure of the monarch is established as divine. That which, in the time of history, would be achieved through conquest, following a sacrifice, is given here as resulting from the different nature of the king, who is associated with a god. Such is, for example, the meaning of the prologue to *Alceste* by Quinault and Lully. Through its use of machines, opera presents a thoroughly mastered world in which technology generates both the real and the supernatural.[129]

Whereas in the earlier *comédies-ballets*, and in the vast and spectacular entertainments organized at Versailles, the king and his courtiers staged and assumed their roles within the monarchy, with the advent of opera, Apostolidès claims, the courtiers became mere spectators, dispossessed, while their king, whose image is forever fixed in public, hid in his apartments with Madame de Maintenon.[130] In this view, the coming of *tragédie en musique* would seem to be a turning point in the monarchy, freezing the image of the king in its prologues, as in a commemorative medallion or coin, and marking the transformation of the court into a passive body which henceforth can only bear witness to the machine of the state as would a spectator. Indeed, the republication of the libretti by Ballard beginning in 1703, under the title of *Recueil général des opéra*, undoubtedly contributed to the impression of a monumental, frozen image of the king. Several critics make similar claims about the advent of opera: that mythology disappeared from life and was fixed on the operatic stage, supplanted by the reality of "history." Apostolidès tells of the destruction of a previously undifferentiated and utopian space of mythology and history, and documents the creation and "autonomization of the major categories of the real, particularly of the field of history."[131] "In the 1670s," writes Jean-Pierre Néraudau in a similar vein, "the time of fiction seemed past, and the time come to enter into history."[132] Néraudau refers repeatedly to the distance taken from mythology, now a mere *divertissement* "which has ceased to be a creative discourse, becoming a catalogue of ornamental stories."[133]

As I have argued, opera can be seen as the endpoint of a series of strategic variations or shifts in the representation of the monarch, and a temporary resolution of some concerns about representation that were raised very early on by the Petite Académie. This is not to say, however, that *tragédie en musique* anchored or fixed an essentially dead image of the king, endlessly troping on mythological fictions which had once been the active material of a bygone "mythistoire." Rather, I have emphasized the ways in which opera simultaneously elaborated, complicated, and problematized the representation of the king. What we witness in early French opera is not so much a grand mythological carcass, shed by a history which had come into its own. Rather, the operatic prologue may be said to convey the "miracle" and "marvels" that, in Chapelain's perspective from the early days of the reign, historical representation might eventually be able to capture; and it accomplished this in ways that developed and expanded the modes of representation crafted in Le Brun's painting.[134] On the one hand, opera created an impression that both history and fable were at the king's command; and it brought the two together in the criss-crossing relations between the prologue and the body of the opera. On the other, by portraying the heroic values articulated in the prologue as derelict, *tragédie en musique* revealed the outcome of that attempt to be, at the very least, uncertain. In this respect, the representation of the king and / or hero in opera, instead of being the expression of a petrified image of the monarchy, coincided with the understanding of glory by writers such as Pascal or La Rochefoucauld which, in turn, prefigured later critical views, such as those of Montesquieu in *De l'esprit des lois*: "if those who direct the conscience or the counsel of princes do not hold themselves to it [the observance of justice in war], all is lost; and if one bases oneself on the arbitrary principles of glory, decorum, utility, rivers of blood will cover the earth. One must never speak of the glory of the prince; his glory will be his vanity; it is a *passion* and not a legitimate right."[135] By Montesquieu's time, the ethical system erected around glory – the keystone of the seventeenth-century monarch's apotheosis – had long since collapsed.

The absence of the king from the operatic stage and his identification in the prologue with the sublime effects of a manifest glory created new possibilities for the politics of encomium. An important disparity emerged, however, between the peerless hero of the prologue and the problematic and threadbare figures of male glory in the operas. In subsequent chapters, I will continue to explore the gaps and disparities opera created within early-modern French culture. As I argued in the introduction, *tragédie en musique* challenged assumptions relating to the poetics of tragedy and the place of music in the theater. The uneasy relation to allegories of glory in *tragédie en musique* points to the problems involved in tailoring opera to a program centered on the representation and celebration of the monarch. The ambiguities and new perspectives opera generated with regard to ancien régime stage representations became one of its greatest assets and weapons.

3 | The ascendance of music and the disintegration of the hero in *Armide*

"La scène invisible hante." [The invisible scene haunts]

Pascal Quignard[1]

Beginning in 1673, Philippe Quinault and Jean-Baptiste Lully (né Giovanni Battista Lulli) created the first French operas as *tragédies en musique* – at once objects of fascination and revulsion. Spectators were seduced; theorists were skeptical. What was one to do with a genre that Aristotle could not have said anything about? What would the sensual distraction of music do to the intellectual force of French tragedy? To many, furthermore, opera was yet another example of ruinous Italian influence. In France, where music-making often had political overtones, Lully carefully sought to distinguish the *tragédie en musique* as something other than an Italian import. By creating a musical fabric that was a near continuum, Lully distanced his work from the discrete alternation of aria and recitative that characterized Italian opera.[2] Because air and recitative were virtually indistinguishable, the musical voice gained a certain consistency and uniformity rather than drawing attention to the operatic form as an alternation of two formally distinct vocal modes. This decision had a decided effect on the operatic characters. Through this specific kind of vocal writing, Lully attempted to create a continuity of character rather than to display the virtuousity of singers. It was in part through this "naturalization" of the musical voice within the context of the French theatrical tradition that Lully created French opera. In this chapter, I will contrast Quinault's and Lully's emphasis on the musical voice with the extraordinary visual impact of early opera. I speculate that their last *tragédie en musique*, *Armide*, staged in the Palais-Royal in 1686 and revived frequently through the 1760s, created a new space for opera within the context of seventeenth-century French aesthetics by placing passion and the musical voice above the supernatural effects that were commonly associated with the genre.

One of the more complex and sensitive aspects of *tragédie en musique* within the context of seventeenth-century theater was the question of visual representation. Seventeenth-century dramatic theory was extraordinarily concerned with determining how things could or should, or should not, be placed before the eyes of the spectator. *Tragédie en musique*, to a greater degree than any other dramatic idiom, highlighted the visual *merveilleux* of supernatural appearances and special effects. Catherine Kintzler has asserted that "opera is not satisfied with the imaginary: it is obliged to represent."[3] Though Kintzler is undoubtedly correct about the general commitment of *tragédie en musique* to magnificent display, *Armide* reveals the question of representation in early French opera to be somewhat more complex than it would appear from her account. For if the liberal use of *le merveilleux* defined early French opera against its spoken counterpart – French classical tragedy – how are we to interpret the fact that the single scene of *Armide* universally recognized by seventeenth- and eighteenth-century commentators as the most moving of any *tragédie en musique* is one in which the visual interest is all but suspended?

One might be tempted simply to point to the music. Yet this reaction would not have been a common one in the late 1680s. Whereas we tend to see the singularity of opera's function as determined by its use of music (if, indeed, we consider opera to be theater at all), music raised more problems than it resolved for Quinault's and Lully's contemporaries. As beautiful as opera may be, as Le Cerf de la Viéville claimed, himself citing Furetière, "whatever draws its principal beauty from the fancywork that the musician adds is nothing but cheap goods."[4] In late seventeenth-century France, opera was considered part of the larger category of letters, as it remained half a century later in the *Encyclopédie*'s system of classification. This situation goes a long way toward explaining the otherwise odd fact that the eighteenth-century poet and dramatist Pietro Metastasio was revered by the French, often compared to Quinault or the great Corneille, whereas the operas that were set by dozens of composers and performed throughout Europe – in London, Madrid, Lisbon, and St. Petersburg – were virtually unknown in France. Whereas there were nearly thirty editions of his works published in France between 1749 and 1869, both in Italian and in French, by 1777 there had been only two isolated performances of his operas in France.[5] Metastasio's reception in France points to the fact that the tragedy was considered the centerpiece of *tragédie en musique*; the music cautiously maintained a secondary and supplementary status. At a time when music was required to play second fiddle to the drama and was often condemned as dangerously sensual, since it was not clear exactly how music might convey meaning, we witness a self-conscious effort in *Armide* to situate opera as something other than second-rate mimesis or a mere play of sound and decoration.

Writing about the tragedies of Pierre Corneille, Marc Fumaroli has suggested that a work of art can reflect upon itself so as to articulate the very conditions under which its forms are possible.[6] Taking up Fumaroli's suggestion in what follows, my argument turns on the preference given to the visual in *Armide* and, more specifically, on moments when the preeminence of the visual is suspended. I argue that the visual profusion of the spectacle is emphatically foregrounded in *Armide*, then pointedly withdrawn, in order to lead the spectator to consider what escapes the visible, that which cannot be represented as such onstage. The analysis that follows will be concerned only marginally with the specific music Lully wrote for his operas. I do not want to suggest that the music of Lully is negligible or unimportant. Rather, my interest lies in the meaning that the voice is given and that it produces in this *tragédie en musique*. I will explore the singular way in which Lully and Quinault link extreme passion to moments in which gaps are produced in the figurative apparatus, in the element of visual representation. Attention is drawn to passion and its vocal manifestations at precisely those moments when the visual spectacle withdraws. In this way, I argue, Lully and Quinault not only made a dramatic (that is to say mimetic) entity of the voice, but by engaging in an aesthetics of the sublime they sought to define early French opera as distinct from its spoken counterpart, as the abbé Terrasson would later do, through different means, in his *Dissertation critique sur l'Iliade d'Homere*. My claim, then, is that aspects of Lully's use of music drew attention away from spectacle per se toward the voice and its particular effects within opera. As I will argue in subsequent chapters, the use of music and of the operatic voice in later works by Marc-Antoine Charpentier and Rameau was increasingly salient because of the effects these elements could generate in relation to the musical fabric itself, as well as in relation to theatrical practices and conventions.

Armide trumps classical tragedy with its own card – the sublime. Through its use of the operatic voice, *tragédie en musique* could be seen as both mimetic – contrary to the claims of opera's detractors, built on the same aesthetic that underlay spoken tragedy – and sublime – something more than spoken tragedy. Rather than framing opera as drama, as have critics from Le Cerf de la Viéville to Joseph Kerman, however, I want to indicate the way in which *Armide* integrates a concern for mimesis with an implicit bid for the operatic sublime, thereby positioning opera somewhere beyond spoken tragedy rather than as derived from it. My analysis is divided into three movements. I begin with the question of the visual in *Armide*, moving to the final scene in act 2 – the moment of visual caesura and the opera's climax. In the second section, I return to an earlier passage in act 1 that prefigures the retreat of the visual that occurs at the end of act 2 and retrospectively reveals its meaning. My analysis concludes with a consideration of how the gap left by the withdrawal of all spectacular elements in act 2, scene 5 raises the issue of the operatic sublime together with that of the musical voice.

OPERATIC VISIONS

Whereas late seventeenth-century tragedy kept *le merveilleux* out of sight – lying dormant in genealogy, occuring offstage, or implicitly omnipresent as *fatum* – *tragédie en musique* placed the supernatural directly before the eyes of the spectator. The poetic rule of *vraisemblance*, concerning the plausibility of appearances, did not necessarily exclude the appearance of gods or supernatural beings or events on the stage. Theorists such as Rapin and D'Aubignac defended the verisimilitude of magic and divine intervention:

Everyone knows that things that are naturally impossible become possible and plausible through divine power or magic; and that the verisimilitude of the theater demands not only the representation of those things that happen in the common course of men's lives, but that it also includes the supernatural, which makes events all the more noble for being unforeseen, though no less plausible.[7]

Deriving from the same theoretical base as the tragedies of Corneille and Racine, but evolving in a different direction, *tragédie en musique* took *le merveilleux* as its fundamental law. La Bruyère remarked on this particular aspect of opera in his *Caractères*: "neither flights, nor chariots, nor transformations are necessary in the *Bérénices* or in *Pénélope* [stage plays by Pierre Corneille, Jean Racine, and Charles-Claude Genest]; but opera demands them, and it is the nature of this spectacle to hold the mind, the eyes, and the ears in an equal enchantment."[8] If tragedy had to do without flying chariots and vast changes of scene, opera absolutely depended on them.

 Armide was no exception. Taken from Torquato Tasso's epic poem *Gerusalemme Liberata* (1581), the subject of *Armide* was a perfect match for opera. In conformity with the exigencies of the operatic stage, the plot makes ample space for visual opulence and *le merveilleux*. As is usual in Quinault's and Lully's *tragédies en musique*, each act is accompanied by a change of scene and includes ornate dances. Jean Berain's drawings for Lully's and Quinault's operas, including *Armide*, give an idea of the sumptuousness of the costumes and set designs. Though *Armide* was not always staged with machines, it was nonetheless conceived with the most elaborate stage technology in mind, allowing for effects such as the aerial departure of Armide and Renaud at the close of act 2, the arrival and disappearance of Hate and his followers as they are swallowed up into the abyss at the end of act 3, and the destruction of Armide's palace at the close of the opera (fig. 4).[9] Drawing from his epic source, Quinault made events such as transformations, arrivals, and departures spectacular in the extreme. This emphasis made *tragédie en musique*, along with the *tragédie à machines* that it replaced, the most visually oriented of spectacles, similar from

Fig. 4. Destruction of Armide's palace, engraving by Jean Dolivan after Jean Berain. Photo courtesy of the Bibliothèque Nationale de France, Cabinet des Estampes, Paris.

this perspective, and from that of the criticism it first received, to early cinema.[10]

In addition to its reliance on staging and machinery, the dramatic poem itself places conspicuous emphasis on the visual. From the beginning of act 1, the plot centers on the effects of seeing and being seen. Sorcery, an obvious metaphor for "female wiles," naturally provides for the spectacle's visual interest, implicitly justifying or accounting for *le merveilleux*.[11] Though Armide can and does invoke magical powers, however, she only uses them as a supplement to the preferred weapon of her beauty and, more specifically, that of her eyes. As Catherine Kintzler has noted, this restraint is part of the law of the genre: "a semi-divine character or a magician must not resort to violent and supernatural means until he or she has exhaused gentler and more ordinary means."[12] As Armide's confidante, Phénice, assures her at the opening of the opera, "Vos yeux n'ont eu besoin que de leurs propres charmes / Pour affaiblir le camp de Godefroi" [Your eyes needed no more than their own charms / To weaken Godfrey's camp].[13] If not precisely a departure from Tasso, the specificity of Quinault's emphasis on the power of Armide's eyes represents a focusing of the epic poem's lush descriptions of the sorceress's physical beauty. Instead of emphasizing the seductive presence and charms of a body from the point of view of the spectator/voyeur, Quinault initially casts the heroine as a warrior – a seventeenth-century Amazon – the supernatural forces of her magic being unnecessary when she can rely on her own self-mastery and the natural power of her eyes to control others. Armide's uncle, Hidraot, sets the power of her eyes above all other conceivable sorcery. Sidonie, a second confidante, adds her own praise to those of the others: "Et ses regards ont, en moins d'un moment, / Donné des lois aux vainqueurs de la terre" [And her eyes, in less than an instant / Subjected the conquerors of the world] (1.3.260). This emphasis returns repeatedly in the opera. Vision and power are virtual synonyms in *Armide*. Whereas Tasso's descriptions gave Armide over to the eyes and fantasy of the knights of Godfrey's camp, and to that of his readers, Quinault places the emphasis on the power of Armide's eyes, and above all on the singular failure of that power.

Only Renaud remains entirely unaffected by her powers: "Par une heureuse indifférence, / Mon coeur s'est dérobé sans peine à sa puissance, / Je la vis seulement d'un regard curieux" [By a fortunate indifference / My heart has effortlessly avoided her power / And I behold her only with a curious eye] (2.1.263). In contrast to Armide's aggressive and seductive eyes, and to the mesmerized countenance of her entranced victims, Renaud views her with some interest, but with emotional detachment. The hero's indifference, a humiliating offense to Armide, is seen as a challenge to her dominance. The entire *tragédie en musique* turns on Armide's failure to move Renaud and on the reversal through which, from dominating others, she in turn is blinded and overpowered by forces beyond her control. Armide's failure is staged first and most poignantly in the final scene of act 2, where the usual visual extravagance of the operatic stage all but disappears. Central to the opera, this scene has undoubtedly received more commentary than any other in Quinault's and Lully's entire corpus. I want to begin by drawing attention to the extremely rich visual evocations of act 2 which relay the emphasis on the visual from the previous act and lead up to the interiorization of the spectacle that occurs in the final scene.

Quinault placed the exquisite *sommeil*, or sleep scene, at the center of act 2, providing ample space for musical and choreographic display. Seeking to destroy Renaud because he has freed her captives and because he has thus demonstrated that he is outside of her influence, Armide and Hidraot join forces to lure him to a meadow. In his monologue air "Plus j'observe," which occupies the whole of scene 3, Renaud points out the sensual beauties of the landscape – the harmonious murmur of a gently flowing stream, the flowers, the wind, and the birds who are silenced, figures of the spectator, spell-bound by the harmonious sounds of nature: "Un son harmonieux se mêle au bruit des eaux. / Les oiseaux enchantés se taisent pour l'entendre" [A harmonious sound joins in the water's murmur. / The spell-bound birds fall silent to listen] (2.3.265). At the end of the air, the hero notices the cool shade, an irresistible invitation for a nap, the high tenor voice finally moving down to repose at the cadence. The ornate spectacle of scene 4 involves a river naiad, nymphs, shepherds, and shepherdesses – all demons in disguise – who surround and envelop the sleeping Renaud with their songs and dances. The concealed presence of Armide and her uncle throughout the scene leaves an ambiguity that is not resolved in the libretto, allowing for the possibility that the entire scene was created ex nihilo, with the wave of a (machinist's) wand. Since Renaud's sleep is not altogether natural, the *sommeil* episode draws attention to the power of Armide and to that of the operatic spectacle itself. Armide's power is thus staged, as it has been from the very beginning, as a figure of the power opera has to fashion a world – its push toward total representation.

The final scene in act 2 breaks radically with the two previous scenes. The rich choreography and varied musical naturalisms (such as the arabesques of quavers figuring the murmur of the stream) vanish and Armide becomes the focal point of the spectator's attention. She hovers near Renaud, weapon in hand. The scene begins with an intense, pondering recitative (see example 4). The moment has finally arrived for Armide to consummate her revenge. The "enemy" in a deep sleep, she has only to strike:

> Par lui, tous mes captifs sont sortis d'esclavage,
> > Qu'il éprouve toute ma rage. . . .
> *Armide va pour frapper Renaud, et ne peut exécuter le dessein qu'elle a de lui ôter la vie.*
> Quel trouble me saisit! qui me fait hésiter?
> Qu'est-ce qu'en sa faveur la pitié me veut dire?
> > Frappons . . . Ciel! qui peut m'arrêter?
> Achevons . . . je frémis! Vengeons-nous . . . je soupire! (2.5.266)

> It was he who freed all my captive slaves,
> > Now let him bear all my fury . . .
> (*Armide moves to strike Renaud, yet cannot act on her intention to take his life*)
> What confusion seizes me; who makes me hesitate?
> What does pity say to me on his behalf?
> > Come, strike! . . . Heavens! who stops me?
> End it . . . I shudder! Vengeance . . . I sigh!

Example 4: "Enfin il est en ma puissance"

Nothing prevents Armide from doing away with Renaud here and now; yet, as the libretto clearly indicates, she freezes, unable to accomplish the act. Along with this sudden inability to act, there is a conspicuous shift away from the visual distractions that filled scenes 3 and 4, and away from the emphasis on the power of Armide's eyes found throughout act 1. Gone are the incidental characters in colorful costumes as are the symmetrical patterns of the dance. The pastoral setting is essentially forgotten. Even Renaud, unconscious throughout

Example 4: *(cont.)*

the scene, is effectively absent as an actor in the drama. The spectacle is reduced to a single tableau, and the spectator is fully absorbed by Armide's monologue.

Critics have recognized act 2, scene 5 as a defining moment in the history of early French opera.[14] Jean-Jacques Rousseau audaciously claimed that this scene, universally recognized as the apogee of *tragédie en musique*, proved the failure of French opera. In his merciless critique of Lully's setting, Rousseau remarked the absence of effective musical

Example 4: *(cont.)*

"expression" in scene 5, which, in his view, turned insipidly around E minor. For Rousseau, there was nothing in the music that would allow the spectator to consider Armide's sudden change of heart.[15] Rousseau famously concluded from his analysis that there was no such thing as French music, and there never would be. Jean-Philippe Rameau returned Rousseau's critique, arguing that Lully was, on the contrary, a master at expressive "modulation," and that the reactions of audiences proved his point.[16] For the purposes of my analysis, what is remarkable is not the authors' particular conclusions about the expressiveness or inexpressiveness of Lully's setting, positions that were largely motivated by the musical polemics of the 1750s, but rather their single point of agreement. Both authors recognize that the dramatic interest of scene 5 is driven by the moment of Armide's hesitation, by the dawning of a reluctant self-awareness on her part. The grand spectacle of opera notwithstanding, the inner scene of passion is revealed as that which has always been present at the center of the tragedy.

The extraordinary insistence on the visual up until this moment makes the point all the more significant. After witnessing the *divertissements* of the preceding scenes, after hearing of Armide's confidence and control, scene 5 marks a reversal. The effect of Armide's *récit* is to point to that which is unmasterable and incomprehensible. Armide senses the presence of a passion that does not yet have a name, and cannot be represented as such. The text and the score figure this gap with ellipses and with repeated rests lasting a full beat or more. In a different version of this same scene, part of Quinault's earlier play, *Comédie sans comédie*, Love personified intervenes to prevent Armide from killing Renaud.[17] In *Armide*, however, Love disappears from the stage, leaving only a nameless hesitation in its place. If Quinault bothered to remove Love from the stage, forgoing any *deus ex machina*, it was in order to emphasize the internal impetus of the tragedy. Initially promising to offer the spectator a visually spectacular act of retaliation, Armide's firm affirmation of scorn in the first act ("Que je le hais!" [How I hate him!], 1.1.256) erodes into a mere wish by the second act ("Que, s'il se peut, je le haïsse" [May I hate him if I can], 2.5.267). Finally, in the third act, the relation has turned entirely inward: "Hélas! c'est mon coeur que je crains" [Alas! it is my heart that I fear] (3.2.269).[18] Act 2, scene 5 marks the definitive interiorization of the tragedy.

Of course, the visual does not entirely disappear from the opera in scene 5. Armide decides to draw on her supernatural powers in the final moments of the scene, inviting her demons transformed into zephyrs to whisk them away to the end of the universe. Yet having evoked an obscure intervening presence ("qui me fait hésiter?") that cannot be presented as such, and by making this evocation central to the entire act, even to the opera as a whole, Quinault and Lully create an effect of caesura. Indeed, *Armide* exploits the spectacular dimension of *tragédie en musique* precisely in order to establish a contrast between the two realms of the internal and the external. When Armide subsequently resorts to magic in spectacular but hopeless attempts to reverse the course of events, instead of signaling her unlimited power over people and things, it points to her own desperation, to her inability to recover her former self-possession.[19] Not only has Renaud escaped her vengeance, but he has done so solely by her own failure to act. If

Armide's eyes were the symbol of her total control before the arrival of Renaud, the lone reference to sight in scene 5 marks a reversal. Not only does her *regard* no longer command, it has a negative effect: "Plus je le vois, plus ma vengeance est vaine" [The more I behold him, the more futile my vengeance] (2.5.266). The scene transforms Armide's seeing from action to passion. Scene 5 is not dominated by seeing as an act (of control, of grasping). Rather, sight leads to passion: she is "ravished," the term she will invoke in act 3. The strangeness of the encounter for Armide and the immensity of the affect are conveyed by the projection of an absence. Renaud is still present on stage; yet, because of the static quality of the tableau – Armide hesitates, Renaud sleeps – because the operatic *merveilleux* has been withdrawn, the scene has the effect of drawing attention to that which has *not* been shown, to secret or hidden desires. The spectator is fully aware that Armide has fallen for Renaud even though she is not; however, this is not to say that Renaud is the object of her desire or could ever be commensurate with it. Representation is made to seem to falter, to lose its object: mimesis is made to appear momentarily inadequate to its task.

At one level of analysis, as Kintzler has so thoroughly established, Quinault and Lully had created a new genre, *tragédie en musique,* that loudly proclaimed its affinity with the aesthetic framework of spoken tragedy. Seen in retrospect, the disappearance of *le merveilleux* in act 2, scene 5, may be understood to comply with the laws of the *tragédie en musique*, since special visual effects would normally be circumscribed in *divertissement* and therefore excluded from what is clearly a dramatic scene. The emphasis on drama and passion, therefore, mark an adherence to spoken tragedy. It is as if Quinault and Lully had decided to present a scene that, through its dramatic intensity and through contemporary commentators' unanimous praise, would manifestly overturn the claims of opera's critics that the new genre had none of the moral stuff of tragedy. *Tragédie en musique* was true theater, they seem to claim in *Armide*, not merely frivolous spectacle. Though this line of analysis is unmistakably tenable, I believe that Quinault and Lully had also created a work that provided opera with an escape from the endless and, for those who championed the new genre, fruitless comparison with spoken tragedy. An aesthetics of the sublime is at work in act 2, scene 5, enlisting the dramatic moment not so much because it spotlights a scene like so many from spoken tragedy in which the effects of passion are disclosed, but because it reveals how opera, through its use of music and focus on the operatic voice of passion, goes beyond what drama can accomplish.

THAT OTHER SCENE

In *Armide*, Quinault and Lully evoke the particular "problematic of the audience" that Herbert Blau has explored: "the pleasure of seeing – what Freud called *Schaulust* (seeing, being seen) . . . is constrained by the desire to see what cannot be seen."[20] "What theater and psychoanalysis have in common," Blau writes, "is the enactment of an obsession with the appearance of an absent cause."[21] Love's disappearance from the stage, indeed the disappearance of all spectacular elements during the moment of crisis, together with Armide's incessant evocation of something or someone intangible bearing responsibility for her hesitation, but which cannot be accounted for by the mere presence of Renaud – all of these signs point elsewhere, to another "scene" that would explain the excessive insistence and urgency of the moment. Given that Armide's dream from act 1, in which she sees herself succumb to Renaud, is in some measure replayed and confirmed in act 2, scene 5, I want to return to the earlier scene in order to supply more ample commentary on Armide's hesitation and the importance Quinault and Lully have ascribed to it.

Troubled, Armide approaches Sidonie and Phénice shortly after the beginning of the opera. A brief prelude introduces the vision as an ominous one, the violins executing restless turns before each downbeat, a pattern that, significantly, returns again in the prelude to act 2, scene 5. She announces that Renaud has appeared to her in a dream:

> Un songe affreux m'inspire une fureur nouvelle
> > Contre ce funeste ennemi.
> > > J'ai cru le voir, j'en ai frémi,
> J'ai cru qu'il me frappait d'une atteinte mortelle.

Je suis tombée aux pieds de ce cruel vainqueur.
> Rien ne fléchissait sa rigueur;
> Et par un charme inconcevable,
Je me sentais contrainte à le trouver aimable,
Dans ce fatal moment qu'il me perçait le coeur. (1.1.256)

A horrid dream fills me with further rage
> Against this hateful enemy.
> I thought I saw him; I shuddered,
I thought I saw him deal me a mortal blow.
I fell at the feet of this cruel conqueror.
> Nothing moderated his severity;
> And by an inconceivable charm,
I felt myself compelled to find him desirable
At the fatal moment that he was piercing my heart.

Dreams are uncommon neither in classical tragedy nor in *tragédie en musique*. In *Armide*, however, if the dream constitutes an oracle, it does so with extreme precision. Armide's dream prefigures, yet also inverts and transposes, the confrontation of act 2, scene 5. From the perspective of the spectator, who only discerns the resemblance between the two after hearing Armide's monologue, the dream scene reappears at the final moment of act 2 precisely like a half-remembered dream. The similarities and differences between the two are telling. Both scenes take place as decisive confrontations between Renaud and Armide. Both set the stage for the victory of one of the protagonists at the expense of the other's life; however, in Armide's dream, the roles are reversed, as is the outcome. Renaud is the aggressor, and he is successful. The dream thus presents the events of act 2, scene 5 in inverted form. In the verses preceding the narration of the dream, Armide remembers that Renaud's victory had been prophesied: "Les Enfers ont prédit cent fois / Que contre ce guerrier nos armes seront vaines" [A hundred times Hades has foretold / That our arms would be useless against this warrior] (1.1.256). Simultaneously anticipating the crusaders' victory over Jerusalem and Armide's own eventual failure, the dream stands out as a moment of truth. At first, Armide hesitates to recount the dream, describing it as an illusion: "*J'ai cru* le voir . . ." [I *thought* I saw him]; "*J'ai cru* qu'il me frappait" [*I thought* he struck me]. She then begins to narrate the scene as if it occurred in fact: "Je suis tombée" [I fell], "Rien ne fléchissait sa rigueur" [nothing moderated his severity] (1.1.256). The dream slowly envelops her. Armide's confidante, Sidonie, paradoxically reinforces the significance of the dream by attempting to explain it away as a fleeting image, her perky triple meter contrasting with Armide's weighty recitative. As in classical tragedy, the confidante's role is to dismiss the tragic, to speak of impossible reconciliations. Given the oracular quality of the dream, however, Armide's aborted attempt to exact revenge on Renaud in act 2, scene 5, appears fatefully unsuccessful from the outset.

One might wonder why the dream is only recounted and thus withheld from sight. Armide's vision thus returns us to the question of *le merveilleux*. As if answering the early critics of *tragédie en musique* who argued that opera had no moral or even mimetic function but was only about sensual pleasure, Quinault shifted the dream to an imaginary site to which the spectator had only indirect access.[22] Certainly, in spoken tragedy at the end of the century, dreams are reported, not represented, because of theatrical proprieties, or *bienséances*; however, the strictures of spoken tragedy do not hold for opera since dreams were often staged in *tragédies en musique* as sleep scenes.[23] Commentators do not seem to have noticed that in the case of *Armide*, there is both a dream and a *sommeil*. When seen in contrast to the *sommeil* of act 2, the heroine's dream creates a layering, an effect of figurative depth. Just as *le merveilleux* sets itself apart from ordinary events that take place on stage, a supplementary theatrical space is created by the dream which is still in compliance with the rules of classical theater since it is not represented on stage but recounted. Armide's dream is given over to the spectator, who will later witness the *sommeil*, as an event that is somehow more "real" or profound precisely because it cannot be seen on stage, but only imagined. In this respect, *Armide* goes against Jean-Marie Villégier's suggestive remark that the *tragédie en musique* is "'tragedy without an *off*,' full tragedy, tragedy without an exterior."[24] As in act 2, scene 5, all that is spectacle, and a fortiori *le merveilleux*, is momentarily eclipsed in the dream. For a brief moment, the entire spectacular apparatus of opera is held in check by the restraint of the dream. The effect of this moment is paradoxical and twofold. It creates, within opera, a distance with respect to operatic conventions (the exigency of representation) and thus a proximity to classical tragedy. At the same time, because it is an effect only opera can realize, because so-called "regular" tragedy cannot play *le merveilleux* and the natural against each other in this way, it draws attention to the instance of difference that exists here, within *Armide*, as a specifically operatic *tour de force*, an act of sublime reticence that is beyond the scope of classical tragedy since the latter does not have the represented *merveilleux* at its disposal.

The dream's absence from the stage is otherwise significant, and its importance reinforced, when it is understood as a phantasm – a daydream giving form to a desire that can be realized only as a fiction.[25] It is a "scene" that is by definition absent and, as such, tells a truth that cannot be presented otherwise. Renaud enters the virtual space of the *dream* to accomplish precisely what Armide will be unable to perform in act 2, scene 5. In her dream, it is Renaud who, unyielding ("Rien ne fléchissait sa rigueur" [Nothing moderated his severity]), strikes down Armide, to whose feet she falls, and to whom she is drawn nonetheless ("Je me sentais contrainte à le trouver aimable" [I felt myself compelled to find him desirable]), at the very moment that she dies by his hand. The death that Armide experiences in the phantasm is also described as pleasurable. If the dream further provokes her rage ("Un songe affreux m'inspire une fureur nouvelle" [A horrid dream fills me with further rage]), it is because it reveals a desire that is persistently denied. The fact that Armide's dream takes the form of an inverted act of vengeance and that she continues to deny her desire remain consistent with the general structure of the phantasm. Laplanche and Pontalis write that "such defences [reversal into the opposite, negation] are themselves inseparably bound up with the primary function of phantasy, namely the *mise-en-scène* of desire – a *mise-en-scène* in which what is *prohibited* (*l'interdit*) is always present in the actual formation of the wish."[26] In the *mise-en-scène* of her desire, therefore, it is Renaud who seeks out the sorceress and who forces a blade into her heart. She supplants the absence of his desire for her by inventing one for him: she has him kill her. If the purpose of the phantasm is to enact unavowed desires, Armide's dream could be seen not only as a premonition of approaching defeat, but as a phantasm about dispossession and loss. In order to account for the strange *jouissance* involved in her own undoing, Armide points to the work of a magic spell unknown to her, indeed unknowable – "Et par un charme inconcevable, / Je me sentais contrainte à le trouver aimable, / Dans le fatal moment qu'il me perçait le coeur" [And by an inconceivable charm, / I felt myself compelled to find him desirable / At the fatal moment that he was piercing my heart].[27]

SPECTATORSHIP AND THE SUBLIME

If we shift now to the perspective of the spectator and his or her identifications, by raising the question of dispossession and foregrounding problems of representation we can discuss how *Armide* points to the sublime. If the sublime is understood as a moment of loss in which representation falters, then Armide's lapse into passion might be seen as an instance of the operatic sublime. The sublime is generally defined as a moment of transcendence founded on a painful and terrifying confrontation with an immense and resistant object – the ocean, magnificent works of art, eternity, infinity, death – that stretches the imagination to its limits and, through this confrontation, allows for a reaffirmation. Describing the sublime moment, Kant writes that "our imagination strives to progress toward infinity, while our reason demands absolute totality as a real idea, and so [the imagination,] our power of estimating the magnitude of things in the world of sense, is inadequate to that idea. Yet this inadequacy itself is the arousal in us of the feeling that we have within us a supersensible power."[28] Like Kant, for whom this moment is *"negative"* in that "the object is apprehended as sublime with a pleasure [*Lust*] that is possible only by means of a displeasure [*Unlust*]," Burke stresses that the sublime is "founded on pain" and submission.[29] The upshot of the sublime experience, however, is an overcoming in which the subject is reaffirmed in its self-presence. "Typically," writes Barbara Claire Freeman, "the sublime involves a moment of blockage followed by one of heightened lucidity."[30] In Kant as in Burke, the overcoming subject is reasserted through the sacrifice [*Aufopferungen*] of an obstacle: "the imagination thereby acquires an expansion and a might that surpasses the one it sacrifices."[31] Freeman notes that "a feminine figure (or traditional symbol of femininity such as water or chaos) [often] becomes a metaphor for the obstacle or 'blocking agent.'"[32] Similarly, Tom Furniss has written that "the sublime is constituted as a corrective to weakness and relaxation" which are characterized by the theorists of the sublime as feminine attributes.[33] "An aesthetic for the strong – those capable of reversing their subjection before the object, text, or other being" – the sublime appropriates, sacrifices, and finally transcends "feminine" weakness and passivity.[34]

Returning to *Armide*, it is indeed the woman who is made to suffer her desire and loss, and the hero who regains self-control through his liberation from (female) desire. In the world of seventeenth-century tragedy, emotion and desire constitute defeat insofar as they mean relinquishing self-control – detachment being the proclaimed ambition of both Renaud and Armide, and the ostensible moral of the opera, put forth, first and foremost, in the prologue. The opera's moral stance is founded on the cold self-sufficiency of personal glory – the stuff of Pierre Corneille's heroic tragedies and of Cartesian models of subjectivity in which passion, seen as lack, must always be held in check. In the prologue, La Sagesse announces the subject of the tragedy to come:

> Nous y verrons Renaud, malgré la volupté,
> Suivre un conseil fidèle et sage;
> Nous le verrons sortir du palais enchanté,
> Où, par l'amour d'Armide, il était arrêté,
> Et voler où la Gloire appelle son courage. (prologue, 253)

> We will see Rinaldo, in spite of carnal pleasures
> Follow a faithful and wise counsel;
> We shall see him leave the enchanted palace
> Where he was held by Armide's love
> And fly to where Glory calls his courage.

Paralleling the sorceress's own ambition ("Mais je fais mon plus grand bonheur / D'être maîtresse de mon coeur" [But my greatest happiness / Is being the mistress of my heart], 1.2.258), though hers is ultimately frustrated – the logical consequence, one might add, of her claim to phallic omnipotence – the monarch receives praise in the prologue as effectively in control: "Il est maître absolu de cent peuples divers, / Et plus maître encore de lui-même" [He is the absolute master of a hundred different peoples, / And even more than this, he is master of himself] (prologue, 251). The foremost spectator – His Majesty – is presented as having avoided the amorous predicaments even magicians and gods could not escape.[35] At the opera's conclusion, a dispassionate and lucid Renaud abandons Armide, having re-established the proper hierarchical relationship between love and glory – in short, the embodiment of the models proposed by the prologue and offered to the spectator. The monarch, theoretically present (though he was not actually in attendance at the opera's premiere), grounds the moral as its ultimate and living referent.

The trajectory of the sublime would thus fit nicely with the moral of Quinault's and Lully's opera. Armide, whose desire is posed as a threat to the self-sufficiency of the warrior-hero – a threat that, moreover, initially defies containment and representation – is overcome; and Renaud, now unhampered and reaffirmed, is free to realize his glory.[36] The sublime moment in *Armide* is captured as the spectator witnesses the sorceress's undoing, her symbolic death in the dream, and the reaffirmation of an ethic of self-sufficiency in Renaud's freedom. In that sense, it is about leaving desire and loss to the woman as her lot: it is about moving definitively into a world of post-Oedipal, indeed post-sexual, glory. Given the context of absolute monarchy, not only under which but specifically *for* which this *tragédie en musique* was created, *Armide* re-articulates a seventeenth-century aristocratic ethic with emphatic phallocentricism.

This much appears clear. Yet the elements of my interpretive puzzle might be seen to fit into place entirely too easily. For one might be justly hesitant to conclude on that note – one that would force the opera's meaning to coincide with its moral and thus reduce the opera to the articulation of a law. At this point in my analysis, therefore, I want to express hesitations or limitations with respect to the argument on the sublime that I have just outlined and its account of spectatorship. First of all, if we take a closer look at *Armide*, the "canonical" version of the sublime outlined above (which is essentially a romantic one) cannot entirely account for the events of the opera, nor does it reflect early-modern audiences' reactions (whether favorable or unfavorable) to the opera. To cite only one instance, Le Cerf de la Viéville's *Comparaison de la musique italienne et de la musique françoise* refers specifically to *Armide* in one passage, claiming that the listener "returns home captivated despite himself, distracted, upset by Armide's unhappiness."[37] For Le Cerf de la Viéville, *Armide* is not really about the triumph of Renaud, who is most often in the background, either absent, asleep, or under a spell. What is recalled and retained, rather than overcome or sacrificed, is the passion of the sorceress. In this view, Armide could not be considered the "blocking agent" through which the hero is reaffirmed. Renaud does not overcome this obstacle by his own will but only through the happenstance of the arrival of his companions and the deployment of counter-magic in the form of the talisman they bear (a shield brought for this purpose). Nor is catharsis operative for the spectator since the spectator is not reaffirmed in any way. On the contrary, following the accounts of contemporaries such as Le Cerf de la Viéville, the spectator continues to be haunted by the figure of Armide. Claude Jamain has argued this point: "As the tragedy draws to a close, the royal image is reconstituted: Renaud contemplating himself in the reflection of a diamond shield, brought by the knights, recovers his power and gives himself over to the service of Heaven. But behind his image, another is there, persistent, and so unfortunate: Armide . . . Armide is the great figure of this tragedy."[38] The operatic moments upon which the most attention was lavished, those which most effectively hold the attention of the listener and spectator – Armide's struggle with herself in act 3, or the duets in act 4, for example, shaped by the gentle flow of parallel sixths – are about succumbing to passion. The two moments considered to be among the most significant and powerful of the entire opera – the dream and the scene of aborted vengeance in act 2, scene 5 – foreground the desire for desire itself, for immobility, for passion; and this desire is presented as central to the tragedy. In the end, neither Armide nor her passion dies; rather, there is a lingering sense of unremitting and unrecoverable loss. The final transcendence and the moral articulated in the prologue cannot be made to explain away the two crucial scenes I have analyzed – the dream scene from act 1 and its strange realization at the end of act 2. Nothing could possibly undo or erase what has taken place in the opera.

The second reason that gives me pause has to do with the nature of the aesthetic object. To see in *Armide* a "discourse" that amounts to nothing more than a reaffirmation of Renaud and everything he stands for is to forget that we are dealing with an aesthetic object in general and an opera in particular. To use keys to explain the opera's meaning, a tactic examined in the previous chapter, is similarly limited. Françoise Karro has suggested that the king created deliberate resonances with the political events of 1685–86 through the choice of Tasso and of *La Gerusalemme liberata*. Karro writes that the opera evokes "the reconquest of a Roman Empire united by faith, a veritable universal monarchy."[39] Armide and her uncle, the king of Damas, are deliberately ambiguous figures, designating not only the seventeenth-century Turks and Louis XIV's dreamed-of conquest against them, but also the protestants: "the king of Damascus is transformed before our eyes into an evocation of Calvin. The magician Armide represents heresy . . . The destruction of Armide's enchanted palace conveys the memory of the demolition, directly following the signing of the Edict [of Nantes], of the Temple of Charenton, a seat of French Protestantism."[40] Though they may add in some measure to our understanding of the opera and its contexts, these political resonances cannot possibly exhaust the meaning of *Armide*, as Karro seems to suggest, particularly given the strong identification and fascination with Armide to which spectators testified. For if *Armide* was supposed to induce pleasure for the final purpose of propaganda or instruction, "it remains unclear," as Frances Ferguson has argued in relation to the aesthetics of the sublime, "why indirection is better than direction and . . . what, other than pleasure, is communicated."[41]

In the final analysis, opera is not about mastering or overcoming desire through the appropriation of figures of passion, but about identification.[42] As contemporary spectators' accounts attest, *Armide* is about identifying with the sorceress, losing oneself in her loss. The first account of the sublime, that of Longinus in his *Peri Hypsous*, differs remarkably from the romantic one that derives from Kant and allows me to focus on identification rather than on the overcoming of the other through self-affirmation. Far from reaffirming the subject in its integrity, the sublime as described by Longinus entails a confusion in which the subject perceives the sublime as if he himself had created it.[43] In Longinus, I would argue, the sublime is not an apotheosis of the subject; rather it is a moment of confusion in which the subject cannot distinguish between itself and the other. The sublime requires a disintegration on the part of the subject and always entails a loss of control. Louis Marin has argued that "the sublime affect-effect is always marked by a modification, a lapse of the subject's identity, a disappropriation of the subject to himself."[44] Sublime moments in opera have a similar effect upon the spectator. Seventeenth- and eighteenth-century spectators who forced themselves to focus on the moral of the story were troubled by Renaud's "emasculation" and by the prominence given to Armide and to her passion. Those who abandoned themselves to the opera had eyes for Armide only.[45] The ultimate negativity of Armide's desire when it is seen as an obstacle to be overcome is transformed through the mechanism of the spectator's identification into the *jouissance* of loss, of the subject's loss in the object. The opera may thus be seen as maintaining a perpetual, and indeed ambiguous, tension between desire and its negation.

The relationship between desire and dispossession that is at the center of Armide's dream in act 1, together with its status as a fantasy not actually representable on stage, brings us to the question of the musical voice. Le Cerf de la Viéville remarked that Armide's monologue "seized" the listener.[46] The listener was powerless to control his experience of the voice or of the passions it aroused: "my heart feels them no matter what I do."[47] In his analysis of Armide's monologue,

Rameau, too, described the "unconscious" and uncontrollable effect of the musical text:

> When the singer notices from the words that she must emphasize [Armide's] confusion at "I shudder," her voice expresses it as if automatically; and without reflecting on the cause that makes her act, without even being aware of it, she finds herself swept up in this expression by the harmony that leads her to it. The listener, on his side, is moved and should not, therefore, ask why.[48]

The characterization of the voice of passion as torn from the subject and forcefully eliciting a passionate response from the listener is a *topos* that returns repeatedly in texts on opera and in other essays on music. In Mably's *Lettres à Madame la Marquise de P . . . sur l'opéra* (1741), opera is said to enrapture the spectator: "a poet must rob me of the use of my mind and my senses, so as to occupy me solely with my passions."[49] Referring to Montéclair's opera *Jephté*, one of the interlocutors exclaims: "Montéclair ravishes me, he transports me, he communicates his enthusiasm to me, and I feel as though infused with the majesty of God."[50] The effect of opera is one of emotional transport, ravishment, penetration. This effect can neither be accounted for rationally, nor prevented: "we transport ourselves to the place depicted on the stage, and that, she added, takes place as if in spite of ourselves. I do not know the reason for this, but the experience is enough."[51]

Texts of a philosophical or "anthropological" bent also remark the particular relationship between voice and dispossession. In his *Essai sur l'origine des langues*, written in the late 1750s, Rousseau describes the musical "accents" of the first language as if he were presenting an ideal musical language for the operatic stage: "these accents which cause us to shudder, these accents to which one cannot close one's ear penetrate to the very depths of the heart, in spite of ourselves conveying the emotions that wring them [from us], and cause us to feel what we hear."[52] For Rousseau, the musical "accent" is associated twice with dispossession and passivity: first, torn or wrung from the passionate subject, these accents then penetrate the listener. The listener cannot ignore the voice: he is affected by it in spite of himself. For Rousseau and others, this effect derives from the origin and peculiar nature of the human voice and is documented in the earliest accounts from antiquity. The focus on Armide's defeat in Quinault's and Lully's opera could thus be seen as a way of foregrounding the effect of *tragédie en musique* on the listener – the pleasure of being affected, of being disarmed. Armide's rapture, presented in the dream as her powerlessness ("Incessamment son importune image / *Malgré moi* trouble mon repos" [*Despite myself*, his unwelcome image / Constantly troubles my rest], 1.1.256), together with Renaud's seduction and fundamental weakness throughout, might be said to stand as a figure for the operatic experience itself.[53]

In the two scenes on which I have focused my analysis, *Armide* could be said to mark a limit of figuration, to evoke another "marvellous" presence – not *le merveilleux*, which is a more or less codified element of epic poetry and *tragédie en musique*, but rather the sublime object of opera.[54] The canonical sublime pertains to vision and is triggered by an image (the poet's *phantasiai*). Yet *Armide* creates the effect of the sublime by pointing away from *le merveilleux* and from visual representation generally.[55] In the dream scene, as in act 2, scene 5, Armide submits to Renaud. Yet is not Armide's submission essentially internal, self-reflexive, without object – submission to desire itself? What could the machinist possibly show us, what could we possibly *see*, what object could possibly be commensurate with desire? Following Louis Marin, for whom the sublime always reflects back onto its own enunciation, the sublime moment of Armide's loss could be said to focus attention inward on a theater of desire and dispossession, and at the same time to produce a self-reflexive gesture pointing to the specificity of opera's function within late seventeenth-century dramatic theory.[56] If Armide's dream reveals dispossession as fundamental to the tragedy, it is in order to evoke the sublime object of opera at the limit of figuration – that is, music, voice, passion. Michel Poizat has suggested that "[t]he voice as object is thus constructed both as lost object and as first object of *jouissance*."[57] *Armide* presents a moment of *jouissance* that turns around an object that is forever being lost, one that is consubstantial with the singer's voice.

With *Armide, tragédie en musique* confronts one of the most crucial and resistant terms of its identity: it awakens a nebulous cluster of meanings around music and the lyric voice embracing dispossession, hysteria, mania, and poetic *fureur*. These meanings explain why the historical moment of the origin of *tragédie en musique*, while borrowing from early seventeenth-century theater, is also that of the decline of the hero, as the père Rapin complained: "we have become gradually accustomed to see heroes on stage, stirred by the love of something other than glory."[58] It is for these reasons that I cannot accept the claims of critics such as Richard Taruskin and Jean-Marie Apostolidès, both of whom view *tragédie en musique* in general as a universe of total mastery. Apostolidès argues that "in the place of a universe without mediation, [opera] presents a conciliatory, unifying myth from which the very notion of conflict is removed . . . Through its use of machines, opera presents a thoroughly controlled world in which technology generates both the real and the supernatural."[59] Richard Taruskin makes a similar claim, suggesting that "the concert of myriad forces in perfect harness under the aegis of a mastermind was the real message, whatever the story."[60] Such claims cannot explain, as Bruce McIntyre has affirmed, why of all of Quinault's and Lully's works their last and most acclaimed opera is the one in which the erasure of the hero is "the primordial function of the story" and, I would add, of the music.[61]

The sublime ecstasy of opera sounds the disintegration and death of the hero; and the death of the hero announces the onset of an age of divas. Writing about the representation of women in opera, Catherine Clément has written that "on the opera stage women perpetually sing their eternal undoing."[62] *Armide* is indeed about the undoing of a woman, to borrow Clément's phrase; but it is also about identifying with the woman who is bereft, who is dispossessed. Arguing against theorists of the cinematic gaze for whom being looked at translates into a position of powerlessness, Linda Hutcheon and Michael Hutcheon, discussing Strauss's opera *Salome*, find that the spectator's gaze upon the female operatic character does not always translate into the spectator's mastery.[63] Quinault's and Lully's final *tragédie en musique* may be said "[to induce] the wish, condemned as effeminate," as Wayne

Koestenbaum writes, albeit with respect to much later opera, "never to reassemble the socialized self, but, instead, to remain in tears forever."[64] As Herbert Blau has suggested, writing about the audience, "what is being listened to appears to be the *listener* . . . [this] is also, as Barthes suggests, a secular form of 'auricular confession.'"[65] Since the tragic hero obviously did not allow for such a model of failure and mourning in early-modern France, opera would create a space for these desires through those of the female protagonist.

My intention has not been to move "beyond" questions of gender in early opera or to play the gender card to further my own hermeneutics of the sublime. Rather, I have been concerned with the sublime in opera at a given historical moment and the way in which it allows me to point to some particular figures of operatic spectatorship and poetics. Because its object is not immediately available or wholly graspable, the sublime "stages" a resistance to representation from within. It is for this reason, I have argued, that a particular form of tragedy, *tragédie en musique*, relied on the sublime to define its own parameters in relation to theater and mimetic modes. *Armide* thus adopted the sublime in order to stake out its claims as tragedy while at the same time flaunting its ability to stretch the limits of that aesthetic. If *Armide* can be said to push the limits of theatrical representation that it assumed as *tragédie en musique*, it may also point to an aesthetics of music that would allow for the loss of objects in general, for a fading of the mimetic paradigm. In *Armide*, the gap opened up by the sublime also points to a historically specific discourse on music, and on opera in particular, involving the relationship between the listener's pleasure and dispossession – a discourse that will undergo further examination in the second section of this book. The connection between music and dispossession contributed to opera's identity from its earliest days and furthermore can be traced to the founding statements of Western musical culture.[66]

After its many revelations, *Armide* ends on a repressive gesture. Renaud has escaped Armide's spell with the help of his two companions who arrived to save him from the sorceress with the help of a magic shield. Armide's aborted attempt at revenge in act 2, scene 5 returns, this time as pure hallucination as her "enemy" flees. In the last lines of the opera, Armide imagines that she has caught up with Renaud as he leaves to join his fellow crusaders: "Traître, attends . . . je le tiens . . . je tiens son coeur perfide . . . / Ah! je l'immole à ma fureur . . . / Que dis-je? où suis-je? hélas! Infortunée Armide!" [Traitor, wait . . . I have him . . . I have his faithless heart. / Ah! I sacrifice him to my wrath . . . / What am I saying? where am I? alas! Poor Armide!] (5.5.287). After this brief illusion, as a final, grandiose gesture of defeat, Armide orders her demons to destroy the enchanted palace, which stands as the memory of her loss: "Démons, détruisez ce palais. / Partons, et s'il se peut, que mon amour funeste / Demeure enseveli dans ces lieux pour jamais" [Demons, destroy this palace. / Away! And if it is possible, may my cursed love / Remain buried in this place forever] (5.5.287). If *le merveilleux* has the last word after all, judging from Jean Berain's sketches for the décor and machines of the final scene, it nonetheless reminds the spectator of the scene that cannot be represented on stage, the scene that no amount of magic or machinery can erase.

Médée was first performed in December, 1693, the only lyric tragedy by Marc-Antoine Charpentier ever to make it onto the stage of the Paris Opéra. Thomas Corneille, lesser-known brother of the famous playwright, Pierre, furnished the libretto. Recordings and stage productions from the 1980s and 1990s by William Christie and Les Arts Florissants have been the stimulus behind much of the attention this extraordinary *tragédie en musique* has received over the past several years, including my own interest here. After examining the opera and its reception history at greater length, I was struck by a detail: the provocative connection between the composer and his central character that emerges from most seventeenth- and eighteenth-century commentaries on *Médée*. Quite consistently, and apparently unwittingly, commentators identified Charpentier with Medea. There is admittedly nothing unusual about seeing the man in his works: indeed, library shelves are full of volumes devoted to variations on this theme. Composers have also been known to hint at possible identifications or close connections between their characters and themselves or their time, as when Wagner wrote of Wotan that "he resembles *us* to a tee."[1] Edward T. Cone has examined an entity he calls "the composer's voice" as emerging from the complex of symbolic gestures involved in accompanied song. A particularly salient example he gives is Milton Babbitt's *Philomel*:

> The dramatic situation requires the soprano to take shape from her electronic surroundings, gradually turning her vocalization into articulate language as the protagonist she portrays, transformed into a nightingale, discovers her new voice. This is a voice in the process of finding itself, but once it has succeeded, there is no question as to its supremacy. So far as I know, this is the unique example of a composition that seems to create its own protagonist, who in turn creates her own

song. As such it appropriately symbolizes the relationship between the vocal persona and the musical persona that envelops and includes it – between the protagonist's voice and the composer's.[2]

Corneille's and Charpentier's *Médée* may be seen as approaching the extreme degree of performativity Cone detects in *Philomel*. In the case of *Médée*, I will argue, the identification of the composer with Medea herself, however small a fragment of reception history in itself, exposes some of the principal fault lines and instabilities that surrounded early opera in France.

Médée and its innovations grew out of an intricate series of aesthetic tensions which developed within the cultural politics of the reign of Louis XIV. First of all, as the previous chapters have established, within the highly regulated network of artistic production that began to cohere around the Sun King in the 1660s, the identity and function of opera were uncertain. The ill-defined genre initially existed in a shadowland somewhere between tragedy, epic, and pastoral. A potentially definitive cultural contribution for the moderns, opera also had at least perceived connections with ancient tragedy. In short, there was no clear consensus on the value or pedigree of *tragédie en musique*. Secondly, because the Italian-trained Charpentier wrote in a genre created in and for the French court, and which was shaped and policed by the Italian-born Lully until his death in 1687, *Médée* was part and parcel of the political and aesthetic tensions that distinguished what was "French" from what was "Italian" in music. This is not the place to give a detailed history of Lully's control over French opera through a series of patents and ordinances during the 1670s, a story that is well documented and has been told elsewhere.[3] The figure of Medea, however, insofar as she can be said to constitute a "return of the repressed" after the death of the powerful *Surintendant de la Musique de Sa Majesté*, is a highly charged one in this situation and merits more attention. The identification of Charpentier and Medea, I will argue, makes sense of these complex and interwoven issues and thereby informs our understanding of early French opera and the contested place it occupied among the aesthetic and cultural productions of absolutism.

In composing *Médée*, Charpentier and Thomas Corneille relied most obviously on Euripides and Seneca. However, Thomas's older brother, Pierre, had also written a spoken tragedy on the subject in 1635; and during his stay in Rome, Charpentier may have been familiar with the *Giasone* of Francesco Cavalli, the most frequently represented opera in seventeenth-century Italy, which premiered in Venice at Carnival in 1649. The most decisive influences, in any event, were Pierre Corneille's version and the two tragedies from antiquity. For Mitchell Greenberg, *Médée* represents the prehistory of Pierre Corneille's career as a dramatist, which begins with myth (*Médée*) before moving on to history (*Le Cid*). Whereas *Médée* reveals "the chaotic forces of nature metaphorized as both woman and mother," Greenberg argues, with *Le Cid* the space of the law was established, however precariously; and the passions, which had burst forth in *Médée*, were henceforth interiorized.[4] If Thomas Corneille returned to the subject his brother had treated, it may be seen as a significant gesture insofar as it referred back to a theatrical mode prior to the development of late seventeenth-century theatrical aesthetics, an attempt to define and justify the existence of opera in the shadow of Corneillian and Racinian tragedy. Since Pierre had written two *tragédies à machines* and been involved at least some in opera – having worked with Molière and Quinault on the *tragédie-ballet, Psyché*, which Lully set in 1671 – one cannot justifiably isolate the two brothers at opposite ends of the aesthetic spectrum. However, Thomas's use of the Medea myth may be understood as a meaningful revision of his brother's early work. One might even go so far as to suggest that Thomas Corneille and Charpentier returned to Medea in order to portray the otherness of opera itself in relation to late seventeenth-century spoken tragedy. In this light, *Médée* could be understood to represent opera, through the figure of the exiled woman, as a "victimized" genre, one whose ostentatious spectacle and music were criticized because they threatened the aesthetic of interiorization and sublimation that dominates so many spoken tragedies by Pierre Corneille and Racine. These very same resources would enable opera, again if we accept the allegorization of Medea, to take spectacular revenge upon those critics, like Boileau, who dismissed the genre on formal grounds ("Ce qu'on ne doit pas voir, qu'un récit nous l'expose: / Les yeux en le voyant saisiroient mieux la chose; / Mais il est des objets que l'art judicieux / Doit offrir à l'oreille et reculer des yeux" [That which one must not see, let a narrative relate it to us: / The eyes upon seeing it would better grasp the thing; / But there are objects that judicious art / Must offer to the ears and draw away from the eyes]) as well as for the immoral content it conveyed to audiences through mellifluous tunes ("Et tous ces lieux communs de morale lubrique / Que Lulli réchauffa des sons de sa musique?" [And all these commonplaces of lewd morals / Which Lully rekindled with the sounds of his music?]).[5] In order to stage this "othering" of opera (Medea seen as *tragédie en musique* in all of its flashy and appalling spectacle) while at the same time performing its vindication (Medea exacting spectacular revenge upon her persecutors), Thomas Corneille distanced himself in the libretto from his brother's representation of Medea by returning first and foremost to Euripides.

The most remarkable transformation from Pierre to Thomas Corneille was that Medea lost her perversely sophisticated and monstrously lucid premeditation. Thomas returned to the human dimension accentuated by Euripides. In Euripides, Medea laments the hardships of a woman's life, asserts her desire for Jason (she repeatedly refers to the marriage bed, *léchos*), and sadly reflects upon her physical attachment to the children ("Oh, how sweet is the touch, how tender the skin, how fragrant the breath of these children!").[6] In Pierre, this aspect of Medea vanished: as he stated plainly in the dedication, "Je vous donne Medée toute meschante qu'elle est, et ne vous diray rien pour sa justification" [I give you Medea in all her evilness and will say nothing in her defense].[7] Pierre's version, like Seneca's, showed Medea from the beginning determined to bring the entire universe to bear upon her vengeance. She appears for the first time in act 1, scene 3, invoking both heaven ("Dieux, garands de la foy que Jason m'a donnée" [Gods, guarantors of the faith that Jason gave me]) and hell ("Filles de l'Acheron, Pestes, Larves, Furies" [Daughters of Acheron, Plagues, Specters, Furies]) in her unbridled rage (1.3.109). She already knows how things will end, and announces her plans to exhibit one final masterpiece of horror in a performance to surpass all the other atrocities she has committed, even the murder of her own brother whose body she had dismembered, scattering the pieces along their path to delay her father's pursuit as she and Jason fled after taking the Golden Fleece from his kingdom:

> Deschirer par morceaux l'enfant aux yeux du pere,
> N'est que le moindre effet qui suivra ma cholere.
> Des crimes si legers furent mes coups d'essay,
> Il faut bien autrement monstrer ce que je sçay,
> Il faut faire un chef-d oeuvre, et qu'un dernier ouvrage
> Surpasse de bien loing ce foible apprentissage. (1.3.111)

> To tear the child to pieces under the eyes of his father
> Is only the slightest consequence that will follow my anger.
> Such minor crimes were my first steps;
> Quite different means will show what I know.
> I must create a masterpiece, and may one last work
> Far surpass this meek apprenticeship.

In contrast to his brother's treatment of Medea, Thomas Corneille returned to the strong sensuality, even tenderness, of Euripides's *Medea*, in large part, as I will argue below, by joining forces with Charpentier. In Thomas's treatment, the course of action Medea undertakes is restrained and absolutely deliberate, slowly spiraling beyond the confines of ordinary rationality, hinting at extraordinary and unthinkable measures. She exhausts rhetorical and amorous argument before moving on to supernatural force.[8] Though she offers a brief indication of the scope of her powers in act 1, scene 1, when the full, five-part array of strings suddenly bursts in wildly upon the recitative, it is only a taste of things to come. In Thomas's version, she does not decide to invoke the "Noires filles du Styx" [Black daughters of the Styx] until the very end of act 3; in contrast, Pierre placed this evocation in act 1.[9] Pursued for the murders she committed to save Jason, Medea has found refuge in Corinth under the protection of Creon. Creon now insists that Medea leave while reassuring her that he will safeguard the children she has had with Jason. Medea hears him out as he announces her exile in act 2, scene 1, and laments her situation ("Ay-je donc merité cette rigueur extrême?" [Have I then deserved such extreme severity?]) before confronting him with her powers at the end of act 4 (2.1.91). Similarly, in act 1, scene 2, and again in act 3, scene 2, Medea complains to Jason about her predicament and allows him the opportunity to renounce Créuse (Glaucè in the Greek myth), Creon's daughter and his new passion, so as to return to her. The decision to murder the children comes later as a surprise, even to her, as was also the case in Seneca. Whereas Pierre's *Médée* fixed her from the very beginning in a form of monstrosity that is already thoroughly developed, Thomas returned to her humanity so that she becomes Medea, as it were, only when forced to do so by everyone else's inability to understand her, and only when she rediscovers and cultivates a recurring aberrance within herself. She rediscovers this identity, in part, through the way the others see her. Jacques Lacan observed that "what I seek in speech is the response of the other. What constitutes me as subject is my question."[10] The question Medea desperately asks herself in dialogue with Creon in act 2 ("Ay-je donc merité cette rigueur extrême?") and the one with which she confronts Jason in act 3, scene 2 ("Ingrat, m'abandonnerez-vous?" [Ungrateful creature, will you abandon me?]), receive no adequate response (3.2.184). She only emerges as Medea (a variation on Seneca's "Now I am Medea"[11]) when she acknowledges or supposes an implicit response, transforming her question into an outraged statement of irreconcilable differences in act 3, scene 3: "Quel prix de mon amour! quel fruit de mes forfaits" [So this is the recompense for my love! so these are the fruits of my crimes!] (3.3.187–88). In the end, Medea produces an answer to her questions, widening the gap that exists between herself and the astonishing mediocrity of the characters who surround her – Jason with his cowardice and self-pity, Creon with his easy lies and blatant political subterfuge, Créuse's naïveté and self-absorption – by assuming and seeking to justify the otherness they see in her. In act 2, scene 1, for example, Creon clothes his own desire to be rid of Medea in his people's fear of her as a potentially dangerous foreigner: "À vous voir dans ma Cour mon peuple s'inquiette. / Il craint ce qu'avec vous vous traînez des malheurs" [Seeing you in my court people are troubled. / They fear that you bring misfortune along with you] (2.1.82–83). In act 5, Medea will act to justify and to make real those projected fears. By killing their children, Medea forces Jason to repudiate her, an act which he had perhaps desired all along but had been powerless to realize until then.

Two of Medea's most obvious distinguishing characteristics, in all versions of the myth, contribute to early-modern commentators' tendency to identify Charpentier with Medea: her status as a foreigner among Greeks, and her knowledge and use of magic to terrible ends. Medea's barbarous otherness and her sorcery come to stand for the foreign roots of Charpentier's art. Charpentier's Italian training with Carissimi was thought to be the source of his penchant for music that was difficult and dissonant in comparison with native French models. Though the Italian music to which Parisians were exposed was at times much simpler than native products, the "difficult" harmonies of Italian violin sonatas had attained exemplary status for many. The Parfaict brothers, for example, noted that after his return from Italy, Charpentier "refused to write anything but very difficult music, music whose harmony and theoretical basis were heretofore unknown to the French. This brought him the reputation of being a barbarous composer."[12] Another writer remarked that Charpentier "imparted to *Médée*, with too much liberality, the misplaced charms of high theory."[13] Le Cerf de la Viéville, with equal venom, referred disparagingly to "the learned [sçavant] Charpentier."[14] The key elements of the resemblance are unmistakable. Medea's identity as a foreigner – as "barbarous" – and her supernatural knowledge came to stand for the supposedly arcane compositional practices Charpentier had brought into France from *outremont* Italy; and the magic that Medea deploys for her revenge evoked the dubious musical wizardry of Italianate harmony. The comparison was thus being used to confirm or rehearse a conviction on the part of the commentators that Charpentier had drawn upon an enigmatic, foreign knowledge (*science*), one with which he conjured up complicated, discordant music with perhaps questionable and certainly bewitching effects ("charms") on the listener.

Médée was not without its supporters: Sébastien de Brossard and, predictably, the reviewer for the enthusiastically modernist *Mercure galant*. However, they were few and far between.

If the identification of composer and character proved to be so irresistible or unavoidable, I want to suggest that it was in some measure deliberately orchestrated by Charpentier himself.[15] Charpentier – a brilliant composer who always worked in the shadow of his all-powerful predecessor, Lully – created a Medea who would embody the foreignness of his work in relation to the normative musicality of late seventeenth-century French compositional practices. In *Médée* we have an exemplary case of a composer and a librettist working together toward the same goals. While Thomas Corneille strove to create a figure for the predicament of *tragédie en musique* in the face of hostility from the proponents of spoken tragedy, staging their repudiation of opera as well as its eventual victory through the figure of Medea, Charpentier's music captured with extreme subtlety the otherness of his work in a musical culture overwhelmingly dominated by the Lullian model. Because both Corneille and Charpentier necessarily worked so closely with their predecessors' models to this purpose, it is perhaps understandable, though accurate only in the most superficial sense in my view, that critics have characterized both the libretto and the composition as derivative products. Thomas Corneille's biographer, Gustave Reynier, makes the hasty claim that the opera is a virtual imitation of Pierre Corneille's *Médée*.[16] Similarly, in her exhaustive book on Charpentier, Catherine Cessac remarks that, though the heated controversy around *Médée* "gives the impression that Charpentier launched a challenge to the genre that Lully had invented and nurtured, it must be acknowledged that *Médée* in all respects falls into the mold of Lully's tragédie lyrique."[17] Cessac can dismiss *Médée*'s entire reception history with this sweeping claim only because her study deliberately sets aside the controversy in order to focus on a "disinterested" analysis of "the work." I propose to offer a more complex picture by engaging the controversy *from within* the musical and textual forms of the opera. By raising the specters of Pierre Corneille's *Médée* and Lully's *tragédie en musique* in a series of performative gestures, Thomas Corneille and

Charpentier elaborated upon, and took a position in relation to, the tensions that surrounded opera in late seventeenth-century France. Judith Butler has clarified the notion of performativity, arguing that "performativity is neither free play nor theatrical self-presentation," but rather is founded on a relationship to constraint: "constraint is . . . that which impels and sustains performativity."[18] If we consider Pierre Corneille's *Médée* and Lully's dominant model as forms of constraint, then *Médée* the *tragédie en musique* can be considered a performative work insofar as it asserts its identity through previous models and a cluster of contemporary perceptions regarding opera itself.

It was, and still is, an aesthetic commonplace to assume that in *tragédie en musique* music inflects or embroiders upon a dramatic text which can be considered already complete in itself, heightening dramatic situations by emphasizing their emotional content. H. Wiley Hitchcock, for example, has noted that "Charpentier's aptitude for exploiting dramatic possibilities, and his skill at embodying musically shades of feeling and emotion are especially striking."[19] No one, I think, would deny Charpentier's extraordinary musical sensibility; nor do I intend to question per se the aesthetic presupposition that is implicit in comments such as these. What I want to suggest, however, is that what truly sets Charpentier's compositional practice in *Médée* apart from that of Lully is not only, and perhaps not even primarily, its ability to express or embody a dramatic text. Rather, by producing shades of difference within and in relation to the overall musical fabric of the *tragédie en musique* itself through his use of dissonance and by opposing the so-called French and Italian styles, Charpentier destabilizes the ordinary relationship between music and text, creating a situation in which the shifting meanings of the compositional practice exceed the expected function of illustration or coloring of the libretto. In other words, Medea is made a musical entity, not so much because her voice is the musical rendering of a text, but because her voice marks its difference in relation to other musical voices. This difference is an extreme instance of what Carolyn Abbate has referred to as the "radical autonomization of the human voice" in song.[20] This autonomization is performative because, like the examples from Rossi's *Orfeo* discussed in chapter 1, it serves to distinguish Medea's utterances from those of the other characters of the opera. At the same time, because Medea the character acts as a figure of *Médée* the work, the performativity of song is expanded, so that Medea's voice is established as the voice of the opera.

Let me move directly to some examples to bring this claim into focus. Because *Médée* was written in a musical culture that was overwhelmingly dominated by Lully, it is not surprising that the work may appear at first glance to be nothing more than a outgrowth of the Lullian *tragédie en musique*. Indeed, it resembles Lully's works in many respects: taking only the most superficial elements, *Médée* begins with a French overture, includes orchestral ballet airs, and demonstrates absolute mastery of the conspicuously French opposition of *petit choeur* and *grand choeur* (in the Passacaille at the end of act 2, for example). Yet during Medea's monologue in act 3, and at a few other extreme moments such as the chorus in scenes 2 and 3 of act 5, Charpentier departs audibly from this style, drawing on musical resources – extremely rich textures and dissonances – that one can find nowhere in Lully and that struck contemporaries as astounding, sometimes offensive, and always as "Italian." These sounds are generally very closely associated with Medea and pointedly contrast with the music of other characters in the opera.[21] Indeed, no other character in the opera receives the emphatic musical treatment that she does. As Geoffrey Burgess insists, "the music of all other characters falls short of her vocal outbursts in both quantity and scale."[22]

In the genre of *tragédie en musique*, the monologue occurs at a moment of extreme tension, one in which a character gives vent to the burden of impossible alternatives and conflicting emotions. Two particularly successful examples from Lully are Alceste's brief lament, "Ah! pourquoi nous séparez-vous?," from act 3, scene 1, of *Alceste*, and Cybèle's "Espoir si cher et si doux" from the final scene in act 3 of *Atys* (see example 5). Though the first is not strictly speaking a monologue, since two other characters are present in the scene, it presents all the defining characteristics associated with Lully's monologues. In Alceste's

Example 5: "Espoir si cher"

lament (not shown), one finds an introductory instrumental ritornello in A minor in which the violins trace a mournful, lilting rhythm, the bass proceeding in descending passages, the second time in a chromatic lament tetrachord. The 14-measure prelude is scattered with dissonances and non-harmonic tones to provide mood and direction: there is the diminished chord in measure 2, several suspensions and appoggiaturas, and the chromatic finish. In the voice, complementary upward and downward minor-6th leaps mark Alceste's exclamations of distress ("Ah!" and "Eh") and also serve to punctuate the beginnings

Example 5: (*cont.*)

of verses. At the end of the passage, a final, emphatic "Ah!" pushes the voice up an entire octave from e4 to e5. These musical resources wonderfully unfold the lament in which Alceste mourns the death of Admète, her lover, and contemplates killing herself in order to save him.[23]

By using Alceste's lament as a foil for my analysis of *Médée*, I do not want to give the impression that Charpentier entirely breaks with the Lullian model, because he clearly does not. Yet the monologue from act 3, scene 3, "Quel prix de mon amour!" does distinguish itself significantly from those of his predecessor, thereby serving to foreground Medea's otherness – both diegetically (the foreignness she carries with her as an outsider among Greeks) and extradiegetically (the foreignness her voice is made to convey in relation to the norms of the genre). The monologue also marks a transitional moment in which Medea reflects on her situation and decides to abandon ordinary resources for supernatural means of action. In the preceding scene, Medea and Jason consider her imminent departure into exile. Jason claims that he must remain behind to fight for Corinth and the safety of the children, but chooses not to mention the fact that he is also in love with Creon's daughter, Créuse. At the close of scene 2, Jason grows impatient with Medea's complaints and walks offstage with an evasive reference to the glory he must uphold, a value which is (conveniently for Jason) always incompatible with feelings of love in French tragedy of the period. As if he cannot quite repress his petulance, Jason leaves Medea with a sickly-sweet imperfect cadence in G on "Adieu," hesitating on the comma at the beginning of the verse ("Adieu, je ne puis plus soûtenir vos douleurs" [Farewell, I can no longer bear your grief]). He then throws away a hasty final cadence in A minor on "gloire" ("Et je dois me cacher vos pleurs / Si je veux en sauver ma gloire" [and I must hide my tears, / If I am to conserve my dignity]), which is, ironically, the last thing on his mind at this moment (3.2.186–87).

Medea, fully aware of his deception, is left alone to lament her situation. Scene 3 opens in D minor with the full, five-part string accompaniment, all muted, drawing attention to the importance of the moment (see example 6). This is the first time the larger instrumental ensemble has appeared in this act, creating an arresting contrast with the sparse recitative of the preceding scene. An intense effect of difference is produced from the start by a sumptuous wash of dissonances – a 9th chord in measure 3, another one enhanced by an augmented 5th in measure 5 – which create a mood that one would be hard pressed to find in Lully. In the first 9th chord, a suspension, the "resolution" to G in measure 4 is already dislocated by the bass shift

Example 6: "Quel prix de mon amour"

Example 6: *(cont.)*

to E♮ in the same measure.[24] This powerful effect is generated within the operatic narrative of *Médée*, in explicit relation to the preceding music – a contrast that was noticed by audiences and commentators from the period.[25] A momentary rift has opened in the musical fabric of the opera.

As the scene opens, the violins (*dessus*) prefigure Medea's vocal line, dissonances wafting through the five-part string accompaniment as if to create a distinct space within the opera, the only one that is adequate to her predicament. It is a space of reflection and rejected desire; but it is also the space of her emphatic otherness. The brief modulation to the sub-dominant (G minor) in measure 2 puts things off balance almost immediately. The resulting tonal ambiguity is repeated and reinforced in the following measures. The vocal B♭ at the end of the first hemistich, "Quel prix de mon a-*mour*" [So this is the recompense for my love!], drops away and is replaced by an unexpected B♮ at the beginning the next hemistich, "*Quel* fruit de mes forfaits" [so these are the fruits of my crimes!] – compounding the wrenching chromaticism of the score

(3.3.187–88). A reorchestration contributes to the effect of the scene. The voice takes over the first violin's initial statement (measures 6–11) while the initial suspended ninth shifts from violas (*hautes-contre de violon*) to violins (*dessus*), the latter brushing against the voice as Medea moves from A to B♭ in measures 7–8. This passage becomes the heart of the refrain: two moments of substantial anguish and dissonance – the two 9th chords – spanning a dramatic pause as the voice leaves B♭, only to make a striking reappearance on B♮, before the score settles into a cadence in measure 11.

Medea makes her way through two chains of thought, each of which is punctuated at the beginning and the end by this anguished refrain where she reflects on the impossible correlation between what she has done for the love of Jason and what she has received in return. In the first, resigned to her situation, she reflects on Jason's indifference and cowardice in the previous scene:

> Insensible au feu le plus tendre
> Qu'on ait veu s'allumer jamais;
> Quand mes soupirs peuvent suspendre
> L'injustice de ses projets;
> Il fuit pour ne les pas entendre. (3.3.188–89)

> Insensitive to the tenderest flame
> That has ever been kindled;
> When my sighs can bring a halt
> To the injustice of his designs
> He flees in order not to hear them.

The second chain of thought, in which she recalls all she has done for him and the extreme lengths to which she has gone, is more violent and dislocated in its rhythms:

> J'ay forcé devant luy cent monstres à se rendre.
> Dans mon coeur où regnoit une tranquille paix,
> Toûjours promte à tout entreprendre,
> J'ay sceu de la nature effacer tous les traits.
> Les mouvements du sang ont voulu me surprendre,

J'ay fait gloire de m'en deffendre,
Et l'oubly des serments que cent fois il m'a faits,
L'engagement nouveau que l'amour luy fait prendre,
L'éloignement, l'exil, sont les tristes effets
De l'hommage éternel que j'en devois attendre. (3.3.190–92)

I forced a hundred monsters to yield before him.
In my heart, wherein there reigned a tranquil peace,
Ever ready to undertake anything,
I succeeded in ridding myself of all trace of nature.
When my natural reactions sought to overcome me,
I made it a point of honor to resist them.
And forgetting all the oaths that a hundred times he made to me,
The new commitment that love has led him into,
Separation and exile are the sad results
Of the eternal homage that I could have expected.

Alternatively extremely agitated and utterly calm during this sequence, the orchestra stops altogether at the verse, "Et l'oubly des serments," leaving the voice alone with a chromatic bass line. The culmination of this second, more dynamic sequence, is drawn out in a mournful, anapestic meter pushed forward in a series of downward-moving, perfect dominant-tonic cadences after which Medea returns once again to an altered version of the refrain which reverts suddenly in the last hemistich ("quel fruit de mes forfaits!") to the same static dissonances that opened the monologue.

One might argue that my sketchy comments on Medea's monologue privilege isolated dissonances and momentary expressive gestures over the kind of large-scale dramatic development and musical consistency that was generally assumed by contemporaries to be the primary features of *tragédie en musique*. My claim, however, is that Charpentier's composition solicits this kind of attention by putting musical resources into play that do not necessarily square with the dominant Lullian model. He does this in order to create an effect of relief or differentiation at both a diegetic and extradiegetic level. Though he certainly also employs what Jean-Philippe Rameau later referred to as "modulation," by which Rameau meant the kind of phrasing that took into account the direction and rhetorical flow of meanings in the text over time, he nonetheless uses dissonances, isolated and in conjunction with other resources, to produce effects that went beyond the orthodox operatic palette of his contemporaries.[26] Whereas Lully was primarily interested in the tonal use of harmony to accompany the dramatic unfolding of the verse, Charpentier used harmony to suffuse entire scenes with particular moods and to produce moments of acute difference, in direct contrast to Lully's more restrained musical rhetoric.[27] The success of this strategy is clearly reflected, as I have noted, in the reactions his music elicited.

It is precisely through this kind of harmonic writing that Charpentier produced an effect of difference – that of his opera in relation to the norms of the genre, and that of Medea as she gradually defines herself in relation to the utterances of the others. It is perhaps no coincidence, therefore, that Seneca's famous line, "Now I am Medea," copied by Pierre Corneille in his spoken tragedy, is never uttered in Thomas Corneille's and Charpentier's *tragédie en musique*. The performativity of this phrase has been given over to Medea's voice, as if, at certain moments, she simply began speaking a strange language, unknown in Corinth, one that she has spoken elsewhere on other occasions. If the music has strayed deliberately from the naturalized Lullian model, Medea has likewise ventured purposefully from the standards of ordinary conduct: "I succeeded in ridding myself of all trace of nature" ["J'ay sceu de la nature effacer tous les traits"], she explicitly states in the monologue, describing the assistance she has given Jason, both supernatural and against nature. Here, Medea refers to past events, specifically to the murder of her own brother whose body she had dismembered and left for her father to find. Medea's ability to erase the voice of nature within herself to accomplish these acts again prepares the contemporary commentators' view of *Médée* as straying from Lully's model and therefore flirting with the unnatural.

Medea must rediscover and deliberately cultivate an "unnatural" voice. The voice is hers; yet, at the same time, it is as if she had adopted a voice that comes from elsewhere, one that returns periodically to inhabit her. Stanley Cavell has remarked on the relation between voice and body in opera, "a relation in which not this character and this actor are embodied in each other but in which this voice is located in – one might say disembodied within – this figure, this double, this person, this persona, this singer."[28] Though Cavell refers here specifically to the effect of the voice on our perception of the gap between singer and character, his discussion aptly describes the gap I have sought to underscore, the one Medea inhabits. Introduced by the orchestra in contradistinction to the harmonic compass of preceding sections, this music of otherness appears in Medea's voice, almost as a voice disembodied *within* her. As I remarked earlier, the voice appears initially in the violins; then, Medea adopts it as her own in dissonant dialogue with the violins. While it may have been common practice for the singer's vocal line to take up the melody of the ritornello, its occurrence in this particular circumstance gains additional significance. The fissuring of Medea as a character who is ostracized by the others and who slowly resolves to inhabit that otherness suits perfectly Charpentier's purpose; for it allows Medea – as a figure of opera and as the voice that corresponds to that figure – to stand *for* the work at the same time that she is an actor in the tragedy. Furthermore, if we accept Cavell's formulation, in *Médée, tragédie en musique* abides by one of the essential marks of the tragic predicament: for in tragedy, paradoxically, characters must take responsibility for situations that are imposed upon them from the outside. In *Médée*, Medea must rediscover a voice that makes her Medea, a voice so emphatically halting at times, as critics have noted, that only the tonal markers in the music continue to give it direction, preventing it from losing all sense of bearing.[29]

Through act 3, Medea seeks something all the other characters refuse her: to unfold herself in grievance and affliction, the consummate realm of lyricism. Confronted by Medea, Creon and Jason often try to cut conversation short: they want to get to the point. Why all this talk, they say to Medea, since you are leaving anyway? "You waste your words," Creon replies to Medea in Euripides.[30] "You should have been far away by now," Creon says in Seneca, "why do you purposely delay matters with speechmaking?"[31] In Pierre Corneille's version, after a lengthy dialogue Creon simply asks Medea to shut up and follow his orders (2.2.123). In act 2 of the *tragédie lyrique*, the divorce between the two camps, between Medea and the others, is even more absolute than in the previous versions. As Medea's *récit* reaches a paroxysm of anguish and musical dissonance in scene 1 ("on m'arrache à moi-même") [I am being torn from myself], Creon blithely chimes in with a little air in triple meter: "Faisons taire les mécontents" [We must keep the malcontents quiet] (2.1.91–92). Medea and Creon inhabit separate musical and dramatic worlds; and the contrast between the two is wrenching. Jason, too, repeatedly begs her to be silent: "Quittez ces détours superflus!" [Cast aside these idle considerations], he urges (1.2.14). Again later, in act 3, he exclaims, "Ah! c'est m'en dire trop, cessez de m'attendrir!" [Ah, you say too much; cease trying to move me to pity]; and, in the same scene, this time more irritably, he tells her, "Je vous l'ay déjà dit, je sens tous vos malheurs" [I have already told you that I feel all your misfortunes] (3.2.186). The others want to walk offstage into silence; they want to resolve all conflict by sending Medea away, thereby rendering her mute. She, however, seeks to suffuse the world, first with plaintive tones, accompanied by flutes, later with her fury, pulling the full, five-part string orchestra along with her. If opera can be claimed generally "to call into question the conventions or conditions making civil discourse possible . . . as though some problem had arisen about speaking as such," as Stanley Cavell has suggested, *Médée* further distances itself from the conventions of Lullian *tragédie en musique* by bringing "uncivil" sonorities into play as well, specifically through the voice of Medea.[32] Medea's music is immoderate in contrast to that of Creon and Jason, figuring *en abîme* the situation of *tragédie en musique* in relation to the spoken theater, as well as that of *Médée* in relation to the works of Lully and Quinault.

Medea's utterances are therefore doubly excessive; and this excess goes hand in hand with the spectacular visual resources that *Médée* puts into motion at the end of act 3. Medea finally invokes the "Noires filles du Styx, Divinitez terribles" [Black daughters of the Styx, terrible divinities] who are brought forth, accompanied by a massive and raucous orchestral intervention; flying demons appear; a subterranean rumble is heard (3.5.205). This invitation to spectacle, included in Seneca but suppressed by Pierre Corneille, is taken up by Thomas Corneille and Charpentier with a vengeance. Supernatural effects are featured at the end of each subsequent act, occasions for Jean Berain to exhibit his décors and costumes, figuring with visual exorbitance the enormity of Medea's acts. When Jason finally screams at her, "Ah! barbare!" in act 5 after discovering the murder of his children, Medea has not merely lived up to the others' estimation of her, she has exceeded their expectations by far (5.8.347). Here, Medea appears before Jason, hovering in the air on a dragon (fig. 5). The visual effects come to a climax during the instrumental section at the close of the tragedy where Medea, in a sensational departure, "fend les airs sur son dragon, et en même temps les statues et les autres ornements du palais se brisent. On voit sortir des démons de tous côtés, qui ayant des feux à la main embrasent ce même palais. Ces démons disparaissent, une nuit se forme et cet édifice ne paraît plus que ruine et monstres, après quoi il tombe une pluie de feu" [flies through the air on her Dragon and at the same time, the Statues and other ornaments of the Palace are broken asunder. Demons are seen to come from all sides, and with flames in their hands, they burn down the Palace itself. The Demons disappear, night closes in and the whole edifice appears to be naught but ruins and monsters, after which there falls a hail of fire].[33] Whereas Quinault's and Lully's *Thésée* (1675) ends with order restored, Minerva having arrived to set things right before Medea could make good on her threats of vengeance, Corneille and Charpentier conclude their opera on a note of sheer unrepentance.[34] As Geoffrey Burgess has argued, "Médée signals the dismantling of the edifice of the *tragédie en musique.*"[35]

If commentators identified Charpentier, the barbarous Italianate composer, with Medea, the monstrous woman, what does that say about the circuits of identification that are set in motion by the work? Catherine Clément suggests that because of Medea's horrendous actions the spectator will identify with Jason.[36] One of the difficulties

Fig. 5. Médée hovering over Jason on a dragon, from *Recueil général des opera représentez par l'Académie royale de musique*, 16 vols. (Paris: Ballard, 1703–45), vol. IV [1703], n.p. Photo courtesy of the Bibliothèque Nationale de France, Paris.

of Clément's approach to opera is that she insists on the absolute antagonism of words and music. As Michal Grover-Friedlander has argued, for Clément, "opera degenerates into an opposition between a text that victimizes women and a music that obliterates that victimization . . . [so that] Murders go unpunished or, worse, unnoticed."[37] To make the libretto into an allegory for the situation of women following Clément is therefore to force oneself into a position in which the effect of the music will always be outside, and in opposition to, the meaning put forth by the text: while the music seduces, the text oppresses. This opposition, it is interesting to note, reproduces exactly the moral objections critics like Boileau made against opera in the 1680s and 1690s. *Médée* strains Clément's understanding of the relationship between the voice and the text, not merely because Medea does not die (though she does force her own exile), but more importantly because Medea's voice has impact not primarily as the singing of a text, but rather as a voice of otherness in a field of voices that do not and cannot truly respond to it. By situating spectatorial identification in Jason, Clément's understanding of *Médée* ignores the very cultural mechanisms that Corneille and Charpentier played upon and upstaged by cultivating the identification between composer and character.

By realigning their Medea with that of Euripides, by distancing their version from that of Pierre Corneille, and by using differentiated voices and musical forms, Thomas Corneille and Charpentier staged the repudiation of Medea as a performance piece designed to represent the situation of lyric tragedy in general and that of Charpentier in particular. In so doing, they distinctly left open the possibility of a sympathetic understanding of the central character. If Pierre Corneille gave us Medea "toute meschante qu'elle est" [in all her evil], it is because his aesthetic foregrounds the pleasure of the act of representation for the spectator, whatever the object of that representation may be.[38] Thomas Corneille and Charpentier certainly do not exclude this form of spectatorial pleasure. Indeed, *Médée* presents the appalling actions of a sorceress in spectacular operatic form, and is therefore, in this instance, in continuity with Pierre Corneille's insistence on the pleasures of mimesis. By returning to Euripides, however, and through the musical luxuriance of Medea's voice, Thomas Corneille and Charpentier brought forth the possibility of an identification with the central character.

Discussing the identificatory mechanisms of fiction, Diderot would later recognize that the erotic and ethical elements that initiate identification revolve around sacrifice.[39] Virtue, the central component of the identificatory gesture for Diderot, is clearly not what characterizes

Medea. In a commentary on Thomas Corneille's works, Voltaire, who could not have attended the opera since its last performances took place the year of his birth in Paris, went so far as to condemn Medea entirely as a subject for the stage, writing that "a poisoner, an assassin cannot touch well-formed hearts and minds."[40] Yet the affective trigger for identification, according to Diderot, the gesture of sacrifice, is central to *Médée*: Medea sacrifices the voice of nature within her to commit horrible acts for Jason, and, treated as she is by Jason and the entire population of Corinth, kills their own children in order to return that sacrifice to Jason at the close of the tragedy. I would suggest that the operatic voice links the representation of sacrifice onstage to the experience of dispossession that the listener undergoes at the lyric theater and which I have described in the previous chapter. This experience of dispossession is obviously not the only one that opera can elicit. However, as Grover-Friedlander has noted, singing is closely associated with the transfiguration of the world and with the realization that this dimension of things cannot occur without a loss. If operatic heroines "resonate, rather than die," it is because "opera kills, at the same time that it attempts to cross over and bring back its dead."[41] Medea resonates in this way. She does not die, but leaves the scene in the air, on a winged dragon. Faced with the unmistakable mediocrity of Jason and her own abjectness in relation to the others, Medea seeks to justify and embody their view of her. It is as if Medea's actions come to fulfill those of her voice, the distinctive quality of otherness that her voice presents from the beginning. For Clément, it is presumed that we identify with Jason and his mediocrity, with his sense of inadequacy and incomprehension when faced with the monstrosity of Medea: "nous sommes tous Jason face à Médée," she writes.[42] This reaction may indeed reflect the way differentiated voices and characters work to elicit paradoxical sympathies and identifications in opera, to make us understand "how small [our] gestures have been until now, how impoverished [our] physicality," as Wayne Koestenbaum has written.[43] It is equally as important, however, to recognize that it is Medea who in the end resonates for us, whose experience of dispossession and whose excessive reaction to that experience made her, for Charpentier, a figure for his opera, and perhaps also for the feeling generated by the operatic experience itself. In this sense, as a figure at once textual and musical, Medea follows closely on the heels of Armide and can be said to justify in advance Terrasson's arguments for the specificity of the operatic spectacle, preparing the way for the unprecedented impact of Rameau's innovations.

5 | The disruption of poetics II: *Hippolyte et Aricie* and the reinvention of tragedy

"La musique . . . C'est l'asème dans le langage." [Music . . . is the a-semantic within language]

Pascal Quignard[1]

Imagine Racine's *Phèdre* as opera. If the idea appears ludicrous or scandalous to us today, it was certainly both in 1733, the year of the premiere of *Hippolyte et Aricie*, the first *tragédie en musique* by fifty-year-old newcomer Jean-Philippe Rameau and his aging librettist, the abbé Simon Joseph Pellegrin. Yet, by 1677, when Racine wrote his last tragedy based on classical (as opposed to biblical) sources, he was no stranger to opera: the new genre was already waiting in the wings. Marc Fumaroli has argued that with *Phèdre* Racine simultaneously staged the apocalypse of classical tragedy by revealing "the passage from muteness to speech, from silence to discourse . . . in order to denounce the theater as criminal speech," and definitively rejected the temptation of opera.[2] Olivier Pot elaborates on Fumaroli's argument, noting that behind the repugnance that Racine's characters exhibit for speech and stage presence ("in everything, it is as though Racinian characters refused to assume their roles") lies a repressed fascination with operatic exhibitionism: "Phèdre's suicide would thus constitute the death certificate of a genre, revealing that which, in neo-classical representation, inevitably had to lead to the point of rupture and of no-return that is opera."[3] The latter makes its fleeting appearance in *Phèdre* through the failed idyll of Hippolyte and Aricie with its pastoral atmosphere and implicit references to Tasso's *Aminta*, an idyll that vanishes like a mirage at the end of the play within "Théramène's narrative, whose funeral oration for Hippolyte is an admirable tableau from a machine opera, in a decor of sumptuous mythology."[4] The melodious, lyrical alexandrines from act 2, scene 2 – "Présente, je vous fuis, absente, je vous trouve; / Dans le fond des forêts votre image me suit; / La lumière du jour, les ombres de la nuit, / Tout retrace à mes yeux les charmes que j'évite; / Tout vous livre à l'envi le rebelle Hippolyte" [I shun you, you are everywhere I go; / In the deep woods, your image haunts my sight; / The light of day, the shadows of the night, / All things call up your charms before my eyes / And vie to make my rebel heart your prize] – are eventually sacrificed along with the rest as illusion.[5] Racine was never closer to opera. In the end, though, Théramène's speech sublimely exorcizes the monstrosity of the operatic stage through the figure of the "monstre furieux" ["raging monster"], "Indomptable taureau, dragon impétueux" ["Half bull he is, half dragon"] that slaughters Hippolyte (5.6.1498–1593; 100). Fumaroli concludes that *Phèdre* represents the "final judgment of the theater on the theater."[6] By the tragedy's close, the theatrical word itself is sacrificed to a silence and an austerity not unlike those practiced at the jansenist convent of Port-Royal des Champs, where Racine was educated. If *Phèdre* can be read as a final statement, a gesture of confession toward a past at Port-Royal and an ingenious *mise-en-abîme* of operatic spectacle in all its excess, then *Hippolyte et Aricie*, as Rameau's first opera, might be read as a response to Racine and a commentary on the situation of the lyric theater in the wake of seventeenth-century tragedy, framing the disintegration or final subsumption of the tragic into the operatic through the lens of *tragédie en musique*.

Racine had used the specter of opera in *Phèdre*, and earlier in the preface to *Iphigénie*, to define tragedy against its lyric rival. In the preface, Racine explained how he found Ériphile, "this other Iphigénie," in Pausanias in order to avoid having to kill the young Iphigénie, and to avoid the other, equally distasteful, option of having her transformed into a doe which Diane then transports to Tauride. By rejecting the latter possibility, Racine implicitly responded to Charles Perrault's *Critique de l'opéra*, a tract written that same year (1674) in support of the lyric theater: "and how would it appear if I concluded my tragedy through the intervention of a goddess and a machine, and through a metamorphosis, which might indeed have found some credibility in the time of Euripides, but which would be too absurd and too unbelievable for us?"[7] Through this critique of machines, and in his rejection of the operatic alternative, Racine sought to distance himself from the then current fascination with *tragédie en musique*. I want to jump ahead to 1733 in order to examine what was at stake for Rameau, Pellegrin, and their public in revisiting Racine's tragedy a half-century later. I will argue that Rameau's work could only succeed by simultaneously embodying and erasing *Phèdre*, and even tragedy itself.

Though *Hippolyte et Aricie* premiered in 1733, it enjoyed three eighteenth-century revivals, the first in 1742, the second in 1757, and the last in 1767. Extensive changes were made to the opera that was performed for each of these years, including changes that were made during the course of the 1733 run. *Hippolyte et Aricie* cannot therefore be considered a fixed entity: the opera's music and text were modified by Rameau and others in response to, and as a result of, the shifting contexts in which it was performed. The "original," in fact, was never performed as such.[8] I have chosen to discuss the opera as Rameau first conceived it in print, not because it is an original or ideal version, but because it represents Rameau's first conception of his encounter with *Phèdre* – an initial encounter he insisted on saving and documenting regardless of the fact that some of its most radical elements were eliminated from performance in the first rehearsals. I will refer to later experiences of the opera insofar as they can be understood as reflections on, or after-effects of, Rameau's encounter with *Phèdre* in 1733.

From its beginnings in the early 1670s with Lully and Quinault, as earlier chapters have established, *tragédie en musique* was seen by critics as the other of spoken tragedy, an object of intense promise and idealization for some, a vehicle of moral danger and aesthetic ruin for others. On the one hand, as a phantasmatic version of ancient tragedy, the "reinvention" of opera held out the promise of resuscitating the mythical presence of Greek theater while correcting its faults. Claude-François de Ménestrier's description of the music of the ancients, for example, published in 1681, bears an uncanny resemblance to Lully's and Quinault's operas, as if *tragédie en musique* had simultaneously reincarnated ancient tragedy and superseded it.[9] Similarly, by 1715, the abbé Terrasson considered that opera had perfected ancient tragedy and remarked that it made both tragedy and epic obsolete.[10] On the other hand, many saw the operatic spectacle and its music as vacuous, sensual pleasure with no rational underpinning – the perverted twin of classical tragedy which it was working to destroy. In his *Traité du récitatif*, first published in 1707, Grimarest noted, for example, the adverse effects of music on declamation itself.[11] Though opera was generally championed by the moderns, commentators on both sides of the divide criticized the preponderance of unheroic affect in opera, often comparing it in this respect to the novel. Antoine Houdar de la Motte, for example, who produced several libretti for the lyric theater, compared operatic plots to those of the novel, referring to a form of "vapid love [that is] worthy at most of our operas and our novels."[12] Anne Dacier, herself a partisan of the ancients and severe critic of La Motte's verse rendering of the *Iliad*, observed of the poets of her day that "with their heads full of nothing but operas and novels, they have only false ideas."[13] With the expansion of dance and *divertissement*, along with the establishment of the new and popular *opéra-ballet* and the rise of the *pastorale héroïque* in the early years of the eighteenth century, even potential supporters saw opera as an increasingly vacuous medium:

> The masterpieces of Quinault, the plays of some of his successors . . . all these tableaux gave way to monstrous sketches, lyric extravagances, even condemned by the true admirers of Music, when applied to such pitiful resources. One cared no longer for Poetry: we made do with song and dance . . . No action at all, not a stitch of plot, neither scenes nor characters. A rhapsody of misplaced Songs, random *divertissements* and, no matter what the story, enchantments . . .[14]

Many saw tragedy as forsaken in the watered-down form developed in the lyric theater. Despite numerous successes in the years preceding *Hippolyte et Aricie*, the Paris Opéra was perceived, as James Anthony has described it, as a veritable graveyard of lyric tragedies.[15]

When Rameau approached Pellegrin for a libretto, these were the meager assets and heavy liabilities of *tragédie en musique*. One can understand the added peril – no small matter – of the choice of subject, one in which Racine had excelled and his last classical tragedy. For an organist known primarily as an arcane music theorist and who, at fifty, had never written for the stage, to "remake" *Phèdre* was a significant move indeed. His choice of the septuagenarian Pellegrin – a holdover from the *grand siècle* – as librettist unquestionably indicates an attempt to mitigate his precarious situation as newcomer. Not unexpectedly, in the first paragraph of his preface, Pellegrin strategically nods to his predecessor, "the most worthy rival of the great Corneille," who was at least as present in the minds of Rameau's contemporaries as Euripides, Seneca, Virgil, or Pradon.[16] "It is Racine himself who furnished me with this episode," notes Pellegrin, referring to his predecessor's defense of Aricie's rightful place in the myth. For all this respect, however, Pellegrin's deference is tempered by a claim that puts *Phèdre*, as classical tragedy, into question:

> Although a noble audacity is one of the most glorious privileges of Poetry, I would never have dared to put a *Phèdre* on stage after an author such as Racine if the difference of genre had not reassured me. Never has a subject appeared more appropriate for enriching the lyric stage, and I am surprised that the great master of that Theater [opera] did not anticipate me in a project that charmed me so much that I was unable to resist it. The supernatural element which permeates this entire story seems to declare openly which of the two forms of spectacle is more appropriate for it.[17]

Pellegrin argues that the *tragédie en musique* so obviously marks its difference with respect to classical tragedy that he does not have to be concerned about the imposing precedent of *Phèdre*. He also delicately sidesteps the problem of direct precursors by naming his work, not *Phèdre* (his respect for Racine "prevented me from giving this Tragedy under the name, *Phèdre*"), not *Hippolyte* (as had Euripides and Seneca), not *Phèdre et Hippolyte* (though Pradon seems entirely forgotten), but *Hippolyte et Aricie*.[18] Moreover, since opera is presumably driven by *le merveilleux*, the subject appears ideal for lyric tragedy. Conflicting divine interests (those of Diane, Vénus, Neptune, Pluton, and Le Destin), Thésée's descent and return from the underworld, lush pastoral settings, Hippolyte's monstrous demise – all of these elements provide ample reserves of spectacle for opera to exploit. And Pellegrin did not hesitate to do so. Machines abound: in the prologue, for example, Jupiter descends from the heavens to resolve a conflict between Diane and Amour. The entirety of act 2, to take another example, is devoted to Thésée's passage to Hell where groups of furies prepare his tortures. After Pluton refuses to release Pirithoüs, the friend Thésée has come to liberate, Mercure finally arrives from above with a message from Neptune seeking Thésée's release. Pellegrin goes as far as to assert that the story is so appropriate for opera that it is startling that Lully ("the great master of that Theater") had not already chosen it. By placing "a *Phèdre*" on the lyric stage, Pellegrin and Rameau believed they were restoring the myth to its rightful place – "a form of repatriation" as Catherine Kintzler has suggested.[19] Though Pellegrin makes a show of listing the ways his dramatic poem respects the exigencies of classical tragedy, the implicit claim manifestly contradicts this deference – it was Racine's strict adherence to the unities that forced him to leave out some of the most important and, of course, spectacular aspects of the story. Despite the lyric theater's reputation for flouting the dramatic unities and overextending the spectator's sense of *vraisemblance*, Pellegrin claims, *Phèdre* is more "reasonable" as opera than as classical tragedy.

The preface gives offerings to the past at the same time that it makes strong claims to innovation and departure, an attitude characteristic of the work as a whole. Pellegrin suggests that *Hippolyte et Aricie* is faithful to the myth in a way that *Phèdre* could never have been. At the same time, he takes just enough of Racine's verse for the libretto to gain the approbation of familiarity from the spectator, seeking the solid ground of Racine's masterpiece without getting close enough to risk being accused of parroting it. The borrowings are oblique: there is generally no correlation between the context of the borrowed text in *Phèdre* and that of its new place in the libretto.[20] *Hippolyte et Aricie* thus comes into existence as a *Phèdre* that has been, first of all, "returned" to its proper place in opera, and second, carefully reconceived and rewritten.

In addition to his use of Racine's tragedy as a gesture of cultural affiliation and appropriation, Pellegrin is also appropriately deferential to Quinault and Lully. The prologue to *Hippolyte et Aricie* stages a momentary commemoration of the prologue to the first *tragédie en musique*, *Cadmus et Hermione* (1673) – also the first fruit of the collaboration between Quinault and Lully. Pellegrin sets the prologue in a woodland retreat where Diane's chaste followers give homage to their protectress. Addressing her pastoral subjects, Diane alludes to Le Soleil's defeat of the serpent Python, the action that occurs in the prologue to *Cadmus et Hermione* and an iconographic commonplace for the representation of Louis XIV: "Vous êtes dans ces mêmes lieux, / Où, sur un monstre furieux, / Un fils de Jupiter remporta la victoire" [You are on the same site, / Where a son of Jupiter won a victory / Over a furious monster].[21] By invoking Racine in his preface, and the *roi soleil* as well, Pellegrin anchors the opera in the canonical tradition of classical tragedy at the same time that he restores *Phèdre* to the genre in which, he claims, it truly belongs. By situating the prologue on the same (rhetorical) site as that of *Cadmus et Hermione* ("ces mêmes lieux"), Pellegrin and Rameau situate *Hippolyte et Aricie* as the successor to the tradition of *tragédies en musique* inaugurated by Quinault and Lully. Again, the gesture is one of superposition, so that *Hippolyte et Aricie* not only continued the work of the recognized masters of the genre, but also staged a replay of the origin of French opera.

Of course, any innovative creator stakes his or her most ambitious claims by making equivocal overtures to the past. Yet Pellegrin appears to have succeeded remarkably well in this by feeding and abetting Rameau's initial proposal to him, and in laying a foundation for the composer's first operatic success before he moved on to work with Voltaire, Fuzelier, Cahusac, and others. He succeeded so well in fact that, even today, Rameau's *tragédies en musique* elicit somewhat paradoxical statements from specialists: they are at once absolutely unprecedented (in their sonorities) and completely orthodox (as lyric tragedies in the Lullian model). Referring to a monologue in *Dardanus*, for example, the musicologist Paul-Marie Masson wrote that "starting with the admirable prelude, which introduces the beginning of the melody, a name comes to mind, a name that Rameau evokes more often than one might think: Beethoven." However, when Masson discusses the structure of the drama, he asserts that "basically, the general idea has stayed more or less the same since Lully."[22] In 1733, Rameau needed Racine, Lully, and Pellegrin to soften the blow his music would make on the public. The *Mercure* reviewer noted that Rameau had produced music "of a new character."[23] The Parfaict brothers later concurred with this assessment of Rameau's originality, suggesting that the work was not simply another *tragédie en musique*, but represented something entirely new: "taking a new direction, which was his own, he set out to become in his genre what Lully had been in his."[24] Rameau had set out to compose a *tragédie en musique*, like those of Lully; yet what he produced was sui generis.[25] The *Année littéraire*'s account of the 1757 revival and the *Mercure*'s 1764 obituary both referred, in retrospect, to the "revolution" Rameau had brought about.[26] Palissot declared that "the performance of *Hippolyte et Aricie* marked an epoch for the nation."[27] This was a revolution for which even Voltaire was unprepared. After attending the premiere of *Hippolyte et Aricie* in October, 1733, Voltaire wrote a brief account of what he saw: "yesterday I attended the first performance of the opera of Aricie and Hippolyte. The words are by the abbé Pellegrin, and worthy of the abbé Pellegrin. The music is by one named Ramau [*sic*], a man who has the misfortune of knowing more music than Lully. He is a musical pedant. He is precise, boring."[28] Hardly an enthusiastic account. Voltaire changed his mind about Rameau very quickly, however. By late November, he had gone back entirely on his earlier judgment; and by 1734, he is calling Rameau, with no trace of his usual irony, "our Orpheus."[29]

As is evident from the 1733 *Mercure* review, spectators could no longer distinctly recognize Lully's *tragédie en musique* in Rameau's work. What had drawn the reviewer's attention and admiration were "the characterized airs, the tableaux," "the chorus and the instrumental thunder [la Simphonie du Tonerre]," "the Hell scene from act 2, the terrifying image of the Fury with Thésée and the Chorus," in other words the instrumental and choral music, the dances, the special effects, and the monologues.[30] No particular mention is made of the traditional

Lullian focus on drama driven by recitative. As his first work for the lyric stage, Rameau produced a *tragédie en musique*, not an *opéra-ballet*; yet it was one that included no less than thirty dances and, as the composer André Campra remarked to the Prince de Conti, enough music to fill ten operas.[31] The 1733 public understood that by transforming the old

Example 7: "Quelle soudaine horreur"

Example 7: (*cont.*)

genre Rameau had created a new one which demanded new modes of theatrical experience. Rameau appeared to his contemporaries to have moved beyond *tragédie en musique*, a genre already in steep decline; but he did so, as Dill astutely remarks, by reinventing it.[32] *Hippolyte et Aricie* was constructed on the ruins of the Lullian tradition, on the one hand, and of classical tragedy, on the other.

The most striking example of the way in which Rameau sought to use music to alter the experience of tragedy in the opera house is the notorious Trio des Parques, in act 2, scene 5, where the three Fates emerge for the second time (see example 7): "Quelle soudaine horreur ton destin nous inspire! / Où cours-tu, Malheureux? tremble; frémi d'effroi. / Tu sors de l'infernal Empire, / Pour trouver les Enfers chez toy" [With what sudden horror your destiny fills us! / Where do you run, unfortunate man? Tremble! Quake with fear. / You are leaving the empire of the underworld / To find Hades in your home].[33] This trio makes use of the enharmonic genre which, in the context of Greek music theory, implied the use of quarter-tones (an interval equal to one-half of a semitone, the distance between the keys on a piano). The legendary affective force of quarter-tones contributed to the enigma and fascination of ancient Greek music and continued to be sought after by theorists throughout the eighteenth century. Rameau insisted that, despite the fact that enharmonic tones are effectively the same degree of the chromatic scale (g♯ and a♭, for example), the ear is struck by the difference between the notes when they are heard in context.[34] Using enharmonic respellings, the trio makes a harrowing chromatic descent in only six bars through F sharp minor to F minor, E minor, E flat minor, and ending in D minor.[35] At one point, the unusual dissonance of an eleventh chord is further heightened by the simultaneous presence of an augmented fifth ("hor*reur*," measure 7). The iambic pulse, which continues almost throughout the entire piece, adds to the feeling of relentless urgency. The trio as it was originally written was never performed publicly in the eighteenth century because of problems that arose during rehearsals with singers who refused to execute the difficult enharmonic modulations of the passage.[36] As Geoffrey Burgess remarks, "initially, Rameau may have expected the singers to distinguish the pitches of the two notes forming enharmonic pairs, an expectation that is likely to have overtaxed both the ability and patience of the performers."[37] However, Rameau had composed it for the premiere, and he made sure that it would be reproduced in the printed score. So, the trio was known to at least some of his contemporaries; and for them it represented the future promise of his works, one that had not yet been fully revealed to the public in performance. Discussing the trio that replaced Rameau's original in performances, the *Année littéraire* remarked in 1757 that "although the melody and the accompaniment of this Trio [the recomposed version] are beautifully expressive, it is yet quite inferior to the one that Mr. Rameau's genius had prepared and which does exist. It will remain useless until the art of performance attains the level of advancement and excellence that this great piece demands."[38] Rameau later noted that he hoped to find another occasion to use these kinds of harmonies; "but that would require docile musicians."[39]

The effect of the enharmonic passage on the spectator was what interested Rameau. This effect was crucial to his conception of act 2, entirely devoted to Thésée's passage into Hell in order to rescue his friend, Pirithoüs – an episode that Racine could not include because of the change of place it required. Indeed, Pellegrin's central contention against Racine in the preface revolves around Thésée's rash condemnation of Hippolyte: "I will admit, first, without attempting to condemn the elegant author who opened the way for me, that his Thésée always seemed too credulous to me, and that a son as virtuous as Hippolyte ought not to be condemned so lightly."[40] What made their version more "reasonable," Pellegrin claimed, was their development of Thésée's character and their elaborate preparation of his final call to Neptune to wreak vengeance upon Hippolyte. The preface details this preparation. First, Les Parques announce to Thésée as he prepares to leave that he will not truly escape hell, because he will find it again in his own home. Second, in *Hippolyte et Aricie*, unlike in Racine's tragedy, Thésée arrives just as Hippolyte reaches for his sword, which Phèdre had seized in order to kill herself. It is at this moment that Thésée recalls the prediction of Les Parques. After both Phèdre and Hippolyte flee, at which point Oenone makes vague insinuations about Hippolyte's guilt, a popular celebration of Thésée's return interrupts the development of the situation. Afterwards, convinced that Hippolyte is guilty of unnatural desires, Thésée asks Neptune to avenge him.[41] The Trio des Parques ushers in this turn of events, prepares Thésée for the worst as he leaves Hell, and uses the enharmonic genre to convey this feeling to the spectator. The spectator witnesses Thésée's encounter with an unfathomable oracle. The sender of this message, Le Destin (Fate itself), is an entity that remains unseen – the vanishing point, as it were, of the entire opera – but whose emissaries deliver this unearthly message in an equally eerie medium. Because Thésée, too, must assume the position of spectator as he listens to his future woes in the spectral voices of Les Parques, the spectator becomes Thésée's momentary analogue, mirroring the situation of rapt attention taking place on stage. Rameau appears to have followed Pellegrin's suggestion in the preface: "the great secret of being approved is to get the spectators to feel that they would be like the actors, if they found themselves in a similar situation."[42]

Whereas the identification that Pellegrin describes was entirely consonant with the aims of tragedy, as it had been described in the writings of influential theorists, the visceral feeling that Rameau hoped to convey, however, was incongruous with those aims. In his *Code de musique pratique* (1760), Rameau mentions the trio and explains that he had used "the enharmonic genre . . . to inspire repulsion and horror."[43] "Repulsion" [*l'épouvante*] and "horror" [*l'horreur*] were strongly coded words for tragedy. Almost a century earlier, La Mesnardière had explained the distinction between horror and terror, the latter being the affect that the spectator of tragedy should ideally experience. Horror was a violent and visceral reaction and was to be avoided in tragedy; terror, however, was grounded in an intellectual identification with the tragic characters that had, at least potentially, salutary moral consequences.[44] As John Lyons writes, "horror has always been linked to the body" and is derived from the Latin *horrere*, meaning "to bristle."[45] Whereas terror produces lessons upon which one can base future actions, horror paralyzes the spectator in the present, stranding him in his body and its reaction to the event on stage.[46] The distinction between horror and terror remained in place in the *Encyclopédie* of Diderot and d'Alembert: *terreur*, Jaucourt wrote, is a poetic and intellectual response based on moral identification; d'Alembert observed that *horreur*, however, causes a physical response ("trembling") which can be described medically.[47]

It is precisely this physical reaction – *horrere* – that Les Parques demand from Thésée: "tremble," they command, "quake with fear." With the trio, Rameau sought to present the transmission of an oracular message along with the physical effects it entailed. Having perhaps heard the original trio performed for a small group of initiates, Pierre Louis d'Aquin de Chateaulyon testified to these physical effects:

We have reason to regret the loss of the Trio des Parques which, because of the singular attention it requires in performance, could not be heard at the Opéra as the composer had initially intended. This trio so affects the senses that one's hair stands on end. There are no words to describe the full effect that it produces, it is beyond agitation, fear, terror. It seems that nature is being destroyed [*s'anéantisse*] and that everything is going to perish.[48]

Rameau sought to make the listener-spectator *feel* this message, not reflect on it per se. In this sense, the trio might be said to evoke something resembling, not so much the reticent sublimity of Théramène's speech, but its monstrous double. In his theoretical treatise, *Génération harmonique* (1737), Rameau argued that the enharmonic genre goes beyond the understanding to take hold of the listener:

One is struck [in the enharmonic genre] by the quarter-tone, without being able to account for it; one is revolted because it is not natural, because the ear is unable to assess it. However, the common harmony, through which the passage from one mode to another takes place, modifies its harshness, the moment of surprise passes in a flash, and soon the surprise turns to admiration in seeing oneself transported from one hemisphere to another, as it were, without having had the time to think about it.[49]

Because the quarter-tone is so removed from the natural basis of sound – the sequence of harmonic partials found in the resonance of physical bodies, or *corps sonores* – Rameau argued that the ear had no basis from which to evaluate it. Quarter-tones reveal the outermost limits of one set of natural harmonies; therefore, "one is revolted" by them. But because enharmonic music uses these tones to pass from one key to another, the listener is subsequently safe, unwittingly "transported" to another harmonic universe. For Rameau, the enharmonic genre constituted a temporarily horrifying, and corporeal, experience of limits.

There is no reason to assume, from Rameau's perspective, that terror and horror are mutually exclusive feelings or that horror necessarily destroys the poetic dimension of theater. Early-modern commentators frequently argue that musical sounds "have a marvelous power to move us"; yet this power is not only natural but also semiotic: "they are the signs of the passions."[50] The composer thus follows a musical poetics, however unwittingly, when he creates opera: "there is therefore a truth in operatic narratives. And this truth consists in the imitation of the tones, the accents, the sighs, and the sounds which naturally belong to the feelings contained in the words."[51] As early as 1726, Rameau had developed a similar position: "just as a discourse is ordinarily composed of several sentences, so a piece of music is ordinarily composed of several *Modulations*, which can be considered as so many *Harmonic Phrases*."[52] Charles Dill has shown that Rameau based this statement on a theory of *modulation*. Unlike our modern use of the term to refer to certain harmonic progressions, Rameau's theory of *modulation* supposed a comparison between poetic and musical syntax, yet going beyond "such matters as whether perfect authentic cadences line up with grammatical periods or dissonant harmonies line up with dissonant emotions."[53] Dill describes Rameau's understanding of *modulation* by borrowing Roland Barthes's distinction, made in relation to visual media, between anchor and relay. To anchor is to label, as in the case of marking conflicting emotions with dissonant harmonies; to relay is to layer meaning in different systems of signification in order to produce a larger narrative.[54] For Rameau, *modulation* describes a large-scale musical strategy that allows the composer to do more than label individual dramatic events, making him a full partner with the poet in shaping the drama. In his analysis of Aricie's act 1 monologue, "Temple sacré," Dill demonstrates Rameau's use of *modulation* to layer meanings. For Dill, Rameau does not simply use individual musical gestures to "comment" on the textual passages they set. Rather, by reiterating textual material set to superficially analogous but in fact dissimilar music, the composer subverts the initial statement and encourages a form of dramatic, recursive listening.

By representing an ineluctable, visceral reaction of horror on stage – "tremble, quake with fear" – and in seeking to produce this same reaction in the spectator as the culminating mood in act 2, however, Rameau had moved in an altogether different direction. This dramatic moment accomplished more than poetics had previously allowed or acknowledged, including, perhaps, his own. The horror Rameau sought to evoke forces the issue of somatic meaning in a way music had never explicitly done before in opera. Rameau sought to generate passionate response in the spectator by using musical events that had as their justification, not only an expressive or dramatic accent, however complex, but a physical response to sound on the part of the listener. As Rameau noted in his *Démonstration du principe de l'harmonie* (1750), the trio went beyond the grasp of the intellect: "[its] effect goes beyond what one can imagine."[55] One could extend this kind of analysis to other moments of the opera; and I would argue that it stands as an albeit extreme example of the way in which Rameau used music in the lyric theater. Another such example is Thésée's appeal to Pluton in act 2, scene 2 ("Inexorable Roi de l'Empire infernal"), which no later than the 1742 revival was accompanied by unusual, obbligato bassoons playing in the upper register. While one might account for the exceptional presence of bassoons standing out against the continuo as an expression of plaintive supplication, this gesture nonetheless also suffuses the scene with a particular instrumental color that cannot be explained away entirely by referring to its role as dramatic anchor or relay. Rameau used instruments in unprecedented ways, particularly the bassoon to which he gave unusually independent lines. Masson documents the fact that contemporary listeners noted and reacted to Rameau's original use of this instrument.[56] Rameau had recreated tragedy as a theatrical event linking musical moments together not only to support or further the dramatic interest but also to produce jolts of somatic response in the spectator.

Hippolyte et Aricie, however, did not end on this note. The contested treatment of act 5 and the modifications that were made to it during subsequent performances are an equally significant, though perhaps less striking, indication that Rameau's opera marked a turning point, both the culmination of directions already taken by earlier *tragédies en musique* and a departure from conventions of the genre. In the original 1733 version, Thésée opens the act to announce Phèdre's guilt and suicide, and to mourn the loss of his son. Just as he is about to cast himself into the sea, Neptune intervenes once again, this time to check his recklessness. Hippolyte lives, it turns out, having only disappeared behind thick clouds in act 4; but Thésée is forever banished from his presence: "Pour te punir d'une injuste vengeance, / Le Destin pour jamais t'interdit sa présence" [To punish you for an injust revenge, / Destiny forever denies you his presence].[57] The set now changes from "Diane's forest," the setting of the previous act, to "delightful gardens which form the avenues of Aricie's forest."[58] Diane and her entourage console Aricie who laments the death of her beloved Hippolyte. The goddess then summons her Zephyrs to bring forth Hippolyte, and the two lovers are reunited in a duet. *Divertissements* follow to close the opera.

Though French opera never strongly adhered to unity of place, set changes in *tragédie en musique* ordinarily occurred between acts. The change of location in the middle of the act was remarked by spectators and critics, and, in reaction, the first two scenes were cut during the first run of the opera: "the first two scenes, which created a certain irregularity against the unity of place through the change of scene within the same act, were cut."[59] For the 1742 revival, then, the spectators no longer had to worry about an irregular and perhaps disturbing change of scene. Now, however, they professed to be disconcerted by Thésée's disappearance: "the fifth act was criticized. One would have liked to see Thésée again there; but this was not the fault of the author of the Poem. This flaw, which was judged necessary in order to shorten it, is not found in the first editions."[60] Whereas the 1733 public was uneasy about the strange scene change within act 5, in 1742, when those scenes were cut, the complaint was just the opposite: Thésée was missed. Indeed, the changes left more than one key issue unresolved. What, exactly, was the nature of Thésée's punishment? What had been Phèdre's fate?

These reactions point to a particular tension that Rameau and Pellegrin had created within their *tragédie en musique*. The strangely syncopated change of scene that Rameau had originally conceived highlights the deliberate dislocation that the pastoral tranquility of act 5 represented for tragedy. It was not unusual for a *tragédie en musique* to end in *divertissements*. However, the particular relationship Rameau and Pellegrin had established with Racine, and the choice of the change of scene *within* the act, point to an overdetermined gesture. As Burgess has remarked, the problem in the change of scene seems to be not so much with the violation of unity of place, but rather with the agency behind the scene change.[61] No divinity or supernatural being provokes the change of scene; no supernatural being transports the characters from one universe to another, as Armide does when she brings Renaud to her enchanted palace. Moreoever, there is an utter absence of continuity: one cast of characters vanishes (Thésée, Neptune) and an entirely new one appears (Aricie, Diane's shepherds and shepherdesses); and time has elapsed to allow for Phèdre's suicide. From the point of view of the represented action (d'Aubignac's "truth of the action"), the passage from Diane's woods to Aricie's forest is absolutely gratuitous. Insofar as there is no underlying dramatic motivation, the scene change appears as Pellegrin's and Rameau's *deus ex machina*. Over the course of its first four acts, the opera carefully develops the characters of Thésée and Phèdre, even more so in the case of Thésée, Pellegrin argued in the preface, than Racine. Yet by act 5, Phèdre has committed suicide, swallowed up by the hell she fears lurks under her steps as she exits in act 4; and Thésée has been banished by Neptune. Phèdre and Thésée have been jettisoned so that the opera can focus exclusively on the young lovers. If the initial 1733 version made the change of scene itself conspicuous in the middle of the act, the shift of focus from one world to another was just as jarring to some spectators of the later version who wanted to see Thésée again. Just as Racine had dispelled the illusion of pastoral and operatic temptations in *Phèdre*, it is as if Rameau and Pellegrin intended to frame a model tragedy in the first four acts of *Hippolyte et Aricie* only to shatter it, or to make it vanish before our eyes in act 5 where we return to the protection of lovers Diane had promised in the prologue. If Rameau had foregrounded the spectator's bodily response to opera in the Trio des Parques, here, through the prominent change of place, he presented *divertissement* in a gesture of utter dramatic gratuitousness as the new condition of the genre first created by Quinault and Lully.

Insofar as the later version subtly controverted d'Aubignac's demands for separation of stage and house, by keeping the scene change between acts, it was in line with new expectations on the part of the audience. Though some may have felt that Thésée's absence was still too abrupt, others found the very contrast between the two acts a source of pleasure: "a well-framed contrast causes great pleasure. For example, I love to see Miss Camargo [a celebrated dancer at the Opéra] appear joyously to wipe away the tears that Thésée has made me shed in the third act of Hippolyte."[62] Or as the *Année littéraire* noted, "it was necessary to give the spectator some respite with an Act of a pleasant nature which would allow him to savor the interest he had taken in the fate of two tender lovers, overwhelmed by the greatest misfortunes."[63] As the title aptly confirms, Rameau's opera no longer even remotely focused on Corneillian heroism, but rather created a space for lovers. Despite the admirable music he sings, despite his efforts to preserve a heroic countenance worthy of the *grand siècle* (even as he descends to Hades to abduct Persephone with Pirithoüs), Thésée has been displaced. In the final analysis, Rameau's opera leaves tragedy and its heroes behind to end in *divertissement*, foregrounding the pastoral love that, as Fontenelle argued, purges life of all the destructive passions because it "tolerates no ambition": "in a word, love purged of everything foreign and harmful that the excesses of human fantasies have added to it."[64]

In my discussion of the trio and of act 5, I have suggested that in order to re-invent *tragédie en musique*, Rameau deployed music and operatic narrative in such a way as to transform a particular conception of tragedy and its effects on the spectator. Operas could no longer be understood, as the abbé Terrasson presciently remarked, as tragedies to which music is simply added.[65] A rejection of the poetic framework that had made opera mimetic in exactly the same way that spoken theater was mimetic, Terrasson's assertion aptly describes Rameau's disruption of poetics. Perhaps Voltaire realized this in the end, praising Rameau for writing in a genre that he had always detested, because he realized that Rameau had produced something new – even if he believed that the composer had destroyed tragedy. As Voltaire perhaps also implicitly realized, it would not be his own desperate attempts to resurrect the genre that would be remembered, but the tragedies of the *grand siècle*, and Rameau's *tragédies en musique*. In a sense, he was right: tragedy, at least as it was conceived by La Mesnardière, d'Aubignac, Racine, or Dacier, was no longer possible.

In the notes to his outstanding 1996 production of *Hippolyte et Aricie*, Jean-Marie Villégier remarked on the problems that Rameau's opera causes for tragedy because of the sovereignty it gives to music. Phèdre and Thésée, in particular, are only shadows of their former tragic incarnations in Racine; yet "they take back their true stature as soon as an air emblematizes them and endows them with a consistency that owes nothing to their evolution from scene to scene – but everything to their immersion in harmony."[66] Reinforcing this distinction in his production, Villégier, working in tandem with costume designer Patrice Cauchetier and choreographer Ana Yepes, decided to isolate different parts of the opera, separating tragic space from *divertissement*, to create a musical revue:

> The characters of the tragedy therefore assume a double function. Sometimes they are partners in a sort of revue, whose guiding themes they announce. Sometimes, promoted to the rank of main attraction, they are allotted a few minutes, minutes that are dilated by the orchestra, to revive in us the memory of their grandeur. A bit like the declaration of Phèdre, recited by Sarah Bernhardt in one of those programs that the public of the beginning of the century enjoyed, could be slipped between a proverb by Alfred de Musset and a grand chorus from *Les Huguenots* . . . Here the tragic cast; there, always renewed, kaleidoscopic, that of the *divertissements*.[67]

The result of this decision is an effect of containment. The elements of the opera that were considered tragic were isolated towards the front of the stage by a wall and proscenium arch that lifted at times to reveal a space of *divertissement* upstage. While he appears favorably disposed toward the preeminence of the musical in Rameau's *tragédie en musique*, Villégier's unwillingness to allow tragedy to be contaminated by song and dance – his desire to maintain a clear distinction between the two – also recalls the early, hostile reception of opera itself. This strategy is at its most extreme at the close of the opera, where, surely not coincidentally, the plot departs most significantly from Racine. Far from the ancient world of Phèdre and Thésée, the pastoral *divertissements* of act 5 usher in the new regime of Hippolyte and Aricie. Phèdre had succumbed to poison offstage between acts 4 and 5; and Thésée had been sent into exile. Yet Villégier insisted on resurrecting the two tragic characters at the end of act 5. As the final gavotte announces the end of the opera, Villégier again reasserted the tragic space – with absolutely no prompting from the libretto – by dropping a diaphanous screen and having Thésée and Phèdre walk across the stage in a somnambulant gait, as the ghosts of tragedy returning to haunt the final joyous moments of *divertissement*.

Conductor William Christie's musical decisions effectively emphasized the separation of worlds Villégier created in his staging. As Rameau originally conceived the passage from act 4 to act 5, the music of the entr'acte returns to the Air des Matelots from act 3.[68] This strategy allowed for tonal coherence in G minor from act 4 through the transition to act 5, and also recalled musically the dramatic circumstances in act 3 that accompanied Thésée's misguided decision to call for vengeance. The Air des Matelots was also retained in the modified 1733 version of the opera, the one in which the first two scenes of act 5 were cut. Though Christie decided to retain the first two scenes of act 5 from the original 1733 opera, he eliminated the Air des Matelots in favor of something more tragic, an instrumental number based on Phèdre's heart-wrenching air, "Cruelle mère des amours." His intention was surely to evoke musically the action that takes place offstage at precisely this moment – Phèdre's suicide. Yet it is worth remarking that this substitution smoothes over Phèdre's abrupt departure from the stage after Hippolyte is presumed dead, resuscitating her in the music, as it were. Perhaps we could see in Christie's decision a reaction to this particularly awkward moment in the opera, as if in response to the criticism of the 1742 spectator that the tragedy and its characters had disappeared too abruptly. Just as Villégier contravened Rameau's original conception of act 5 by returning an exiled Thésée and a lifeless Phèdre to the stage, Christie made Phèdre's presence felt as the act opens in order to ease the otherwise abrupt transition. In this way, the production of Villégier and Christie could be said to revisit and replay many of the issues we have seen surrounding early opera in France.

For my part, I would like to consider *Hippolyte et Aricie* as a homage to the monstrosity that Racine's *Phèdre* so brilliantly evoked, albeit a homage that makes its own claims for a different kind of theater. For it was the hybridity of opera, so often denounced by commentators, that Rameau sought to capture, *a contrario*, for the benefit of the *tragédie en musique*. He sought this out through the kind of contact with the spectator that is exemplified in the Trio des Parques and in the changes to the end of the opera that explicitly staged a resistance to tragedy. Commenting on Racine's *Phèdre*, Olivier Pot has remarked that "monstrosity serves – in the etymological sense (*monstrare*) – to 'show' what discourse cannot represent, but which it nonetheless figures and causes to exist at least intentionally in language . . . the final appearance of the monster in Théramène's narrative enables the passage from the scene of language to the imaginary scene, from the figure of words to the figuration of phantasm."[69] If what Rameau sought to present was the luscious "horror" of *tragédie en musique*, what better place to start than *Phèdre*'s own sublime monstrosity?

Part II | Opera and Enlightenment: from private sensation to public feeling

"Ulysse n'a jamais dit que le chant des Sirènes était beau . . . [il a dit] que ce chant 'remplit le coeur du désir d'écouter.'"

[Ulysses never said that the song of the Sirens was beautiful . . . (he said) that the song "filled the heart with the desire to listen"]

Pascal Quignard[1]

A central aspect of opera's aesthetic and moral monstrosity in early-modern France was its association with compulsion and ecstasy. Taking this enduring association as a point of departure for the second part of my study, I will argue that eighteenth-century views of musical affect brought about a transformation in the Renaissance understanding of music as a specific form of magic. Whereas Renaissance theoreticians believed that music had occult properties endowing it with the ability to affect the body and soul in sometimes predictable ways, eighteenth-century writers saw in music a form of "therapy" and a catalyst for sympathy – a trigger for a deep-seated intersubjectivity. Seen in this light, both magic and sympathy could be considered as elements within a vast discursive continuum concerning music and its effects which has taken specific forms in given historical and cultural circumstances. As Philippe Lacoue-Labarthe has suggested, the connection between music, ecstasy, and submission "seems very much to be the first and last word on music in Western philosophy."[2] While it is not the point of this line of inquiry to open the floodgates to ahistorical meditations about "the power of music," an ancillary purpose of my endeavor nonetheless will be to begin to come to terms with the larger picture of an ongoing Western discourse on music and affect, as I bring my analysis to bear more specifically on its eighteenth-century manifestations. By charting a course through early-modern speculations on music, its relation to the listener's body and mind, and the effects of identification and dispossession that were associated with it, I propose a more ample understanding of the ways in which eighteenth-century writers and composers attributed to music in general, and to opera in particular, the power to create sympathetic responses in the listener-spectator. My principal claim, which lies at the end of this trajectory in the following chapter, is that opera came to be understood in the eighteenth century as fostering an otherwise elusive capacity for generating sympathy and identification; and, therefore, that it held a distinctive position in the emergent realm of the aesthetic – the aesthetic being invested from the beginning with the mission of reconciling the multiple inflections of individual, subjective feeling with the general traits of a common humanity.

To make claims of such consequence with regard to opera will undoubtedly seem strange, if not incomprehensible or absurd, given the marginalization and trivialization of opera in the twentieth century, exemplified by Theodor Adorno's characterization of the genre as a commodified "bourgeois vacation spot."[3] The most prevalent image of opera today, reflecting Adorno's stance, is that of a tawdry yet grandiose entertainment, isolated not only from everyday life but also from the truly transformative potential of other forms of high art. Unlike painting or poetry or narrative fiction, there is some sense in which opera remains frozen within a late nineteenth-century aesthetic and therefore lost to any contemporary relevance. Opera may aim to be great art; yet, as Longinus described the sometimes overburdened task of the sublime, at every moment it risks foundering instead upon "the tinsel reefs of affectation."[4] Even many opera-goers share a view of the spectacle as a wonderfully pleasurable, though ultimately fatuous or kitsch, distraction. Though there may be elements of this modern attitude in early-modern Europe, as in Madame de Sévigné's fascination with her own paradoxical attraction to the "ridiculous" and "detestable" novels of La Calprenède, opera emerged in France under cultural circumstances distinct from our own.[5] In the eighteenth century, opera's cultural identity was in flux and its potential effects upon listener-spectators were open to heated debate, both on the side of its advocates – in their enthusiastic claims for the genre – and of its critics – in their shrill insistence on the spectacle's senselessness or on the moral dangers it posed.

Our understanding of the Renaissance musical culture out of which opera emerged has been greatly enriched in recent years by the work of Gary Tomlinson.[6] Within the Renaissance model of the universe as *discordia concors* (that is, harmony produced from difference or discord existing within a larger unity), as Tomlinson has shown, harmony was central to the world and its functioning and was often taken as a key to, or a model for, the universe. Within the realm of the human, music was considered to have a profound impact on men and women, both as a mode of communication with the divine and as a cure for soul and body. Carlo Valgulio's *Contra vituperatorem musicae* (1509), for example, gave music the power to heal "warring parts of the soul" and to align the soul with the world: "if we bring in music, with its most sweet connections and its very suave intervals, we shall be able to tune, almost like strings, the contrary and diverse motions of our souls, and we shall always be able to make them consonant among themselves."[7] Ultimately based on the place music held in a harmonious cosmos, these effects were considered possible because music brought about a form of magical mimesis or communicative bond between musician and listener, as Ficino claimed:

> Song is a most powerful imitator of all things. It imitates the intentions and passions of the soul as well as words; it represents also people's physical gestures, motions, and actions as well as their characters and imitates all these and acts them out so forcibly that it immediately provokes both the singer and the audience to imitate and act out the same things . . . [it] not only possesses motion and displays passion but even carries meaning like a mind.[8]

Similar views on musical "possession" and its therapeutic values were common currency in mid-sixteenth-century France. In his *Dialogues* (1556), for example, Louis Le Caron argued that music restores "the good form [*bienséance*] and gracious harmony that is in oneself," disposes the mind toward greater thoughts, and purges it of adverse ones.[9] Music "educates manners, softens anger, calms irritations, and tempers ill-ordered passions."[10] Lyrico-musical furor for Pontus de Tyard, as for Ficino, constituted "the unique way in which the soul can find the path that leads to the source of its sovereign good [*Summum bonum*] and final bliss."[11] Tyard treated music more specifically in his *Solitaire second*, a detailed music treatise in the form of a dialogue between the *solitaire*, whom one imagines as a wizened sage, and Pasithée, his female interlocutor, beginning and ending with philosophical considerations on the art of music. A long, vigorous life, the *solitaire* argues, is guaranteed "him whose soul is at ease and whose passions, affects, and emotions remain well tempered, whose humors are kept in balance, without excess."[12] He singles out music in this quest for temperance because it is "understood by the most reputable group of sages to contain all the perfections of symmetry, and retained as the image of the full circle of knowledge [*toute l'Encyclopedie*], seems so powerfully to me to provide us with the true image of temperance, that he who does not understand music must think that the soul is crippled and powerless."[13] Throughout his work, Tyard established music as the mediator between macrocosmic and microcosmic orders, a resonant bridge between a universal order and the particular ratios and proportions of individual bodies – an ideal relation of congruence and concord through the intervention of music that would later be considerably transformed in eighteenth-century aesthetics.

Renaissance theorists, then, understood music as an omnipresent force in the universe, an agent of connections between cosmic orders and a mode of access to the nature of things. Within this framework, the musician acted as a conduit between the musical cosmos and the listener, attuning him or her to the universe, producing a tempered rapport between self and world. The health of the listener depended on a temporary detachment or "madness" through music – Ficino's *furor* – which would allow him or her to reconnect with the divine order of things. Timothy J. Reiss notes that "*furor* was not some kind of vague madness. It was *ruled* by a harmonic order, and it aimed to create the same in its hearers."[14] By the end of the sixteenth century, however, these conceptions were on the wane. The notion of music's power and its strong connection to human affect remained, but increasingly without the integrated cosmological framework that had generated these conceptions in the first place. Tomlinson draws on the work of Michel Foucault to describe the waning paradigm of music and magic as it gave way to an analytic and representational scheme, based upon Horace's notion of imitation – *ut pictura poesis*. Distinguishing these two *episteme*, Foucault wrote that "the activity of the mind will no longer consist in *drawing things together*, in setting out on a quest for everything that might reveal some sort of kinship, attraction, or secretly shared nature within them, but, on the contrary, in *discriminating*."[15] The similitudes of Renaissance thought in Foucault's work correspond to Tomlinson's views of musical magic; and Foucault's seventeenth-century paradigm of analysis and discrimination correlates with Tomlinson's view of opera as "representational" after Monteverdi. The old paradigm did not entirely or immediately disappear, Tomlinson stresses; yet, magic is gradually naturalized and the idea of music as imitation or representation displaces music as universal harmony. For Tomlinson, beginning in the seventeenth century, music was no longer at one with the world, but served as a tool for representing the world.

As a guiding principle to the composition and meaning of music in the seventeenth and eighteenth centuries, the ideal of imitation – *ut pictura poesis* – is most often understood by modern commentators to refer to the use of music to represent sounds that occur in the natural world. Seventeenth- and eighteenth-century theorists often discussed this type of imitation, through which vocal music might reproduce the accents of the human voice in passion whereas instrumental music could imitate the sounds of the wind, waves, or bird calls. Of both subspecies of imitation, the abbé Dubos wrote:

> There is therefore a truth in opera's songs [*récits*]. And this truth consists in the imitation of the tones, the accents, the sighs, and the sounds which naturally belong to the feelings contained in the words . . . The truth of imitation in an instrumental piece consists in the resemblance between this piece and the sound it proposes to imitate. There is truth in an

> instrumental piece composed to imitate a storm when its melody, harmony and rhythm make us hear a sound similar to the howling of the winds and the roar of the waves which collide together and crash against the rocks.[16]

The type of imitation described here by Dubos involves the coordination of the object of representation (human passions, waves) with the musical material used in such a representation. A different sort of mimetic relationship pertained between music and listener, a relationship that appears to have interested seventeenth- and eighteenth-century writers at least as much as the above type of imitation: "just as an orator, using transitions, guides his listeners to ideas that did not seem contained in his first subject, so a composer, with the help of modulation, arouses in our soul extremely varied passions."[17] Music not only imitated the sound of the passionate voice or of the objects of nature; it also induced passion. Accompanying the naturalization of musical magic and the late sixteenth-century rhetorical turn in musical composition, exemplified by the proto-operatic ideal of *recitar cantando*, was the assumption that the moral grounding of musical effects depended upon a mimetic rapport between music and its listeners, a relationship between musical "motion" and the "movements" of the soul.

For many seventeenth-century theorists, musical affect was governed by mimesis – not only an imitation in the sense of a reproduction of sounds, but perhaps more importantly a kind of "resonance" or "harmony" between human beings and music. This conviction would continue to guide reflection on opera in the eighteenth century. Marin Mersenne used an ancient example to bolster his claims for the beneficial effects of song on the soul: "each virtue," Mersenne wrote, "is like a specific cord in the soul whose harmony drives away passions and vices, like the sound of David's harp drove away demons." He elaborated further on the tight connection between music and the physical and moral state of the listener, remarking that "the ill effects of dissonances, and the displeasure that they cause the ear, allow us to understand the disorder that passions and vices bring to life; thus, there is nothing in harmony that does not serve morals."[18] In this passage, Mersenne argues that there is a process of reflection, a form of mimesis, connecting the audience members and their passions to the musical patterns they hear. Mersenne's claim about the mimetic connection between music and the soul was not unlike Ficino's earlier views: "I note therefore, first of all, that it is an infallible rule for music [*chants*] that one must follow and imitate the movement of the passion which one wishes to excite in the listener."[19] His friend, René Descartes, agreed, arguing that a direct correspondence existed between the *"varia mensura"* of duple and triple meter, the inherently different orders reflected in them (*"duplici genere battutae"*), and the corresponding passions induced in the listener.[20] Recalling Jean-Antoine de Baïf's experiments with measured music and the emphasis he had placed on rhythm in his Académie de Poésie et de Musique in the late sixteenth century, theorist Nicolas Bergier noted that the powers of music "vary according to the different mixtures and the order of the long and short periods [*temps*] in poetic feet, whose various interactions produce various passions and affections in our souls."[21] Discussing musical mimesis in early-modern Europe, Timothy Reiss remarks that "what was 'imitated' might be actions and feelings, but only insofar as they *moved* similar affects in the recipient."[22]

By means of music – its intervals, modes, temperaments, meters, rhythms, and so on – the passions of the listener could be "retuned" so that "the well-tempered soul would act in accord with prudence, justice, temperance and wisdom."[23] This understanding of music and its effects no longer necessarily assumed the existence of a divine, cosmological harmony which would guarantee essential connections between entities; rather, it disclosed and attempted to elucidate through musical sound a world of specifically human morality and affect, health and infirmity. Joining the literary paradigm that shaped musical thought in this period with the somatic concerns summarized above, two classical poetic values can be identified as the basis of an early-modern understanding of the experience of music: catharsis and mimesis. A tempering (catharsis) of being would be triggered by way of the listener's "resonance" (mimesis) with music. This general framework was adapted in order to conceptualize and describe the moral dimensions of opera and its effects upon listener-spectators.

It is with these developments in mind that I take exception to the starkness of Tomlinson's Foucauldian opposition between the episte-mological presuppositions of musical magic and the representational convictions of *ut pictura poesis* which subsequently gained predomi-nance. This shift occurred, for Tomlinson, in tandem with a dilution of purpose and depth that occurred when Italian opera withdrew from the closed aristocratic and academic speculations responsible for its birth in Italy to become increasingly present in courtly and commer-cial life. For Tomlinson, the representational, anti-inwardlooking, and brilliant Marinism of Monteverdi's late opera, *L'incoronazione di Poppea* of 1642, replaced the Petrarchan outlook of impassioned, introspective oratory characteristic of *L'Orfeo* of 1607.[24] Opera had abandoned the magic of the world and the immediacy of passion for the distance of representation and showiness. He concludes: "Not until the midday sun of romanticism melted the ice did Italian music regain the fluid or-atorical passion it had lost at the end of the Renaissance."[25] My purpose is not to evaluate Tomlinson's view of the evolution of Italian opera; however, the abrupt shift he describes from one set of epistemological assumptions to another is altogether too tidy and does not do justice to an ongoing preoccupation with the force of music. Musical mimesis, as it was understood beginning in the seventeenth century, I argue, carried over recognizable elements of the Renaissance tradition that associated music with obscure forces and correspondences. The decisive rupture that Tomlinson, following Foucault, places between the epistemology of resemblances of Renaissance thought and the analytic and repre-sentational paradigms of early-modern thought obscures paradoxical continuities. Where Tomlinson sees only opposition and departure, I want to draw attention to the fascination with occult musical effects that persisted beyond the indisputable gap separating a world fueled by Aristotelian essentialism from one that was driven by Cartesian or Newtonian mechanics.

In many ways, certainly, seventeenth- and eighteenth-century com-mentators wrote about music in very different terms from their Renaissance counterparts. Other discourses – most often philosophico-medical, containing anthropological, utopian, and, in a wide sense, political inflections – came to take the place of the far-reaching cosmological speculations of the Renaissance. In the eighteenth century, interest in musical magic – the "artless power and hidden energy" that Tyard had identified with music – was transformed into a concern with the natural effects that music had on the body and soul of the listener.[26] Integrating mechanical and moral frameworks, eighteenth-century commentators sought to understand the sympathetic resonances that music generated in its listeners. Today, commentators tend to imagine a categorical distinction in the eighteenth century between a "scientific" or physical model for music, in which musical sound would influence individuals through purely physical properties, and a verbal model, in which music acts as a language, as a sign of our passions. John Neubauer, for example, summarizes the history of music theory as "the alternating dominance, the frequent battles, and the occasional peaceful coexistence of verbal and mathematical approaches to music." Neubauer identifies the imitation of the passions with the first approach and argues that the rise of instrumental music in the nineteenth century was supported by a neo-Pythagorian revival of mathematical views of music.[27] Yet, as writers naturalized their descriptions of musical effects in the eighteenth century, the two paradigms often blur and merge. Indeed, if mimesis is understood as a form of compulsive modeling or as a "sympathetic resonance" that occurs when our minds and bodies come into contact with musical sound, then the distinction between music as a physical "science" and music as a language with moral effects becomes less pronounced. In other words, it is difficult to isolate the effects of the sounds "themselves" from the effects of the music when it is considered as a discourse. Some eighteenth-century writers with materialist inclinations even tended to erase this distinction entirely, placing the poetic and moral on a continuum with the physical. Through the analysis of some examples of philosophico-medical discussion of musical effects, we can gauge the degree to which consideration of the power of music, while transformed by new concerns that emerged in Enlightenment culture, remained a constant source of fascination and of anxiety.

The impressive history of music that Jacques Bonnet completed from the manuscript of his brother, the abbé Pierre Bourdelot, described the effects of what the authors called "natural" music, which was their term for a latter-day *musica mondana*. Bonnet and Bourdelot examined the unexpected, and often unexplained, ways in which music appeared to be connected to the world. Because music could produce ripples in water, break mirrors, and other demonstrable phenomena, Bourdelot and Bonnet noted that "those authors, like Ovid, who have stated that music had the power to animate inanimate objects did not take their stories as far from the truth as people think."[28] The natural effects of music also extended, they suggested, to human beings:

> A famous doctor of the court assured me that he had cured a lady of the highest quality who had become mad of a passionate love through the unfaithfulness of her lover. He had a partition created in this lady's chamber for musicians so that she could not see them. Three concerts were given each day, and at night airs were sung that indulged her pain and others to help bring her to her senses, which were drawn from the most beautiful passages of the operas of Lully.[29]

If opera's detractors accused Lully and Quinault of corrupting their spectators, here Bonnet and Bourdelot claimed that these operas could be shown to possess a cathartic effect. After a number of other similar examples, Bourdelot and Bonnet concluded that music acts on the passions through the body's connection to the soul: "this indisputably proves the sovereign effects of music on the passions, which can be dissipated or moderated through the effects of the sympathy that surely exists between musical harmonies and the organs that are situated in the folds of the brain, or the pineal glands, for the functions of memory and the faculties of the soul."[30] Music alters the mind, and therefore affects the passions through the sympathetic resonances it produces there. In this early eighteenth-century work on the history of music and its effects, we are closer than Tomlinson would lead us to believe to Renaissance theoretician Franchino Gaffurio's understanding of the harmony inherent in human beings.[31] Much has changed; yet the certainty of musical effects remains a constant preoccupation.

In his later work on the history of music and dance, *Histoire générale de la danse sacrée et prophane*, Bonnet regards musical magic with a fair degree of skepticism; yet, in the end, it is impossible for him to distinguish musical magic from natural music with any degree of clarity. In a chapter entitled "On the Elementary Music attributed to Aerial Spirits and to the Oracles of Antiquity," Bonnet tells of a mysterious enchanter who, very much like the pied piper of Hamelin, once visited the city of Nuremberg to lure away the children of the city:

> A kind of phantom or tall man, of prodigious size, passed through this
> large city and who, playing the flageolet, went down every street; and
> all the children who heard him set about following him as if by
> enchantment. He assembled as many as 800 of both sexes and led them
> out of the city; and afterwards, they disappeared so completely that
> whatever searches the parents of these children were able to undertake,
> it was never discovered what had become of them.[32]

Bonnet attributes widespread belief in tales such as this one to the credulity of simple people; yet he notes that these tales do not discredit "natural" music. "The Church Fathers and the most profound Philosophers of Antiquity," Bonnet writes, "claim that it was upon the principles of natural music that God created the universe and that he fashioned its shape using the first matter." Saint Augustine referred to this music as "universal harmony"; and the philosophers of antiquity, too, believed that "everything that moves in nature acts only according to the principles of natural music."[33] The distinction between musical magic and "natural" music, between the hypnotic effects produced by the pied piper of Nuremberg and the therapeutic qualities of Lully's operas, Bonnet finally concludes, cannot be determined with any confidence: "since all the occurrences of this supposed celestial, or natural, or elementary music that I relate appear either miraculous or natural, I will not undertake to say anything decisive regarding it: this sublime matter is above my understanding."[34]

Though Bonnet was unable to distinguish the natural from the supernatural in the wide assortment of musical effects that he sought to describe, others looked more closely at the implications of music for their understanding of health and illness. Even a relatively brief examination of eighteenth-century philosophical medicine reveals considerable interest in the effects of music and sound, in part fueled by the increasing attention given to sensibility.[35] Claude-Nicolas Le Cat, a chief surgeon at the Hôtel-Dieu in Rouen and perfecter of several instruments for lithotomy, gave considerable attention to music in his treatises on sensation and the function of the nerves. Le Cat was a contemporary and sometimes rival of Albrecht von Haller, the latter having gained renown as the first to establish the distinction between irritability and sensibility, the former a property of muscle tissue and the latter a property of nervous tissue. Le Cat rejected Haller's account because of the weight and centrality it gave to irritability conceived as a purely mechanical process. For Le Cat, since "to feel and to think are the same thing," irritability and sensation were intertwined with the functions of the soul, a hypothesis that was confirmed, in his eyes, by the observation that sensation continues even when the body has ceased to function.[36] "A thousand facts prove," he wrote, "that the soul is still in all the organs" for a short while after death.[37]

In his *Traité des sens*, first published in 1740, Le Cat established the importance of sensation as a dynamic principle of existence. Sensations, he argued, tell us of our needs and allow us to communicate with other beings. More generally, we have sensations "in order to enjoy the world where we are placed."[38] Of all the senses, hearing and sight are foremost for Le Cat because they are most actively involved in "our commerce with other Beings."[39] Though Le Cat devoted more space in his treatise to sight than to hearing, he argued that hearing is superior to sight because our ears can distinguish individual sounds from a multitude, whereas our eyes cannot refract colors.[40] After a lengthy discussion of the mechanics of hearing, Le Cat suggested that music joins "all these mechanistic perfections" with "those delicate, reflective sentiments which distinguish [man] from all other animals."[41] Le Cat also recounted the well-known story of a musician who moved Alexander the Great to violent emotions with one tune and then calmed him with another. Bringing the discussion into the present, Le Cat noted that Lully "seems to have undertaken to resuscitate that music of pathos, those sounds which go to the heart," implicitly comparing the effects of his operatic airs to those of the ancient musician's lyre.[42] In support of his argument that musical effects were not the exclusive property of ancient music, Le Cat referred to a modern Venetian whose lute made the Doge "pass successively from melancholy to joy, and from joy to melancholy, with so much art and force that the Doge, who no longer felt in control of his emotions [*mouvemens*], ordered him to cease his enchantments."[43] By using the term "enchantment," Le Cat placed music and magic in close proximity to each other. Comparing contemporary opera to ancient music, he also claimed that opera had taken great strides toward reclaiming the powerful effects attributed to the music of the ancients.

For many eighteenth-century medical doctors like Le Cat, the ability of music to move its listeners made it "very pertinent to health."[44] Since most illness was caused by an imbalance in the "animal fluid," which Le Cat referred to as "the soul of sensation," the senses were "very well suited to modify the character of this fluid and to excite through it, in the entire machine that it animates, healthy changes." Le Cat again distinguished hearing as exemplary in this regard: "of all the senses, the hearing is the one in which man excels beyond all other animals, in relation to harmony; there is no sense that moves [man] like it does."[45] Concluding his examination of the medicinal effects of musical sounds, Le Cat referred to incidents of fever cured by music and documented in the *Histoire de l'Académie des Sciences* in 1708 and 1717; and he described in detail the process by which music can cure tarantula bite. This latter description is worth citing at some length because of the detail Le Cat was able to provide of the musical cure:

> Everyone knows of Saul's cure by David's harp, and few have not heard of the story of the tarantula. The bite of this large species of spider is not more painful than that of a large ant or a bee; however it is followed by very dangerous occurrences, such as melancholy, suffocation, lethargy, delirium, and death. Music is the only remedy for this dangerous illness. An excellent musician must be brought, and he must try out various tunes on various instruments, since not all are suitable in this instance. The instruments that fare the best are the bagpipes, the tambourine, the guitar, the lute, and the violin. The best tunes are fast, cheerful ones.
>
> When the musician has found the salutary tune and instrument, he will notice that the lethargic patient moves his hand to the beat, then his

arm, and progressively his entire body; after which he begins dancing at a startling pace, which lasts for six entire hours. When he is obviously weary, he must be put warmly to bed and, when he is judged to have sufficiently rested, the musician gives him another serenade. This exercise is continued until it is clear that the sufferer feels weary and that he begins to regain consciousness. These signs of recovery ordinarily occur after seven or eight days; at that point the sufferer believes that he is coming out of a profound sleep and recalls neither his illness nor all the dancing that he has been made to do. He is still left with a dark melancholy, and sometimes the attack returns every year, at which point one must resort once again to music.[46]

The music acts as a cure because it affects the body and mind of the sufferer in such a way as to restore equilibrium to the animal fluid, which had previously been knocked out of balance by the tarantula bite.

Joseph-Louis Roger, a doctor associated with the Montpellier school, published his *Tentamen de vi soni et musices in corpore humano* in 1758. Roger divided musical effects into mechanical and moral ones, yet noted that these effects operated simultaneously and could not always be isolated one from the other. As his translator, Etienne Sainte-Marie, a member of the Société Médicale de Montpellier, noted in the 1803 French edition of the *Tentamen*: "music acts directly upon the mind and the nerves," yet at the same time it constitutes "a moral treatment."[47] For this reason, Sainte-Marie argued, music is particularly effective on "the nervous disorders" which join the physical with the moral: "one will find in this book verified observations of catalepsies, hysterical or hypochondriac ailments, malignant fevers, nervous or humoral melancholies, epilepsies, cured by music. Frequent concert-going has also dissipated certain rheumatisms, migraines, nostalgia, etc." (xxix). Music can deter a person who is driven to suicide because it "rejuvenates the imagination, renews the sensibility, and brings back hope to the soul" (xxviij–xxix).

In the first part of his treatise, Roger considered the phenomenon of the *corps sonore*, or resonant body, examining also the air as a *corps sonore* before moving on to describe the transmission of sound in the ear. Roger examined wind instruments and the voice to show that when these instruments are played, or when a singer sings, "the air undergoes not only a tremor, but also vibrations identical to those that occur in strings" (13). After discussing the phenomenon of sympathetic resonance in strings, he suggested that the human body may be said to function in a similar way: "the organ of hearing, and even the entire human body, can be considered as instruments of this kind; for the influence that music exerts on us depends in part on the greater or lesser ease with which the viscera, the bones, the nerves, and the humors of the human body resonate and quiver" (29). Sainte-Marie echoed this view, remarking that "one can therefore consider the body [*la machine animale*] as a musical instrument which has its particular tones, chords, resonance, and timbre" (316).

With Roger's general principle established, the second part of the *Traité* is devoted more specifically to the influence of music on human beings, beginning with a short history of music. Roger noted that music was often associated with "absurd magic" by the ancient pagans since it was observed to have curative powers (116). The problem with accounts of musical effects for Roger, as Bonnet had noted earlier, was the difficulty in separating fact from fiction: "once reason had shattered the magic scepter, several authors, both ancient and modern, sought to return the greater part of these marvels to music since it had almost always been used in magic spells; but they committed a grave mistake in not taking pains to distinguish truth from falsehood" (120–21). In a world driven by reason, Roger argued, it was of the utmost importance to preserve the verifiable truth of musical effects from the superstition of "magic." Both Kircher and Mersenne were guilty, in Roger's eyes, of credulity, the latter for example claiming that "hens flee at the sound of a guitar whose strings are made from fox gut" (125). The authentic explanation for musical effects, Roger suggested, may lie in the "harmonic fibers that we have in our ears" or perhaps in the love of order which we seek in all things (130). In any event, musical effects were a proven fact for Roger, since the principles of harmony exist "in the souls of all men," despite the many variations individual taste may exhibit (131). All objects, and therefore a fortiori the external and internal organs of the human body, react to sound because they exist "in harmonic relation" with sound (146).[48]

There should be no doubt, Roger insisted, that musical sounds create motion in inanimate fluids and solids – the water that ripples or the glass that vibrates at the sound of a musical instrument (147–59). Animals, too, are affected by music: "the sound of the fife tempers the ferocity of bears"; "swans allow themselves to be charmed by the sound of a guitar"; and fish are attracted by song (164–65). Music can be observed to affect human beings specifically through the nerves. However, Roger noted, "those who have attempted to explain all the effects of music through the movement and the vibrations in the nerves have proposed a vague and far too general theory" (184). Our experience of sound does not depend on the vibration of the nerves but on the effect it has on "the nerve fluid." Sounds have "physical" [*mécanique*] effects; but they also affect the soul "which determines, as is well known, the course of nerve fluid in the nerves" (206–07). Nerve fluid, because it can remain for some time in the nerves, endows them with "movement and feeling, depending on whether it flows in greater or lesser quantity in their tissues" (242). The soul re-equilibrates the nerve fluid by moving it about the body to combat the disease resulting from its imbalance: "every time, therefore, that nerve fluid is suddenly channeled to some part of the body, in order to produce pain or illness there, if the soul can recall it into the nerves that it has abandoned and render its distribution more balanced, the pain and illness will immediately cease, as if by magic" (242). The soul therefore serves as a regulator for the nerve fluid; and the changes it effectuates occur *comme par enchantement*.

Music acts in precisely the same way. In support of his claim, Roger referred to the widely accepted view that music, like rhetoric, moves the passions of the soul: "each musical composition has, like discourse, its periods. Each period has its members, its ideas which are more or less vivid, more or less fresh. These ideas correspond to the various passions of which man is susceptible: they paint courage or fear, joy or sadness" (218–19). Music imprints these passions on the soul "unbeknownst to us, and even sometimes despite us" (220). Roger did not elaborate on any significant difference between the rhetorical (moral) and the physical action of music. Music moves the soul and alters the flow of nerve fluid simultaneously: "at the same time that music distracts the soul, and occupies it with gentle pleasure, it conveys to the nerve fluid and the animal spirits a movement which serves to explain several other of its effects" (241). Roger argued that of all the senses "the sense of hearing is in general the best suited to distract the soul," which is why music is considered both salutary and potentially dangerous. On the one hand, music can cure nervous disorders and maintain balance in the nerve fluid and animal spirits. On the other, as Sainte-Marie remarked in his preface, disorders associated with nostalgia are risky to treat with music since it can often intensify the disorder rather than alleviate it (xxix). Roger, too, noted that because of its power "Muslims dread music" (235).

In describing the therapeutic uses of music, Roger used the term *sympathie* quite frequently. A hysterical or epileptic girl was cured by the sound of a gunshot in one example cited by Roger because of the *sympathie* produced in the eardrum and the nerves by the sound (194). The naturalization of musical effects is most clearly illustrated by Roger's hypothesis, after a passage in which he recounted the biblical story of how David cured Saul with the music of his harp, that "it was perhaps a bout of hypochondria or of hysteria that Saul experienced" (248). The effects Roger described, and which he believed could be used to cure many illnesses, were based on the "sympathetic resonance" of the human organism with all kinds of sounds, but particularly with musical sounds. Like Bonnet, Roger remarked on the difficulty of his subject and admitted that it was not yet possible to understand fully the effects of music; yet his aim was to show that, because of the fundamental nature of human sensibility, music could constitute an effective form of medical treatment (251–52). For Roger, it was imperative to distinguish the sympathy that existed between sounds and objects or living organisms from the occult resemblances that, Mersenne had claimed, made chickens flee at the sound of guitar strings made from fox gut. Whereas the latter belief constituted a ridiculous form of superstition, the former was verifiable and could be harnessed for its curative powers.

Eighteenth-century writers in areas of inquiry other than medicine and in countries other than France also understood listeners' reactions to music as a form of sympathy. Francis Hutcheson, in *An Inquiry Concerning Beauty, Order, Harmony, Design*, argued that although beauty is universally derived from a sense of "uniformity amidst variety," music may play upon different experiences and temperaments: "when our ear discerns any resemblance between the air of a tune . . . to the sound of the human voice in any passion, we shall be touched by it in a very sensible manner, and have melancholy, joy, gravity, thoughtfulness excited in us by a sort of *sympathy* or *contagion*."[49] Around the turn of the century, Leibniz, too, identified the mimetic or sympathetic component of musical experience in the orderly "impulses" which "proceed together in order but with a certain variation." "Through our hearing," Leibniz argued, "this creates a sympathetic echo in us, to which our animal spirits respond. This is why music is so well adapted to move our minds, even though this main purpose is not usually sufficiently noticed or sought after."[50]

Similarly, in 1769, Daniel Webb observed the isomorphic relation between musical "movements" and those of the passions:

> We are then to take it for granted, that the mind, under particular affections, excites certain vibrations in the nerves, and impresses certain movements on the animal spirits.
>
> I shall suppose, that it is in the nature of music to excite similar vibrations, to communicate similar movements to the nerves and spirits. For, if music owes its being to motion, and, if passion cannot well be conceived to exist without it, we have a right to conclude, that the agreement of music with passion can have no other origin than a coincidence of movements.
>
> When, therefore, musical sounds produce in us the same sensations which accompany the impressions of any one particular passion, then the music is said to be in unison with that passion; and the mind must, from a similitude in their effects, have a lively feeling of an affinity in their operations.[51]

In a note Webb referred to two ways of accounting for the effects of music. The first was to consider music as sounding number (*harmonici numeri*), the order of music being reflected in the order of the soul. Webb cited Athanasius Kircher's *Musurgia universalis* (1650) as the source of this view among the moderns. For the second, Webb referred the reader to Aristotle's definition of the imitations of music as "simulacra morum et affectionum." For Webb, however, whether one accepts the view of music as the manifestation of an essential order or as a representation of the passions, in both cases music exhibits what Webb termed a "principle of assimilation" – music's ability, in other words, to compel the listener to conform to its example.[52]

In arguing that the human organism reacted in sympathetic resonance to music and in suggesting that medical knowledge could tap into this phenomenon in its mission to maintain the equilibrium that sustains good health, doctor-philosophers like Roger were in agreement with writers like Webb. Jean-Baptiste-Joseph Lallemant, like Roger, divided music into mechanical and moral effects. Also like Roger, he subscribed to the rhetorical and physical effects of music: "melody acts on the passions in two ways, either by expressing the movement that it inspires, or by the simple impression that rhythm makes on the ear."[53] The first – musical expression – is based on a rhetorical model. The second – the physical effects of sound on the body – is founded on the mechanism of sympathetic resonance. In both cases – since music expresses passion and triggers movements in the soul of the listener through its own movements – a mimetic principle is at the heart of our reactions.[54] For Lallemant, our sympathetic reaction to music could be verified by noting that slow tempi generate similar movements of the passions, such as those that produce sadness, whereas brisk ones produce joy and excitement. As was the case for the other doctor-philosophers, however, since music was considered a form of oratory, it was difficult for Lallemant to distinguish rhetoric from reflex. At the origin of music, Lallemant contended, were "melodic impromptus in which the throat, independently of reflection, expresses in its way the well-being of the entire body."[55] The first melody was a reflex reaction in response to feelings of satisfaction. Yet for the listener-onlooker,

Lallemant wrote, reflecting perhaps equally on primeval encounters and on the effect of contemporary operatic scenes, the reaction of the other becomes a sign to which he or she responds mimetically: "through a hidden impulse independent of will, it so happens that we are naturally given over to the passions whose effects we see in others."[56]

In his *Traité de l'existance, de la nature et des propriétés du fluide des nerfs*, published in 1765, twenty-five years after the *Traité des sens*, Le Cat staked out a somewhat different position, elaborating on his earlier views on the effects of music. Le Cat viewed nerve fluid as the primary mechanism of sensation: "it is, as we have said, the instrument of movement and of sensation; it is a mediating substance between the soul and the body."[57] He suggested that there were two possible scenarios to account for the function of the nerves: they might communicate between the muscles and the brain in and of themselves, or they might accomplish this task through the mediation of nerve fluid. Arguing against the first possibility, he remarked that "several doctors . . . have considered these [nerve] fibers as so many strings similar to those of musical instruments, as so many strings capable of all kinds of vibrations, of all tones, through the impressions of external objects."[58] According to this model, the vibrations of the nerves themselves communicate sensation directly to the brain and, through the *sensorium commune*, to the soul. Le Cat argued that this model could not account for the intricacy of the contraction of the muscles, which is triggered by a mechanism internal to the body, not by any external stimulus. Here, Le Cat remarked, unraveling the musical metaphor, the musical model falls apart: "there are no longer any external objects here to draw sounds from them, and if one were to suppose that there were, where would simple and more or less harmonious or dissonant modulations get us? . . . where in the animal economy are the strings analogous to those with which the Gaviniés and the Mondonvilles [celebrated violinists and composers] draw such touching sounds?"[59] The body, in Le Cat's 1765 work, does not resonate like a violin at the touch of a bow.

The conclusions Le Cat drew regarding music in his treatise on nerve fluid are indicative of a shift in the description of musical effects in the eighteenth century; yet, in 1765, this epistemological change was not far-reaching. For Le Cat, nerves could not be said to work like the strings of a musical instrument. The nerve branches did not have the same elasticity or resistance, and they were much too diffuse.[60] Unlike Roger and many others, by 1765 Le Cat had taken a position against the view of the body as a musical instrument. He did not contest the fact that people reported being moved by music; and he firmly believed that these effects could be observed and used by the medical doctor in order to restore and maintain health. However, he argued that the mechanism of music (resonance) and that of our sensibility (for Le Cat, the circulation of nerve fluid) were not isomorphic. Our bodies cannot be understood as musical organisms.

The naturalization of musical effects to which Tomlinson refers can be traced from seventeenth-century writers to Bonnet, Le Cat, Roger, Lallemant, and others. This naturalization involved a shift in the ways in which writers accounted for musical effects, yet it did not entail a waning of their fascination with the natural power of music. A parallel form of naturalization has been traced by Peter Kivy, who has argued that Aristotelian mimesis came to be overshadowed in the eighteenth century by "the demands of a pure musical syntax."[61] For Kivy, an increasingly influential "arousal theory" of music – one that we might associate with Le Cat's 1765 treatise – excluded Aristotelian mimesis over the course of the eighteenth century.[62] Music arouses passions because it is a stimulus, not because we react in sympathetic resonance to its imitations of the passions. Kivy's own account, however, and the above discussion of the psycho-physiological understanding of music, reveal how slippery the distinction between mechanism and mimesis was for eighteenth-century writers. For the purposes of his argument, Kivy would like to distinguish "'pure' musical pleasure" and "'pure' musical form *per se*" from the mimetic behavior described by much of the medical literature.[63] However, as I have attempted to establish, the two were utterly intertwined during the eighteenth century; and

Le Cat's 1765 qualifications were not widely shared. In 1785, for example, Michel Paul Guy de Chabanon came out very strongly against the Rousseauian view that music imitates the passions: "the expression of song does not consist in the imitation of the inarticulate cry of the passions."[64] Yet despite this position with regard to music as imitation, or perhaps precisely because of it – because, as he argued, music is not *created* to imitate the passions – Chabanon insisted that the emotional qualities we perceive in "the musical language" were natural, not conventional:[65]

> High-pitched sounds have something light and brilliant about them which seems to invite the soul to gaiety. Compare the high strings of a harp to the low ones of the same instrument, and you will feel how much more readily the latter make the soul receptive to love. Who knows if the broad undulations of the long, relatively loose strings do not communicate to our nerves similar vibrations, and if this condition in our body is not that which produces affectionate feelings? Man, believe me, is but an instrument; his fibers respond to the strings of the lyrical instruments which strike and probe them.[66]

Chabanon's position against music as imitation – that music was "sensation" not "sentiment" – did not prevent him from suggesting that we respond to music mimetically, that the vibrations of the bass strings of the harp, echoing in our own *corps sonore*, impart to us the feelings they naturally evoke.[67] Over the course of the seventeenth and eighteenth centuries, as musical effects were naturalized, the notion of the resonant human body, both in medical writings and in other areas of inquiry, became the predominant way to account for the effects of music. When mimesis itself disappeared, as in the case of Le Cat's 1765 treatise, musical effects nonetheless remained a constant source of fascination. In eighteenth-century opera and reflections on opera, this fascination with the effects of music was exemplified through a marked preoccupation with sensibility and sympathy.

"Mes larmes coulaient, et j'y trouvais une espèce de douceur; quand le coeur est véritablement touché, il sent du plaisir à tout ce qui lui prouve à lui-même sa propre sensibilité."
[My tears flowed, and in this I found a sort of sweetness; when the heart is truly touched, it feels pleasure in everything that proves to it its own sensibility]

Claudine-Alexandrine Guérin de Tencin[1]

My purpose in the previous chapter was to set aside, if only temporarily, the particular history of aesthetic ideas – constructed around antithetical episteme – that we have inherited from Foucault. I argued that music was considered over a very *longue durée* – from Renaissance magic to the mimesis of the seventeenth and eighteenth centuries – as exploiting certain dispositions of the individual that would foster good health and well-being in the world, and as facilitating mutually beneficial and pleasurable connections between individuals. Some eighteenth-century commentators were skeptical of musical effects, particularly those recounted by the Greek historians. The highly ironic Pierre Jean Baptiste Nougaret wrote: "A singular thing that no one will ever have suspected is that music is a sovereign remedy to many ills; if we believe the Greeks, it is more effective than all the secrets of medicine."[2] Although Nougaret did assert that music had been proven to remedy tarantula bite, his skepticism quickly returned: if only all illnesses, he exclaims, could be cured with a prescription for a little music.[3] Similarly, d'Aquin de Chateaulyon was skeptical about the stories of miraculous musical effects from ancient history; and he remarked with irony that "one will recall that it is the custom to embellish stories, and besides, we take our place alongside the Greeks since we also have in our century music that puts people to sleep."[4] Noting that in ancient Greece medical and musical knowledge was inseparable, he observed: "How everything changes. I defy Mr. Blavet at present to do as much: the best flute sonatas will never cure the gout."[5] In the place of magic, d'Aquin de Chateaulyon suggested that *la sensibilité* was the key to the musical effects that were incontestable in the eyes of eighteenth-century observers:

> Today no one can put into doubt the fact that lively and brilliant music is the only cure for Tarantula bite; and to use examples that I have right here before me, I know people for whom an opera by Rameau was worth as much as the consultation of [all] the Molins and the Vernages [famous medical doctors]. They were quite ill upon their arrival, and they left cured. I am speaking only of those who have sensitive ears.[6]

The naturalization of musical magic thus took two, often interconnected, routes in the eighteenth century: the first passed into medicine, as I argued in the previous chapter; the second made its way into what the eighteenth century called "moral philosophy" and involved the specific problem of sympathy. The present chapter will take as its focus this second direction.

Most eighteenth-century commentators described the connections facilitated by music as forms of sympathy. For Renaissance writers, music promised to involve the individual in the cosmos through the interlocking orders of *musica mondana*, *musica humana*, and *musica instrumentalis*. The mimetic and sympathetic effects associated with the operatic experience in the eighteenth century were imminent, not transcendent, and constituted the promise of a moral commonality through which the individual spectator could shed his or her isolation to become part of a larger community. Sympathy encompassed both the relationship of the listener-spectator to the operatic spectacle and the bond established between spectators. In each case, this relationship was described as a form of identification or common feeling. For many eighteenth-century writers, the extraordinary effect of music in general, and of opera in particular, was its ability to absorb the listener-spectator: the listener, in some sense, *becomes* that which he or she hears or is otherwise transformed by it.

After mid-century, I will argue, the broad cultural investment in sympathy – evidenced in fiction and philosophical writings as well as in the theater – took root in the newly reinvented genre of the *opéra comique*, a genre which, in the eyes of contemporaries, was particularly well suited to sympathy.[7] For the generation of the *philosophes* and their successors, *opéra comique* came to be identified as the theatrical genre that spoke most powerfully to the heart; at the same time, composers and librettists exploited the connection between *opéra comique* and sentiment, so that feeling became an unavoidable presence in their works, whether thematically, textually, or musically. Of course, the *tragédies* that dominated the stage of the Académie Royale de Musique had also long been associated by audiences and theorists alike with sentiment, and particularly with love, as earlier chapters have documented. As the abbé Batteux remarked: "it is also noteworthy that in most of the tragedies made to be set to music, what is most interesting is not the action itself but the sentiments that emerge from the situations brought about by the action; whereas in other tragedies, it is the activity of the hero itself which is striking and astonishing."[8] My particular claim with respect to *opéra comique*, which I will support through an analysis of individual works and eighteenth-century commentary about the genre, is that *opéra comique* made sympathy an integral part of its identity and success. Beginning with an examination of the notion of sympathy and its various eighteenth-century inflections in philosophy and dramatic theory, I will move on to examine the ways in which *opéra comique* drew on the culture of sympathy. By placing theoretical works before stage works in my discussion, I do not mean to suggest that theory preceded practice in this case; nor do I claim that *opéra comique* was derived from theoretical questions or polemical stances, whether consciously or unconsciously. Indeed, *opéra comique* had developed long before theoreticians were truly able to account for it. A preliminary discussion of the larger cultural preoccupation with sympathy will therefore serve primarily to facilitate the subsequent analysis of individual works.

The interrelated questions of sympathy and identification had a long and involved history in the eighteenth century, a history that I will be unable to recount here in any comprehensive fashion. However, I would like to pursue a few lines of inquiry in order to expose some

204 Aesthetics of Opera in the Ancien Régime

of the central issues at hand. At the beginning of Diderot's *Jacques le fataliste*, Jacques tells a story that raises the paradoxical question of sympathy. Jacques tells of his enlistment in the army and the battle of Fontenoy, where he was shot in the knee:

> Jacques – . . . Ah! monsieur, je ne crois pas qu'il y ait de blessure plus
>   cruelle que celle du genou.
> Le maître – Allons donc, Jacques, tu te moques.
> Jacques – Non, pardieu, Monsieur, je ne me moque pas. Il y a là je ne sais
>   combien d'os, de tendons et d'autres choses qu'ils appellent je ne sais
>   comment . . .

> *Jacques* . . . Ah, sir, I believe there is not a crueler wound than that on
>   the knee.
> *The Master.* Come now, Jacques, you exaggerate.
> *Jacques.* No, by heaven, sir, I do not. There are in a man's knee I know not
>   how many bones, tendons and other things whose names escape me.[9]

Shortly thereafter, Jacques repeats his claim about knee wounds and his master reiterates his response word for word. The narrator intervenes here to explain that, at that very moment, his master's horse slips and falls, and his master with it. During the fall, his master's knee strikes a rock and he is soon forced to concede to Jacques entirely on the subject of knee injuries:

> Lorsque les deux chevaux essoufflés reprirent leur pas ordinaire, Jacques
>   dit à son maître: Eh bien, Monsieur, qu'en pensez-vous?
> Le maître – De quoi?
> Jacques – De la blessure au genou.
> Le maître – Je suis de ton avis, c'est une des plus cruelles.
> Jacques – Au vôtre.
> Le maître – Non, non, au tien, au mien, à tous les genoux du monde.
> Jacques – Mon maître, mon maître, vous n'y avez pas bien regardé;
>   croyez que nous ne plaignons jamais que nous . . . Il cherchait à faire
>   concevoir à son maître que le mot douleur était sans idée, et qu'il ne
>   commençait à signifier quelque chose qu'au moment où il rappelait à
>   notre mémoire une sensation que nous avions éprouvée.

When the two horses, winded, fell back to their normal pace, Jacques
  said to his master: "Well, sir, and now what do you think of it?"
The Master. Of what?
Jacques. Of a knee-wound.
The Master. I agree with you completely; it is one of the worst.
Jacques. That is to say, if it's *your* knee?
The Master. No, no, no. Yours, mine, all the knees in the world.
Jacques. Oh, my master, my master, you haven't thought that out well!
  You must know that we never pity anyone but ourselves . . . He was
  trying to show his master that the word 'pain' was without meaning,
  and that it started to mean something only when it recalled to our
  memory a sensation that we had already experienced.[10]

After complicating the question further by bringing in the example of
the pains of childbirth – sensations a man could never feel – Jacques
and his master leave the problem hanging, unresolved. Jacques asserts
that he cannot possibly sympathize with the suffering of childbirth
since, being a man, he cannot possibly have that experience; whereas
the master could now endorse Jacques's statement about knee injuries
since he had just had an analogous experience. Jacques then returns to
the story of his loves.

As Jean Starobinski has noted in a splendid article on Diderot and
the art of demonstration, Diderot raises here the formidable problem
of sympathy and identification which Mandeville, Addison, Rousseau,
Condillac, and others had treated in a more abstract line of inquiry.
The problem is that of the other's pain. If indeed we are generally
capable of sympathy, Starobinski writes (and Jacques has raised his
doubts on the matter), is it a spontaneous phenomenon or does it occur
through a self-reflexive process of imagining one's own past suffering
through the present ills of others?[11] In *De l'art de raisonner*, written for
the instruction of the Prince of Parma, Condillac argued that, since
other forms of evidence are lacking in this instance, one must resort to
analogy in order to acknowledge the sensibility of others: "you observe
that I have organs like yours; and that I react as you do to the influence
of objects on my senses. You conclude from this that, having sensations

yourself, I also have them."[12] Adam Smith likewise made sympathy an indirect phenomenon through imagination since, as he pointed out, "we have no immediate experience of what other men feel."[13] Because of this epistemological gap, the experience of sympathy was seen as anchoring the belief that individuals were connected, by virtue of their basic humanity, to others. For many writers, sympathy – the basis of our "commerce" with others, as social interaction was referred to in the eighteenth century – was the foundation of society and of the economic exchange that led to the prosperity of nations.[14] Sympathy was thus a cornerstone of Enlightenment thinking.

The word "identification," Pierre Force has suggested, first appeared in French in Rousseau's *Discours sur l'origine et les fondements de l'inégalité parmi les hommes*.[15] Writing of *la pitié*, Rousseau noted: "In fact, commiseration will be all the more energetic as the witnessing animal identifies itself more intimately with the suffering animal. Now it is evident that this identification must have been infinitely closer in the state of nature than in the state of reasoning."[16] For Rousseau, Force remarks, "the intensity of our pity is determined by the degree of our identification with the sufferer. Thus if pity is the foundation of morality, identification is the foundation of pity."[17] Rousseau altered earlier moral philosophy in several ways. Whereas competing views made sympathy mechanical (Shaftesbury and Hutcheson), Rousseau derived sympathy from the imagination and saw it as spontaneous rather than reflective, contra La Rochefoucauld. Helvétius, like La Rochefoucauld in this respect, made self-love primary, and saw identification as a secondary impulse, arguing that "one never values in another but one's own image and likeness."[18] Unlike La Rochefoucauld or Helvétius, Rousseau placed identification first. Force argues that Adam Smith, after having reviewed Rousseau's *Discours*, borrowed from it when he published his *Theory of Moral Sentiments* three years later.[19] He concludes that Smith means exactly the same thing when he says "sympathy" as Rousseau when he refers to "identification": that is, an "imaginary change of situation."[20]

Though Rousseau saw only perversion in the projected selves created for the benefit of others, as Elena Russo has noted, Reid, Hume, and Smith saw the self as "a social and relational entity that emerges to consciousness through a process of identification with the other where the imagination plays an essential part."[21] Some even saw sympathy as organic in nature. Referring to the Chevalier de Jaucourt's article on sympathy in the *Encyclopédie*, Anne C. Vila has remarked that "Jaucourt's descriptive language not only makes moral sympathy analogous to organic sympathy, but actually suggests that the former is little more than a higher-level expression of the primordial mechanism by which all vital entities communicate."[22] Instead of seeing human sociability as a dichotomous interplay of selfish and altruistic motives, in their accounts of sympathy eighteenth century writers considered the complexity of the presence of others and of our interactions with others "in enabling persons to be persons," as Frances Ferguson has termed it.[23] Sympathy was a phenomenon that not only potentially connected all beings, but was basic to the individual subject. In other words, the eighteenth century clearly recognized that identification with others was essential to one's sense of self.

Diderot's dramatic theories furnish a framework through which we can begin to understand the mechanism of sympathy in the theater. Though the repertory of the Opéra-Comique did not generally include plays as sober as *Le Père de famille*, as Karin Pendle has noted, the *sensibilité* that pervades Diderot's dramaturgy was nonetheless a substantial component of the repertory at the Opéra-Comique beyond the mid-century.[24] Diderot's theories present new ways of understanding the relationship between the stage and the audience which extend far beyond his own meager dramatic production and have significant bearing upon the history of the lyric theater. It is surely not mere coincidence that the metaphor Diderot uses for touching the spectator in *De la poésie dramatique* is a musical one: "poet, are you sensitive [*sensible*] and discerning? strike this chord [referring to honesty] and you will hear it resonate or quiver in every soul."[25] The *Entretiens sur le fils naturel* (1757) launched the idea of creating a "serious genre," neither comedy nor tragedy, which Diderot tested in *Le Fils naturel*.[26] In *De la poésie dramatique* (1758), Diderot suggested the possibility of inventing a form of drama that would be "in between the serious genre of

Le Fils naturel and comedy."[27] One of the most significant priorities of his dramatic theory was to bridge the gap between self and other by making identification a more effective aspect of the theatrical experience. In the *Entretiens sur le fils naturel*, Dorval tells his interlocutor of an encounter with a village woman who was mourning her husband whom she had unknowingly sent off to his death. Great passions like this one, Dorval remarks, are ideal for the theater: "what the artist must find is that which no one could hear without immediately recognizing it in oneself."[28] The gap between the experience of self and other, which later became the subject of the unresolved discussion between Jacques and his master in *Jacques le fataliste*, disappears in Diderot's vision for theater where the passions of characters represented on stage are immediately recognized by the spectators within themselves: "it is by going to the theater that men will escape the wicked men whose company they keep; it is there that they will find those with whom they would wish to live; it is there that they will see the human race as it is and will reconcile themselves with it."[29] Identification was reinforced, not through the traditional focus on exemplary types (as they are foregrounded in the titles of Molière's plays, for example – *L'Avare, Le Misanthrope, Le Bourgeois gentilhomme*) but rather by staging situations through the use of tableaux and the representation of social conditions: "it is not, properly speaking, characters that one must place on the stage, but stations [*conditions*]."[30]

As David Marshall has shown, the immediacy that Diderot's model presupposes is mitigated by the fact that the characters are, and must be, absent for theater to have its effect.[31] This is the gap that constitutes spectatorship in the theater, and sympathy *as* spectatorship in eighteenth-century philosophical texts. In his *Theory of Moral Sentiments*, Adam Smith remarked that the passions of others elicit our sympathy only when perceived at a distance:

> We are disgusted with that clamorous grief, which, without any delicacy, calls upon our compassion with sighs and tears and importunate lamentations. But we reverence that reserved, that silent and majestic sorrow, which discovers itself only in the swelling of the eyes, in the quivering of the lips and cheeks, and in the distant, but affecting, coldness

of the whole behaviour. It imposes the like silence upon us. We regard it
with respectful attention, and watch with anxious concern over our
whole behaviour, lest by any impropriety we should disturb that
concerted tranquillity, which it requires so great an effort to support.[32]

When sorrow is consciously presented for our consumption, when
it "calls upon" us, we react with disgust. Respect and distance are
required to produce a sympathetic response. Likewise, in order to be
effective, Diderot argued in *De la poésie dramatique*, the spectator in the
theater must be excluded: "the spectators are but the unacknowledged
witnesses of the thing."[33]

Whatever the mechanism behind the effect of immediacy Dorval
describes, however, the theater undoubtedly can generate real feeling
in the spectator. Indeed, as Jay Caplan has argued, the absence of the
spectator actually constitutes the force of his or her presence. Noting
the specific effect of Diderot's theatrical tableaux, Caplan writes: "it
asks the beholder to be partial to the suffering of the represented characters, and thereby also to define himself as the missing part or fragment that the tableau has not really lost, at least ideally."[34] In Diderot's
theatrical writings aesthetic distance does not imply detachment, but
rather a certain form of intense involvement. The beholder takes the
place of the one who comes to console, to comfort. In order to sat-
isfy this particular pleasure, however, the pain of the other becomes
necessary. Reflecting on the function of distance at public executions
in the eighteenth century, via Burke's thoughts on the topic, David
Bromwich notes: "Far from being rendered certain of our detachment
by a sense of aesthetic distance or immunity, we are brought close to
the source of that self-division that makes us by no means choose to
do what we are eager enough to see once it is done."[35] In art and in
some cases in life (as in Burke's public execution), we venture close
to pain because this involvement allows us to imagine ourselves as
redressing injustice or as consoling a sufferer, and simply because we
are involuntarily curious.

If the act of recognizing another's passion in oneself summarizes the
identificatory purpose of theater for Diderot, it is equally important
to recognize that desire also contributes to that theatrical aesthetic.

Caplan notes that "the sensuous moralism of a Diderot or a Greuze, for example, relies upon the ironic juxtaposition of an ethical prohibition and its transgression. By excluding grieving widows, loving mothers, and virgins as objects of desire, moral law invites its own transgression. In fact, the pathos that sets these prohibited objects apart signals their desirability."[36] To show a woman in tears and thereby to force the spectator to "break down in tears," as he noted in *De la poésie dramatique*, represented for Diderot the apogee of theatrical success.[37] The tearful woman is simultaneously an object of desire and an object of sympathy. As an object of male desire, she invites a certain kind of interest; as an object of sympathy, she is an occasion to verify what Enlightenment writers described as our natural tendency towards good actions.

The interrelated questions of identification and of desire came to be articulated in more explicit terms, and ones perhaps more familiar to us today, by Freud. Freud, it should be recalled, saw his work as an effort to wrestle them from unregulated, unscientific discourses and therapeutic practices involving sympathy (*Einfühlungs*), hypnosis, trance, and suggestion.[38] "Identification," he wrote in *Group Psychology and the Analysis of the Ego*, is "the earliest expression of an emotional tie with another person."[39] In Freud's view, the Oedipal scenario produces the model for appropriate kinship relations, directing identification towards the same sex and guiding desire across the sexual divide towards members of the opposite sex: "it is easy to state in a formula the distinction between an identification with the father and the choice of the father as an object. In the first case one's father is what one would like to *be*, and in the second he is what one would like to *have*."[40] For Freud, these relations are maintained and regulated by a threat, which Jacques Lacan designates as the Name of the Father. In the Freudian model and its Lacanian elaborations, therefore, sexuality is structured by desires and fears concerning lost objects which take the form of mutually exclusive fantasies of having and being. Diana Fuss has remarked, in part as a critique of the pathologizing of homosexuality by the Freudian tradition, that "Freud's entire theory of subjectivity rests on this rather precarious but pervasive distinction between object-choice and emotional tie."[41] Similarly, Judith Butler has argued that the opposition between desire and identification is at best problematic.

"To identify," she writes, "is not to oppose desire. Identification is a phantasmatic trajectory and resolution of desire; an assumption of place; a territorializing of an object which enables identity through the temporary resolution of desire, but which remains desire, if only in its repudiated form."[42] Butler and Fuss assert that identification and desire are inseparable and that the former is the mechanism through which identity develops out of a relation with others. This inseparability indicates the crucial place that identification has within social relations. As Fuss argues, "identification is the point where the psychical/social distinction becomes impossibly confused and finally untenable."[43] The fact that every identity is based upon an identification, itself embedded in desire, changes our sense of the social bond and our sense of self. Mikkel Borch-Jacobsen has argued that Freud's assertion of a social / emotional tie (*Gefühlsbindung*) depends on the persistence of a hypnotic, mimetic relation to others – a "rapport *sans* rapport" – which leads to the consideration of an original "alteration" by others before the Oedipal triangle, before the ego.[44] Borch-Jacobsen concludes: "to affirm that 'the earliest emotional tie with another person' is identification is, in effect, to assert that affect as such is identificatory, mimetic, and that there is no 'proper' affect except on the condition of a prior 'affection' of the ego by another."[45]

Though psychoanalysis emerged out of a repudiation of sympathy as it had previously been conceived, Freud's notions of identification and desire, as they have been read by recent critics such as Fuss, Butler, and Borch-Jacobsen, nonetheless exhibit a strong affiliation to those Diderot described beginning in the 1750s as part and parcel of the experience of spectatorship. In making these fleeting connections between the eighteenth-century history of sympathy and twentieth-century psychoanalysis, my intention is to highlight the question of our essential engagement with others, which Borch-Jacobsen calls a mimetic relation to others. In the eighteenth century, it was the recognition of this engagement with others that drove the fascination with sympathy and related issues that we see both onstage and in philosophical reflections on human identity and conduct. I have argued above that eighteenth-century philosophical discussions of sympathy resituated identity and feeling as relational, not essential, through their description of the intertwined urges of desire and identification. I have also established that in eighteenth-century dramatic and philosophical theories sympathy was described as inherently theatrical. Having situated sympathy as a function of identity as both relational and theatrical, I would like to turn now to the ways in which *opéra comique* was touched and shaped by what must be recognized as a truly modern preoccupation with sympathy. Because the *Entretiens sur le fils naturel* conclude with a brief sketch for an *opéra comique* which Dorval proposes to his interlocutor, Diderot leaves an invitation to consider the ways in which the lyric theater might correspond to the dramatic ideals that his theories propose. He presents opera as both the best and the worst of theater: at its best, it is sublime, better even than spoken tragedy, the queen of dramatic arts; at its worst, it's more ludicrous than the lowest farce.[46] By bringing opera back into "the real world," as opposed to the "enchanted regions" of the Académie Royale de Musique, Diderot suggests that new talent in a new context could transform the operatic practices inaugurated by Quinault and Lully: "a great composer and a great lyric poet would repair all the damage."[47] Indeed, in *Le Neveu de Rameau*, which Diderot may have begun in the early 1760s, nearly all the references that "Lui" makes to operatic airs are taken from the repertory of the Opéra-Comique.[48]

Two successful eighteenth-century stage works will serve as convenient, but in no way absolute, beginning and end points for the discussion at hand: the first, *Le Devin du village* (1752), an *intermède* by Jean-Jacques Rousseau; the second, Étienne Nicolas Méhul's and François-Benoît Hoffman's *Stratonice* (1792). *Le Devin du village*, performed on October 18, 1752 at Fontainebleau and on March 1, 1753 at the Paris Opéra, though not strictly speaking an *opéra comique*, was later identified by many eighteenth-century commentators as a major impetus for the development of the genre. The plot of *Le Devin* is simple: through his "powers" – actually, his common sense and understanding of human relationships – a village seer reunites a troubled couple (Colin and Colette) who genuinely love each other despite the wayward designs of a lady of the local *petite noblesse* who has taken an interest in Colin.[49] In *Stratonice*, first performed on May 3, 1792 at the Comédie-Italienne, the kind doctor Erasistrate detects a mutual love hidden beneath the anguish of Antiochus and Stratonice, who is betrothed to Séleucus, Antiochus's father and king of Syria. By compelling him to assume the virtues of sacrifice, Erasistrate convinces Séleucus to renounce his marriage and preside over the union of his son and Stratonice. *Le Devin* and *Stratonice* exhibit very obvious differences. The former takes an image of ordinary country life as its setting; the latter, on the contrary, involves the affairs of kings and princes and is set in the ancient world. *Le Devin* is sung throughout whereas *Stratonice* contains spoken dialogue as well as accompanied recitatives and *ariettes*. Nevertheless, some striking similarities connect the two works. A form of specialized and curative knowledge (whether magic or medicine) is present as a dominant trope and serves a similar purpose in each work. In *Le Devin*, the soothsayer, whose business ordinarily involves solving problems and curing ailments through the powers of divination, is able to settle a young couple's predicament simply by reading into their hearts. In *Stratonice*, the doctor engages in a systematic medical diagnosis of Antiochus's affliction. In the end, however, rather than invoke any specialized, medical knowledge, like the village soothsayer he makes use of his understanding of "human nature" to cure the ills of a broken family. In both cases, a certain form of opera serves as the medium for these romantic and familial reconciliations. Like the soothsayer, the doctor acts as a figure of analytic distance, rather than engaging in the drama himself as an impassioned participant: both characters remain outside the emotional fray. Each provides a necessary frame for the situation which invites our interest, pity, sympathy, and identification. Paradoxically, as characters on the margins of the passions that drive the stories, abstracted from the emotional turmoil, they provide the spectator with an entry into the drama.

Each of these works exhibits several key elements – thematic and structural – that are central to my approach to *opéra comique*. Each focuses on passion, sacrifice, and reconciliation – both within the self and with others. Each makes sympathy the key to the resolution of the problem and thereby invites the interest and sympathy of the spectator. In Rousseau, Colin must make the connection between Colette's feigned lack of interest in him, staged by the Devin in order to bring Colin back, and his own distraction; and, in Méhul's *opéra comique*, Séleucus must place himself in his son's position before he is able to make his sacrifice. Finally, each work brings about this realization through figures of distance whose arcane knowledge (magic and medicine) turns out to be, simply, a sound understanding of human feeling. In a sense, the lesson of *opéra comique* is akin to Dorothy's realization in the film version of *The Wizard of Oz* that she never really lost what she was looking for in the first place. *Opéra comique* functions through an identification that presents itself as a return to the self, and through the realization and reinforcement of self that comes from this identification.

Because only scant attention has been given to *opéra comique* by commentators, in comparison with other forms of opera, some general background is in order before we continue. The *opéras comiques* of the second half of the eighteenth century have a distinctly hybrid genealogy. Though some scholars point to distant medieval origins in Adam de La Halle or to the *comédie-ballet* created under Louis XIV by Molière and Lully, *opéra comique* was for all intents and purposes a creation of the eighteenth century.[50] In 1714, the Paris fair theaters at the Foire St Germain and the Foire St Laurent made a series of agreements with the Opéra which allowed them to present certain kinds of spectacles (plays with music and dance) and to call themselves the Opéra-Comique. The official, state-sponsored institutions – the Comédie-Française and the Académie Royale de Musique – managed to have various restrictions imposed on the fair theaters which affected the number and kind of instrumentalists, singers, and dancers employed by the fair theaters, and determined the precise ways in which song and text could be used. Because of heavy competition (*Le Mercure galant* reported that the Comédie-Française and the Opéra were deserted at the opening of the Opéra-Comique at the Foire St Laurent on July 25, 1715), the Comédie-Française prevented the fair theaters from exploiting spectacles other than marionette shows and acrobatics from 1718 to 1724.[51] Adding to the competition in 1716, the Duc d'Orléans recalled to Paris a troupe of Italian actors who became known as the Comédie-Italienne, giving Italian plays and, more frequently over the years, works by French playwrights. Strife with the Comédie-Française was ongoing and led to closure of the fair theaters from 1745 to 1752. However, as Michel Noiray has pointed out, the often-told story of the many skirmishes and open wars between the official theaters and the Opéra-Comique and the numerous constraints placed on the latter have made us forget the degree to which these two poles of the Parisian theater scene depended on each other during the course of the eighteenth century: "without the serious genres, the creators of vaudevilles would have been deprived of a vital source of inspiration; without parody, tragedy, lyric tragedy, and *opéra-ballet* would not have benefited from the crucial soundboard of the comic theaters, where the opera public went with the same assiduity as the lower classes."[52]

In the first half of the eighteenth century, *opéras comiques* were most often *en vaudevilles*, a term that refers to the practice of mixing spoken dialogue with popular tunes sung to new words. These works – parodies of *tragédies en musique* and other comic works of various stripes – functioned in part through audience participation, the incipit launching the spectators into a well-known refrain, known as a *timbre*, to which the new words would be sung. As Bruce Alan Brown has noted, the public needed only the *timbre* in order to bring back the tune.[53] Examples of *opéras comiques* from this period can be found in printed sources deriving from Alain René Le Sage's repertory and in early works by Charles Simon Favart.[54] Because there was no need in the eighteenth century to print the tunes, however, these works present many obstacles for researchers and have generally not benefited from modern productions.

Though the dispute opposing Italian and French opera of the early 1750s, known as the Querelle des bouffons, had relatively little impact in the end on the development of the *tragédie en musique*, it can be identified as an impetus for the creation of the new *comédie mêlée d'ariettes* in which dialogues were interspersed with newly-composed *ariettes* and ensembles.[55] Writing in 1765, Grimm characterizes the new genre thus: "the genre of *opéra comique*, which has been established in France for a few years, in which the airs are sung and the scenes are declaimed."[56] The Bambini troupe sojourned in Paris from 1752 to 1754 to perform *opera buffa* and intermezzos, among which was Pergolesi's *La Serva padrona*, the work that launched the Querelle des bouffons. In the heat of the scandal, Antoine Dauvergne and Jean Joseph Vadé emulated Italian models in *Les Troqueurs* (1753), which was seen retrospectively as a watershed in the development of *opéra comique*. Jean Marie Bernard Clément and Joseph de Laporte wrote in their *Anecdotes dramatiques* that "it is the first musical work of this genre to be created and performed in France. A few years before, a troupe of Italian *Bouffons* were allowed to perform, on the stage of the *Opéra*, intermezzos by Pergolesi and other Italian composers. It is to these two different periods that one must trace the taste of one part of the Nation for these new spectacles."[57] However, perhaps because *Les Troqueurs* included recitative and airs but no spoken dialogue or *vaudevilles*, opinions differed. Another commentator claimed that *Le Maréchal ferrant* by Antoine-François Quétant and François-André Danican Philidor, given in 1761 at the Foire St Laurent and mixing *ariettes* with *vaudevilles*, represented the beginnings of the new *opéra comique*.[58] For Nougaret, *Les Troqueurs* was the first "Drame-Bouffon," though Michel-Jean Sedaine's *Blaise le savetier*, with music by Philidor, was the first work in the "new genre" of *opéra comique*.[59] In any event, by the mid-1750s, the *opéras comiques en vaudevilles* were being pushed aside by the new *comédies* which integrated borrowed music, such as songs based on popular *timbres*, with newly composed music in a style often resembling that of popular songs, the whole framed by spoken dialogue. The competition between the older and newer forms of *opéra comique* was amusingly staged in *Le Procès des ariettes et des vaudevilles* (1760) by Charles-Simon Favart and Louis Anseaume. By the 1760s, nearly all *comédies mêlées d'ariettes* could boast newly composed music and the genre took off in popularity.[60] By 1769, Bricaire de la Dixmérie could claim that "the plays with *ariettes* have caused the plays with *vaudevilles* to be forgotten."[61]

The status of the Opéra-Comique was regularized in 1762 when it was merged with the Comédie-Italienne and moved into the Hôtel de Bourgogne.[62] With the fusion of the two troupes, as Karin Pendle has noted, "the triumph of the plays with *ariettes* over the plays with *vaudevilles* was reinforced."[63] By this time, the *vaudevilles* had all but disappeared and were often retained only in the concluding sections of plays. Because the phrase *mêlées d'ariettes* could not adequately characterize many of these works, which increasingly tended toward strong sentiment and the *larmoyant*, or tear-jerkers, alternative terms such as *mêlée de musique* or *mise en musique* were also used.[64] The Opéra-Comique, now annexed to a state-sponsored theater, had come of age and was attracting spectators from the other theaters in droves:

> It is true that the doormen of the Opéra Comique are being suffocated, and that the *Blaise le savetiers*, the *Sancho-Panças*, the *la Brides*, the *Mère Bobis*, and so many other similar characters [from *opéras comiques*] have caused the *Orosmanes*, the *Rhadamistes*, the *Alcestes*, the *Phèdres* and the *Armides*, etc. [tragic characters], to be entirely forgotten ... In short, the majority of the public has deserted Molière's theater in order to run to that of Pantalon. *Zaïre* no longer brings tears to the eyes, except to Russian eyes, and it is only the English who come to admire the beauties of *Le Misanthrope*.[65]

Three years later, in 1769, Grimm confirmed Bricaire's observations and attributed this success in part to the joining of the Comédie-Italienne and the Opéra-Comique:

> [The Comédie-Italienne] has only made a solid living for itself since the new genre of *opéra comique* was joined with it. Since this time, the Théâtre-Italien has constantly outdone the other theaters of Paris. And since there is nothing more punishable than to please the public the most, it is obliged to pay the Académie Royale de Musique an annual fine of thirty-five thousand *livres* in order to have the permission to amuse us. Despite this burden and a great many others, it is said that the actors' share at this theater is as much as twelve or fifteen thousand *livres* per year.[66]

The impact of the Opéra-Comique was such that the king, in the letters patent of the Comédie-Italienne of March 31, 1781, suggested that the development of new operas on the stage of the Opéra-Comique had led to the complete transformation of the by-now venerable Opéra:

French music, which was once the object of the indifference or the scorn
of foreigners, has today spread throughout Europe, since *Opéra-bouffons*
are performed in all the northern courts, and even in Italy ... it is works
of this genre that have formed French taste ... and which, finally,
prepared the transformation [*révolution*] that has occurred on the very
stage of our Académie de Musique, where masterpieces are applauded
today whose merit would have been neither understood nor enjoyed if
they had been performed twenty-five years earlier.[67]

Louis XVI claimed that the flowering of *opéra comique*, which had
previously occupied only the passing interest of "slumming" nobles
in the fair theaters, led to the internationalization of French music.
Ironically, just as the fair theaters had operated in competition with the
official theaters in the first half of the century, as the Opéra-Comique
established itself as a primary attraction, new theaters emerged on
the boulevards from about 1759 offering alternative fare – parodies,
pantomimes, acrobatics, farces – not unlike that of the first fair theaters
early in the century.

A relatively neglected subcategory of opera, *opéra comique* has often
been maligned by musicologists and literary scholars alike as ridiculous, superficial, and unworthy of serious consideration. Those who
have ventured into this territory have tended to privilege the phenomenon of the fair theaters from the early years of the eighteenth
century over later developments because of the contestatory associations of these early productions. Robert M. Isherwood has explored
the admittedly fascinating history of the ways in which the fair theaters
circumvented the restrictions placed on them by the official theaters.
Because of its focus on fair and street culture, however, Isherwood's
work considers only the early history of the Opéra-Comique before
the Comédie-Italienne co-opted the Opéra-Comique, in his terms,
"by taking it over." He focuses exclusively on the counter-cultural aspects of the fair theaters, their "struggle," their attempts "to combat"
the privileged theaters, and the comic weapons "in their arsenal."[68]
Similarly, Maurice Barthélemy praises the fair theaters and the pre-
Favart *opéra comique* for its "strange freedom" and "disdain for all
decorum," its "gaiety" and "insolence."[69] His valorization of the fair

theaters is underscored by his abhorrence of the later, sentimental *comédies:* "this display of artifice, this simple-minded sentimentality would take *opéra comique* on to glory . . . one must realize that the public of the past did not have any better taste than today's."[70] For commentators such as Barthélemy, once *opéra comique* loses its counter-cultural edge by finding success and becoming established, when it turns toward the bad taste of sentimental, bourgeois themes, it is no longer worthy of scholarly attention.

The transformation of *opéra comique* around the mid-century also raised the hackles of some eighteenth-century commentators, but for very different reasons. As Couvreur and Vendrix have shown, many regretted the fact that *opéra comique* had adopted spoken dialogue and deplored the sense that, in so doing, it had pretensions to high drama.[71] For these critics, by adopting serious subjects and attitudes, *opéra comique* was taking on airs and overstepping its prescribed bounds. L.-H. Dancourt, for example, complained that the genre's exaggerated representation of ordinary characters revealed its misplaced ambitions for an aristocratic pedigree: "people swoon, they go into raptures upon hearing a little country girl sing, [or] a peasant, a soldier, with all the tones and accents that good sense once reserved for Armide, for Castor and Pollux."[72] Others simply refused to discuss *opéra comique* because it was understood that, of the lyric genres, only the noble *tragédie en musique* was worthy of lengthy commentary. In comparison to its high-brow cousin, *opéra comique* received meager attention. Even Marmontel, a top-billed and prolific librettist of *opéras comiques,* gave only minimal attention to the genre in his theoretical works, preferring to support his reflections on the poetics of lyric theater with standard references to the operatic patrimony, which in the mid-eighteenth century consisted of the works of Quinault and Lully.[73]

Still others objected to the new *opéra comique* because they found the mixture of speech and song that defined the genre untenable. Diderot was favorable to the use of simple declamation in *opéra comique*; Grimm, however, condemned this mixture, calling it "barbarous," and preferred "an intermediate declamation between song and ordinary discourse, adapted to the uneven pace of the stage, and from which the transition to the singing of the air would not be shocking: this is what is called recitative."[74] For all his complaints about the new genre, however, Grimm did not favor the earlier form of *opéra comique*, which he found vulgar: "it is true that the dreadful genre of old *opéra comique*, which consists of vaudevilles and short airs, never fails to have an effect on me. I leave worn down, harassed, as if from a fit of fever."[75] Charles Collé's comments about the *comédie à ariettes* are perhaps the strongest:

> Some day our descendants will find us truly stupid for having applauded so extravagantly at this hybrid genre, which is nothing but a monstrous assortment of farce and opera, a genre that eliminates all theatrical illusion and which I find equally opposed to reason, to the truth and perfection of nature [*à la vraie et belle nature*], and to the original institution of theater and of true dramatic poetry – it is the *sodomy* of all this.[76]

Opéra comique, for Collé, was a sin against nature – monstrous, perverted theater.

Though they recognized the awkwardness of the mixture of speech and song, many commentators considered that composers and librettists needed time to develop its possibilities and the public time to grow accustomed to it. If Collé imagined the attitudes of future generations, Bricaire de la Dixmérie referred to the strangeness of *tragédie en musique* to the spectators of the 1670s and 1680s in order to place the jarring novelty of *opéra comique* into perspective:

> It has been claimed that this mixture of songs and spoken dialogue is not natural and creates a shocking contrast. This may be true to some extent, but these reasons cannot argue with pleasure. This genre seduces even those who rise up against it . . . Our forefathers must not have been any less surprised to see Cadmus, Hercules, and Roland speak while singing for the first time. Let us proscribe nothing that can please us.[77]

Bricaire recalled the strangeness of the by-then familiar genre of the *tragédie en musique* in order to remind his readers that theatrical conventions are no less conventional because they happen to have been accepted. Bricaire suggested, as Pierre Corneille had before him, that pleasure is the ultimate criterion of theatrical representations; and that, though it may now be startling to spectators, *opéra comique* undeniably has its pleasures.

One of the strengths of the *opéra comique* – making it the spectacle which, "however incoherent, however bizarre it is, pleases perhaps more widely than all the others and is less likely to cause boredom" – was its mutability.[78] Chabanon remarked that the *opéra comique* distinguished itself from other forms because of the alternation of speech and song that some critics had found distasteful:

> It is distinguished by the greatest of advantages, variety – a much more powerful appeal than strict verisimilitude. It unites all the advantages of song and speech: it occupies the mind and allows it to absorb what is spoken, imposing only the light duty of judging the appropriateness of the songs. In short, through the moments of respite that it provides the ear, it renews one's taste and instinct for music.[79]

Proposing like Diderot the dismantling of the traditional genres of comedy and tragedy, Chabanon also praises the effortlessness with which *opéra comique* passes from sadness to gaiety: "in *opéra comique* there is no need to modulate in order to move from a sad situation to a joyful one."[80] If *opéra comique* was problematic for its critics because one could not tell what it truly was, this openness was seen by others as part of its success. Reviewing *Le Déserteur* by Sedaine and Pierre-Alexandre Monsigny, Grimm wondered about the coordination of the complex mixture of emotions drawn from the spectator by *opéra comique*: "an important question . . . is to know at what point good taste can allow and authorize this mixture of tragic and comic, this continual passage from pathos to the ridiculous and from the ridiculous to pathos." A page later, however, after imagining the dramatic potential of a sequence of situations for the operatic stage, Grimm concluded that "it is therefore certain that one can laugh and cry at the same time," since that is precisely what is demanded by the complexity of human situations.[81] Barnabé Farmian de Rozoi argued that *opéra comique* was neither comedy nor tragedy, and referred to it as "this new, intermediate genre."[82] For Nougaret, "it is difficult to determine the true genre of the new spectacle."[83] Garcin identified so many different sub-types of *opéra comique* that he eventually gave up on identifying it as belonging to or embodying a single genre. In the end, he adopts the omnibus term "French music," revealing the degree to which *opéra comique* defied generic categorization and the degree to which it had taken the place of other forms of music as the premier, international expression of French culture: "I call French Music the new genre that has emerged in the past few years."[84] Contant d'Orville went so far as to characterize *opéra comique* as a total art form, involving the entire range of situations and emotions:

> At the birth of the lyrico-comic genre, the styles of pastorale and farce were the only ones associated with this kind of drama. Now there is nothing to which it cannot aspire: scenes of pathos, striking situations, horrible tableaux, it is open to everything, it embraces everything. This genre, which can be contained in no single genre, unites all of them – fair spectacle [*parade*], shepherd's play [*bergerie*], fairy tale, pastorale, comedy, tragedy.[85]

Many commentators, however, were in agreement that the Académie Royale de Musique was the proper place for supernatural subjects in opera, whereas the Opéra-Comique was the realm of the "human." In the article, "Opéra," of his *Eléments de littérature*, Marmontel wrote: "The character of this spectacle has varied so much recently that it would be difficult to define it, unless one were to distinguish two genres, one taking the supernatural world as its basis, the other reduced to simple nature."[86] This difference between the grand subjects of the Opéra and those of the Opéra-Comique, limited to "simple nature," is highly significant. The genre of the novel again surfaced as a model for opera in its representation of the everyday: "what [Samuel] Richardson was in his books, I would like a composer to be in the theater. When a woodcutter, dragging himself onto the stage like an exhausted man, arrives in order to confide his pains to me, to describe his work and the details of his domestic woes, and admits naively, taking a bottle from his bag, that he finds consolation in wine, I pay back his confidence with a real interest."[87] It was by staying within "the confines of ordinary society" that *opéra comique* sought to move the spectator: "we seek to press your heart, to move your soul, to endear it to us and sometimes to wring tears from it."[88]

One of the most intriguing discussions of the specificity of *opéra comique* and its effect on the spectator can be found in Jean Laurent de Béthisy's medico-musical pamphlet *Effets de l'air sur le corps humain* (1760). Béthisy began his text with an argument, like those discussed in the previous chapter, that relied on the naturalization of musical effects. He remarked that music should naturally be expected to affect us quite strongly, "through the considerable vibration [*ébranlement*] that it causes in our organs."[89] Italian music had several advantages in this respect over French music. By avoiding choruses, the Italians "never interrupt the melody and avoid the dissonance and the hulla-baloo of our French operas" (14). Their instrumental accompaniment is "admirable" because it doesn't distract from the voice or divide the attention of the spectator (14–15). The Italians had also rid their the-aters of machines, "a phenomenon of barbarous times" (16). However, according to Béthisy, Italian art had many drawbacks. Although opera was considered the premier musical art form in Italy, their operas were "distanced from the natural, disjointed, and of little interest to the Italians themselves: everything happens there in the ear" (10–11). Resurrecting the time-worn characterization of Italian music as super-ficial, sensual, and difficult, rather than heartfelt or natural – a charac-terization I explored earlier in relation to Marc-Antoine Charpentier's *Médée* – Béthisy remarked that the Italian aria was over-wrought and ultimately lost the listener in a surfeit of notes: "in their infinite vari-ations, soon one no longer recognizes anything. They make a kind of pedal point of each note; and in the scales that they make a point of running through at every moment, the most difficult and the most dubious sounds are always the most applauded. Shall I say it? – their song appears to be nothing but a debauchery of the throat" (12). The artificial qualities of vocal pyrotechnics, and the unnaturalness of the singers themselves ("their eunuchs, their unnatural falsetto"), were, perversely, highly praised values in Italian opera (13–14). Finally, Italian theaters were so large that the grand effect of the spectacle as a whole is lost (16).

Béthisy noted that French opera was still in its infancy: "we are still only at our dawn" (21). After the monotonous Lully, "Rameau woke us up with a start," opening up French music to "a new route" (22). Taking a detour into the question of the origin of languages, Béthisy argued that whereas most spectators only considered "singing [*le chant*] as a trifle [*une chanson*]" – a pleasurable diversion – in truth song maintained a vital connection to "the cry of nature," the first expressions of human feeling (25–26). Whereas words are only understood by the inhabitants of the areas in which a given language is spoken, sounds communicate through sensation and are therefore universal: "when we will have [identified] the sound of each passion, with their gradations and nuances, it will be easy to move them in whichever mode we choose, causing the appropriate vibration of the nerves. This is the true and righteous object that any composer must strive to attain in his work" (32–33). Relying on Rameau's *Démonstration du principe de l'harmonie* (1750), Béthisy argued that the effects of music on the listener derived from its natural connection to passion: "I am deeply persuaded that music could render us calm and virtuous, could inspire in us the honest and the beautiful" (34). Béthisy described the mechanics of these effects:

> Passionate feeling is communicable; it causes another who hears its accents to experience the same state . . . when a passion renders a sound, by forcing out sound waves [*globules* – his is a corpuscular theory of sound propagation], their configuration is communicated instantly from one person to another and, striking the cellular tissue of him who is within range of this sound, these waves constrain his nerves to take the same configuration and occasion the same sentiment: this is the mechanism and the effect of the communication of sounds. (48–50)

In justification of his claims, he cited at length the 1730 edition of Philippe Hecquet's *De la digestion et des maladies de l'estomac* (1712), which described the beneficial effect of the ordered regularity of music on the mind (62–71). The musical effects described by the ancients, as when "using music David calmed Saul's frenzy," derive from human pre-history and can be resurrected in opera (57): "it seems to me that our operas could contain a music in which all the passions would be communicated and would be assumed by us through the inherent vibration [*ébranlement*] that the voice of these same passions would produce in us" (36).

The three specific references that Béthisy made to composers or works are to "the monotonous Lully," Rameau (who, he said, gave the French a start and made them receptive to new musical forms), and *Blaise le savetier* (21, 22, 37). Béthisy claimed that the spectator of 1760 needed a sentimental re-education: "men have lost sight of the natural for so long that it is necessary to bring them back to feeling little by little, just as after certain illnesses one must teach people to think anew" (38). By arguing that Rameau had made the French public receptive to new music, and by citing *Blaise le savetier* in the concluding pages of the text as exemplary of the musical effects he had been discussing, Béthisy appears to suggest *opéra comique* as the vehicle for this re-education.[90] *Opéra comique* was the preeminent genre in late eighteenth-century France because it was centered on feeling, not on the spectacular but unnatural machine effects of the Académie Royale de Musique, which Béthisy criticized.

The importance of sentiment, and the preeminence of *opéra comique* in its depiction, were echoed by many commentators. Inquiring about the specificity of what he called "le drame lyrique," Rozoi reasserted the primacy of feeling: at the origin of humanity, "to feel was the first need, and to think the second."[91] It is important, Rozoi argued, to distinguish between *opera buffa* and *opéra comique*, which, erroneously, were often considered interchangeable. Many commentators wrongly assumed that *opéra comique* was concerned merely with entertainment and pleasure, as *opera buffa* in fact was, in Rozoi's estimation: "this genre [*opéra comique*] had long been regarded as entirely dependent on a pretty *ariette*."[92] Whereas *opera buffa* engages only "wit" [*l'esprit*] and "gaiety," *opéra comique* is focused on intense feeling.[93] As a result, Rozoi claimed, "it is evident that the purely farcical [*bouffon*] genre is easily and quickly exhausted."[94] Mere laughter is beneath serious interest: "compare this equivocal genre in which sentiment and taste can have no part . . . to passages such as those that the likes of Grétry and Monsigny have given us."[95] Chabanon agreed, remarking that "song moves us through its natural properties; it can be joined with laughter only through the effort of imitation." Music communicates directly with the soul, whereas pure comedy only touches the mind. It is for this reason, Chabanon argued, that *opéra comique* moved toward serious subjects: "consider the characteristics of the art of sounds, and you will see that its need for sympathetic subjects is self-evident. The Opéra-Comique had scarcely been established when the sentimental genre [*le genre pathétique*] immediately joined forces with it."[96] Indeed, as one commentator remarked, serious subjects can be very well suited to the stage of the Opéra-Comique: "you call the stage on which you see tragedy, *la Comédie*, and no one finds this wrong. One can therefore place very serious plays that are full of pathos on the stage of the Opéra-Comique."[97] For Rozoi, the centrality of feeling to *opéra comique* made it preferable even to the grand spectacle of *tragédie en musique*:

> A man, an enthusiastic friend of the arts, cries out: "True genius is being lost; great opera demands those beautiful subjects which belong to it! . . . " Ah! do you believe, injust man, that all the advantages of the genre created by Quinault are not as dear to us as they are to you? Well then, let us cede for an instant to your wishes; let us place on this stage [the Opéra] the proud *Arsène*, the good *Fée*, and the tender *Zémire* [*opéra comique* characters]. The celebrations, the pomp, the visual magic will perhaps be magnificent; but what about the sentimental scenes, the details of love, fear, pride, arrogance; the gradations of hate or jealousy; the multitude of incidents, which add to the interest, to the acting, to the perfection of all the aspects of the art – what will become of these resources that are so valuable to musical genius?[98]

Opera buffa was therefore identified as the realm of superficial laughter, *tragédie en musique* that of pomp and magnificent stage effects, and *opéra comique* that of feeling.

As Couvreur and Vendrix have suggested, because of its focus on sentiment and feeling, identification was a central mechanism of spectatorship at the Opéra-Comique, "whereas classical [seventeenth-century] comedy and tragedy based their aesthetic on the notions of verisimilitude and decorum which did not presuppose the identification of the spectator with the characters."[99] For Marmontel, the use of pathos encouraged sympathy and identification, and this particular form of spectatorship led to a heightened awareness of self and of the relationship between oneself and others: "where is the usefulness of pathos? In the exercise of sensibility, which I regard as a great benefit, and in the effect of example: for, in ceasing to fear for the fictive character whom I have just seen in danger, I do not stop fearing for myself."[100] Marmontel argued that "sentimental [*attendrissant*] comedy" was perhaps even more morally useful than tragedy, "seeing that it concerns us more directly, and therefore the examples that it offers touch us more markedly."[101] The focus on sympathy and identification was all the more effective in *opéra comique*, commentators remarked, because of the genre's attention to the supposed universal appeal of *petits sujets*, or minor subjects:

> Thus, at least in subjects relating to passion, the morality of the example is common and the interest universal . . . It is not only for kings that the clemency of Augustus is a model to follow; and when Alcides [Hercules], the most valiant of men, descends from the heavens to encourage his friend Philoctetes to pardon the Atridae for the most conspicuous ingratitude, and the cruelest abandonment, it is no less an example for the people than an example for heroes. Morality is for all states. The duty of the small and the duty of the great are like two concentric circles, which have the same spokes.[102]

While in his *Poétique Françoise*, Marmontel claimed that both tragedy and sentimental comedy had a moral dimension for ordinary spectators, in the article, "Action," from his *Eléments de littérature*, Marmontel suggested that "low" subjects made the focus on the humanity of its characters even more moving than tragedy: "one expects a hero to accomplish great things, and one is not surprised by it. But when sublime sentiments come from an ordinary soul, nature (who alone is responsible for them) is all the more satisfied; and humanity delights in these examples which honor it."[103] True pathos results not from great interests of state, in and of themselves, but rather from the representation of internal, domestic conflicts and tensions that result from the intersection of the domestic and the outside worlds. Marmontel continued:

> The moment of highest pathos in the Portuguese conspiracy is not the one where all the people, armed in an instant, rise up and break their chains, but the one in which an obscure woman appears suddenly with her two sons, in the middle of the band of the conspirators, draws two daggers from underneath her dress, gives them to her two children, and says to them: "Only bring these back to me stained with Spanish blood."[104]

Marmontel was exuberant about the possibilities of such a scene, if only poets were willing to take full advantage of them. Like Diderot, Marmontel had uncovered the central mechanism of the new *opéra comique*: "to believe that we need titles to move and to touch us is to insult the human heart and to fail to understand nature. The sacred names of friend, father, lover, spouse, son, mother, and, above all, man – these are the qualities of pathos."[105] Marmontel recognized that representations of the domestic should be the focus of a new kind of theater because, as Samuel Weber has argued, "'the family' serves as the chief conduit between the singular and the general in human affairs."[106] *Opéra comique* would focus on this aspect of theater and thrive because of it – witness the enormous popularity of Marmontel's and André-Ernest-Modeste Grétry's *Lucile* (1769) and that of its emblematic quartet, "Où peut-on être mieux qu'au sein de sa famille?"

Mary Hunter has remarked on the various performative strategies that *opera buffa* adopts in its rhetoric of pleasure, rejecting the claim that these are mere side-effects of opera.[107] Hunter examines one category of performance – sentimental utterances – which are usually sung by heroines and do not address the audience, yet cannot exist without the "'eavesdropping' presence of the auditorium audience." This type of music is performative, Hunter remarks, because it "draws attention to its own beauty, in part by being divorced from the stage action, in part by emphasizing the singing (rather than the declamatory) qualities of the voice, and in part by displaying an unusually sensuous surface in the accompaniment." Hunter calls these moments "performances of absorption" and argues that "they *demand* sympathy and identification by enacting a pretty or pitiable scene, and by virtue of the music's beauty."[108] Hunter also explores the gender issues inherent in such representations:

> But just as the power of the "performance of absorption" paradoxically depends both on the presence of an audience and on the illusion that it is not there, the permissibility of that power depends on its exercise in the service of a demonstration of powerlessness; sentimental heroines make their strongest appeals to the audience when they have least control of the stage action . . . the sentimental heroine exercises a "performative power" out of proportion to her capacity to affect the action of the drama. That power, however, is confined to situations where she is essentially pleading for sympathy.[109]

Emphasizing the ways in which identity is stretched or reconfigured through these performances, Hunter notes further that "the sentimental mode in the throats of many of opera buffa's women draws on the 'noble' capacities of the audience to respond with sympathy and generosity and redefines the relations between gender and class."[110]

Hunter's characterization of the performativity of the sentimental utterance in *opera buffa* recalls the ways in which eighteenth-century theorists discussed the exercise of human sympathy and its pivotal contribution to the act of spectatorship through the appeal of the performance to the audience. Taking some examples from the repertory of the French *opéra comique*, I now want to explore the ways in which these issues were framed in lyric stage works from the second half of the eighteenth century.

Tom Jones, with words by Antoine Alexandre Henri Poinsinet and music by Philidor, premiered at the Comédie-Italienne on February 27, 1765. Grimm attributed the failure of the work to "the dull and sullen Poinsinet," though he commended Philidor, noting that "there are some quite beautiful things in the music."[111] After revision by Sedaine, with some minor changes to the music undertaken by Philidor, *Tom Jones* took to the stage a second time, on January 30, 1766, this time to general acclaim.[112] After its success in 1766, *Tom Jones* was performed throughout Europe. The libretto draws together early scenes from Henry Fielding's novel. Whereas M. Western expects his daughter, Sophie, to marry the wealthy nephew of Alworthy, Sophie has fallen in love with Tom Jones, Alworthy's low-born ward. Sophie rejects the nephew, Blifil, angering both M. Western and his sister, Mme. Western, both of whom are intransigent in their expectations for her marriage. Once their mutual affection is discovered, Jones is banished and Sophie decides to run away from home. Finding themselves in an inn for the night, Sophie and her companion Honora are harassed by drunks (who open act 3 with a quartet). Jones appears just in time to rescue them. After everyone arrives at the inn, having come out in search of Sophie, the honest Quaker Dowling reveals that Jones is in reality a nephew of Alworthy and that Blifil, who was entrusted with documents to prove Jones's birth, has been deceiving everyone. This turn of events brings about the final union of the two lovers.

Feeling and sympathy are foregrounded at several salient points in the work, moments that were recognized as such by eighteenth-century commentators. Furthermore, these instances occur in situations of triangulation, not entirely unlike those from the repertory of the *opera buffa* discussed by Hunter, in which the spectator is implicitly included in the drama as the one who overhears an important revelation or who is counted on to react sympathetically. One such moment occurs at the opening of the work. Honora confides to Sophie that, hidden in the garden, she has overheard Tom Jones speak of his love for her as he strolled in the grove. Re-enacting the scene, she sings Jones's words to Sophie (the *ariette*, "Oui toutte ma vie la Belle Sophie"), who, after listening breathlessly, is characterized by the stage directions as "troubled" and is unable to put a complete sentence together.[113] Just as Honora has overheard Jones pouring out his emotions in the presumed solitude of a grove, the spectator eavesdrops on the inner feelings of both Jones and Sophie. All the paradoxical elements of absorption are present in this example. The spectator witnesses both the framed scene – Tom Jones in the garden – and the scene of the telling, which refers back to the first. Sophie is moved because she now knows that

Jones loves her just as she loves him, and because she, too, has just witnessed the garden scene in its re-enactment. The representation of Jones's song *en abyme* functions so well precisely because the effect is predicated on the spectator's presumed absence; yet the spectator is also necessarily present, just as Sophie is both absent and present to Jones as he walks in the grove. The representation of the garden scene, set in the *salon* of M. Western, is a moment of privacy, a moment in which the spectator is excluded, yet also present, peering simultaneously into the garden and into Sophie's domestic space. As Samuel Weber has argued, "what constitutes the theatricality of a scene is not simply its visibility, not simply the fact that it is seen, but rather that it is seen *by another*: someone who remains, qua observer, external to the scene."[114] Sophie's speechless reaction to Honora's *ariette* is appropriate insomuch as it offers up to the spectator in the auditorium the extreme emotion with which she is overcome.

The contrast between the eloquent and beautiful "speech" of Honora's *ariette* and Sophie's stammering response frames the moment as one that is laden with feeling. The association between speechlessness and feeling was fully exploited by librettists and composers in the latter part of the eighteenth century.[115] In *Tom Jones*, the contrasts between the prosaic or mundane on the one hand, and the poetic or expressive on the other, are aptly conceived. Sophie's aunt, Mme. Western, is obsessed with the political events about which she reads in each issue of the gazette, and with her own ability to interpret and find solutions to the problems of the world: "non, contre toutte raison le Dannemark prend les armes, on s'était arrangé sur une confédération. On avait projetté des articles, et point du tout: en vérité, il est bien pénible d'arranger des gens qui ne veulent pas s'entendre" [no, against all reason Denmark is taking up arms. A confederation had been arranged. Articles had been drawn up, but no chance: in truth, it is very trying to work with people who do not want to get along with each other].[116] Yet it is Mme. Western who, despite her intense preoccupation with politics (she does nothing but wait for the latest issue of the gazette), recognizes that Sophie is in love. After Sophie sings of her amorous troubles and anxieties, but before discovering that the object

of her love is Jones, Mme. Western reacts with sympathetic identification, again figuring the reaction of the spectator: "tu me charmes,
tu me rapelles des momens! . . . " [you charm me, you remind me of
moments! . . .].[117] M. Western is portrayed as a simple-speaking, honest man in contrast to Blifil's stiff and, as it is discovered later, deceptive
character. In response to his sister's astonishment that he can spend
all his days at the hunt, M. Western replies: "je paye mes ouvriers tous
les mois; je compte avec mes fermiers tous les ans; je bois avec mes
amis tous les jours" [I pay my workers every month; I count with my
farmers every year; I drink with my friends every day].[118] However, for
all his bonhomie, M. Western refuses to listen to what his daughter
truly wants. As is clear from the example of Honora's *ariette* discussed
above, song is equated with the revelation of feeling and with sympathy. It is interesting to note, however, that Dowling the Quaker, one
of the most morally upstanding characters in *Tom Jones*, is a speaking
role. The ability of *opéra comique* to bring opera down to earth while it
strikes a deep sentimental chord within the spectator is emblematized
in the contrast between the sensible (in the modern English sense),
represented by Dowling, and the *sensible*.

Two key *ariettes*, both sung by Sophie – "C'est à vous que je dois
la vie" from act 2 and "O toi qui ne peux m'entendre" from act 3 –
illustrate the shift *opéra comique* undertook in this period to increasingly strong sentimental subject matter. In the first, Sophie pleads with
her father, explaining to him that she does not want to marry Blifil
(see example 8): "C'est à vous que je dois la vie, / Vos bontés me
la font chérir; / A la voix de votre Sophie, / Que votre ame daigne
s'ouvrir / Ecoutez son coeur qui vous crie" [It is to you that I owe my
life; / Your favors make me cherish it; / To the voice of your Sophie, /
Deign to open your soul; / Listen to her heart that calls out to you].[119]
Tom McCall has signaled the importance of the father–daughter dyad
in eighteenth-century theater, arguing that tears shed onstage are
closely connected with the bourgeois mercantilism represented in
domestic tragedy through the common theme of emotional and monetary capital that binds the family together.[120] In her *ariette*, Sophie draws
on the sentimental link between father and daughter in the family

Example 8: "C'est à vous"

economy in order to elicit a sympathetic response from M. Western, calling for him to open his soul to her "voice" and to listen to the "cries" of her heart, the latter plea emphasized by a pulsating heartbeat in the bass and the use of accidentals (a minor sixth and a major seventh) on the words "coeur qui vous crie." Characteristically, the audience is both implicitly included through the spectatorial figure of the father who listens to the *ariette* onstage, and excluded as one who "overhears" this domestic scene between daughter to father. Garcin commented on the strong effect of this *ariette*, emphasizing the spectator's tears: "the sadness of the modulations bends the hardest soul to pity. There

Example 9: "O toi qui ne peux m'entendre"

is hardly a note in this number that does not cost the listener a tear."[121]

Garcin continues his discussion of *Tom Jones*, identifying "O toi qui ne peux m'entendre" as "unquestionably the most moving [*pathétique*] air in *Tom Jones*, and one of the most beautiful show-stoppers [*morceaux d'effet*] in the entire repertory."[122] This *ariette*, beginning with expressive, incantatory leaps in the voice, starts *lento* shifting abruptly to allegro at the words, "viens accours" [come quickly], signaling Sophie's unsettled emotional state (see example 9).[123] "O toi qui ne peux m'entendre" differs from the previously discussed *ariette* in that Sophie is alone, absorbed in thought. The poignant, cantabile line of the voice contrasts first with a repeated rhythmic figure in the bass, then with the sustained B♭ in the bass as the voice descends diatonically and with slow deliberation from its highest point. Because the scene takes place in the solitude of her hotel room, emphasized by the lone candle she holds in her hand, the spectator is unambiguously excluded from the scene. Sophie, moreover, stresses the absence of Jones – "toi qui ne peux m'entendre," which is re-emphasized in a revised 1771 version of the libretto by the line, "Qui ne peux receuillir mes pleurs" [You who cannot catch my tears].[124] The exclusion of the spectator and the absence of Jones, patently underscored in the text, make Sophie truly alone. The impossibility of Tom Jones's presence, however, constitutes an invitation to the spectator who is there listening to Sophie's lament. Scaling the wall that Freud saw fit to erect between identification and desire, the identification that song effectuates in *opéra comique* (according to Garcin, "there is not a single musical inflection in this air that does not contribute to making the listener enter into the situation of the one who sings") is seconded by the way in which it elicits desire on the part of the male spectator.[125]

The final vaudeville, celebrating the restoration of Jones's identity and the union of the lovers, ends with a chorus. "Voir des heureux, l'estre soi même . . . c'est le triomphe des bons coeurs" [To see those who are happy, to be happy oneself . . . is the triumph of good hearts].[126] Despite the final push toward the singularity of union and the resolution of differences, the ways in which the sentimental *ariette*s of *Tom Jones* are framed as heard, and overheard, by others confirms the strong tendency of eighteenth-century moral theory, examined earlier in this chapter, to focus on feelings of affliction. The spectator's propensity for sympathy is tested and exercised through the spectacle of the unhappiness of others. It is the spectator's reaction to the woman in tears that proves "the triumph of good hearts." The ending of *Tom Jones* is consistent with Mary Hunter's assertion that ensembles "raise questions about the nature of individuality in their presentations of, and inexorable drive toward, undifferentiated group utterance."[127] Because sympathy requires the exclusion inherent in spectatorship and the difference of situation it implies, as both eighteenth-century moral theory and my analysis of *Tom Jones* reveal, while the final vaudeville celebrates the union of the group (with the sole exception of Blifil, whose deceitfulness is condemned) it nonetheless also recalls that the feeling *opéra comique* generates is also predicated on the difference of situations (between father and daughter in the *ariette*, "C'est à vous") and on isolation (in "O toi").

The sympathy on which *opéra comique* focused its energies was conveyed effectively and forcefully through the *ariette*, and this focus confirms what many commentators had explicitly recognized: that music was central to the focus on sentiment in *opéra comique*. This fact seems so obvious to us today as to be beyond dispute. However, in a culture that traditionally gave first billing to the poet, rather than to the composer, it remained to be proved. The composer was given unusual prominence on the title page of scores and even libretti from the 1760s onward. As Sedaine wrote, "invention and design . . . cede the honors to music."[128] The new *ariettes* were distinct from the vocal writing of most *tragédies lyriques* and, as such, caught the public's attention. By 1770, it would appear, at least by one estimation, that the Comédie-Italienne was "the only place where there is music that anyone wants to hear."[129] As David Charlton has cogently argued, whereas the practice of associating new words to popular vaudevilles in the old *opéra comique* "forces the audience to think in a textual, not a musical, way," music was a driving force behind the new genre.[130]

The newfound prominence of music did not imply that the text was no longer important. Charlton has argued that most opera commentators today do not take proper account of "the fact that spoken dialogue is present in some of the finest repertory works even today" and falsely assume that characters in opera sing all the time.[131] The fact that opera characters sing, Charlton suggests, in no way suspends the literary qualities of the works in which they exist: that is, one should not exclude "the possibility that audiences in the past perceived the speech–song alternation as operating across a perceived continuum, expecially when verse was used as the medium of spoken dialogue."[132] Indeed, it is an indisputable fact that the alternation of spoken words and song contributed to the sentimental construction of sympathy in *opéra comique*. The flexibility of *opéra comique* derived from the fact that it was written, Chabanon argued, as "isolated numbers," so that the spectator is taken into the dramatic logic of musical numbers rather than the textual movement of the libretto.[133] Even more clearly, Lacépède remarked:

> What needs to be said except that these different numbers, being
> separated by purely declaimed sections with which they have, as it were,
> no relation, are more closely compared with each other? Perhaps as a
> result they need to be more diversified and to resemble each other less,

because they are neither preceded nor immediately followed by any singing that might make them stand out? Being moreover heard in a sort of isolated way, mustn't they each offer an entirety and present a whole that is much more independent than in works in which music reigns from the beginning to the end?[134]

Given Lacépède's insistence on a musical logic, it is worth remarking in passing, at the risk of opening up a vast area of musicological debate that it is not within the means of this chapter to address, that new uses of the orchestra also contributed to the effect of *opéra comique*. Relying on accounts of eighteenth-century spectators, Charlton notes that "the orchestral contribution may have existed as an equivalent to the novelist's authorial voice."[135] In a scene from *Les Fausses apparences, ou l'amant jaloux* (1778) by Grétry and Thomas d'Hèle, for example – one that is strikingly similar to the finale in act 2 of *Le Nozze di Figaro*, to the point of wondering about Mozart's dramatic models for this sequence – Léonore tells her lover Don Alonze and Don Lopez, her father, that it is not a man who is hiding in her closet, as they suspect; rather, a woman who is seeking protection. A spare, impatient figure in the bass appears in response to Léonore's story, as if to mark time, returning in the end simply to the note on which it began. Above this figure the score indicates: "on this motif [*trait*] Lopez appears to say, 'perfect'."[136]

The reactions of Garcin and Diderot to the mixture of spoken dialogue and song are illustrative of the new directions in which *opéra comique* was urging audiences. For his part, Garcin disagreed with the assumption that music was the principal object of opera.[137] He conceded that music did render the presentation of sentiment much more palpable to spectators: "the sequence of ideas is too rapid in ordinary speech: the great usefulness of song is to fix them and through this to make them more perceptible."[138] Yet, Garcin always worried about the possibility that music would take the upper hand: "if song causes one to forget the words, if the music conquers and subjugates the poetry, opera itself is no longer anything but the withered remains of the art that once dominated the soul of an entire people."[139]

Discussing *Rose et Colas* (1764), by Sedaine and Monsigny, Garcin contrasted the brilliant musical virtuosity he (and many others throughout the eighteenth century) associated with Italian opera with the dramatic focus of French products: "the best beginning is not the one that shines the most, but the one that grasps most profoundly the poetic idea."[140] While Garcin argued that music should be subordinated to the poetry, Diderot took a different stance in his review of Garcin's *Traité du mélodrame*. Diderot presented a critique of Garcin, praising the emphasis the chevalier de Chastellux had placed on music in his 1765 *Essai sur l'union de la poésie et de la musique*, though he indicated that a dramatic or narrative dimension was also necessary to sustain the spectator's interest:

> He [Chastellux] claims that in the pleasure of our sensations there is something inexplicable because it is purely organic; and he is right. Beautiful chords, well prepared and sequenced, flatter my ear, setting aside any feeling in my soul, any idea in my mind; although in truth I would not listen long to music that had only this quality. I have never heard a good instrumental piece, especially an *adagio* or *andante*, without interpreting it, and sometimes so aptly that I hit upon precisely what the composer had proposed to depict. I will also never abandon the advice that I gave to a skillful harpsichordist. "Do you want to create good instrumental music," I told her, "and always make your instrument speak to me? Put Metastasio on your music stand, read through one of his arias, and let your mind go."[141]

Diderot acknowledged the effect of music qua music on the listener; yet he insisted on some form of narrative behind that music. When it tells a story, music has "the divine ability to move us, torment us, to bring the most varied accents to our ears, and to make us imagine all kinds of apparitions, to make our tears flow or to make us burst into laughter."[142] The effect of *opéra comique*, therefore, is the studied result of a complex association of narrative means involving spoken words, song, ensemble numbers, and orchestral intervention.[143]

In the opening sequence of *La Fausse magie* (1775) by Grétry and Marmontel, sung and spoken text function in tandem to produce a situation in which song reveals the "truth" whereas speech, at least at first, appears unaware or self-deceiving.[144] Lucette is in love with Linval, but Lucette's older tutor and guardian, Dalin, also has his eye on her. To make matters worse, Linval's sexagenarian uncle, Dorimon, also has vague notions of wooing Lucette. Following an *ariette* sung as an aside in which Lucette tells of her longings, she eventually confides in Madame Saint-Clair, her aunt, after the latter surmises that her niece is in love. Madame Saint-Clair reveals (in song) her own story, which mirrors that of Lucette: an old and unwanted suitor was send packing by a watchful, sympathetic aunt. The two *ariettes* – Lucette's and Madame Saint-Clair's – respond to each other sympathetically across a divide of spoken dialogue in which Lucette, ineffectively, attempts to hide her troubles. This opening sequence forms a bond between the two women of different generations, a bond which is reinforced when Lucette and Linval sing a duet, as Madame Saint-Clair listens, in which they recall the moment of their first love. Figuring the sympathy and identification that is expected of the spectator, Madame Saint-Clair, who had once been in precisely the same situation as Lucette, reacts to the duet with emotion in an aside directed to the audience: "Comme tout cela m'interesse! / Je me sens le coeur tressaillir, / Quand je vois deux amants s'aimer avec tendresse" [How all of this touches me! / . . . I feel my heart flutter / When I see two lovers love each other dearly].[145]

Madame Saint-Clair imagines a strategy to favor the aims of the two lovers and to rid "D'un fol amour deux vieilles têtes" [Two old heads of a crazy love] (92). Dalin, who believes in prognostication and astrology, has told Madame Saint-Clair about a disturbing dream he has had in which "a young hen is guarded by a gallant old cockerel. A watching kite abducts the hen; the cockerel promptly changes into a gosling."[146] Madame Saint-Clair announces to Lucette and Linval that a band of "charlatans" is on its way and suggests, in the middle of an impressive quartet on which the *Mercure* lavished praise, that they leave everything up to her (125; see example 10).[147] The charlatans to which she refers turn out to be gypsies; they arrive, and a series of palm readings takes place, each framed as an *ariette*. Linval, whose future appears rosy, has his hand read first. When a gypsy scrutinizes Dalin's

Example 10: "Vous allez voir dans peu" (before palm reading scene)

Example 10: (*Cont.*)

hand, however, after glimpsing festive celebrations in his future the predictions suddenly turn bleak: "L'heureux destin si tout resemble à ce festin! / Mais j'entend l'orage qui gronde. / Ah quelle crainte vous poursuit? / Je vois dans l'horreur de la nuit / Le noir soupçon qui fait sa ronde. / Oui je vois l'amour qui s'enfuit" [What a fortunate destiny if everything resembles this feast! / But I hear a storm rumbling. / Ah, what fear pursues you? / I see in the horror of night / Dark suspicion making the rounds. / Yes, I see love taking flight] (146–47). Dalin answers petulantly (*"avec humeur"* [angrily]): "C'est la ce que dit ma Planette? / Elle n'a pas le sens commun. / Voyons à présent, si quelqu'un / Lira plus clairement dans la main de Lucette" [That is what my planet says? / It makes no sense. / Now let's see if someone / Will read Lucette's hand more clearly] (147). Linval, disguised as a gypsy, now reads Lucette's palm. Dalin provides a running commentary, in recitative, as Linval sings of Lucette's charms. Abuptly, the reading changes course, half-veiled allusions to Dalin's ominous dream appear, and the music permanently shifts to E flat, the key associated with the dream (see example 11). Charlton explains:

> The libretto instructs: "The music recalls the dream." So the tonality
> becomes E flat as the 'fortune-teller' affects to see a change in her future,
> while Grétry recalls thirty-five bars closely based on [the earlier dream
> *ariette*] in order (i) to show Dalin's act of memory, (ii) to remind us of the
> content of the dream, and (iii) to portray Dalin's assumption that the
> fortune-teller is witnessing the substance of the dream. Through the
> agency of the orchestra Dalin's imagination is perceptible on both active
> and passive levels.[148]

In this scene, spoken dialogue is skillfully juxtaposed to sung sequences, themselves interwoven with recitative, to create a complex, dialogical effect. The orchestra, too, participates in the "magic," returning in the horn part to some of the same music that was part of the original statement of the dream in scene 5 (71, 153).[149] The *Mercure* recognized that Grétry used the orchestra as an "actor," noting his "prodigious gift for varying musical forms, his particular talent for making actors of all the instruments, his exquisite taste for grasping, embellishing

Example 11: "Mais quelle métamorphose" (palm reading)

Example 11: (*Cont.*)

Example 11: (*Cont.*)

Example 11: *(Cont.)*

Example 11: (*Cont.*)

and fortifying the particular language of feeling or of the passions."[150]
Solo *ariettes* are juxtaposed with spoken dialogue at the beginning of
La Fausse magie in order to spotlight the interiority represented by song
and, through the spectator-participant figure of Madame Saint-Clair,
to provide audience members with a conduit for their sympathy and
identification. As the work progresses, increasingly complex configurations of song, recitative, speech, and orchestral music allow Grétry
and Marmontel to produce multiple layers of meaning.

Grétry used music in similar ways in his other stage works. In
Richard Coeur de Lion (1784), Grétry and Sedaine made a song the key
to a crucial recognition scene. In act 2, Richard overhears and recognizes the voice of Blondel, his squire, as he sings a song Richard once
wrote for his beloved Marguerite: "Quels accents! Quelle voix! ... je la
connais!" [what melodious strains! what a voice! ... I know that voice!].
Richard responds by joining in; and in act 3 Blondel in turn recognizes
Richard by his voice: "Sa voix a pénétré mon âme" [His voice pen-
etrated my soul].[151] The song thereby creates a situation in which

Richard, Blondel, and Marguerite, who have been separated by the course of events, can be reunited. Music can also complicate matters, rather than resolving them. In a rather complex quid pro quo from *Les Fausses apparences*, a nighttime duet reconciling the lovers Alonze and Léonore is interrupted by Florival who, believing that Léonore is his beloved Isabelle, sings a serenade, scored for two backstage mandolines, below Léonore's window.[152] The serenade immediately creates a rift between Alonze and Léonore, whose duet quickly turns bellicose.

In *La Fausse magie*, Linval's gypsy performance, replete with an incantatory song and an orchestral "recreation" of the dream while Dalin prosaically comments on the action in recitative, appears to the spectator as false magic which is stripped away in order to reveal the truth, represented all along by sympathy and feeling, in the final sequence. As Dalin pleads for a spell to set things right, he gives the gypsies two talismans: a ribbon that belongs to Lucette and his own signature. After a preparatory chorus, a gypsy asks Dalin to kneel in front of a mirror on the ground into which he then gazes. When Lucette appears in the mirror, followed by Linval, Dalin understands. The signature has been his acquiescence to the marriage of the two young lovers, which is now being performed in the mirror.[153] Before the final chorus, Madame Saint-Clair concludes on the events of the day:

> Veut-on que la bonne aventure
> N'ai rien de douteux ni d'obscur
> Le plus facile et le plus sure
> C'est d'interroger la nature.
> Chacun de nous a son devin
> Qui ne repond jamais en vain.
>   (*le refrain en choeur*)
> On sait assés quand on est sage
> Ce que promet le lendemain
> Mais ce n'est pas sur notre main
> C'est dans nos coeurs qu'est le presage. (184–85)

> Do you want the adventure
> To have nothing dubious or obscure about it?

The easiest and most reliable way
Is to consult nature.
We each have our own fortuneteller
Who never answers in vain.
  (*chorus*)
When one is good it is easy to know
What tomorrow promises.
Yet the omen is not written on our hands
But in our hearts.

Linval draws the final lesson – "Pour être heureux avec ma femme /
Je ne lirai point dans les Cieux. / Je lirai mon sort dans ses yeux
[To be happy with my wife / I will not read in the heavens. / I will read
my fate in her eyes] – while Lucette responds in kind: "Je lirai le mien
dans ton ame" [I will read mine in your soul] (186). Just as Rousseau's
soothsayer had used common sense to resolve the difficulties between
Colin and Colette, in *La Fausse magie* divination functions as a kind of
smoke screen which dissipates to reveal a natural, domesticated form
of magic: sympathy. Giving absolute priority to sympathetic feeling,
because "We each have our own fortuneteller / Who never answers in
vain," *La Fausse magie* endorsed the centrality of sympathy that had
been established by eighteenth century moral theory.

A paradigmatic instance of the focus of *opéra comique* on sympathy
and identification can be found in *Zémire et Azor* (1771), a beauty and the
beast story by Grétry and Marmontel. One of the most popular and
internationally successful *opéras comiques* ever, *Zémire et Azor* saw 271
performances through 1797, and another 294 over the course of the first
half of the nineteenth century.[154] It was so successful from the start that
it set the directors of the Opéra into a panic. Feeling the need to take extreme measures to combat the insurgency of the Comédie-Italienne,
they resurrected what was considered at the time to be Rameau's
consummate masterpiece: "the success of *Zémire et Azor* frightened
the Académie Royale de Musique ... it went to the greatest lengths
to remedy the situation and brought out the shrine, *Castor et Pollux*,
patrons of the Académie."[155] *Zémire et Azor* focuses on the bond between a bourgeois father and his daughter, on the sacrifice of this

daughter, and on her sympathy and eventual love for a strangely dis-figured prince who has been given a beast-like appearance until such a time as he can inspire love. Returning from commercial exploits in the east, Sander and his slave Ali are miraculously saved from a shipwreck in which Sander has lost his fortune. Magically, a table overflowing with food and drink appears and the two weary travellers indulge them-selves, Ali to comic excess. Sander remembers his youngest daughter Zémire's wish that he bring her back a flower from his travels and he plucks a rose to take to her. The Persian prince, Azor, who suddenly appears in frightening form, challenges Sander for taking advantage of his hospitality. In exchange for having taken the rose, Sander must either sacrifice one of his daughters to Azor or die himself. Back home in Ormuz in act 2, Sander is despondent. Zémire finds out the truth of her father's situation from Ali and pleads with the latter to take her to Azor. Ali relents in the end, and as act 3 opens we find Zémire in Azor's palace. Though she is initially terrified at seeing Azor, Zémire soon perceives his noble character. Because Zémire misses her family, Azor conjures up a magic picture in which she can see and hear them. Finally granting her wish to visit them, Azor allows Zémire to return briefly to Ormuz in act 4. Meanwhile, Azor despairs in his gardens. Zémire appears, searching for Azor. As she calls to Azor and gradually emerges from offstage, she realizes during the course of an extended monologue that she loves him. Upon her declaration, the scene trans-forms to an enchanted palace where Azor sits on his throne, restored to his original beauty. The fairy who had originally caused Azor to be transformed into a beast reunites Zémire with her family and presides over the wedding.

From the cutting of the rose in act 1 – a highly sexualized sym-bolic act – the plot centers on the special bond between Sander and his favorite daughter, and turns on an ineluctable need for sacrifice: "La pauvre enfant ne savait pas / Qu'elle demandit mon trépas" [The poor child did not know / That she was asking for my life].[156] Sander's financial ruin after the sinking of his ship is mirrored in an impending loss within the family: Sander must give his life or turn his daughter over to Azor. If Sander agrees to the latter arrangement, however, Azor promises him unlimited wealth. As in many other eighteenth-century plays, emotional wealth is made equivalent to monetary capital.[157] Zémire's ability to muster the necessary emotional and moral resources is therefore at the core of the work. With Sander's property lost at sea, the rose becomes a symbol both of a commodity that is beyond wealth, establishing the transcendent value of bourgeois family feeling, and of the eventual restoration of the family's monetary ease. Zémire recognizes the transcendent quality of the rose as a symbol of familial emotion as she muses on her father's gift: "Une rose? c'est peu de chose. / De sa main, elle est sans prix" [A rose is not worth much. / But from his hand, it is priceless] (68 69). Sexual desire, symbolized in the rose, is transformed and channeled through the emotional circuits of family feeling.

At various points in *Zémire et Azor*, feeling and sympathy are explicitly connected to the voice and to the act of hearing the voice, figuring *en abyme* the desired response of the spectator. Some *ariettes* reproduce "performances of absorption," to borrow Hunter's phrase, in which a lone onstage character is lost in thought, as was the case with Sophie's lament, "O toi qui ne peux m'entendre," from act 3 of *Tom Jones*. Similarly, upon Zémire's final return to the enchanted palace in act 4, she calls out for Azor, lamenting that "en vain ma voix t'appelle" [in vain my voice calls to you] (204). Grimm noted the remarkable use of the orchestra in this scene: "to imitate the echoes of the barren place where the scene takes place, the composer placed horns and flutes in the flies, which repeat twice, each time more softly, the lines of the horns and flutes in the orchestra" (see example 12).[158] In a general sense, the orchestra can be said to function as a dialogical element in the narrative. However, in this case, because Zémire's offstage voice is echoed by the distant calls of horns and flutes, the play of dialogue between present and absent entities is highly accentuated.[159] Zémire is present somewhere in the woods and we hear her call; yet, she is offstage. Azor is technically absent, since he is separated from Zémire who calls out to him; yet, he is present in the grounds of the palace. Meanwhile, the instruments hidden in the flies call out to and dialogue with the orchestra.

Example 12: "Azor"

Vocal expressions of feeling and calls for sympathy most often occur in *Zémire et Azor* in another's presence. In act 2, when Zémire entreats Ali to take her to Azor so that she may sacrifice herself for her father, Ali cannot resist Zémire's tears ("je m'attendris" [I am touched], he says) and finally succumbs to her demand (99). As Tom McCall has

Example 12: *(Cont.)*

argued, "tears are the phenomenalized, physiological indicators of mimetic identification": "tears [serve] as the exchange rate or conversion factor for the flow of capital between individual feeling and public morality."[160] Ali's individual reaction serves as a conduit to the potential for public feeling inherent in the audience. When Azor appears before Zémire in act 3, she faints; yet once he begins to sing, she is perplexed, forgetting her fear on seeing him, fascinated by the "charm" of his voice. The discrepancy between Azor's visual appearance and his character is of course central to the original story of *La Belle et la bête*. In *Zémire et Azor*, the discrepancy functions to highlight the emotional appeal of song as an effective measure of the truth. Azor's appearance may deceive, but his voice reveals the truth of his feeling: "Ah quel tourment d'être sensible" [Ah, what a torment it is to have feelings], he sings at the opening of act 3 (106). After hearing Azor, Zémire remarks: "Mais, vous m'attendrissez" [But, you have touched me] (134). Azor, in turn, desires to hear her voice (*accens*). Zémire, thinking of her distant family, sings a lament, and Azor, moved, wonders how he can reduce her suffering: "Vos chants pour moi sont une plainte. / Hélas! je ne puis réussir / A calmer les regrets dont votre ame est atteinte. / Ne puis-je au moins les adoucir?" [Your song is for me like a lament. / Alas! I am unable / To stop the regrets that afflict your soul. / May I at least ease them?] (146). Just as we have seen in *Tom Jones* and *La Fausse magie*, the spectator on the stage renders the reaction desired from the spectator. In act 3 of *Zémire et Azor*, the two eponymous characters each serve in turn as the spectator of the other, witnessing and above all *hearing* the voice of the other. In addition to the desire and identification elicited by Zémire, Marmontel's discussion of the costume he imagined for Clairval further emphasizes the conception of Azor as a man – not a beast – with whom the spectator could identify. Reluctant to play an ugly character, Clairval expressed his reservations to Marmontel: "'How can I possibly,' he told me, 'make a role attractive in which I am hideous?'"[161] When Marmontel saw the frightening creature's costume that had been readied, he was horrified and ordered the costumer to redo everything, asking him, "Who told you that Azor was a beast?"[162] Judging from a contemporary engraving, authenticated by Marmontel's description of his specifications for the costume, Azor was visually striking, and far from being a monster.

Zémire requests to be allowed to see her father and her sisters one last time. Azor consents, but warns her: "Dans un tableau magique ils vont ici paroître; / Mais si vous approchés, tout va s'évanouïr"

Example 13: tableau magique

[They will appear here in a magic frame; / But if you come near, everything will vanish] (146). In act 2, scene 6, Sander, Fatmé, and Lisbé appear within a picture frame, their images teleported to the palace, as Zémire and Azor look on (see example 13). At first, the image is mute and Zémire sees only their gestures of despair at her disappearance (the sisters are compassionate, unlike their models in *La Belle*

Example 13: (*Cont.*)

et la bête, so that family unity prevails) without being able to hear their voices: "Ah, mon pere! ah, mes soeurs! . . . / Helas! comme il est triste! / Il pleure. Sa douleur resiste / Au soin que leur amour prend de le consoler. / Il me cherche des yeux. Il semble me parler. / Ses bras vers moi semblent s'etendre" [Ah, my father! ah, my sisters! . . . / Alas!

Example 13: (*Cont.*)

how sad he is! / He is crying. His sorrow resists / The care their love takes to console him. / He is seeking me out with his eyes. It is as if he is speaking to me. / His arms seem to reach out to me] (147). Zémire narrates and interprets the images she sees. Emphasizing the fact that her father's words and those of her sisters are inaccessible to her, she

Example 13: (*Cont.*)

pleads with Azor to allow her to hear them. The magic picture thereby underscores the absence of those sounds that otherwise would have accompanied the image. Azor had decided not to reproduce the sound for fear that their voices and laments would have an excessive effect on Zémire, the onstage spectator of this scene. When Zémire asks him if

Example 13: (*Cont.*)

he definitively refuses to allow her to hear their voices, Azor responds: "Non mais je suis sur, helas, / Qu'en vous obéissant je me trahis moi même. / Leurs plaintes vont me rendre odieux je le vois" [No, but I am sure, alas, / That in obeying you I will betray myself. / Their tears will render me odious, I know] (147). In the end, Azor consents to this additional request and a muted instrumental prelude arises to introduce an equally distant and ethereal familial trio, "Ah! laissez-moi la pleurer," the voices emerging from the tableau. The score clearly indicates that "the accompanying instruments are behind the stage" (147). The hallucinatory or dream-like quality of the entire scene is emphasized in the distant accompaniment and through a "hypnotic repeated figure" in the trio, first appearing in the horns, then moving on to the voices, which Grétry identified as having been inspired by a visit from Diderot.[163] Charlton remarks that "the blended tones almost consciously hark back to the offstage trombones of supernatural scenes in Baroque opera."[164] The effect of the *tableau magique* was unanimously praised. Grimm observed that "this number is accompanied only by clarinets, horns and bassoons placed behind the magic picture, and the orchestra keeps quiet. It is very charming and made the greatest effect."[165] The *Mercure* remarked that the tableau produced a strong reaction on the spectators: "one will never be able to give sufficient praise to the muted Trio of the father and his two daughters who appear in the magic picture. It has a tender pathos which brings tears to one's eyes."[166]

The *tableau magique* exhibits all the elements I have identified as specific to the ideological makeup of *opéra comique* in the late eighteenth century: sacrifice, tears and sympathy, and identification through spectatorship. The scene is carefully modulated, progressing from the spoken dialogue of Zémire and Azor who are viewing the mute image, to a remote instrumental accompaniment once Azor activates the sound, and finally to the trio. When Zémire rushes toward the magic picture, it vanishes just as Azor had predicted it would; and the scene reverts to the barrenness (for Zémire) of a tête-à-tête. The initial dialogue between Zémire and Azor insists on the fact that the tableau is voiceless. Moved by the images of their suffering, Zémire desires to experience the full emotional impact of their voices; and Azor recognizes that these voices will have an overwhelming effect on her: "their tears will render me odious, I know." Indeed, it is their voices (in song) that produce an irresistible sympathetic reaction in Zémire. She throws herself at the tableau just at the point when her family calls for her return: "Oui je la vois je crois l'entendre qui m'appelle. / Ah ma Zemire sans toi j'expire / Revien … " [yes, I see her; I believe I hear her calling me. / Ah, my Zémire, without you I will die / Come back …] (149–50). The tableau vanishes and one last isolated "come back" is heard as the orchestra fades away, smorzando. The *tableau magique* is a performance of absorption which, as such, "demand[s] sympathy and identification."[167] A figure of the spectator, Zémire is fully absorbed in the spectacle she witnesses, and now hears the effects of her sacrifice on Sander, Fatmé, and Lisbé. Her unconscious reaction to the tableau, too, acts as a mimetic call for the spectator's sympathy and identification.

Rozoi confirms my reading of the scene in his *Dissertation sur le drame lyrique*, in which he opposes the caustic voice of the critic, overly involved in the many musical *querelles* of the day, to the pleasures of the ordinary spectator:

> Cantankerous critic, enemy of my heart and of yours, I was going to give myself over to a delicious sensation; you might have shared it … Yet you reason when I only want to feel! You dare to place yourself between me and the tableau that was before me. But, when Zémire thinks she sees her father and her sisters, if he who says that he is looking after his pleasures were to place himself between her and these three beings that she hears and sees, that is truly when he would be a monster. This is your situation and my own.[168]

By depicting a situation in which the critic stands in between the spectator and the spectacle, Rozoi explicitly remarks the spectator's and his own identification with Zémire, whose desire to be with her family is thwarted by the fact that the scene is only a simulation, controlled by Azor. The sympathetic spectator *becomes* Zémire: "this is your situation and my own." But just as the spectator must be excluded in order to be absorbed, as we saw in connection with Diderot's dramatic theories, the *tableau magique* provides distance necessary – both visually and aurally – to produce the strong identification that Rozoi describes. The moment of spectatorship on stage is reproduced, traversing the necessary divide separating stage from spectator, in the audience's tears. At the moment of the final transformation, when Azor is restored to his true appearance, Zémire is amazed and remarks on the power of her sympathy, for it is precisely her sympathy, transformed into love, that has produced this miraculous change: "Quel bonheur! quel prodige! / Et c'est moi qui l'opere" [How fortunate! how amazing! / And it is I who have made it happen] (210). The "real" effects of the spectator's sympathy are thus confirmed in those of Zémire's feeling.

As the foregoing analyses reveal, the particular sentimental effects of *opéra comique* resulted from the genre's complex association of spoken words and song, and from the ways in which this association solicited spectators' desires and identifications. Charlton has suggested that the relationship between spectator and stage at the Opéra-Comique was enhanced in part because music was accessible to opera-goers (it was sold with the libretti) and in part because spectators took singing lessons in order to be able to do justice themselves to the music of these works:

> Audience participation hardly argues for an assumption that words and music, already learned, were forgotten as soon as the stage soloist began. It argues for dramatic understanding and for enhanced perceptual continuity between spoken and sung episodes. Today's (or tomorrow's) theorists ought not shirk the fact that audiences studied and memorised the best music and texts, as playgoers memorised their Racine. Did this practice enhance 'authorial voice' or usurp it? Presumably it usurped some of the performer's authority, until vocal music became too difficult to be regarded as common property . . . Narrative in these *ariettes* struck contemporaries with all the force of a revelation; in our terms they again point to a way of multi-voicing, imaginatively opening out the small space at the Hôtel de Bourgogne into other landscapes and 'lives' offstage.[169]

It has been my contention that the particular dynamic set in motion by the lyrical and narrative nexus of *opéra comique* became the locus for a spectatorial experience foregrounding the primacy of sympathy. The contours of this experience were detailed in eighteenth-century theoretical writings treating sympathy from a medical and / or moral perspective in which the health and well-being of the individual were understood through the individual's sympathetic interactions with others. The *opéras comiques* I have examined above underscore the benefits and pleasures of sympathetic response and, through performative gestures in which sympathy is featured onstage, attempt to draw the audience into this dynamic. In light of contemporary theories of sympathy, listening to the *ariette* may have been construed as a way for the spectator to encounter, through the experience of the other, the moral basis of his or her own identity – a way of coming into contact with the boundary between singular and shared human experiences. By eliciting these kinds of responses from spectators, *opéra comique* helped to elaborate and furthermore sought to put into motion the dynamic of identification described in eighteenth-century moral treatises and later theorized (as the earliest emotional tie to others) by Freud. Beaumarchais described the twin acts of spectatorship and identification thus: "What is morality? It is the fruitful result and the personal application of reflections that an event draws from us. What is interest? It is the involuntary feeling by which we adopt this event, feeling that puts us in the place of him who suffers, in the midst of his situation."[170] The Opéra-Comique became a place in which these mechanisms could be encouraged and affirmed through acts of spectatorship and identification, fueled in part by the desire that is embedded or sublimated in that identification, as is evident from the plots of many *opéras comiques* and as recent re-evaluations of psychoanalytic theory confirm.

Musical magic in the Renaissance placed the body and soul within a larger, hierarchical framework, in which human feeling was a channel to a higher-order divine or cosmological totality. Eighteenth-century musical "magic" was founded on a world that had been naturalized and was resolutely imminent, but which nonetheless involved a space of human feeling that transcended the boundary between self and other. Scott Bryson has made the distinction between affirmation "through submission to an outside order" – royal or cosmological – and identification, which he characterizes as the hallmark of bourgeois drama.[171] By championing and identifying itself with a culture of sympathy, *opéra comique* embodied the new forms of "value, subjectivity, and legitimacy" that Jay Caplan has identified with "post-absolutist culture" in France.[172] To attend an *opéra comique* therefore constituted a social act of participation in cultural values and beliefs that were quite distinct from those that had existed several decades earlier. As I will argue in the following chapter, the Académie Royale de Musique itself was not exempt from these changes.

8 | Architectural visions of lyric theater and spectatorship

Previous chapters have explored the importance of sympathy and identification in eighteenth-century operatic culture by examining the emergent culture of feeling and the ways in which opera participated in this culture. Leaving the Hôtel de Bourgogne, the seat of the Opéra-Comique from 1762, the current chapter returns to the Académie Royale de Musique to explore the impact of these developments on the premier operatic venue of eighteenth-century France. Rather than turning my attention to specific examples from the operatic repertory during this period, however, I propose to investigate the ways in which unexpected though not entirely unpredictable fires, which ravaged the Paris Opéra in 1763 and again in 1781, inadvertently helped open the lyric theater to a new conceptualization, both dramatic and architectural. The architectural proposals for new opera houses that resulted from these fires encouraged forms of spectatorship that developed along with the new culture of sympathy.

In comparison with the enormous number of projects that arose during the second half of the eighteenth century, few new theaters were built during the first half of the century, and the lyric theater in particular remained within the structure of the old *jeu de paume* which defined the spectacle principally through vertical movement and depth. After the fire, with new theaters already built or planned in Lyon, Besançon, and Bordeaux, a new Parisian theater was needed to replace Richelieu's old *salle* in the Palais-Royal and the operatic spectacle that it framed. Although bits and pieces of the traditional repertoire continued to be staged in various incarnations through the end of the ancien régime, the fires freed architects and designers from the spaces inhabited by the *tragédie en musique* developed by Lully and continued in the eighteenth century by Rameau. As concepts of the genre itself changed, the theorization of spectatorship also moved in new directions. The supernatural effects (the *merveilleux*) of the *tragédie en musique*, such as the appearance of flying gods and goddesses, were increasingly criticized and rejected. Taking attention away from the vertical movement created by the machines, the architects of the lyric theater began to emphasize the horizontal space of the stage and moved to create an inclusive, circular space for the audience, bringing the spectator into closer contact with the stage and altering the relationship between spectators. The architectural model for this space was found in Italy, in the ruins of Greco-Roman temples and amphitheaters. I want to examine a few of the architectural projects – most of which were never realized – that arose following the fires in the Palais-Royal, giving particular emphasis to the one contained within the *Lettres sur l'opéra* by Charles-Nicolas Cochin, the famous engraver, because of the interrelations he articulates between architecture, musical theater, and social space. Jean-Marie Pérouse de Montclos has remarked that "the theater is without doubt the program that was the most profoundly affected by the evolution of public architecture in the eighteenth century."[1] More than this, though, the theater became a space of predilection for testing concepts of public architecture. As projects for new Parisian theaters multiplied, designed for both the lyric and "regular" genres, there appears to have been an increasing emphasis on the theatricality of all public space. My argument is concerned with the public space to which architects and planners referred, the space that they hoped to shape. Of primary interest to me is the solidification of "the architectural project" as a construction of spectatorship and a projection of public values at the end of the ancien régime. I see the architectural project as articulating mimetic relationships that come together in the theater, as coordinating various representations. This chapter does not make claims for all theater during the period, but rather seeks to draw out tendencies that marked the architectural imagination in late eighteenth-century France in the shift from absolutist to post-absolutist conceptions of the theater, while evoking the complex ideological motivations that are embodied in individual architectural projects. I will argue that the move to eliminate divine intervention at the Opéra, together with the new conception of the theatrical experience implicit in this move, favored the architectural creation of a self-reflexive public space.[2] However, as it appeared in designs by Boullée and De Wailly toward the end of the century, this public space became increasingly closed, overdetermined, and uninhabitable.

Cochin's *Lettres sur l'opéra* (1781) elaborated on his earlier *Projet d'une salle de spectacle* (1765) and slightly modified the original conception, adapting it for the Opéra, whose theater had just burnt to the ground for the second time in twenty years. Like other proposals of the period, Cochin's *Projet* substituted an elliptical design for the deep, rectangular *jeu de paume*. Although it was a relative novelty in France, the idea was not new. Italian theaters, of which Palladio's *Teatro Olimpico* was the most celebrated in France, were almost always elliptical or oval. Cochin, Jacques Germain Soufflot, and Gabrielle Dumont traveled to Italy between 1749 and 1751, stimulating theater design in France in the second half of the eighteenth century through "a series of projects that adapted the Roman amphitheater or its Palladian derivation to French uses."[3] Yet Cochin and others claimed that the Italian theaters were too immense, and that echos and ambient noise impeded the clarity of the voice (fig. 6). The smaller, elliptical shape would be ideal for the new type of operatic spectacle Cochin advocated, which parallels in many respects the aesthetic Diderot proposed in his writings on the theater. Cochin noted that the machines were given much more attention than they deserved and that "magic and enchantment [supernatural effects] have become obsolete . . . these gods and goddesses and so many other imaginary beings have ceased to be of interest to us."[4] He stressed the importance of eliminating the flying machines and cut-out clouds that were standard in operatic performances: "I still remember the *vol* in *Phaéton*; nothing could be more ridiculous than four cardboard horses and sixteen legs dangling in the air" (62).[5] In his *Entretiens sur le fils naturel*, Diderot had presented a similar argument, making the larger claim that the emergence of new philosophical systems, establishing new connections between the mind and the world, should be accompanied by shifts in the way in which art represents the world: "Men of genius have recently brought the philosophy of the intelligible world into the real world. Will one of these men not render the same service

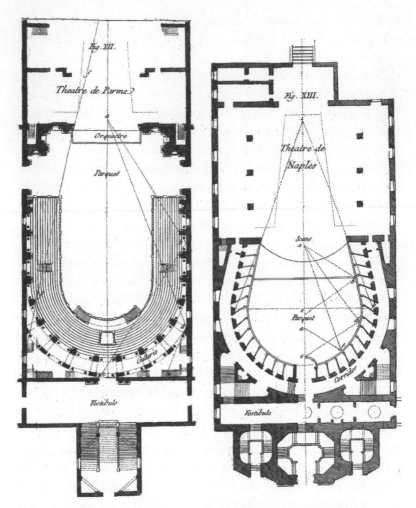

Fig. 6. From Pierre Patte, *Essai sur l'architecture théâtrale* (Paris: chez Moutard, 1782), 210. Photo courtesy of Special Collections Department, University of Iowa Libraries, Iowa City, Iowa.

to lyric poetry, bringing it from enchanted regions to the earth that we inhabit? . . . a great musician and a great lyric poet would repair all the damage."[6] Following Diderot's logic, the machinery driving the special effects of opera should no longer constitute the central interest of the spectacle because knowledge itself had undergone a profound shift. The accord reached in philosophy between the intelligible and the real, which Diderot characterizes as a move from "enchanted" metaphysics to "real" philosophy, should find its analogue in the realm of theatrical and operatic performance, bringing it, too, into the "real" world. As I argued in the previous chapter, *opéra comique* had already begun to respond to many of these concerns. As the premier theatrical institution of the ancien régime, however, the Opéra was slower to change. The real world does increasingly appear at the center of the debates on theater design, though; calls for "truth" and "reality" were tied to an approach toward theater that would place more emphasis on human stories than on those featuring gods and goddesses. More significant for my purposes, however, is the architectural reality of seating arrangements, of corridor design, and of the placement of the building within the city. If the stage became "real" instead of supernatural, it is equally important to recognize that architecture used the theatrical experience to coordinate theater "proper" with an architectural "staging" of spectatorship in the larger conception of the auditorium and its site in the city. Taking these calls for reform in theatrical representation as a backdrop, I want to examine the architectural program that likewise sought to reshape the experience of spectatorship.

ARCHITECTURE AND THE PLACE OF SPECTATORSHIP

In the place of a theater of supernatural effects, Cochin, like Diderot, would substitute an opera centered on drama and affect – a spectacle that would cultivate a different set of relations between the stage and the audience. Contained within the architectural specifications of the *Lettres sur l'opéra* is a (physical) reconfiguration of the spectacle itself and of its relation to the spectator. The elliptical shape of the theater, Cochin notes, would bring the audience as a whole closer to the stage, twenty feet closer than they were at the Comédie-Française (fig. 7).[7] Cochin's plan sought to make the space of the stage and that of the

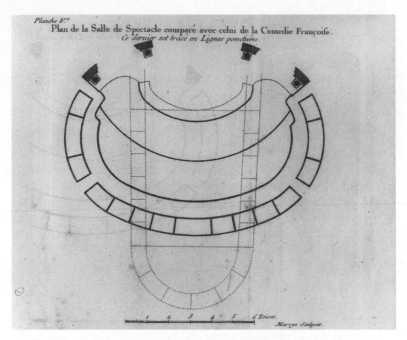

Fig. 7. From Charles-Nicolas Cochin, *Projet d'une salle de spectacle pour un théâtre de comédie* (London and Paris: C.-A. Jombert, 1765), 44. Photo courtesy of Special Collections Library, University of Michigan, Ann Arbor.

audience converge. To this end, he suggests a protruding lip which would bring the actor towards the center of the ellipse, where he would be "as if in the middle of the audience" (6). Cochin also shows concern for the acoustical clarity and presence of the voice in his design. The elliptical shape is optimal in this respect, as Pierre Patte argued in his *Essai sur l'architecture théâtrale*, a compendium and reiteration of recent developments in design, because of "the invaluable advantage it has of being able to concentrate the voice towards the listeners in all its plenitude."[8] The Chevalier de Chaumont faults the Italian designs for their lack of attention to the voice: "we have been to Italy, we have taken & copied theater designs; but we have not taken the time to examine closely everything related to the voice . . . we only strive to embellish theaters without going into further details."[9] The voice is crucial to theater, and particularly to the lyric theater in which music constitutes the affective link that joins together the elements of the spectacle and the members of the audience. Louis-Sébastien Mercier adopts a musical metaphor to describe how the playwright will "make a sort of instrument of the spectator which he will make resonate as he wishes: once master of the heart, the mind and reason obey."[10] By stirring the emotions, music establishes a condition favorable to belief which, once it is free of "the mind and reason," should lead to the impassioned reconciliation of humanity that Diderot imagined in his writings on the theater. In his treatise on architecture, Ledoux emphasized the effect of music on the audience: "when will we cease compromising such invaluable accents? . . . See what sounds can do to the multitude." Ledoux identified the orchestra as a "voice" which, as such, "must not be apparent"; he thus placed it in a pit between the stage and the auditorium so that the music arises from the stage as the unseen voice of drama.[11] The disappearance of the orchestra as a collection of instruments led to its imaginary reconfiguration as a single voice. For many writers, the lyric element of musical theater brought about a reconciliation, the uniting of the multitude in a singular, affective experience. In France, the old *jeu de paume* enclosed a long, fancifully decorated echo chamber; and many of the new projects, as Chaumont argued, simply changed the shape without reforming the interior design. Cochin's project redesigned the auditorium, eliminating the deep backstage corridors (*coulisses*) and other extraneous spaces in order to improve the acoustics. The *Lettres sur l'opéra* drew together and attempted to integrate the dramatic, acoustic, and visual aspects of the operatic spectacle through the circular organization of the theater.

In addition to acoustical concerns (such as favoring wood and stone construction for their enhanced resonance), Cochin's project marks a desire for a high degree of intervisibility and intercommunication between spectators. Architects and theorists complained about the division that the loges and their décor inflicted upon the unity of the theatrical space. Remarks on the desire for private boxes for distinguished spectators, and complaints about it, were common in the writings of the period throughout Europe. Seventeenth-century Dutch theaters, for example, were equipped with curtains for each box. Francesco

Milizia, in his *Del Teatro*, describes theater boxes as "un caos di teste e di mezzi busti" [a jumble of heads and busts][12] In France, the loges were referred to as chicken coops (*volières*) for two reasons: first, because they were usually vertically constructed, so that their occupants appeared in boxes one atop the other; and secondly, because those seated in the loges were locked in by an attendant from the beginning of the play. André Roubo attributes this practice to opulence and "Italian jealousy."[13] Though practices such as these were criticized, eighteenth-century French cultural and social habits continued to make certain unavoidable requirements on the design of the *salle*:

> The Ancients had imagined disposing seats in an amphitheater with rows of tiered seats, but this disposition, as we have remarked, seems too contrary to our manners, to our social practices, to our morals...
> Women, long accustomed to being the principal ornament of [the theater], would not be done justice on these tiered seats, on which they would appear isolated and jumbled together.[14]

Similarly, when it was decided that the chandelier would be raised in order to focus more light on the stage rather than on the auditorium, spectators complained that they would no longer be able to use their libretti and that women could no longer attend the opera with the aim of being seen, since in the diminished light their charms would be unavailable to idle male gazers.[15]

The compromises that the architect envisaged involved aesthetic and practical considerations that tended to fragment and divide the *salle*. Although Cochin's project fell short of the equality implicit in Boullée's project for a Parisian opera or the hierarchical social utopia of Ledoux's theater in Besançon, Cochin sought nonetheless to create a practical equality in the seating and an effect of unity in his design for the loges: the result being that "one can say that there is no bad seat [in the house]" (13). Rather than placing the loges in perfect aplomb, his project staggered them, ascending towards the back of the theater. The design would eliminate the *volière* effect of stacked boxes and, as Cochin noted, would allow for "a smaller number of women to sufficiently ornament the spectacle" who could "see and be seen" more easily (26–27, 34).[16] Cochin emphasized that because of the terraced effect, the spectators could carry on conversation without straining from one level of loges to the next. The architectonics draws attention towards the center of the structure, linking the staged spectacle to the audience and creating a space of intervisibility and interaction in the audience. In most theaters, which date from "the time when we preferred polite society to convenience," the view is blocked at many points by the pillars separating the loges (12). Cochin's project seeks to move away from the rigidity of these designs by establishing a triple effect of transparency: from actor to spectator, from spectator to actor, and from spectator to spectator. Those seated in the loges would be interconnected in a complex way with the operatic performance, both as subjects and objects of spectacle. In the seventeenth and early eighteenth centuries, as Henri Lagrave has remarked, "the disposition of loges on the side . . . has the effect of directing the axis of sight, and the bodies of spectators themselves, towards their neighbors facing them, rather than towards the stage where the action takes place," and hence, "the stage is quite clearly de-centered in relation to the vast majority of spectators."[17] Lagrave describes a social (and, of course, theatrical) space that is physically isolated from the events taking place on stage. In direct opposition to this configuration, Cochin imagines an inclusive theatrical space. The stage, no longer isolated at the end of a rectangular hall, would instead be brought into the space inhabited by the audience; and the audience itself – particularly its female half, the half to which Cochin and Patte referred – fans out in a public display that defeats the traditional parcelling of multiple, intimate boxes.

I would argue, then, that Cochin, in his architectural layout and his description of the activities that would take place within that layout, attempted to consolidate a particular space of spectatorship and to reinforce the idea of an interactive community of spectators by way of theatrical experience. Through his insistence on the presence and clarity of the voice and on the relative proximity of the actors, Cochin's project refined a new concept of spectatorship and of theatrical representation. One aspect of Cochin's work in this area is his move to hide certain aspects of the spectacle from the spectator. At the same time that he brought the actor toward the center of the auditorium, Cochin proposed a curtain to conceal the mechanics of scene changes between acts. Cochin also suggested that the area he set aside for the orchestra – a pit between the stage and the *parquet* – would create precisely enough distance between the singers and the audience so that the efforts of the singers – often resulting in contorted facial expressions and raucous vocal sounds ("éclats de voix") in close proximity – would not be apparent to the spectator. Combats would also be placed farther towards the back of the stage so that their artificiality would not impinge upon the dramatic experience. Cochin emphasized that combats had previously taken place at the front of the stage, precisely so that the spectator could see that they were not real; but this effect was no longer considered desirable. The *Lettres sur l'opéra* articulate a balance between distance and proximity: the audience is close enough so that "the most far-removed [spectators]... can see & hear distinctly" without the echo of the old *jeu de paume*, yet the design maintains enough distance so that the action falls within the bounds of an aesthetic of the natural (26). With its machines, the *tragédie en musique* had attempted to produce marveled and amused spectators. Cochin sought to create an architecture conducive to a different kind of spectacle, one which offered a new role to the audience. The theater would be constructed as a whole including the actor and the stage, on the one hand, and the audience on the other, the lip of the stage integrating the two spaces. At the same time, an effect of truth would be encouraged by maintaining a distance between certain actions taking place on stage and the spectator. The proscenium arch (*avant-scène*) is an important architectural figure of this distance.[18] Patte notes that the spectators who were seated there were too close to the action to frame it as real, and that the loges in the *avant-scène* hampered the effect of the voice.[19] Because the proscenium marks the symbolic boundary of two spaces, as Patte argues, the loges that contaminate that boundary should be eliminated. In Cochin's project, the arch marks the boundary between stage and audience, figuring at the same time the distance necessary for the audience to frame properly the events as "natural" (that is, as a certain kind of fiction), while the circular construction of the theater as a whole unites these two spaces. If combats no longer took place at the front of the stage, it was because an idea of spectatorship and reception had changed and with it, a conception of the space that framed and defined that experience.

From this standpoint, what Cochin and other theorists, such as Diderot, refer to as "truth" in theater has less to do with an invariable or timeless concept of verisimilitude, as it has often been understood, than it has with a series of representational or presentational (*Vorstellung*) relationships – the relationship of the spectacle to the audience, of the audience to the spectacle, and of the audience to itself. When Cochin argues that the combats should be farther away from the spectator, he does not alter the relationship of the theatrical performance to that which it represents (the combat), but he does modify the relation of the spectator to that performance. Cochin's project reveals a desire to refashion theatrical representation, not by changing the mimesis carried out through dramatic events, but by altering and exerting control over the space in which representation occurs. By carefully manipulating the space of spectatorship (this manipulation being, after all, the function of design), theater architecture attempted to control a series of more or less contiguous spaces: the stage, the auditorium, and eventually the area surrounding the theater. Segregated yet linked by the architecture, these different spaces would form a mimetic continuum, connected by an architectural vision that sought to express an ideal of community. It could be argued, then, that the "truth" of the theater, as defined by theorists such as Diderot, in some measure lies in the affective experience of the spectators as projected by the architecture, and in the (imaginary) community implicit in that experience. This kind of community is precisely what Diderot had in mind in *De la poésie dramatique* when he sees an entire audience in tears following a play on the death of Socrates. Imagining the scene he has just conjured up, Diderot exclaims, "what naturalness! what truth!"[20] The "truth" of the

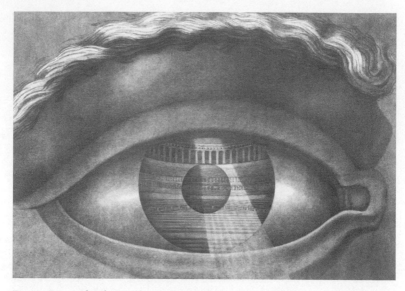

Fig. 8. From Claude-Nicolas Ledoux, *L'Architecture considérée sous le rapport de l'art, des moeurs et de la législation*, 2 vols. (Paris: chez l'auteur, 1804), 1:224. Photo courtesy of the Environmental Design Library, University of California, Berkeley.

performance to which Diderot refers no longer concerns the events on stage, but rather another presence that is generated as an after-effect of those events: a reconciliation, an extended moment of collective pathos. Cochin's project reveals a conscious attempt in theater design to control mimesis and its effects, and through them, to unite the audience as a community, both as subject and object of representation.

The reciprocal relationship between the stage and the community of spectators, mediated by the proscenium arch, is clearly figured by Claude-Nicolas Ledoux in his drawings for a theater in Besançon. In a startling and often reproduced image, which Ledoux calls a "coup d'oeil," an eye is located onstage into which we gaze to see the seats and the rear of the theater reflected in its pupil (fig. 8). Here, the semi-circle arranges the audience as in the public theaters of antiquity; and there are no divisions between loges to interrupt the continuity of vision, from the back of the auditorium to the front. Seen in Ledoux's "coup d'oeil," the tiers of seats are themselves "staged" as seen by the eye of the stage which has been given the role of spectator. It is unclear whether the beam of light illuminating the rows of seats comes from the back of the theater, striking the eye which looks back toward the spectators; or whether it is the result of an invisible machine, enclosed within the recesses of the eye. Abandoning the standing *parterre*, but nonetheless maintaining and even reinforcing the articulation of social status, Ledoux, as Anthony Vidler has shown, creates an unprecedented degree of visibility, and complicates or even collapses the relative position of stage and spectator. The eye also figures the importance of the proscenium arch, whose object is, according to Pierre Patte, to "prepare the opening of the Theater."[21] The opening should serve as an *encadrement*, framing the stage and acting as a transition from the *salle* to the theater itself: "the eye, as Ledoux pointed out, was indeed the 'first frame' through which the world was seen, and remains the frame of vision for each individual member of the audience."[22] The theatrical experience of the audience peering through the proscenium arch reproduces a natural schema: that of the subject's vision of the world. The proscenium also figures the merging of singular visions into a collectivity: all eyes being directed towards one aperture.

Cochin's project does not move so directly toward the Greco-Roman fantasy Ledoux creates through the representation of a community of spectator-citizens, even if he insists on a certain equality in the seating. What Cochin's project does establish in this direction, in conjunction with the play of distance and proximity, is a movement from the stage, to the theater, and to the public spaces outside the opera house. This movement is initiated through the disintegration of the perfectly closed perspective of the classical stage. The traditional opera stage in France presented a series of movable frames for the scenery (a *galerie de chassis*) which were fixed in slotted groves, directing the perspective towards a unique vanishing point located at the rear of the stage. Borrowing the perspective *per angolo* from Servandoni, who had been active at the Académie Royale de Musique in the 1720s and '30s, Cochin proposed a tri-partite stage which would create a panorama instead of the tight depth of French theaters:

[The Italian designers] dared to present their objects at an angle, which makes them more picturesque, offers the spectator a pleasing view, and whose perspective escapes his criticism, since the converging lines move toward points that he cannot examine.

Ils osaient présenter leurs objets sous un point de vue pris sur l'angle, ce qui les rend plus pittoresque, & offre au spectateur un coup d'oeil agréable, & dont la perspective échappe à sa critique, les lignes fuyantes tendant à des points qu'il n'est pas à portée de juger. (64–65)

What is new in this statement is not the description of staging *per angolo*, but Cochin's theorization and rendering of it.[23] For Cochin, it is a question of projecting a space of belief, a space that is invested with something other than, but nonetheless receives the approbation of, rational judgment. Fully adopting the recommendations of Italian stagecraft, the operatic spectacle would abandon the comprehensive, unique perspective from the front of the stage to the back curtain.[24] The *Lettres sur l'opéra* endorsed Servandoni's stagecraft, and proposed an architectural space that would do justice to it, incorporating the stage perspective into the complete experience of spectatorship. Cochin suggests that Servandoni, by forcing the vanishing point beyond the walls of the theater, created a representation which was more "truthful," escaping the criticism of the onlooker because it escapes his/her inspection. Because the vanishing point moves beyond the stage, a point of reference was suggested outside the confines of the theater itself, an area that could be imagined but which was not open to direct inspection ("dont la perspective échappe à sa critique"). This space escapes the direct observation of the spectator and thus exists beyond her/his rational mastery.

The disappearance and reconfiguration of space in Cochin's project – produced by the retreat of the vanishing point – introduces an aesthetic predicated on the withdrawal of the object which would later be theorized by Kant. If the aesthetic judgment for Kant moves away from the object to bring to the foreground the mental state and capacities of the spectator and their communicability, so Cochin's description of the stage makes objects unavailable to the spectator so as to bring the imagination into play. Through his/her ability to imagine objects that cannot be depicted on stage, the spectator is brought into the work of representation and this work becomes the basis of a collective experience. In Kantian terms, the withdrawal of the vanishing point in the perspective *per angolo* lays the groundwork for the creation of a communal feeling of subjective purposiveness in representation. The mimetic capacity of the spectator is thus stimulated by the dramatic and architectural protocol outlined by the *Lettres sur l'opéra*. The attention to distance (of actions and grimaces on stage) and proximity (of the audience to the actor and to itself), together with the perspective *per angolo*, is not so important because it plays with the presence or absence of objects per se, as it is for the pleasure and the awareness of this pleasure that it generates within a community of spectators. It is in this respect that architecture's interest in mimesis has less to do with the events depicted on stage than it does with a relationship created between persons through a particular form of mental activity.

If Cochin's description of staging allows us to discuss what Kant would call the communicability of subjective purposiveness elicited by representation, the architectural specifications lead us back to a concrete rendering of that aesthetic experience: the Diderotian image of spectators weeping over the death of Socrates. This activity on the part of the spectator is what Diderot had in mind in *De la poésie dramatique* when he referred to the reconciliation of the theatrical image and individual conduct: "it is by going to the theater that men will escape the wicked men whose company they keep; it is there that they will find those with whom they would wish to live; it is there that they will see the human race as it is and will reconcile themselves with it."[25] In the theater, the "wicked" is abandoned for the "good," and the individual spectator is reconciled with humanity. Diderot's formulation suggests a kind of projection through which the moral character of the representation is superimposed on the spectators. The referent in this passage is purposefully equivocal: the people Diderot describes as "those with whom they would wish to live" and "the human race" are both the abstract models of theatrical representation – the characters of the play – and the moral "becoming" of the audience. He suggests that the theater can reconcile the particular and the general – a reconciliation that appears to Frances Ferguson "not merely as one epistemological problem among others but as *the* characteristically aesthetic epistemological problem."[26] Perhaps more than any other, it is the issue of the singular and the general that is omnipresent in late-eighteenth-century theater architecture. Rétif de la Bretonne touches on this mechanism of collective identification: "let us see what we are in other men, that is what will interest us, engage us, and intensely move us."[27] One might object that in the case of Diderot, I am conflating morality and politics, and that Diderot frequently appears more interested in the moral experience of the isolated and excluded beholder than he is with the kind of communal experience so often evoked by Rousseau. Yet his writings on theater, such as *Le Paradoxe sur le comédien*, show a reiterated concern with the influence of spectacles on taste and culture (*moeurs*). In *Le Paradoxe*, the first interlocutor concludes that the influence of theater could be widespread: "do you doubt that the national spirit is affected by it?" Diderot also compares the actor to the Roman orator in his effect on the public as a whole.[28] Similarly, in the *Correspondance Littéraire* of January 1, 1765, Grimm notes the exemplary politics of Greek and Roman theater, emphasizing the collective acts of spectatorship that took place within the space of the city:

> For the ancients, tragedy was a political institution, a religious act; for us, it is a diversion which allows the idle population that fills the capitals and large cities to pass a few hours of the day. In Greece and in Rome, the people attended spectacles as a collective body; by going to the theater, they satisfied a duty ... If the people of Athens or Rome could see our most moving tragedies represented, those we call masterpieces, they would surely judge them as meant for the amusement of children.[29]

In Cochin's response to this problem, the community of individual spectators that the architecture moves to unify is projected, via the *per angolo* perspective of the stage and the music, to an "imaginary" space of public feeling that is neither inside nor outside the theater. In his design, Cochin has sought to create a "publicness" in and through spectatorship.

My analysis of the architectural evocation of public space may be seen to differ significantly from Jürgen Habermas's conception of the public sphere. Most importantly, Habermas's conception of the public sphere is not theatrical, but is based on rational discussion, open debate, and the exchange of ideas.[30] The public spaces I describe are spaces of performance, not of liberal exchange, which would associate them, at least aesthetically speaking, within the feudal world of "representative publicness" as Habermas envisions it. However, given the model of the public sphere put forth by Habermas, it may not be contradictory to claim that the public sphere may be asserted, represented, or contested in cultural forms that are not essentially dependent on the liberal exchange of ideas. Indeed, Habermas's bourgeois public sphere does not arise only out of rational debate. It also arose out of literary models which "staged" certain forms of subjectivity that were "audience-centered": "the empathetic reader repeated within himself the private relationships displayed before him in literature; from his experience of real familiarity (*Intimität*), he gave life to the fictional one, and in the latter he prepared himself for the former."[31] As this model of literary consciousness allows, there is room for a performative sort of public awareness, even within an essentially non-theatrical conception of the public sphere. In any event, my intention here is not to dispute the applicability of Habermas's model of the bourgeois public sphere to eighteenth-century France: that critique would be beyond the scope of my study and has been undertaken by others.[32] Rather, I want to draw out the aesthetic and political dimensions of some exemplary theater architecture in the late eighteenth century through its figuration of public space. I have argued that Cochin's project involves a move away from traditional absolutist theater practices – a system that Cochin identifies with a spectatorship of *politesse* and its attendant social practices and spaces. His design favors not only "comfort," as he suggests in opposition to the rigidity of *politesse*, but moreover it emphasizes quite different social structures and configurations which correspond to new conceptions of theater and spectatorship. Architecturally and aesthetically, this shift occurs through the integration of spectator and spectacle in the elliptical design, the play with proximity and distance that goes hand in hand with this manipulation of space, and the retreat of the vanishing point. All of these elements signal a change in theater that we can identify as a shift towards post-absolutist conceptions of spectatorship. Moving away from the concept of the princely theater, Cochin's design stretches the requirements of theatrical space in the ancien régime as it provides the spectator with new spaces, and hence new identities.

MUSICAL THEATER AND CITY SPACE

In Cochin's design, the exterior architecture and setting were designed to complete the effect initiated by the complex stagecraft and the disposition of the auditorium, and to solve certain practical problems. Every architectural proposal for an opera house in the second half of the eighteenth century showed an overriding concern with preventing fire: with theaters burning all over Europe – in Vienna, Milan, Stockholm, Venice, Bologna, Lyon, Mantua, Amsterdam, and Saragossa – it was an absolute imperative that the theater be isolated from neighboring structures.[33] Entry and exit had to be facilitated in case of fire, and this concern led to the separation of the theater from surrounding structures which contributed greatly to the monumentalization of the theater as public architecture. Inside, the corridors would be enlarged, monumental staircases would be constructed, and open galleries would be built to enable spectators to leave the building safely in the event of fire. In addition to providing safe access, these spaces also reinforced the sense of public unity and presence which Cochin sought to create in the theater itself. The enlarged staircases and galleries offered areas that would in effect "stage" large numbers of theatergoers in harmonious procession, giving a sense of moment and proportion to their arrival and departure. Modern theaters would be public theaters, and as such they would provide an impression of openness and easy access. The idea of the theater as public monument, isolated from other structures, can be linked to an eighteenth-century desire to create an enlightened *polis*, modeled after the harmonious relationship that was perceived between Greco-Roman architecture on the one hand, and the political and social accomplishments of those cultures on the other. Blondel, in his *Cours d'architecture*, for example, sees architecture as a sign and expression of the political health of a nation: "simple Roman Citizens proclaimed their love for their country by the roads that they had built." Subsequently, however, "architecture suffered the same misfortunes that divided & destroyed the Roman Empire."[34] In a similar linking of architecture and social concerns, Diderot comments in the *Essais sur la peinture* on the effect of the open and isolated temples of the ancients which are "accessible from all directions: the image of security. Even kings secure their palaces with doors."[35] As Marvin Carlson has suggested, the "correlation between regularized city spaces and an orderly society proved enormously attractive to theorists and to those in power in seventeenth- and eighteenth-century Europe."[36] These statements reveal a degree of conflation, or confusion, of aesthetics and politics: powerful, harmonious architecture is the sign of a secure and morally sound nation.

Toward the end of the century, architectural projects for the theater show an increasingly insistent concern with regulating the spaces inside and outside the theater – the neighboring district the theater can shape, to some degree, by its presence and the larger urban landscape that contains it and of which it becomes a symbol. Both Boullée's project for an opera house and Cochin's *Lettres* are indicative of this concern. Isolated from the neighboring structures, yet symbolically linked to the King and the (cultural) wealth of the state through its proximity to the Louvre, the opera would create a separate cultural space in which spectatorship and citizenship could blend – a space modeled on a fantasy in which eighteenth-century France would recapture the public life of ancient Rome. The neoclassicism of late eighteenth-century theater architecture (which is already present in the projects of Cochin and Roubo, and becomes omnipresent in Boullée's) announces a desire to refashion social space. Through the articulation of a series of public and scenographic spaces, the architect sought to re-invent the spectator as the figure of the Roman citizen, superimposing him on a series of imaginary scenarios of moral community – the architecture assuring the mechanism of transference through the regulated proximity of the stage and projecting both inward and outward through the perspective *per angolo* that Cochin promotes, linking the singular experience of the spectator with a feeling of community. The architect answers Voltaire's call to cast aside the image of Paris as a city of "Goths and Vandals," of "obscure, confined, hideous" spaces in order to create the open public spaces of a new Rome.[37] If the isolated temple is an "image of security," as Diderot suggested, it is because this architecture creates a sense of public space and life. Impassioned through the experience of the lyric theater, unified by the architecture, opera spectators would be transported from the spectacle on stage (theatrical scenes of domestic and public virtue) to an ideal public space of moral and civic values.[38] Jean Starobinski has commented on the moral thrust of all late eighteenth-century architecture: "[bringing] architecture back to its elementary figures and the materials to their true nature, one sees a choice that is not only aesthetic but also moral . . . the moralising pathos, in the theoretical writings of Boullée and Ledoux, is in no way an inadvertent addition . . . it is the very meaning of their undertaking that they reveal by making an eloquent pedagogy out of architecture."[39]

Existing Paris theaters were not consonant with these aims. Voltaire complained of the "inconvenient" layout and "disgusting" qualities of the quarter surrounding the existing opera at the Palais-Royal, and of the "suffering" and "confusion" [*embarras*] inflicted upon the spectators as they attempted to find their seats or leave.[40] The Berlin opera, built in 1745 for Frederick the Great, offering a monumental classical facade and expansive vistas, became a model of the modern, rationalized cityscape – everything the Paris Opéra was not. Paris lacked such a monument. After the 1763 fire, the Opéra was rebuilt as a modest dependency of the Palais-Royal because the Duc d'Orléans refused to have the elaborate entrance he had just built there eclipsed by a monumental facade. Carlson has pointed out the importance of the isolated structure for conceptions of public space in the eighteenth century. He notes that "in order for the almost invisible public theatres of the seventeenth century to become significant elements in these new urban designs, the theatre itself had to be regarded in a new way. The rulers who had the power to effect urban changes had to begin considering the signifying possibilities of the theatre as a cultural monument rather than as a private possession."[41] Isolating the theater from other structures was a crucial aspect of this general tendency.

The Place du Carrousel was generally agreed upon as the ideal site for a new opera (now the site of the underground shopping mall that opened in the early 1990s as part of the Grand Louvre). The Carrousel was in close proximity to the symbolic center of the nation, yet there the opera would stand out against the backdrop of the Louvre from which it would be physically separated. None of the designs for this site, including that of Cochin, would ever be realized. Boullée's proposal, to cite an example that differs in some important ways from Cochin's design by carrying its innovations to their limits, offers monumental access from all four sides of a circular structure which appears to contain a sphere. In Boullée's work, the globe stands as a metaphor for the universe, and a fortiori, the "public sphere." Similarly, Ledoux speaks of the glory of the circle: "all is circle in nature . . . It is there, yes there, that man returns to his primitive state and recovers the equality that he should never have lost. It is on this vast stage, suspended in the skies, in circles within circles, that he takes part in the secret of the gods."[42] In an initial conception, Boullée considers the various pleasures of spectators who come to stroll and enjoy the sights around the "jardin de la révolution (ci-devant le Palais-Royal)": "the Public would arrive from all directions, drawn either by the lure of the theater, the promise of a stroll, or by the desire to enjoy the sight of this great gathering of people."[43] In the end, choosing the Carrousel over the Palais-Royal, Boullée indicates his desire to focus on the monumental effects of architecture, on the image of the theater: "this last site [the Carrousel] is majestic. There I have situated my theater isolated on all sides" (55). Boullée remains concerned with many practical matters of spectatorship, including the danger of fire and the need to provide a space that would be in proportion to our limited senses of sight and hearing; "but," as he insists, "the Theater should nonetheless be as large as possible" (59). In one drawing, spectators are depicted leaving the theater, slowly making their way down the massive steps in front of the building which dwarfs and governs their movements through its projection of monumental meaning. The building is animated by the spectator-citizens it determines as a community, highlighting the moment of their emergence from the theater and linking the operatic performances in the globe with the urban space upon which the building imposes itself and which it seeks to control. The theater frames the spectators inside as well as outside:

> Being careful to offer the most agreeable sight [*tableau*], I thought I would succeed by placing the spectators such that it would be they who would decorate my theater and constitute its principal ornament. Indeed, it is by bringing together the fair sex, situated so as to replace the bas-reliefs of my architecture, that I think I have succeeded in giving the mark of elegance to my tableau. (61)

Although Boullée may seem to highlight the living presence of the spectator and to oppose this presence to the static conception of design embodied in the traditional use of bas-reliefs, the spectator is in fact swallowed up by the architecture, taking the place of the bas-relief. The spectator's aimless promenade disappears in the later project so that she can reappear as ornament, contained within the building as an architectural effect. Through its strong formal geometry that incorporates the spectator, the opera house creates and structures a utopian, urban space. The effect of the monument, according to Boullée, should be one that draws attention to its massive and singular presence: "a colossal monument must excite our admiration . . . its proportion must diminish everything that surrounds it" (98).

I do not intend to create an absolute opposition between Boullée's proposal and that of Cochin. Indeed, they share many of the same references and concerns, and both are strongly interested in the publicness of theatrical architecture. Yet I would argue that Boullée's architecture clarifies, to the point of overdetermining, the theatrical spaces (audience, actors, society) described in the *Lettres sur l'opéra*. It collapses the subtle play with differences – the play with concealment and disclosure, distance and proximity – that characterizes Cochin's design by imposing a massive and uniform architectural control over spectatorship. The spectators who would constitute the true spectacle of his opera house, according to Boullée, are the abstract projections of an enormous architectural idea. Whereas Cochin's spectators were carefully situated within the real and imaginary concerns of eighteenth-century spectatorship, Boullée's spectators people his plans to give life to an architectural program. The open space of identity – the play between the singular and the collective – that appears in Cochin's project is shut down, because overdetermined, in Boullée's conception of architecture: "what is architecture? Will I define it with Vitruvius as the art of building? No . . . one must conceive in order to do" (27).

What is frequently referred to as the "monumentalization" of theater architecture in late-eighteenth-century France has a definite socio-political meaning. To create a monument is to focus a massive effect of meaning at a site; the monument acts as if it stands for something, refers to something, renders that something concrete, gives it a place in the world and thus makes it real. The monumentalization of the theater, as it was imagined in the eighteenth century, reveals a desire for the spatial embodiment and consecration of morals, hence for overwhelming moral control over the citizen who inhabits this space, and for a performative closure in design that assures inviolability. Through unrelenting architectural control upon the site (like that, for example, of New York City's Lincoln Center), the theater as public monument is able to create a fiction of public space – in other words, to impose certain criteria on public space by framing it – precisely insofar as it displaces the existing city and its inhabitants. Unlike Paris's Opéra Bastille or the nineteenth-century Palais Garnier, Lincoln Center is "a kind of supermonument," Marvin Carlson remarks, "an entire artistic enclave within the city." The project was seen as a foundation for "the upgrading of surrounding areas," particularly the "slum area" around Lincoln Square, north of Columbus Circle.[44] Similarly, in suggesting a new location for the "Comédie," Rétif de la Bretonne recommends that the areas surrounding the theater be cleaned up, both aesthetically and hygienically, by demolishing the existing houses:

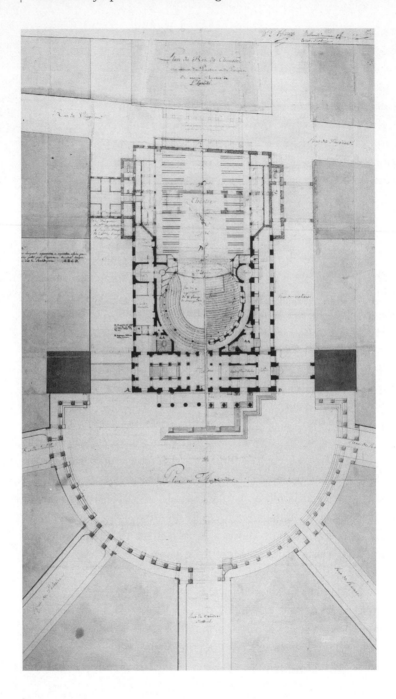

[It would be appropriate] to demolish, on the one hand, all the houses up to the Hôtel-du-Premier-Président, & all those that are situated between the rue Sainlouis & the Palais up to the rue de la Barillerie; and on the other hand, everything that borders on the Quai-de-l'Horloge, & the entire section of the rues Sainbarthélemi & de la Barillerie that masks the Palais: thus the Theater, entirely isolated, would have multiple exits. One senses what a beautiful sight [*coup-d'oeil*] would be created.[45]

The closure that Scott Bryson shows to be one of the defining characteristics of eighteenth-century bourgeois drama extends to the ideal spaces defined by certain theater architects. Because they create their own spaces and the citizens who would inhabit them in the cleanliness and abstraction of architectural theory, these projects would respond to Voltaire's call for more decorous surroundings and for more decent citizens who would not appear to foreigners and visiting dignitaries as "Goths and Vandals." The move toward public theaters in the late eighteenth century brought with it, in its idealism, some opposed and conflicting tendencies and aims. I have argued that the architectural project came into its own as a public project. While aspects of Cochin's project appear to open the theater of the ancien régime to new concerns with public space, the monumentalization of the theater in Boullée's design reveals a mystification of those ideals. The presence of the spectator has been eclipsed by the massive effect of the project.

The effort to monumentalize the theatrical experience (both the lyric and "regular") and to extend that experience, in parallel spheres, from the stage to the audience, led architects out of the theater into the urban landscape surrounding it. Charles de Wailly's project for a large public *place* outside his Odéon theater, elaborated around the height of the Terror in 1794 primarily for spoken drama, is one such scheme (fig. 9).[46] De Wailly's project implicitly recognizes the social pedagogy of architecture that Starobinski remarks, and moreover

---

Fig. 9. From Charles de Wailly, "Plan d'aménagement de la place du théâtre français, transformée en aire de rassemblement public, avec gradins et tribune d'orateur" (1794). Photo courtesy of the Bibliothèque-Musée de la Comédie-Française, Paris.

emphasizes design as a form of power and constraint. In his drawings, a colonnade of Doric columns – that order being the most appropriate one for the authoritative definition of a space of public virtue – extends from either side of the theater, forming a semi-circular passageway around the public *place*. In another drawing, not reproduced here, seated muses reign over the arches that open onto side streets. These side streets – rue de Molière, rue de Racine, rue de Voltaire, rue de Crébillon – fan out in all directions, symbolically bringing the history of theater to its culmination in the modern structure that was designed to fuse spectator and citizen and thus complete the civil education that was the basis of d'Alembert's argument for the theater in the *Encyclopédie* article, "Genève." The "Plan du Rez de Chaussé au niveau du Parterre et du Parquet du nouveau theatre de l'Égalité" shows the "place en amphithéâtre" which mirrors the theater building itself and whose extended circle symbolically contains it: spectatorship is contained within, and duplicates, the relations of the social body. Furthermore, the two principal spaces, the outdoor amphitheater and the Odéon theater itself, are mediated by the steps of the theater and the "tribune d'orateur" which slightly encroach on the geometrical perfection of the semi-circular, outdoor amphitheater, connecting one space to the other. The relationship of the stage to the spectators is thus duplicated once again in the larger scheme by the relationship established between the orator at his podium and the people assembled in the *place*. The theatricality of de Wailly's architectural plan is striking. De Wailly sketches three interconnected spaces: the first two consist of the auditorium and the stage, which slightly interconnect through the lip of the stage, with the third and largest being that of the public *place* containing the two others. Both the space of the spectacle, and that of spectatorship and citizenship, are controlled by a meta-representational scheme, revealing a desire to give birth to the "real" through utopian control over the imaginary. As if it wasn't enough to design the theater building, that space also had to be contained and determined within another design.

The more modest innovations of Cochin's *Lettres sur l'opéra*, concerning the acoustical and visual ease of the spectator as well as fostering a sense of community, have given way to a mystifying vision of the spectator as citizen. In Cochin's *Lettres sur l'opéra*, spectatorship and community are above all based on the aesthetic and shared experience of singular persons. In de Wailly's additions to the Odéon, the person vanishes while a vision of the Nation or the People appears: there is no longer any singular body to have pleasures or discomforts. The idealization and effective disappearance of the spectator into ideology in de Wailly's plan reveal one direction of architectural theory in the late eighteenth century. However, the "political correctness" of projects such as de Wailly's – reproducing as it did a revolutionary vision of spectatorship as citizenship – did raise social questions that the aesthetic concerns of Cochin's proposal could not or did not resolve. One such issue is that of the *parterre*, an issue that dogged French theater through the end of the eighteenth century. As a figure of the architectural repressed in the eighteenth century, the *parterre* returns in each theater project as a (particularly French) problem which, for lack of a better solution, is "resolved" through more detailed attention to other areas of the design in a form of compensation until it was eliminated just before the Revolution. The debate surrounding the *parterre* involved many issues relating to long-standing custom, finances, morality, and public health. Ravel interprets the debate on seating the *parterre* as an indication of shifting relations between the public of theater spectators, on the one hand, and actors, authors, and the authorities, on the other hand. Ravel argues that the move to seat the *parterre* in late eighteenth-century France, by clearly attempting to control the access and conduct of spectators, "prompted a wide spectrum of the literate, theater-going population to analyze the problem in overtly political terms."[47] The particular interest of Cochin's project, though, is that it fuses the architectural and aesthetic transformation of the musical theater with a new view of spectatorship. Cochin's architecture explicitly enhances intervisibility as an aesthetic element of spectatorship, not only between the different groups of spectators, but also between the different public spaces of the theater and the city. From this standpoint, it reveals a concern for the articulation of operatic spectacle and public space. Cochin's architecture facilitates the various identifications of the spectator through the play of proximity and distance at the same time that it demonstrates a concern for the spectator's ease and safety. The

Lettres sur l'opéra takes into account the mechanism of the spectator's identifications at the theater, and attempts to create a space in which to engage them.

Initially built as the Théâtre-Français, Peyre's and de Wailly's Odéon theater was renamed the Théâtre de la Nation (1790), later the Théâtre du Peuple or the Théâtre de l'Egalité (1794), and was baptized the Théâtre de l'Europe toward the close of the twentieth century in wishful anticipation of the realization of the Maastricht treaty. The Odéon theater – named, renamed, occupied during May and June of 1968, and renamed again – reveals the extent to which the theater and its site have been involved in claims to, or on behalf of, various publics. Given that the many projects that emerged after the 1763 fire were addressed to the state and sought its financial backing, it is not surprising that they articulated connections between theater, architecture, and the social body. As Grimod de la Reynière explained from the vantage point of the final years of the eighteenth century, the Opéra has, "in every era, drawn the attention, the protection, and the assistance of the government; it has always been seen as a truly national enterprise," and therefore all the more worthy of the state's financial support since what it has taken in "has never, at any time, been able to offset its expense."[48] He remarked further that the opera performed the important service of representing the French nation to important visitors from other nations: "the Opéra is also the principal objective of foreign travelers in Paris, and the first theater to which they decide to come."[49] Indeed, architecture always evokes an idea of community or nation through its ability to imagine, define, and control space. Louis XIV had mastered the theatrical display of politics (as well as the political use of theater) in the previous century: the fêtes staged at Versailles during the 1660s, for example, sought both to display the power of the state, and to cultivate a particular relationship between the subject and the king. If opera was no longer so clearly a vehicle for absolutist ideology in the eighteenth century, it nonetheless continued to be involved in the creative definition of new national and social spaces through the configurations imagined by its architects and designers.

de la musique

"It would be fair to say that music criticism becomes postmodernist when it proceeds by deconstructing the concept of the extramusical."

Lawrence Kramer[1]

The second half of the eighteenth century saw an enormous proliferation of writings on the origins and development of human culture. Many of these writings took music, and opera in particular, as exemplary forms of human expression and therefore as keys to understanding human affect and its impact on the development of society. The previous two chapters have established the increasing importance of sympathy and feeling in eighteenth-century operatic culture. The aim of this final chapter is to pursue that inquiry still further through one writer who endeavored to valorize the culture of feeling by constructing an anthropology in which acts of operatic identification are represented as those through which humanity and the bonds of sociability originally emerged.

An important figure at the end of the eighteenth century, though he is relatively unknown today, Bernard Germain Étienne Médard de la Ville-sur-Illon, Comte de Lacépède, led a double life. He was a naturalist who followed in the footsteps of Buffon, specializing in reptiles and fish; but he also composed music and wrote an influential theoretical volume on music. He corresponded with d'Alembert, met Gluck in 1777, studied with the composer François-Joseph Gossec for a few years prior to 1781, and held important positions at the Jardin des Plantes, then the King's collection of exotic and domestic wildlife, plants, and minerals. Several of his musical works – a *Cyrus*, an *Alcina*, an *Omphale* – were accepted by the Paris Opéra but never made it to the stage. He apparently destroyed his own setting of *Armide*. According to the only scholar to my knowledge who has explored the details, though Lacépède was unable to distinguish himself through composition, he did successfully influence later composers such as

Jean-François Le Sueur and Hector Berlioz. Particularly important in this regard was Lacépède's "development of the *genre instrumental expressif,* his particular attention to individual instrumental timbres," and his dramatization of the orchestra.[2]

In this chapter, I will focus on his authoritative treatise, well over 700 pages long, *La Poétique de la musique*, first published in 1785. As Lacépède conceived it, the treatise was directed at both composers and amateurs – a general, cultivated public: "this work is written for young artists who aspire to follow in the footsteps of the great composers, and for those who, without any knowledge of the the the art of Music, seek to recognize the beauties of the works of the great masters."[3] With the *querelle* between the Gluckists and Piccinnists behind him, if only by five years, Lacépède could propose a triumphantly universal musical poetics, citing the works of Gluck most often, but also occasionally those of Niccolò Piccinni, Antonio Sacchini, Marin Marais, and others.[4] Ora Saloman has identified prophetic elements in *La Poétique de la musique* by reading backwards from Berlioz through the forgotten works of the first quarter of the French nineteenth century to Lacépède, who stands as a precursor. Saloman focuses almost entirely on the notion that instrumental music was liberated from earlier aesthetic models and their dependence on poetics, justifying this reading through the more extensive role Lacépède gave the orchestra. However, because Lacépède understood the orchestra as a "voice" that "speaks," one could easily see the opposite in his treatise – that is, a strong connection to standard eighteenth-century theories of musical meaning. Indeed, given its title, *La Poétique de la musique* would appear to be one of the last great statements of music theory as poetics, at once the *summa* and swan song of eighteenth-century musical aesthetics. Lacépède's treatise gives overwhelming preference to opera over other musical forms – one whose music was considered to function along rhetorical lines – and specifically to the *tragédie lyrique*. He described at great length the representation of character and passion in music, and nearly excluded instrumental music entirely, to which he concedes twenty-odd pages at the end of the second volume. For

Lacépède, music represents passion by presenting "the signs of the emotions" and thus constitutes "a kind of language" (1:80, 1:99). This view applies to instrumental music as well: the composer should write a symphony, he argued, "as if he were working on a grand aria in which one or several voices would seek to express more or less spirited affections" (II:331). Lacépède's aesthetics would thus appear to constitute essentially a restatement of the mimetic principle articulated most clearly for music in Batteux's *Les Beaux Arts réduits à un même principe* of 1746.

Both of these diametrically opposed views tend to fossilize certain elements in his work and pass over what is most eye-opening in relation to aesthetic tendencies in the 1780s by making Lacépède into either a precursor of the music of the 1820s or a latter-day theorist of the 1740s. In order to explore more fully what distinguishes Lacépède's enterprise from earlier aesthetic statements – that of a Batteux, for instance – we must begin with the peculiar first chapter on the origin of music, in which Lacépède reinvented the story of Adam and Eve as if it were the sketch of a secular opera for which the music and libretto had not yet been written out in full – something like a plan for a specific production with detailed stage directions and long descriptive passages to set the scenes. The treatise sets the scene with a description of the world in never-ending spring. A fully satisfied man appears in this paradise; and his first words emerge as song. In its moral tone and language of emotion, passages of Lacépède's treatise are reminiscent of the contemporaneous novel, *Paul et Virginie* (1788), by Bernardin de Saint-Pierre. Yet, the writing gives the distinct impression that an operatic sketch is being elaborated because of constant reference to the voices and singing of the characters, and to specific musical qualities such as intervals, vocal dynamics, and harmonies. What is unusual about the chapter, in short, is that it narrates a story about the origin of music as if it could, or should, be recreated in performance. The question of the origins of music and the secularization of human origins were, of course, favorite topics of eighteenth-century French writers and their counterparts across the Channel in Edinburgh and across the continent in Berlin. Music had also figured prominently in earlier writings on the origins of language and culture by Condillac, Rousseau, and others. Lacépède's decision to represent the origin of humanity in a lengthy narrative that reads like a virtual opera is, however, exceptional. One wonders about the motivation behind this decision and, furthermore, why he chose to place this unusual story at the head of a poetics of musical composition. I will examine these questions by taking a closer look at the first chapter and its resonances throughout *La Poétique de la musique*.

After the short preface, Lacépède launched into a narrative that is extremely reminiscent not so much of Genesis as of the story of the first man that Buffon wrote in 1749 for the second volume of his *Histoire naturelle*. Buffon sought to describe the discovery of the world and of subjectivity through sensation. Without necessarily reversing the direction of Buffon's narrative, Lacépède turned inward, staging the disclosure of passionate subjectivity and, above all, intersubjectivity through a narrative of passionate being in the world. The lyric voice is the vehicle of these discoveries, mirroring the close connection between opera and sensibility that was established by theorists and composers of *opéras comiques*. The treatise begins with an overwhelmingly lush description of paradise:

> In these blessed fields where an endless spring reigned, where the sun sent only rays tempered by the breath of the soft zephyrs, the earth, forever covered by fresh greenery, displayed nothing but expanses of flowers and trees laden with fruit. Fountains murmured quietly; they spilled out a delightful freshness within the sweet-smelling wood. The most pleasant scents lingered in the air. Under the thick foliage of these enchanted woods, the birds sung melodiously. (1:1–2)

The stage has been set for the entrance of the first character. As Paul Alpers reminds us, pastoral is not really about landscape but about the representative shepherds that inhabit it.[5] Lacépède's man is one of these pastoral figures. He arrives on the scene in order to provide a vocal, human response to the natural surroundings in which he finds himself:

> The man, happy and content, drifting through these fragrant, blossoming fields with his female companion, intoxicated with pleasure and delight, celebrated his joy. His voice came to life. The spoken word was inadequate for expressing his feelings: fleeting sounds that vanish as soon as they are spoken, indistinct nuances, accents that are too close together could not act as the signs of a long outpouring, intense sensations or impetuous passions. With effort, he was able to sustain his voice. He raised and lowered it rapidly. Cries of joy intermingled with his tones. He sang. (12)

Glancing back at what must have been Lacépède's model, vocal expression takes the place of Buffon's narrative of progressive sense impression.[6] Song is portrayed as the result of the inadequacy of words for the expression of intense feeling. Stong emotion calls for clear, sustained vocal tone – something the indistinct vocalizations of spoken language cannot supply. Lacépède continued his story, moving on to describe how dance and poetry naturally spring from the corporeal and verbal rhythms of the voice. The idyllic mood of the text is complete; yet almost immediately, for an unknown but apparently necessary reason, the man's companion (who, it must be noticed, has not yet been allowed to say a word) disappears. At its origin, in Lacépède's view, lyricism is primarily, even exclusively, a male prerogative. Perhaps he followed in this the ancillary status given to woman in Genesis. However, there is also an operatic precedent for this view of lyricism, namely that of the Orpheus myth. In a passage reminiscent of the story of Orpheus and Euridice and its various operatic versions, nothing comes close to offering Lacépède's man any consolation for his loss despite the astonishing beauty of his surroundings – nothing, that is, except his own voice:

> He cried out; he wept while repeating his tender complaints. It is no longer simply a language he is using; it is a composite of several signs joined together, of several expressive and profound qualities. The various

feelings which dominated the wretched man – bitter sorrow, touching regrets, sweet melancholy, ardent apprehension, gloomy sadness, sometimes consoling hope – one after the other move his soul and his accents. They raise, lower, hasten, delay, and modify his voice into long and sustained tones, piercing and broken cries, deep bass inflections, and almost breathless sobs. [Thus,] true music appeared. (1:5)

The first man's initial vocalization is an expression of unfettered joy. Speech is transcended even before Lacépède could mention it in his narrative, and song emerges as the only expression adequate to the man's feelings. Fading almost immediately, however, this moment has virtually no temporality: "he only experienced a few instants of delight" (1:3). Lacépède's musical poetics is inflected with an overriding anthropological vision. The particular vocal sounds on which Lacépède focused his narrative are deemed authentic because they are understood to be consonant with the true condition of humanity. As Lacépède claimed, "lasting happiness has never been man's lot" (1:3):

> From pain and sorrowful melancholy comes true music, this living representation of all the passions and, above all, of the most profound ones, [a music] which engraves them so deeply and ignites them so rapidly in our souls, which summons such delightful tears, which provokes such sweet emotions, and such intimate delights in all sensitive souls who have experienced or who are experiencing misfortune, and consequently, alas, in all those who have received the precious and fatal gift of sensibility. (1:6)

What Lacépède subsequently referred to as "true" music is forever marked by the first man's painful loss. The liminal moment of joy at the beginning of Lacépède's narrative is recalled throughout *La Poétique de la musique*, but only because it has been forever lost, and because it is a moment whose loss we perpetually re-enact. From this point onward the original moment of joy remains inaccessible; or, rather, it can only be recalled through the voice of nostalgia. In contrast to "true" music, Lacépède rejected the inauthenticity of the *chanson*, understood as a popular song or ditty. The simple, joyous expression of the *chanson* derives from everyday pleasures, pleasures of circumstance. Only truly profound music can embrace the temporal depth of memory.

Slipping from the story of origins to commentary on the uses of music in the present (one might remark on the extensive use of the pronoun *nous*), Lacépède argued that modern music continued to derive its effects from an original grief: "music retains the mark of its origin; born from tears and sorrow, from profound affections, music only succeeds in depicting sad events, piercing sensations, melancholic situations, somber and profound feelings" (1:6). Even when music tries to present serenity or evoke joy, Lacépède claimed, it inevitably leads the listener back to tears (1:7). Lacépède proposed evidence for this claim when, after a bout of theorizing, he returned to his original narrative at the point where the first man's companion returns. The couple creates the first duet, the man singing "true music, not mere song [*chanson*]," the woman accompanying him at the octave (1:18). Happiness should be the emotion of the moment, yet the music retains something of the melancholy and suffering of their separation: "he no longer dwells exclusively in the present moment; he can wonder about the past and the future . . . he lost the happiness he relished; he can therefore lose it again" (1:17). The separation has created a depth to the man's subjectivity and experience: "he is happy and yet he is on the verge of tears" (1:18). The a-temporality of the *chanson* – an unreflective present – has given way to the resonances of past experience and reflections on events to come in the temporal depth of the authentic lyric voice.

Like Rousseau before him, Lacépède used a representation of the lyric voice as a way of articulating an anthropological model. (When seen from this angle, his double life in music and natural history no longer seems quite so strange). Again like Rousseau, Lacépède had recourse to a fiction linking together a series of original human moments in order to ground a particular understanding of music in the 1780s, the mythical past serving to explain how things came to be as they were then. This fiction about the origins of music also supported an understanding of human intersubjectivity and its historical and anthropological origins. Lacépède departed from the Rousseauian model, however, when he staged a loss at the origin of music because he saw loss as *the* original, formative human experience. Where Rousseau foregrounded an original plenitude to better set the stage for the degradation that continued to affect music and culture in the eighteenth century, Lacépède foregrounded the musical expression of loss as a necessary, indeed desirable, reflection of human subjectivity. Lacépède also flatly contradicted Rousseau in arguing for harmony as natural.[7] For Rousseau, loss occurred because an original plenitude had been misdirected or subsequently covered over; Lacépède saw loss as a more constructive element of human existence. Like other elements of Lacépède's narrative, the focus on loss derives from pastoral conventions. Paul Alpers notes that "pastoral convenings are characteristically occasions for songs and colloquies that express and thereby seek to redress separation, absence, or loss. The inaugural poem of Western pastoral, Theocritus's first Idyll, brings herdsmen together for the pleasure of hearing a lament for Daphnis."[8]

More to the point, however, Lacépède's understanding of loss also recalls the dispossession that has been discussed in earlier chapters and which appears to have always been an unavoidable element of Western musical understanding, at least since Plato's view of lyricism as unthought. Lacépède's man experiences a loss of the object of his affection and, at the same time, a loss of self, a loss of control. The lyric voice – the act of singing – was described by Lacépède as an involuntary, and necessary, reaction to this experience. Indeed, although Lacépède later claimed that music came after words, music is represented in the order and emphasis of his narrative as the first truly meaningful language. His treatise never discusses the origin of the spoken word. For Lacépède, these original moments of loss, expressed in music, return at the other end of history, in the eighteenth-century present. Of course, this return might be seen as part and parcel of the logic of origins, and the very reason that the narrative of origins that begins *La Poétique de la musique* appears so much like an opera in the first place. More striking, however, is the fact that operatic lyricism is understood to frame a defining moment in human subjectivity. In Lacépède's conjectural anthropology, the act of *listening* to music in the present mirrors the original experiences to which it is inextricably linked. Lyricism, both at its origin and in the present, necessarily entails a moment of dispossession in which outside forces act upon the soul. Music forces the listener to "shed tears" (1:7); and the effect of music is described by verbs that denote emotional coercion or possession: music fires the passions, and the listener is captivated (*entraîné*) by the voice (1:6, 18). In Lacépède's treatise, an anthropological view of operatic spectatorship hinges on a generalized anthropology based on a representation of the lyric voice, as if only opera could epitomize the foundation of humanity. In the first chapter of the *La Poétique de la musique*, opera represents this origin, just as the origin represents opera; and, implicitly at every performance, this same origin is re-enacted in the opera house. The listener is defined as a mirror, or refractor, or distiller of the experience of loss recalled by the operatic voice. This loss can rightfully emerge only as song, since only the lyric voice was perfectly tuned to the frequency of humanity at its origins. In the opera house, listening to the tenor or soprano is just such an experience of loss; yet it takes place in a controlled environment. Lacépède's argument is thoroughly Aristotelian here, reiterating for the *tragédie lyrique* what Aristotle had said about ancient tragedy: the lyric voice reproduces the momentary pleasure "of having taken delight in the power of being moved" (1:16). The pleasure of these representations is one of controlled loss, one whose fullness will end almost as soon as the music stops but which will continue to have effects beyond the walls of the theater.

"True" music is always about self-knowledge for Lacépède: "all that saddens us, all that evokes somber thoughts, all that gives rise to deep feelings, naturally brings the soul to withdraw into itself, to contemplate and judge itself" (1:8–9). *La Poétique de la musique* defines virtue as a self-awareness arising from self-examination, the entire process being triggered by the musical experience: "we recognize ourselves in the features that it offers us ... whoever we may be, whatever misfortune may have befallen us, it seems to say to us, *I, too, have felt that and I, too, bear its unfortunate marks"* (1:14). Lacépède characterizes the act of listening to music as both a dialogue and a moment of intense identification. The listener in the present, who is represented as utterly alone or isolated in contemplation through the effects of the music, re-experiences the solitude of loss and the dialogue with self that arose in the first man after he had lost his companion:

> Sad and melancholy, he sets out into the densest forest, looking for the most untamed and solitary spot. He calls out to his companion and is heartened to hear an echo just as sad as he repeat the name of the one he has lost with the same emotion. This voice, alas, which is only his own, carries nevertheless a gentle illusion into his soul. He believes that he hears a being similar to himself, a hapless being like himself who shares in his sorrow. (1:3–4)

Using the musical voice as interlocutor (represented as an echo), the listener in the present re-initiates the dialogue with self Lacépède places at the origins of humanity. Because of its origins in loss, and because this loss also defines what it means to be human, music is at once an imaginary interlocutor in the process of self-discovery – a mirror – and a normative measure of universal virtue ("whoever we may be"): "thus, only the virtuous man can savor with tranquility the tender emotions that true music inspires; only he can delight in all the sensations it provokes. The enemy of virtue can seek only mirth and frivolous songs" (1:9). Taking a step beyond its status as a guarantor of human feeling, music becomes a test of a man's virtue, of his sincerity and fidelity. Lacépède develops this line of thought in a later section on the musical representation of friendship, to which I will return below.

The further reflections Lacépède offers on his claim for the foundational nature of melancholy and sorrow are based on the fundamental importance he ascribed to the minor mode. His argument is twofold, and both of its aspects blend music history with anthropological reflections on musical culture. First, Lacépède presents a general overview of the development of harmony in Western musical history. The major mode is given precedence over the minor mode because it is said to be found in nature whereas the minor mode emerged only after the invention of the art of musical composition. Rameau had argued this point by showing that the major chord could be derived from the natural resonance of harmonic partials in the *corps sonore*, or resonant body. The derivation of the minor chord, however, caused theoretical problems that were debated throughout the eighteenth century. As recently as the seventeenth century, Lacépède remarked, composers almost always concluded their works with a major chord, even those composed in the minor mode, because they were historically "less separated from the origin of the arbitrary establishment of dissonances and of the minor mode" (1:190). Composers necessarily relied on the major chord in these instances because the minor chord was an invention of the art of harmony – conventional and therefore "arbitrary." The precedence of the major mode would thus appear to contradict the importance Lacépède attributed to the minor mode for musical expressions of sorrow. However, if "the ear is never truly satisfied . . . except when it hears perfect chords, identical to those that nature produces," for expressions of sorrow – those to which Lacépède attributed fundamental importance in human experience – the minor mode is still preferred because it does not effectuate a complete resolution, because it leaves something to be desired (1:188).

In the second part of his argument, Lacépède questioned the anthropological significance of Rameau's discovery of the natural origin of the major triad by noting the prevalence of the minor mode in "primitive" cultures. If one were to examine, he claimed, "the nature of the airs the Negroes sing to better endure their toils and their sorrows . . . watering with their sweat the earth to which they are chained and which their hands must endlessly labor . . . to what sort of songs did their misfortunes give rise? Songs that are almost always in a minor key" (1:191–92). Reflecting current views of race, Lacépède implied that because black slaves were further from civilization and therefore closer to nature than Europeans they bore witness to the primacy of the minor triad as the expression of the fundamental sorrow and loss that shape all human experience.[9] In casting sorrow as essential to the existence of blacks in the eighteenth century, his claim also incidentally naturalized the continued practice of slavery.

The next episode in Lacépède's narrative directly addressed his aim of transforming compositional practices by infusing music with an anthropological vision and mission, a project begun some thirty years earlier by Rousseau. A new "scene of suffering" appears in the text. Cruel invaders, who have descended upon the two primordial lovers, capture and separate them:

> They are seized, separated, and taken away by force. They escape from the hands of their ferocious abductors; each one flies back towards the other; they are torn once again from each other's arms . . . the spoken word cannot express their cruel situation. The accents of pain and burning passion: this is their language. They know it already, this sublime language. Fragmented tones, sharp cries that issue from a breaking heart, the shuddering of helpless rage, the deep and terrible sounds of the furor which moves them, these are their words and their sorrowful adieux. The first pathetic duet is thus formed. (1:23–24)

As anthropological fiction, the above passage is a projection of Lacépède's musical ideals back to an original moment. Once again, Lacépède's argument is based on what was by the 1780s an orthodox assumption: that music, as a form of communication or expression, was like a language. Yet in this passage, music is both fragmented, remaining beneath the threshold of the word, and extended beyond the monody of speech, clearly stretching the limits of the linguistic model so that it resembles what Michel de Certeau has referred to as "glossolalias":

> From the clamor of voices [*sabbat de voix*] overrunning and breaking up the field of statements comes a mumble that escapes the control of speakers and that violates the supposed division between speaking individuals. It fills the space between speakers with the plural and prolix act of communication and creates, mezza voce, an opera of enunciation on the stage of verbal exchange.[10]

Like glossolalia, Lacépède's scene of separation and desperate communication between the two lovers – a pre-figuration of opera – toys with the limits of meaning in its imperative to *say everything* without the support of content, "destroying the possibility of articulating meaning, [yet attempting] to restore a way of talking [*un parler*]."[11]

The lovers' voices are fragmented into pre-linguistic utterances, cries, and vocal tones. But these utterances are also multiplied into polyphony through their simultaneity. At once pre-linguistic (before the conventions of language) and beyond language, music can thus be said to have numerous advantages over speech: "it is a language that is more moving, more full of energy than ordinary language" (1:51). For Lacépède, the obvious advantage of music over other forms of expression is that it can be polyphonic. He argues that "having several voices at its command, each capable of representing feelings and events with more or less intensity, music can easily express several different things simultaneously" (1:130). This view of the multiple possibilities of polyphony leads to an argument in favor of expanding the range of possible harmonies through the use of quarter-tones, tones that are unavailable on the ordinary chromatic scale: "this reveals how much more expressive our music would be and how much more truthfully it would render the feelings it wishes to convey if, instead of contenting ourselves with dividing whole-tones into two semitones, we divided them into four, eight, and so on" (1:67). Both pre-linguistic and beyond language for Lacépède, music opens up a full range of glossolalic possibilities for the expression of passion, possibilities currently available neither in conventional language nor in ordinary musical practices. The detour that Lacépède took through the origins of music before arriving at the heart of the matter – his poetics – turns out not to be a detour at all, but rather reveals the importance he ascribed to certain conceptions of humanity and culture for the meaning of opera in the eighteenth century, from the point of view of both composers and audiences. Subsequently, through references to works by recent composers and through specific advice on musical and dramatic compositional techniques, the treatise aims to realize the promise of the first chapter: that is, to recreate *that* music, the music that was and remains fundamental to humanity.

Venturing beyond the fiction of origins framed in the first chapter, we might wonder exactly how the anthropological model Lacépède establishes there impinges upon the topic he proposes to address in the treatise as a whole – that is, music in the eighteenth-century present. Part of the answer to this question lies in an implicit connection between the scene of separation and pathos cited above and the late eighteenth-century aesthetics of sentiment and sensibility, which I examined from a somewhat different angle in previous chapters. Bringing this connection under scrutiny, I want to suggest that Lacépède saw opera as a way of engaging contemporary medicine, moral philosophy, and aesthetic theory in common cause. All of these areas brought their sights to bear on the body and its various modes of sensation and expression, of action and reaction, either from a diagnostic perspective or as a means of representing passion, conduct, and their complex relationship. *La Poétique de la musique* supported the notion that the lyric theater acted as a barometer of, and a moral influence upon, social relations. Lacépède's clear articulation of the part opera did and should play in the culture of sensibility, and the larger role he attributed to the entire musical fabric (beyond the voice alone), bore out while expanding Enlightenment views of musical meaning.

Sensibility was central to eighteenth-century conceptions of the body and its role in the formation of subjectivity and the development of knowledge.[12] The late eighteenth-century fascination with sensibility developed from increased attention to sensation, rather than innate ideas, as a foundational element of human understanding of the world from the mid-century. The models used to describe the mental processes involved with sensation varied through the century. John W. Yolton proposes the following roughly chronological outline of eighteenth-century physiologies in England: "(1) the scholastic theory of species, (2) the physiology of animal spirits and brain traces, (3) the physiological application of Newton's subtle elastic fluid (the aether), and (4) the Hartleian theory of vibrations."[13] In France, influential Cartesian theorists such as Nicolas de Malebranche were associated with theories of animal spirits and brain traces, and Charles Bonnet, among others, with the theory of vibrations. The Swiss physiologist Albrecht von Haller, author of *Elementa physiologiae* (1759–66) and an influence on Condillac's *Traité des animaux*, developed his own theories of irritability, discussed in chapter 6. As Ann Jessie Van Sant has shown, citing Laurence Sterne, terms such as sensibility and sentiment weave through different discursive contexts and meanings, from the delicacy and refinement of mind to the physiological model of nerves and their vibration:

> In the popular language of sensibility, in fact, we can see not only a mixed but an imaginary physiology. "There is a sort of pleasing half guilty blush," Yorick simultaneously announces and confesses, "where the blood is more in fault than the man – 'tis sent impetuous from the heart, and virtue flies after it – not to call it back, but to make the sensation of it delicious to the nerves."[14]

Sterne's character quite easily conflates moral response and physical reaction. This conflation was the result of eighteenth-century medical models of sensibility and, as I will argue below, is crucial for understanding the larger aims of aesthetics in France as well. In the eighteenth-century context, the conflation of sentiment and sensibility was the result of physiological models where the heart was the center of feeling and the brain that of thought.[15] References to music often drifted into the language of sensibility. As Van Sant notes, "heartstrings" was originally defined by Johnson and others as a physiological term. Similarly, for Sterne, writing of compassion:

> In benevolent natures the impulse to pity is so sudden, that like instruments of music which obey the touch – the objects which are fitted to excite such impressions work so instantaneous an effect, that you would think the will was scarce concerned, and that the mind was altogether passive in the sympathy which her own goodness has excited.[16]

We might be tempted to see in Sterne's view of sympathy a quasi-materialist twist on, or revival of, the old scholastic notion of *musica*

humana. In both systems, the human organism responds to the deter-
minations of outside forces (objects, images, people) independently
of subjective will through what one could call a kind of *Stimmung* –
a tuning or mood – which sets the emotional tone. Though Martin
Heidegger's use of the term is of course radically different, nevertheless, *Stimmung* fittingly characterizes affect as a way of being in
relation to things, a way of being that one cannot circumscribe or
elude.[17]

Recent scholarship has established close parallels between medical theory and experimentation in the area of sensation, on the one
hand, and the literary and dramatic focus on sensibility from Diderot
to the end of the century. "The fusion of literal internal systems
and metaphor, of actual and imaginary physiology," Van Sant notes,
"is sometimes difficult to sort out."[18] Anne C. Vila argues similarly
that sensibility should not be considered the exclusive property of
any single field of knowledge; rather, it was "a polysemous concept,
a notion that not only cut across disciplinary boundaries, but represented several different things at once." Vila reads Diderot's novel,
La Religieuse, as bridging the gap between the novel of sensibility and a
philosophico-medical discourse on sensation and its effects.[19] Another
scholar, Stefano Castelvecchi, encourages us to develop a "critical ear"
for eighteenth-century sentimental operas by drawing out the close
relationship between contemporary "psychiatry," notably that of the
physician Philippe Pinel, and scenes of therapy staged in Marsollier's
and Dalayrac's *opéra comique* entitled, *Nina, ou la Folle par amour*
(*Nina, or The Love-Distressed Maid*).[20] Indeed, if one were to examine
a sample of the philosophico-medical works published in France during the second half of the eighteenth century, one would find that for
many authors – Lallemant, La Mettrie, Béthisy de Mézières, among
others – the effects of music were exemplary of the general effects of
sensation on the human organism from a medical perspective. To tap
sensation would be to gain access to a truer, deeper understanding of
humanity.

If one reconsiders Lacépède's operatic narrative in light of the contemporary interest in sensibility, the "fragmented tones," the "sharp

cries," and the "shuddering of helpless rage" to which the reader's attention is drawn, all point to the body and its pre- or post-linguistic vocal sounds and corporeal movements. As it is described in *La Poétique de la musique*, opera reveals subjectivity and, above all, intersubjectivity, in their most rudimentary and truest forms through vocal utterances that do not appear in ordinary language, or that reappear only in extreme moments. Operatic music reveals the truth of intersubjectivity in its mood – its *Stimmung* – which would otherwise remain unspoken because it is beyond or below the threshold of language, beyond or below the grasp of meaning that can be articulated in the ordinary linguistic parceling of reality. By resuscitating the presumably hidden fundamental tones of humanity, opera accomplishes something other cultural forms cannot, according to Lacépède, by recalling and commemorating foundational human moments to which we can no longer otherwise gain access in an advanced culture. Opera is engaged in a process of recovery through which the listener-spectator returns to witness the spectacle of origins, of his or her origins. Thus, Lacépède argued, the dominant expression a composer will choose for a particular dramatic moment will generally be "the first expression given to these airs or songs, following their resemblance to natural harmony, or to the cries of the passions" (1:97). The operatic voice affords a unique kind of ventriloquism by speaking in a language that could never otherwise be resuscitated in its first form. For Lacépède, music – particularly operatic music – is implicated in a moral and anthropological vision claiming universal applicability. On the one hand, the natural resonance of physical bodies establishes the basic harmonic structure of music for human use, whether it be vocal or instrumental. On the other, from the perspective of the proto-history Lacépède staged in the opening pages of his treatise, the original operatic moments of humanity determine, once and for all, the basic representational configurations of music: "it is no more possible in music to decide to use new signs to express such and such a passion than to decide, in painting, to represent a square surface seen head-on by a triangular one seen from the same position" (1:52). But just as the advent of perspective in painting can be shown to have gained impetus from the cultural and scientific initiatives of its time, Lacépède's assertion of a hegemonic musical discourse issues from his humanism and from the anthropology of the passions that appears throughout *La Poétique de la musique*.

In this framework, spectatorship takes on an additional meaning: that of being true to the resonances of one's own humanity, to the original human scene with which Lacépède began his treatise. By resuscitating these original moments, opera might produce a model of humanity which could be put to use in the present. Lacépède saw in the experience of opera an act of adherence, on the part of the spectator, to an implicit socio-anthropological vision. As Lawrence Kramer has written about the musical experience generally, "listeners agree to personify a musical subject by responding empathetically to the music's summons. Their pleasure in listening thereby becomes a vehicle of acculturation."[21] The action that takes place on stage engages and calls forth the reaction and emotional participation of the spectator. A glance at some of Lacépède's preferred operatic scenes confirms this assertion. Each of these scenes focuses on some kind of loss, preferably that of death, and frames the spectator at the margins of the drama – excluding the spectator in order to accentuate his presence all the more – by making him privy to crucial information that the characters ignore.[22] Lacépède in this way defined the ideal operatic scene as one that engages the spectator in the vicarious experience of the character's loss. The scenes Lacépède singled out for particular attention are drawn from three eighteenth-century opera texts that would have been familiar to his readers: (1) Pietro Metastasio's *Ciro riconosciuto*, a tragedy set by the most famous composers of *opera seria* (Galuppi, Leo, Jommelli, Duni, Hasse, and Niccolò Piccinni), (2) two versions of *Iphigénie en Tauride*, one by Piccinni, the other by Christoph von Gluck and his librettist, François Guillard, and (3) *Alcyone*, an early eighteenth-century *tragédie en musique* by Marin Marais and Houdar de la Motte which underwent revivals beyond mid-century. Lacépède was drawn to specific scenes from these operas because they all focus on situations in which the spectator's affective state is foregrounded when he or she is privy to knowledge that is hidden from a character or group of characters. He remarked that, in general, "if the interest of a dramatic situation comes from the fact that a character ignores what it is most important for him or her to know, and depends on the opposition of the actual feelings of the actor with those that he should have, then the composer should give the character feelings even more contrary to those that should grip him or her" (1:132–33). The lyric theater in its ideal configuration, for Lacépède, revolves around a narrative of ignorance and revelation, and of concealment and disclosure, through which the listener-spectator's affective response is specifically brought into play through the affective contrast of knowing and ignorance, inclusion and exclusion.

Lacépède highlighted in particular opera's ability to negotiate multiple degrees of concealment and disclosure through the simultaneity of spoken or sung dialogue, orchestral accompaniment, and staging. Lacépède deliberately chose scenes in which words no longer suffice, where the dialogue or monologue is on the verge of splintering into fragments, no longer able to contain the affect it is supposed to represent in words. These moments of excess in which the text falters allow the music and the body, in its vocal and gestural manifestations, to come forth. As Castelvecchi has suggested in relation to *Nina*: "the person overwhelmed with emotion is often incapable of continuous discourse; the amount of the unspoken (interrupted speech, silence, bodily signs) unveils the communicative limits of verbal and rational language."[23] Tellingly, none of Lacépède's operatic examples go as far in this direction as his own narrative of origins where he presented the first couple's use of the sublime language of "fragmented tones, sharp cries that issue from a breaking heart, the shuddering of helpless rage" (1:23–24). For, as de Certeau has suggested, glossolalia is manifestly utopian.[24] In *La Poétique de la musique*, opera seeks to restore and to give voice to something that by definition is lost and cannot be brought back intact. By this logic, Lacépède's treatise represents opera as eluding ordinary linguistic meaning by crying out for the necessity of a communication that is denied, impossible, or excessive. Here, as it so often does, opera flirts with the edge of reason. His operatic examples, therefore, should be taken as the metaphorical equivalents, within the musical and stage conventions of the 1780s, of the unreachable, primordial scenes he evoked in his story of origins.

In Metastasio's *Ciro riconosciuto*, the mention of tears, gestures, and drastic changes in facial expression are common and accompany the many suspicions, changes of fortune, and disclosures that fill the tragedy. The text begs for attention to the voice, face, and body on stage: "Se tornasse il Fellone . . . Eccolo. Oh come / Tremo in vederlo! . . . Numi, quel volto / Come trovo cambiato! Intendo: è questa / Une vendetta. Il mio tacer t'offese: / Mi punisci così . . . Oh Dio! / Perché quel fiero sguardo?" [What if the villain returned . . . I see him. Oh, I shudder at his sight! . . . What do I see? / What a transformation! I understand; my silence offends you / and you want to punish me for it . . . Heavens! / Why such a terrible expression?].[25] The hidden identities and mistaken affinities found at every twist and turn of the complex dramatic situation are always present beneath the surface of the visible in textual allusions to unexplained surges of passion ("What mean these heaving sighs, these swelling tears, / Why flutters thus my heart?"); and these truths repeatedly threaten to break out into the open.[26] As gaps or shifts in the dialogue and as moments of intense emotional struggle, these situations also provide conspicuous opportunities for the composer. One critic has argued that:

> in Metastasian theater, the description of the physiognomy of the characters and of its variations is an actual theme in which speech can and must assimilate the spectacle into itself both because it holds the vicarious function of an impossible mimesis or an impossible vision, and because, instead of being improper according to the *bienséances*, it substitutes its own acceptable violence for representation on stage.[27]

As opera, however, *Ciro riconosciuto* has at its disposal mimetic resources other than speech, even though it is the dialogue, as we see above, that frames these moments of excess. In this opera, the body always potentially speaks a different language, a language that reveals a truth against or beyond appearances. Lacépède called for the music to do likewise.

In the scene that he singled out for particular attention, the stage is set for an ambush in which Cyrus, in hiding under the name of Mithridates's son, will be killed by his own father who has been in exile for years and thus could not recognize him. In the specific dialogue Lacépède describes from act 3, scene 1, Mandane, Cyrus's equally long-lost mother, speaks to Mithridates, giving vent to her rage against her son whom she takes for Mithridates's son and whom she believes to be her son's murderer. All of Lacépède's preferred dramatic elements are present: the hidden truth of Cyrus's identity, Mandane's blindness to the fact that she has set a trap for her own son, and Mithridates's (and the spectator's) full awareness of the tragic situation. Lacépède set the scene thus:

> [Mandane] speaks to Mithridate whom she believes to be the father of the murderer, and the instigator of Cyrus's death. She describes with the bitterness of cruel irony, all the horror of the situation she believes will soon be his. To take her revenge on him in the most horrible manner, she slowly drives a dagger, as it were, into his breast. And just as the spectators, beside themselves, are about to exclaim, "wretched woman, you are speaking of yourself," she says to him, "learn how it feels to lose, to mourn a son." (1:133–34)

Alternating between the spectator's urge to respond, which is barely held in check, and the situation of the protagonist, Lacépède's description represents the spectator's reaction as impinging upon the drama itself, making it part of the scene. As in Diderot's dramatic theory, the spectator is always on the verge of stepping into the scene in order to enter into dialogue with the characters. The narrator of Diderot's *Entretiens sur le fils naturel* explains that while attending his interlocutor's play, "forgetting at several points that I was a spectator . . . I had been on the verge of getting up and adding a real character to the scene."[28] Similarly, Castevecchi reports that during performances of Paisiello's *Nina*, Neapolitan audiences "screamed at the protagonist on stage in the vain attempt to console her."[29] Lacépède suggested that the music could cultivate this urge and enhance the emotional impact of the scene by occupying any number of dialogical positions in relation to the situation:

> The composer must exalt the feelings of hate and vengeance which envelop the heart of this wretched mother. He must give her a contentment so distant from the horrible despair into which she will be plunged once the whole of her misfortune is revealed. He must allow the cry of maternal tenderness that resounds within Mandane's heart to dominate only so as to show to what degree her rage stifles all the other sentiments which should prevail in her soul. (1:134)

For Lacépède, the orchestral and vocal writing should produce layers of contrasting meanings, allowing the operatic situation to come forth in all its complexity. The role of the music is to maintain a focus on the situation as a whole so that "the spectator may never lose sight of all the anguish and horror in the situation, and so that the accompaniment may convey the voice of nature, repulsed, crying out in a dreadful and plaintive tone: 'Wretched woman! you are sacrificing your own son'" (1:135). Lacépède sought to maintain and heighten the tension that was built into the dramatic situation. However, he also raised the stakes by stretching the dramatic situation beyond the dialogue, beyond the visual representation of singers and stagecraft, into the audience and into the liminal or excessive meaning generated by the music and, one imagines, by the grain of the voice in those moments when speech fragments or falters into cries and lamentation. Other voices are brought into play – those of the spectators and that of the music – voices that are either in principle unspoken (in the case of the spectator) or "speak" in a different language. These voices are provoked by the impending loss at the center of the dramatic tableau; and loss, one will remember, marks the origin of the lyric voice itself.

Lacépède's discussion of *Alcyone*, which he gives as an extended example at the end of his general discussion of the operatic air, focuses on similar elements. As is quite frequently the case for early French opera, the story of Alcyone is drawn from Ovid's *Metamorphoses*. Unbeknownst to Ceyx, king of Trachis, the magician Phorbas, whom

Ceyx considers an ally but whose ancestors once ruled over Trachis, has used his powers to thwart Ceyx's marriage to Alcyone. In the scene Lacépède discusses (act 2, scene 2), Ceyx visits Phorbas to ask for his help. Lacépède's description of the music differs radically from the original score of 1706; and it is difficult to determine how much of this situation to attribute to changes made in the score or in performance at the Opéra during its revivals throughout the century, and how much to attribute to Lacépède's own narrative license in his dramatic retelling of the story. Particularly glaring are the differences in orchestration. Where Lacépède mentions howling trumpets and horns, and the "dreadful blows" of timpani echoing the king's despair, the original score mentions only violins, violas, cellos, recorders, flutes, oboes, bassoons, and continuo. However, as Alice Renken has asserted, the original orchestration is never entirely clear and revivals later in the eighteenth century testify to drastically altered productions of the opera.[30]

Lacépède emphasized the ability of the orchestra to add other voices in order to provide a multiple counterpoint to Ceyx's lament. As the king addresses the gods, reflecting on his loss ("Je touchois au moment où la beauté que j'aime / M'eût rendu plus heureux que vous" [I was on the verge of the moment where the beauty I love / Was to make me happier than you]), the music proffers a very different discourse:

> All the while in the moments of silence that Ceyx's song presents, the second violin and the bass unremittingly play for him the figured accompaniment that was the sign of his sorrow: they continuously sound, though in a muted way, the cry of his despair. They warn him, as it were, that the happiness with which he vainly attempts to intoxicate himself is lost. (II:164–65)

In striking parallel to Lacépède's narrative of origins, the scene from *Alcyone* he chose to discuss presents a fleeting but already tainted moment of nostalgic happiness that rapidly dissolves into loss and despair. Another similar moment appears at the end of Ceyx's air, though here again the differences between Lacépède's account and the orchestral resources reflected in the printed score reveal either Lacépède's zeal in recalling *Alcyone* to suit his utopian view of the ideal operatic air or the changing conditions of operatic performance in the decades before the Revolution. Discussing the moment at which Ceyx is on the verge of repeating the final line of this air ("l'excès du désespoir où vous livrez mon coeur" [the extreme despair to which you submit my heart]), Lacépède remarked that "he can no longer speak; rage stifles his accents. Nothing comes forth other than broken, ascending sounds" (II:166). The orchestra responds to Ceyx's "sobs" with "frightful clamor." As was the case in Lacépède's operatic story of the first man and woman, Ceyx's air ends beyond words in sub-linguistic vocalizations and orchestral rumble, these being the only possible expressions adequate to his loss. The successive moments of loss, illusory recollection, and terminal grief that characterized the fundamental and defining experience of the first man are resurrected in Ceyx's air. This moment of commemoration is realized, Lacépède suggested, when the original experience echoes in the ear of the listener.

The last example I will discuss, Gluck's *Iphigénie en Tauride*, is the only one for which it is possible to hear the music that Lacépède found so compelling. He mentioned Gluck's opera during a particularly lengthy analysis of the treatment of *l'amitié*, or male friendship, in operatic composition (I:218). As in the chapter on the origin of music, where he depicted the origin of music as an operatic narrative, Lacépède's analysis of friendship is indistinguishable from re-enactment and relies heavily on the reader's presumed capacity for identification. The passages on friendship also bridge the gap between the biblical heterosexuality of original song, triggered as it is by the man's loss of his female companion, and the revival of Greco-Roman notions of homosociality so important for eighteenth-century art. As always, loss is at the center of the tableau, the most satisfying representations of friendship being for Lacépède those that place two men in a situation of mutual sacrifice, where one risks losing the other. Here, sacrifice must be complete and unconstrained:

> even faithless to the holy laws of friendship. He pities him [his friend]; he forgives all the wrongs that he endures from him; he is distressed by it,

but he cherishes him for it nonetheless. He sacrifices all his happiness for
that of his friend; he wants to die for his Orestes, and accepts that he be
unaware of [this sacrifice]. His soul merges with that of his friend; and it
has no longer anything but the same desires, the same emotions, the
same affections. (1:215)

This particular representation of friendship inevitably leads to the ultimate sacrifice confronted in friendship. Death is both the ultimate loss
and the moment of ultimate fulfillment during which the homosocial
friendship is fully consummated.

Lacépède referred his reader to a duet between Orestes and Pylades
in act 3, scene 4, of *Iphigénie en Tauride*. Because it has been prophesied
that a foreigner would take the life of the king of Tauris, the two men
are imprisoned upon their arrival there. The priestess Iphigenia can
save only one of them and finally decides to send Orestes, whom she
does not recognize as her brother, back to Greece. Orestes, who can
only save his friend's life by offering to die for him, begs Pylades to leave
in his stead. In a brief recitative and in the ensuing duet, each of the two
friends insists on sacrificing himself for the other, moving through a
kaleidoscope of emotional phases. In the recitative, the doubts and in-
securities of reciprocated love are emphasized as Orestes's voice quizzi-
cally rises a 4th from b♭ to e♭' ("M'aimes-tu?" [Do you love me?]) over
an unsettled dominant chord in first inversion. Then, after a breathless
rest, unable to wait for a response, he calls out again ("Parle!" [Speak!]).
Pylades painfully responds: "O Dieux! Tu l'oses demander?" [Oh Gods!
You dare ask?].[31] In the air that follows, each man pleads with the gods
to make the other bend in his resolve, to spare the other's life. Finally,
Orestes's desperation, echoed in defiant yet apprehensive arpeggia-
tions in the strings, leads to the mention of the Eumenides who have
been tormenting him ever since the brutal revenge he exacted on his
mother, Clytemnestra, for the murder of Agamemnon. The orchestra
is increasingly disturbed, upward-streaking arpeggios entangled with
edgy tremolo passages, until Orestes begins to hallucinate, seeing the
Eumenides before him and taking his friend for one of his netherworld
tormenters. Orestes finally loses consciousness in his fury and falls

into Pylades's arms. The contest for magnanimity in friendship cannot end in concession, but only at the moment when Orestes loses consciousness in a gesture that functions as sympathetic prefiguration of the death of Pylades: "Où fuir? . . . Eh! quoi! Pilade & me fuit & m'abhorre! / Il me livre à leurs coups! . . . arrêtés . . . ah! grands Dieux!" [Where can I hide? . . . What! Pylades flees me, abhors me! / He delivers me over to their blows! . . . stop . . . ah! great gods!]. The orchestra relentlessly pounds out a diminished seventh chord while Orestes mistakes Pylades for one of his persecutors, singing a tritone from c' to f♯' ("Arrêtez"). He returns to c' as if to repeat what he has just exclaimed but can only reach up a minor third to e♭' before losing consciousness. As Orestes's soul mate, Pylades responds in perfect sympathy, mirroring the interval Orestes has just sung in his response ("Eh quoi!," e♭" to c").[32]

The image of friendship Lacépède found in Gluck's opera stands as an ideal in contrast to what he claimed to see around him in life: "oh celestial friendship, why do your pure flames not consume all souls? Why do so few mortals have you in their hearts when they all have you on their lips? And why has your name, which only virtue should pronounce, been so often used to conceal dark acts of treason and sinister plots?" (1:216–17). In a statement of near Revolutionary tenor, Lacépède recalled the distinction he had made earlier between the unimpeachable seriousness of virtue and the speciousness of gaiety, between the deep sentiments inspired by the *tragédie lyrique* and the pleasing but superficial veneer of the chanson. Music written for the trials of friendship, like that of Gluck's *Iphigénie en Tauride*, would put virtue back into the hearts of men, virtue being a "passion which truly elevates us above ourselves" (1:217). It would fulfill this aim through the introspection this kind of music naturally produces, according to *La Poétique de la musique*, allowing men to hear the resonances of their own original humanity. In this way, Lacépède made the argument for the truth of sentiment as it is presented in opera, and for the value of the feeling that its representations generate in the spectator.

The experience of operatic music, as it is described by Lacépède, is one in which the spectator is reconciled with his original humanity through the summons of the lyric voice, by answering its call. The operatic moments Lacépède described implicate the spectator in scenes in which he or she is invited to participate by identifying with a character or characters and by responding affectively to the operatic spectacle. Indeed, Lacépède's spectators are always on the verge of calling out to add another voice to the opera. The spectator undergoes a reconciliation with the origins of his or her humanity through an emotional engagement in what could be described as a flashback of "collective memory," vicariously returning the spectator to the moment at which the original conditions of passionate response to loss activated intersubjective feeling. In her study of tears, Anne Vincent-Buffault has argued that the "extraordinary experience of the 'delicious moment,' in which people would weep, unable to speak, in each other's arms, evoked the dream of a new social bond. Curiously these feasts of tears came about at the moment when the political system became based on the individual." "Tears," she writes, "revealed sociability and the true nature of relationships."[33] This new form of sociability, based on eighteenth-century writers' perceptions of ancient Greek social bonds, is central to the ideal of intersubjective sympathy that Lacépède proposed through opera.

The implications of Lacépède's reflections for eighteenth-century aesthetic thought are equally important. In the model of spectatorship advanced by *La Poétique de la musique*, the operatic experience corroborates the translatability of sensation that was the universal goal of Enlightenment epistemology. The prominence of sensation in the eighteenth century resulted in a new understanding of intersubjectivity – understood as the equivalence of, or the relative interchangeability of, each individual's experience of the world. Lacépède's representation of the lyric voice and of operatic spectatorship foregrounds and attempts to substantiate this understanding. Framed within the context of eighteenth-century sensationism, a central but implicit aim of *La Poétique de la musique* may have been to provide compelling proof of the existence of a *sensus communis* – the sensibility that shapes humanity. Eighteenth-century writers, such as Rousseau and Adam Smith, saw the imagination as the faculty that allows us to engage and identify with the feelings of others, in principle regardless of rank or social relationship.[34] Describing the effect of operatic music in similar terms, Lacépède suggested that music facilitates and maintains this mechanism by provoking the feelings and tears of the spectator. In opera, music serves as a vehicle for the representation of loss in order to provide a guarantee of our humanity in the sympathetic response of the spectator.

| Conclusions

By the 1780s, the centrality of absolutist politics and pageantry to *tragédie en musique*, along with the heated debates about the evils of operatic spectacle, were part of a relatively distant past. In the context of continued tensions between the "French" and "Italian" styles, and continued anxiety over the place of opera within French literary culture, the concern with individual and collective feeling that came to dominate opera in eighteenth-century France implied significant institutional and aesthetic change. Just as the characteristics of operatic music, text, and performance were considerably revised during this period, cultural assumptions and meanings integral to opera also changed. In discussing the intimate connection between music and power or powerlessness its ability to draw the listener outside him- or herself – I have also attempted to underscore salient continuities which, despite these changes, underlay opera in France from its inception to the Revolution. This study, in short, bears witness to persistent continuities while documenting a shift within opera and discourse on opera from one set of assumptions about the individual, the collective, and their multiple relations, to another. In the France of Louis XIV, the central issue facing opera was that of its identity and function, both in relation to the absolutist state and, more decisively in the long run, to other forms of theater. Part of the "problem" of opera during this time – its function as an affective nexus – came to be identified as one of its central features in the eighteenth century. If opera in France after the mid-eighteenth century was expected to bear the burden of displaying, evincing, or effectuating the communicability of feeling, if opera served as a medium through which affect could be experienced as demonstrative of virtue and shared as such, then it may be seen as directly implicated in the eighteenth-century formation of the aesthetic domain. For as I noted in the previous chapter, aesthetics was founded on the particular cognitive realm of feeling. By way of conclusion, I would like to assert that the connection between opera and aesthetics distinguishes the operatic experience and the aesthetics of the eighteenth century from those we have inherited from our more recent past.

At least three major changes have made their mark on the aesthetic domain since the end of the eighteenth century. First, rather than being concerned with feeling in general aesthetics has taken the art object as its exclusive focus. Second, aesthetic attention is understood as disinterested, since art is considered "an object of taste outside truth and morality."[1] For Kant, individual aesthetic judgments coincide precisely because of their disinterestedness (because they are not based on contingencies) and because taste is presumed to be shared.[2] The move away from interest in aesthetics may have resulted from concerns, expressed particularly forcefully by Jean-Jacques Rousseau, about the confusion of aesthetic and moral attention, that "the interest provoked by aesthetic representation comes at the expense of an interest in the very objects to which the representation might seem to direct one's attention."[3] As a result of the retreat of aesthetics into disinterestedness, however, "questions of truth, goodness, efficacy, even pleasure (since our interest in art is 'disinterested') are eliminated at the outset."[4] Third, the aesthetic has come to appear indissociable from the promise of transcendence, the promise that divided consciousness can be reconciled, the barrier between subjectivity and objectivity breached. The heightened value given to art in modernity derives most obviously from Hegel, who saw art as an accord between spiritual content and sensual existence.[5] Beauty is valuable for Hegel because it takes us beyond the sensible to the Idea. In this framework, art constitutes "a visibility of invisibility as such, or ideality made present."[6] This last development in particular has been seen as problematic by many recent commentators. As Christopher Norris has put it, the illusion of "aesthetic ideology" is that it promises "to reconcile subject and object, mind and nature, concepts and sensuous intuitions," promises that are utterly illusory.[7] Jean-Joseph Goux has persuasively explained that over the past two centuries, by seeking answers to metaphysical questions in art, we have asked far too much of it.[8] Some, such as Lacoue-Labarthe, have simply called for an end to aesthetics itself. Others, like Goux and Thomas Pavel, have suggested a newfound attention to the more modest aims of pleasure in art.[9]

The situation *before* Kant is significantly different. First of all, in the eighteenth century aesthetics was not primarily concerned with art. As Jean-Luc Nancy points out in a fascinating essay on why several arts developed rather than just one, the question of "art" misunderstands the field of aesthetics in the eighteenth century, when no such singular entity can be said to exist, but only *les beaux-arts, les belles-lettres,* or the liberal and mechanical "arts."[10] Renato Barilli, too, has remarked that the many fields "we would group together under the common rubric of aesthetics did not in fact constitute a unified totality."[11] Aesthetics arose out of the many developments in philosophy and medicine that I have discussed in relation to questions of sensibility, sympathy, and taste. *Cognitio sensitiva* (the entire complex of physiological and psychological perceiving) was the bedrock of aesthetics.[12] Aesthetics attempted to come to terms with the ways in which these modes of perceiving and experiencing were shared. It is therefore mistaken to assume, as have many critics, that aesthetics and taste have always referred to exhaustively individual, im-mediate preferences.[13] Eighteenth-century aesthetics maintained an ambiguous tension between that which was "touching" (a particular feeling) and that which was "beautiful" (a universal judgment).

The concerns that shaped eighteenth-century opera were articulated within the cultural idioms and aesthetic issues of its day, and were therefore centered on the experience of passion, of intersubjective feeling, and of pleasure. During the nineteenth century, opera was spared much of the aesthetic overvaluation that befell the symphony. Because of its increasing association with bourgeois values, because of its attachment to words, opera was generally not taken to embody the transcendental. I would argue that if opera continues to mean something to us today, it is therefore surely not because we are under the spell of "aesthetic illusion," or simply because we have fallen irremediably into bourgeois tastes. Eighteenth-century opera and its close link to the aesthetic domain reveal that at one time in its history opera was considered a way of coming to terms, aesthetically, with what it is to be human. The operatic experience does not bring with it transcendence, but rather an experience of estrangement in which one is brought into some form of contact with others through feeling. Opera grounds us in the human. Even at its most extreme, even when the soprano is hitting that note beyond all other notes, opera remains grounded in meanings, in bodies, in the feelings of listener-spectators. Indeed, part of its pathos lies in the tension between the unworldliness of its presentation and the feelings which it can elicit. My hope is that, having reconsidered a number of key issues and flashpoints in the history of early-modern French opera, we can become attuned to its many pleasures and can gain a more informed understanding of the early aesthetic culture through which it was shaped.

NOTES

The publisher has used its best endeavors to ensure that the URLs for external websites referred to in this book are correct and active at he time of going to press. However, the publisher has no responsibility for the websites and can make no guarantee that a site will remain live or that the content is or will remain appropriate.

INTRODUCTION

1 Bernard le Bovier de Fontenelle, *Entretiens sur la pluralité des mondes* (Paris: M. Guerout, 1687), 14–16. All translations are mine unless otherwise noted.
2 See Philippe Lacoue-Labarthe, *Le Sujet de la philosophie* (Paris: Aubier-Flammarion, 1979), 281; and Henry Staton, *Eros in Mourning* (Baltimore: The Johns Hopkins University Press, 1995), xii.
3 See, for example, Jane F. Fulcher, *The Nation's Image: French Grand Opera as Politics and Politicized Art* (Cambridge: Cambridge University Press, 1987).
4 Catherine Kintzler, *Poétique de l'opéra français de Corneille à Rousseau* (Paris: Minèrve, 1991).
5 Ibid., 177n75.
6 Peter Kivy, *Osmin's Rage: Philosophical Reflections on Opera, Drama, and Text* (Princeton: Princeton University Press, 1988), 15.
7 See Anne C. Vila, *Enlightenment and Pathology: Sensibility in the Literature and Medicine of Eighteenth-Century France* (Baltimore and London: The Johns Hopkins University Press, 1998).
8 See, for example, Gary Tomlinson, *Music in Renaissance Magic: Toward a Historiography of Others* (Chicago and London: University of Chicago Press, 1993), 221.

I SONG AS PERFORMANCE AND THE EMERGENCE OF FRENCH OPERA

1 See Marc Fumaroli, *Héros et orateurs* (Geneva: Droz, 1990), 499; and Henry Prunières, *L'Opéra italien en France avant Lulli* (Paris: Champion, 1913), 141 50.

2 See William D. Howarth, ed., *French Theatre in the Neo-Classical Era, 1550–1789* (Cambridge: Cambridge University Press, 1997), 159.

3 For a listing of several works that were presented in some form, but not fully staged, or planned but never performed, see Neal Zaslaw, "The first opera in Paris: a study in the politics of art," in John Hajdu Heyer, ed., *Jean-Baptiste Lully and the Music of the French Baroque* (Cambridge: Cambridge University Press, 1989), 7–23.

4 Prunières, *L'Opéra italien en France avant Lulli*, 77.

5 Ellen Rosand, *Opera in Seventeenth-Century Venice* (Berkeley and Los Angeles: University of California Press, 1991), 4; [Théophraste Renaudot], *Gazette* (l'impression de Lyon) (December 21, 1645), 1180. For a discussion of *La Finta pazza* in its Venetian context, see Rosand, *Opera in Seventeenth-Century Venice*, 110–24.

6 François Maynard, *Les Oeuvres de Maynard* (Paris: Augustin Courbe, 1646), 8.

7 Charles Coypeau d'Assoucy, *Poësies et lettres* (Paris: Jean Baptiste Loyson, 1653), 66.

8 [Théophraste Renaudot], *Gazette* (l'impression de Lyon) (March 14, 1647), 202, 212.

9 François and Claude Parfaict, "Histoire de l'Académie Royale de Musique depuis son établissement jusqu'au présent," Nouv. Acq. Fr. 6532, Bibliothèque Nationale de France, Paris, 1:1–2. The passage reproduced in italics is crossed out in the manuscript.

10 Prunières notes that during the Fronde, *Orfeo* was the pretext for many malicious poetic attacks on Mazarin (Prunières, *L'Opéra italien en France avant Lulli*, 144). See Prunières's lengthy discussion of the reaction against *Orfeo* and Mazarin (ibid., 86–94, 102, 113, 148). He also notes that the queen used opera to stage her return to Paris in 1654 after the defeat of the Frondeurs with representations of *Le Nozze di Peleo e di Theti* by Buti and Caprioli (ibid., 150).

11 Rosand, *Opera in Seventeenth-Century Venice*, 45.

12 Ibid., 333. See also Geoffrey Burgess's illuminating discussion of the acceptibility of song in relation to text (Geoffrey Vernon Burgess, "Ritual in the *tragédie en musique* from Lully's *Cadmus et Hermione* [1673] to Rameau's *Zoroastre* [1749]," Ph.D. dissertation, Cornell University, 1998, 141–200).

13 Luigi Rossi, *Orfeo*, ed. Clifford Bartlett, 3 vols. (Redcroft, Bank's End, Wyton, Huntingdon: King's Music, [1997]), 1:22. All subsequent citations

and translations included in the text follow this edition, referring to volume and page numbers. I have occasionally made slight modifications to the translations for the sake of clarity.

14 Rosand, *Opera in Seventeenth-Century Venice*, 247.

15 The ending of Striggio's 1607 libretto differs from the 1609 score, the latter introducing a cloud machine and thereby making possible Orpheus's final ascent. See John Whenham's discussion of the questions surrounding this alteration in Stanley Sadie, ed., *The New Grove Dictionary of Opera* (1992; London: Macmillan, 1997), s. v. *"Orfeo* (i)."

16 François Hedelin, abbé d'Aubignac, *La Pratique du théâtre* (Amsterdam: Jean Frederic Bernard, 1715), 35–36.

17 Ibid., 38–39.

18 John D. Lyons, "The Barbarous Ancients: French Classical Poetics and the Attack on Ancient Tragedy," *MLN* 110.5 (1995), 1143.

19 D'Aubignac, *La Pratique du théâtre*, 37–38.

20 [Charles de Marguetel de Saint-Denis, seigneur de] Saint-Évremond, "Sur les opera," in François Lesure, ed., *Textes sur Lully et l'opéra français* (Geneva: Minkoff, 1987), 86–87.

21 Burgess has pointed out the ways in which the prologue, *divertissement*, and the ritualistic chaconne challenge d'Aubignac's prescriptions (Burgess, "Ritual in the *tragédie en musique*," 137).

22 D'Aubignac, *La Pratique du théâtre*, 132. The reference to "the economy of satyric tragedy" refers to its mix of serious and comic actions.

23 On the *ballet de cour*, see Margaret McGowan, *L'Art du ballet de cour en France, 1581–1643* (Paris: Centre National de la Recherche Scientifique, 1963), and Marie-Françoise Christout, *Le Ballet de cour de Louis XIV: 1643–1672* (Paris: A. et J. Picard, 1967).

24 Perry Gethner, "Comedy-Ballet and Court Festivities: Three Extreme Scenarios," *Cahiers du dix-septième* 3.1 (1989), 207. See also Charles Mazouer, *Molière et ses comédies-ballets* (Paris: Klincksieck, 1993), 12.

25 The machine plays existed in contradistinction to the neoclassical genres, a fact that can be gleaned from the comments of Donneau de Visé, who himself wrote several machine plays, when he refers to the regular plays as *"pièces unies"* [unified plays], implicitly recognizing the machine plays as an odd assortment of bits and pieces (Perry Gethner, "Staging and Spectacle in the Machine Tragedies," in David Trott and Nicole Boursier, eds., *L'Age du théâtre en France / The Age of Theatre in France* [Edmonton: Academic Printing & Publishing, 1988], 231). As Gethner notes, these plays

"do not form as homogeneous a corpus as the standard generalizations
might lead us to expect . . . [because] singing and dancing, unlike the
machines, were among the components deemed dispensable"
(Perry Gethner, "On the Use of Music and Dance in the Machine
Tragedies," *Papers in French Seventeenth-Century Literature* 15.29
[1988], 463).

26 René Rapin, *Les Réflexions sur la poétique de ce temps et sur les ouvrages des
poètes anciens et modernes*, ed. E. T. Dubois (Geneva: Droz, 1970), 99.

27 Jean Laurent Le Cerf de la Viéville, sieur de Freneuse, *Comparaison de la
musique italienne et de la musique françoise*, 2nd ed., 3 tomes in 1 vol.
(Brussels: François Foppens, 1705), 1:147.

28 Antoine-Louis LeBrun, *Théâtre lyrique* (Paris: Pierre Ribou, 1712), 5.

29 Antoine Furetière, *Recueil des factums*, 2 vols. (Paris: Poulet-Malassic et De
Broise, 1859), 1:173.

30 Jean-Baptiste Dubos, *Réflexions critiques sur la poésie et sur la peinture* (Paris:
École nationale supérieure des Beaux-Arts, 1993), 153.

31 Pierre Bourdelot and Jacques Bonnet, *Histoire de la musique et de ses effets*
(Paris: Cochart, 1715), 46.

32 Antoine-Louis LeBrun, *Théâtre lyrique*, 13.

33 Ibid., 12.

34 Samuel Chappuzeau, *Le Théâtre françois* (Lyon: Michel Mayer, 1674), 53.

35 François de Châteauneuf, *Dialogue sur la musique des anciens* (Paris: Noël
Pissot, 1725), 102.

36 Saint-Évremond, "Sur les opera," 82.

37 André Dacier, *La Poëtique d'Aristote* (Paris: Claude Barbin, 1692), xii.

38 Ibid., 82.

39 Ibid., 83.

40 On the debates surrounding theater, see Sylviane Léoni, *Le Poison et le
remède: théâtre, morale et rhétorique en France et en Italie, 1694–1758* (Oxford:
Voltaire Foundation, 1998), 121–76.

41 Antoine Arnauld, "A M. Perrault, de l'Academie Françoise, au sujet de la
satire sur les femmes par M. Despreaux," *Lettres*, 9 vols. (Nancy: Joseph
Nicolai, 1727), VII:413, VII:431. For another similar depreciation, see Jean de
La Fontaine, "A M. de Niert," *Oeuvres diverses*, in *Oeuvres complètes*, ed.
René Groos, Jacques Schiffrin, and Pierre Clarac, 2 vols. (Paris: Gallimard,
1954–58), II:617–18. For a discussion of these issues, see Perry Gethner,
"La 'Morale Lubrique' dans les opéras de Quinault," in *Les Visages de*

l'amour au XVIIe siècle (Toulouse: Université de Toulouse-Le Mirail, 1984): 145–54.

42 Arnauld, *Lettres*, vii:26. It is interesting to note similarly negative characterizations of Italian opera. In *Della perfetta poesia italiana* (1706), Locovico Antonio Muratori, like Arnauld, degraded operatic music as effeminate (see Edward Lippman, *A History of Western Musical Aesthetics* [Lincoln, Nebr. and London: University of Nebraska Press, 1992], 139).

43 Quoted in Etienne Gros, *Philippe Quinault: sa vie et son oeuvre* (Paris: Champion, 1926), 723.

44 Saint-Évremond, *Les Opéra* (Geneva: Droz, 1979), 69.

45 Ibid., 104–05.

46 Saint Évremond, "Sur les opera," 81.

47 Pierre de Villiers, *Poëmes et autres poësies* (Paris: Jacques Collombat, 1712), 359.

48 Ibid., 364.

49 Ibid., 373.

50 Saint-Évremond, "Sur les opera," 118. Giovanni Maria Crescimbeni echoes Saint-Évremond across the Alps in his *La bellezza della volgar poesia* (1700), faulting opera for ruining tragedy and comedy (Lippman, *A History of Western Musical Aesthetics*, 138).

51 Villiers, *Poëmes et autres poësies*, 368.

52 Ibid., 357, 373–76.

53 "Those who would like to defend Quinault against Boileau's attacks cannot deny that the characters of his tragedies are too unmanly" (Germain Boffrand, "Vie de Philippe Quinault," in Philippe Quinault, *Théâtre contenant ses tragédies, comédies et opéra*, 5 tomes in 1 vol. (1778; Geneva: Slatkine, 1970), 1:14.

54 Adrien Baillet, *Jugemens des sçavans sur les principaux ouvrages des auteurs*, 4 tomes in 9 vols. (Paris: Antoine Dezallier, 1686), 4:321.

55 Gustave Lanson, "Notice," in Racine, *Théâtre choisi* (Paris: Hachette, 1896), 7.

56 Gustave Lanson, *Histoire de la littérature française*, 2 vols. (Paris: Hachette, 1951), 1:537.

57 Quoted in Gros, *Philippe Quinault*, 731.

58 Gros, *Philippe Quinault*, 731.

59 Ibid., 731–32.

60 Ibid., 732.

61 Ibid.

62 Ibid., 743.

63 Ibid., 741.

64 Antoine Adam, *Histoire de la littérature française au XVIIe siècle*, 4 vols. (Paris: Éditions Domat, 1954), IV:392, IV:267.

65 Ibid., 266.

66 Ibid., 268.

67 Antoine Adam, Georges Lerminier, Édouard Morot-Sir, et al., *Littérature française* (Paris: Larousse, 1967), 1:280.

68 Joan DeJean, *Tender Geographies: Women and the Origins of the Novel in France* (New York: Columbia University Press, 1991), 9–10.

69 Gros, *Philippe Quinault*, 75.

70 Patricia Howard, "The Positioning of Woman in Quinault's World Picture," in Jérôme de La Gorce and Herbert Schneider, eds., *Jean-Baptiste Lully: Actes du colloque Saint-Germain-en-Laye–Heidelberg 1987* (Laaber: Laaber-Verlag, 1990), 194, 198.

71 Jean-François La Harpe, *Lycée, ou cours de littérature ancienne et moderne*, 16 tomes in 19 vols. (Paris: H. Agasse, 1799–1805), 12:205, 12:208.

72 Roger W. Herzel, "Racine, Laurent, and the *Palais à Volonté*," *PMLA* 108.5 (1993), 1080.

73 La Harpe, *Lycée*, 12:210.

74 Joan DeJean has attested to the innovative quality of Terrasson's thinking when she refers to him as "a true pre-Enlightenment figure" (*Ancients Against Moderns: Culture Wars and the Making of a Fin de Siècle* [Chicago: University of Chicago Press, 1997], 178n58). See DeJean's discussion of the highly polemical years that saw the publication of Terrasson's *Dissertation* (ibid., 97–108).

75 Dubos, *Réflexions critiques*, 154.

76 Le Cerf de la Viéville, *Comparaison*, 1:157.

77 Ibid., 2:10.

78 The tendency to demystify ancient music is exemplified by Châteauneuf's *Dialogue sur la musique des anciens*. Referring to passages from Plutarque, one of the interlocutors, Callimaque, attempts to explain away the supposed force of music by pointing to the specific circumstances in which these effects occurred: "I would tend to think that a wild man [*un frénétique*] who was being calmed by the Lydian mode was already very close to the end of his fit. Similarly, when we are told that Terpander calmed a revolt in Lacedaemonia with his lyre, it is

because the common people, always capricious and inconstant in nature, soon grow tired of fighting. Often even before they tire the slightest distraction, by drawing attention to itself, is capable of dissipating the disturbance. It is quite possible, then, that Terpander, who knew the character of the masses, understood that by presenting himself with his musician's garb, he would certainly cause a diversion; and it is possible that the supernatural qualities of this event amount to nothing more than this" (11–12).

79 Jean Terrasson, *Dissertation critique sur l'Iliade d'Homere, où à l'occasion de ce Poëme on cherche les regles d'une Poëtique fondée sur la raison, & sur les exemples des Anciens & des Modernes*, 2 vols. (1715; Geneva: Slatkine, 1971), 1.220. Subsequent citations are given in the text.

80 On the music of the ancients, Perrault notes that "all the subtleties of music, judging from their writings, were contained in the modulation of monodic song [*d'une seule partie*]; and they used consonances only as we do in the hurdy-gurdy or in the bagpipe where drones are tuned to the fifth and the octave" (Vitruvius, *Les Dix livres d'architecture de Vitruve* [Paris: Jean Baptiste Coignard, 1684], 165n31). In what follows, Perrault remarks that contemporary audiences have spurned the complexity of "modern" counterpoint in favor of a revival of the simplicity of "ancient" practices based on the expressive solo voice (ibid., 165–66n31).

81 Rodrigue and Chimène are principle characters in Pierre Corneille's *Le Cid* (1636).

82 DeJean, *Ancients Against Moderns*, 64. In her discussion of the term, "public," DeJean argues that "the opening up with which the new public was associated was a democratization, not of spectatorship, but of readership" (ibid., 37). Though Terrasson may appear to have "the public" in mind primarily as an audience for theater, his use of the term also encompasses the kind of public literary opinion DeJean discusses in relation to Donneau de Visé and *Le Mercure galant* (ibid., 65).

83 See Charles Perrault, *Critique de l'opéra* (Paris: Louis Billaine, 1674).

84 *The New Grove Dictionary of Opera*, s. v. "Opera (iii)."

2 THE OPERA KING

1 Louis Marin, *Portrait of the King*, trans. Martha Houle (Minneapolis: University of Minnesota Press, 1988), 8, 121.

2 Marie de Rabutin-Chantal, marquise de Sévigné, *Correspondance*, ed. Roger Duchêne, 3 vols. (Paris: Gallimard, 1972–78), II:479. See also William Brooks, "Lully and Quinault at Court and on the Public Stage, 1673–86," *Seventeenth-Century French Studies* 10 (1988), 107.

3 Jean Chapelain, "A M. Colbert," *Lettres*, 2 vols. (Paris: Imprimerie Nationale, 1883), II:362.

4 Ibid.

5 On seventeenth-century conceptions of allegory, see Bernard Beugnot, "Pour une poétique de l'allégorie classique," in Marc Fumaroli, ed., *Critique et création littéraires en France au XVIIe siècle* (Paris: Éditions du Centre National de la Recherche Scientifique, 1977), 411, 417.

6 In his dissertation on the *Ursprung des deutschen Trauerspiels*, Walter Benjamin considers allegory as a form of writing, "not a playful illustrative technique, but a form of expression . . . " (*The Origin of German Tragic Drama*, trans. John Osborne [London: NLB, 1977], 162). From the perspective of the early twentieth century, Benjamin contrasts the romantic symbol with allegory, noting that "[w]hereas in the symbol destruction is idealized and the transfigured face of nature is fleetingly revealed in the light of redemption, in allegory the observer is contronted with the *facies hippocratica* of history as a petrified, primordial landscape" (ibid., 166).

7 Paul Duro, *The Academy and the Limits of Painting in Seventeenth-Century France* (Cambridge: Cambridge University Press, 1997), 189. See also Norman Bryson, *Word and Image: French Painting of the Ancien Régime* (Cambridge: Cambridge University Press, 1981), 40.

8 Jennifer Montagu, *The Expression of the Passions: the Origin and Influence of Charles Le Brun's Conférence sur l'expression générale et particulière* (New Haven: Yale University Press, 1994), 43.

9 After painting *The Queens of Persia at the Feet of Alexander* (1660–61), Le Brun began the series on the battles of Alexander. The largest of these is nearly 13 meters long. See Duro, *The Academy and the Limits of Painting*, 93–98.

10 For more on these tapestries, see Daniel Meyer, *L'Histoire du Roy* (Paris: Éditions de la Réunion des Musées Nationaux, 1980), 127–40.

11 Ibid., 129.

12 Daniel Meyer clarifies and documents the complex evolution of this work in the third series, *la troisième teinture*, which is the one he chose to

study. Le Brun produced a drawing which Van der Meulen used to create a more complete sketch of the scene. This sketch was later taken up by Baudoin Yvart for the tapestry design, which remained in this form until it was finally woven in 1731–32 (Meyer, *L'Histoire du Roy*, 86).

13 Ibid.

14 Joël Cornette, *Le Roi de guerre: essai sur la souveraineté dans la France du Grand Siècle* (Paris: Payot, 1993), 131.

15 François Bluche, *Louis XIV* (Paris: Fayard, 1986), 360.

16 Cited in Michel Gareau, *Charles Le Brun: First Painter to King Louis XIV* (New York: Harry N. Abrams, 1992), 43.

17 Charles Perrault, *Parallèle des anciens et des modernes en ce qui regarde les arts et les sciences*, 4 tomes in 1 vol. (1688–97; Munich: Eidos Verlag, 1964), 1:227.

18 Ibid., 1:116–17. See also Duro's discussion of this passage (*The Academy and the Limits of Painting*, 190).

19 Duro, *The Academy and the Limits of Painting*, 194.

20 Lydia Beauvais and Jean-François Méajanès, *Le Brun à Versailles*, exhibition catalogue from the Cabinet des Dessins (Paris: Musée du Louvre, [1985]), 24.

21 Alain Mérot, *French Painting in the Seventeenth Century*, trans. Caroline Beamish (New Haven: Yale University Press, 1995), 263.

22 Beauvais and Méajanès, *Le Brun à Versailles*, 28–29.

23 Ibid., 25.

24 Cited in ibid., 33.

25 *Le Mercure galant* (September, 1680), 295.

26 Beauvais and Méajanès, *Le Brun à Versailles*, 33.

27 Cited in Duro, *The Academy and the Limits of Painting*, 194–95.

28 Ibid., 195.

29 For references to these designs, see Beauvais and Méajanès, *Le Brun à Versailles*, 37. See also Mérot, *French Painting in the Seventeenth Century*, 264; and Peter Burke, *The Fabrication of Louis XIV* (New Haven: Yale University Press, 1992), 188.

30 Cited in *Colbert: 1619–1683*, exhibition catalogue (Paris: [Hôtel de la Monnaie], 1983), 311.

31 See Paul Duro's remarks on the framing devices – false stucco frames for the historical paintings and more complex swags and garlands for the mythological scenes – that Le Brun used to articulate the various

modes of representation he deployed (*The Academy and the Limits of Painting*, 199–200).

32 Ernst H. Kantorowicz, *The King's Two Bodies: A Study in Mediaeval Political Theology* (Princeton: Princeton University Press, 1957), 20–21.

33 Thomas Kavanagh, *The Esthetics of the Moment* (Philadelphia: University of Pennsylvania Press, 1996), 137.

34 For other discussions of this painting, see ibid., 135–38; Gareau, *Charles Le Brun*, 70; and Montagu, *The Expression of the Passions*, 44.

35 Le Brun appears to have planned another series of tapestries devoted to the military campaigns of 1672 along the Rhine and in Holland, this time incorporating mythological figures. These tapestries, however, were never executed (Meyer, *L'Histoire du Roy*, 133).

36 Jean-Marie Apostolidès, *Le Roi-machine: spectacle et politique au temps de Louis XIV* (Paris: Minuit, 1981), 66. Apostolidès affirms that "the imaginary of antiquity structures the social reality of the seventeenth century; it organizes it by giving it a comprehensible form and meaning" (67–68).

37 See J. Melet Sanson's remarks in the exhibition catalogue, *Colbert: 1619–1683*, 447; and Manuel Couvreur, *Jean-Baptiste Lully: musique et dramaturgie au service du prince* ([Brussels]: Marc Vokar, 1992), 43–63. In an uncharacteristic gesture of continuity with respect to the work of his predecessor (even though Perrault was replaced by Félibien), Louvois maintained the Petite Académie after the death of Colbert and even doubled its size. In 1683, La Chapelle, Racine, Boileau et Rainssant joined Charpentier, l'abbé Tallemant, Félibien, and Quinault (Couvreur, *Jean-Baptiste Lully*, 46).

38 Chapelain, *Lettres*, II:273. At the end of his letter, Chapelain suggests other means of spreading the king's glory by drawing attention to massive or impressive objects: "the ancients have left us illustrious examples which still hold the gaze of all nations in respect, such as pyramids, columns, equestrian statues, colossi, triumphal arches, marble and bronze busts, the bas-reliefs, all historical monuments to which one could add our rich tapestry works, our frescoes and our engravings which, though of less longevity than the others nonetheless last a long time." He adds that these objects "belong to arts other than that of the Muses" and are therefore beyond the scope of his letter (ibid., II:277).

39 Ibid., II:273.

40 Ibid., II:274.

41 René Rapin, *Les Réflexions sur la poétique de ce temps*, 40.

42 Chapelain, *Lettres*, II:275.

43 Paul Pellisson-Fontanier, *Oeuvres diverses*, 3 tomes in 1 vol. (1735; Geneva: Slatkine, 1971), 2:323–24.

44 Chapelain, *Lettres*, II:275, II:275n8.

45 Ibid., II:275.

46 Ibid.

47 Jean Racine, *Oeuvres complètes*, ed. Raymond Picard, 2 vols. (Paris: Gallimard, 1950–52), II:201.

48 Chapelain, *Lettres*, II:274, II:276.

49 Ibid., II:276.

50 On October 5, 1672, Roger de Rabutin, comte de Bussy, wrote to Jean Corbinelli, complaining that "if I were [the King's] historian, I would not do as Boileau did in an epistle that he addresses to the King [on the crossing of the Rhine] when he makes a fiction out of the actions of his campaign, because, he says, they are so extraordinary that they already very much seem like fiction . . . I would say the thing plainly and without so much fuss" (quoted in Raymond Picard, *La carrière de Jean Racine* [Paris: Gallimard, 1961], 363). We can read in Bussy's letter a perceived confusion between panegyrics and history, for an epistle is clearly not intended to replace historiography. However, his letter does express anxiety about maintaining a clear distinction between history and fiction, also one of Chapelain's concerns with respect to narrative poetry.

51 "After Charpentier declined, since he had not received the secret memoirs that he had requested, the king undertook to dictate his own memoirs to the Président de Périgny and to Pellison, his historiographer. These two secretaries never belonged to the Petite Académie. Boileau and Racine, historiographers since 1677, entered [the Petite Académie] only in 1683. *L'Histoire du roi*, at least in its literary form, eluded the jurisdiction of Chapelain and Perrault" (Couvreur, *Jean-Baptiste Lully*, 48).

52 Duro, *The Academy and the Limits of Painting*, 198.

53 Beauvais and Méajanès, *Le Brun à Versailles*, 33.

54 Montagu, *The Expression of the Passions*, 44.

55 *Le Mercure galant* (December, 1684), 3, 8–9.

56 Ibid., 18. See also the explanations of each image in Jean-Baptiste Massé, *La Grande galerie de Versailles, et les deux salons qui l'accompagnent* (Paris: chez la Veuve Amaulry, 1753).

57 Duro, *The Academy and the Limits of Painting*, 207. Claims such as those of Montagu, above, and Duro pointing to allegory's necessary reliance on external narratives must nonetheless be tempered by the fact that these accounts were written not only for those who could view the paintings at Versailles, but also for the many who could not and who therefore necessarily relied on narrative explanations of the allegorical figures. In this sense, descriptions such as those in the *Mercure galant* functioned, as did the accounts of the eighteenth-century salons published in Grimm's *Correspondance littéraire*, to transform the visual into narrative for the benefit of an absent public.

58 Sarah R. Cohen, *Art, Dance, and the Body in French Culture of the Ancien Régime* (Cambridge: Cambridge University Press, 2000), 31.

59 Jean-Pierre Néraudau, *L'Olympe du roi-soleil: mythologie et idéologie royale au Grand Siècle* (Paris: Les Belles Lettres, 1986), 122; and Nicole Ferrier-Caverivière, *L'Image de Louis XIV dans la littérature française de 1660 à 1715* (Paris: Presses universitaires de France, 1981), 66.

60 Néraudau, *L'Olympe du roi-soleil*, 124.

61 Cited in ibid., 128.

62 Cited in ibid., 130.

63 For a brief description of the festivities at Versailles in 1664, 1668, and 1674, see Martin Meade's introduction to André Félibien, *Les Fêtes de Versailles: chroniques de 1668 & 1674* (Paris: Dédale, 1994), 5–18.

64 Cohen, *Art, Dance, and the Body*, 51.

65 Ibid., 73.

66 If this appearance was his last in a ballet, it is important to note that Louis XIV continued for some time to dance at balls, in effect performing for an audience, and that he encouraged the Dauphin in his own dancing. However, the symbolic framework inherent in the court ballet made it a very distinct form of representation. Cohen has described some of these distinct qualities, in particular the importance of the proscenium stage in court ballet (ibid., 29–38). On Louis XIV's departure from the stage, see Charles I. Silin, *Benserade and his Ballets de Cour*, The Johns Hopkins Studies in Romance Literatures and Languages, extra volume xv (Baltimore: The Johns Hopkins University Press, 1940), 384. Mark Franko erroneously gives the date of Louis's last appearance in the *Ballet de Flore* as July 18, 1668 (*Dance as Text: Ideologies of the Baroque Body* [Cambridge: Cambridge University Press, 1993], 122). Néraudau concurs

with Silin in noting 1669 as the date of this ballet (*L'Olympe du roi-soleil*, 132) as do Ferrier-Cavevière (*L'Image de Louis XIV*, 66n80) and Christout (*Le Ballet de cour de Louis XIV*, 116).

67 Several commentators claim or suggest that Louis did appear in the February 4th festivities and was replaced only for the second performance on February 14th. See Néraudau, *L'Olympe du roi-soleil*, 138; Manuel Couvreur, *Jean-Baptiste Lully*, 189; and Christout, *Le Ballet de cour de Louis XIV*, 119, 156. However, these commentators base their accounts on Robinet whose panegyric brief on the *divertissement* was based on the *livret*, which had been printed in advance of the performance. His *Lettre en vers à Madame* from February 8, 1670, reads: "Il y parêt le Dieu de l'*Onde*, / Et le *Dieu* de Mont *Parnassus*, / Avec tant d'éclat que rien plus, / Qui fait que tout chacun admire, / Ce redoutable, & charmant Sire: / Qui, sans contrefaire ces Dieux, / Est, par ma foy, bien plus / Dieu qu'eux" [He appears as the God of the *Waters* / And as the *God* of Mount *Parnassus* / With a radiance never before seen, / Which caused everyone to admire / This awesome and charming Sire / Who, without imitating the Gods / Is, in faith, even more godlike than they] (Charles Robinet and Jacques Laurent, *Le Théâtre et l'opéra vus par les gazetiers Robinet et Laurent*, ed. William Brooks, *Papers on French Seventeenth-Century Literature* 78 (1993), 28. Robinet corrects himself on February 22nd: "Mais c'est tout ce que j'en puis dire, / Sinon que nôtre *Auguste Sire* / Fait danser, & n'y danse point, / M'étant trompé, dessus ce point, / Quand, sur un Livre, / j'allay mettre, / Le contraire, en mon autre Lettre" [But that is all that I can say of it, / Except that our Noble Sire / commands the dance but does not dance himself / Having been mistaken on this point, / When, relying on a book, / I wrote / The contrary in my other letter] (ibid., 29). For clarification of this episode, see Molière, *Oeuvres complètes*, ed. Georges Couton, 2 vols. (Paris: Gallimard, 1971), II:1413–14.

68 See Racine, *Théâtre complet*, ed. Jacques Morel and Alain Viala (Paris: Dunod, 1995), 306.

69 Nicolas Boileau, "A M. de Losme de Monchesnai," *Oeuvres complètes*, 4 vols. [Paris: Garnier Frères, 1870–73], IV:253.

70 Louis Racine, *Mémoires contenant quelques particularités sur la vie et les ouvrages de Jean Racine* [1747], in Racine, *Oeuvres complètes*, I:48.

71 Néraudau, *L'Olympe du roi-soleil*, 137, 143.

72 Abby E. Zanger, "The Spectacular Gift: Rewriting the Royal Scenario in Molière's *Les Amants Magnifiques*," *Romanic Review* 81.2 (1990), 187n20, 188.

73 Barbara Russano Hanning, *Of Poetry and Music's Power: Humanism and the Creation of Opera* (1969; Ann Arbor: UMI Research Press, 1980), 2.

74 See ibid., 271.

75 Cited in Jean-Pierre Néraudau, "Du Christ à Apollon: les chemins d'une mythologie de la cour," in *La Tragédie lyrique* (Paris: Cicero, 1991), 15.

76 Siegbert Himmelsbach, *L'épopée ou la 'case vide': La réflexion poétologique sur l'épopée nationale en France* (Tübingen: Max Niemeyer, 1988), 251, 239.

77 Terrasson, *Dissertation critique*, ii:209. Similarly, for Rémond de Saint-Mard, opera borrowed *le merveilleux* from epic poetry (*Réflexions sur l'opéra* [1741; Geneva: Minkoff, 1972], 20).

78 Couvreur, *Jean-Baptiste Lully*, 332–33.

79 Néraudau, "Du Christ à Apollon," 19.

80 Jean Duron, *"Atys,* 'opéra du Roi,'" *L'Avant-scène opéra* 94 (1987), 21.

81 Buford Norman, "Le Héros contestataire dans les livrets de Quinault: politique ou esthétique," in Roger Duchêne et Pierre Ronzeaud, eds., *Ordre et contestation au temps des classiques*, Papers in French Seventeenth-Century Literature 73 (1992), 291–92.

82 Ibid., 296.

83 Ibid., 293.

84 Brooks, "Lully and Quinault at Court and on the Public Stage," 107.

85 Patricia Howard has suggested that "there is no place for the role of love in Quinault's school for heroes" ("The Positioning of Woman in Quinault's World Picture," 199).

86 Gros, *Philippe Quinault*, 721.

87 Perrault, *Critique de l'opéra*, 44. Geoffrey Burgess compellingly presents the opera prologue as a form of performative ritual and examines chaconnes and passacailles of *tragédie en musique* as ritualistic reaffirmations of order. Burgess argues that *tragédie en musique* performs the reconciliation of glory and love ("Ritual in the *tragédie en musique*," 80, 582) while nonetheless remarking the ways in which opera "obfuscated the force that empowered the *régime*" and "served as a forum for the critique of power" (ibid., 651, 507).

88 Perry Gethner, "La Magicienne à l'opéra, source de subversion," in Roger Duchêne et Pierre Ronzeaud, eds., *Ordre et contestation au temps*

des classiques, Papers on French Seventeenth-Century Literature 73 (1992), 306.

89 Hélène Himelfarb, "Un domaine méconnu de l'empire lullyste: le Trianon de Louis XIV, ses tableaux et les livrets d'opéras (1687–1714)," in Jérôme de La Gorce and Herbert Schneider, eds., *Jean-Baptiste Lully: Actes du colloque Saint-Germain-en-Laye–Heidelberg 1987* (Laaber: Laaber-Verlag, 1990), 294.

90 Buford Norman, "'Le Théâtre est un grand monument': l'évocation du passé et des passions dans l'*Alceste* de Quinault," in Volker Kapp, ed., *Les lieux de mémoire et la fabrique de l'oeuvre, Papers on French Seventeenth-Century Literature* 80 (1993), 323.

91 See Bluche, *Louis XIV*, 426.

92 On the pastoral genres and the emergence of *tragédie en musique*, see Kintzler, *Poétique de l'opéra français*, 210–26.

93 Philippe Quinault, *Livrets d'opéra*, ed. Buford Norman, 2 vols. (Toulouse: Société de littératures classiques, 1999), I:III, I:II4.

94 Ibid., II:5.

95 Ibid., II:198, II:201.

96 Cornette, *Le Roi de guerre*, 14–15.

97 Le Cerf de la Viéville remarked that "*Armide* is the women's Opera, *Atys* the King's Opera, *Phaéton* the People's Opera, and *Isis* the Musicians' Opera" (*Comparaison*, 1:102). According to Antoine de Léris, *Atys* was revived numerous times (in 1678, 1682, 1689, 1699, 1708, 1709, 1725, 1738, and 1740) and parodied throughout the first half of the eighteenth century, a sure sign of its success. Among other versions, there was the *Arlequin Atys* at the Théâtre Italien, Sticotti's *Cybele Amoureuse* in 1738, and Carolet's *Polichinelle Atys* given by the Marionettes de Bienfait at the Foire Saint-Germain in 1736 (Antoine de Léris, *Dictionnaire portatif historique et littéraire des théâtres*, 2nd ed. [Paris: C. A. Jombert, 1763], s.v. *Atys*).

98 Philippe Quinault, *Atys*, ed. Stéphane Bassinet (Geneva: Droz, 1992), 55. Subsequent citations to the prologue in my text refer to page numbers in this edition. In citing the opera itself, references are to act, scene, and page numbers.

99 Perry Gethner, "La Mémoire agent de consécration et génératrice du spectacle," in Volker Kapp, ed., *Les lieux de mémoire et la fabrique de l'oeuvre, Papers on French Seventeenth-Century Literature* 80 (1993), 298. Burgess

has also noted the importance of time in the prologue to *Atys* ("Ritual in the *tragédie en musique*," 284–94).

100 Claude-Charles Guyonnet de Vertron, *Paralèlle de Louis le Grand avec les princes qui ont esté surnommez Grands* (Paris: Le Febvre, 1685), 52.

101 Racine, *Oeuvres complètes*, II:201.

102 Marin, *Portrait of the King*, 8.

103 Quinault, *Livrets d'opéra*, I:59, II:108, I:232, I:111, II:251.

104 Jean Duron, "Commentaire musical et littéraire," *L'Avant-scène Opéra* 94 (1987), 38, 40.

105 Quinault, *Livrets d'opéra*, I:61. See also the critical edition of the libretto with supporting documents: Philippe Quinault, *Alceste*, ed. William Brooks, Buford Norman and Jeanne Morgan Zarucchi (Geneva: Droz, 1994).

106 Quinault, *Livrets d'opéra*, II: 199.

107 Charles Cotin, "Ode pour le roy," *Réflexions sur la conduite du roy* (Paris: Pierre Le Petit, 1663), 31.

108 *Encyclopédie ou dictionnaire raisonné des arts et des métiers*, ed. Denis Diderot and Jean le Rond d'Alembert, 28 vols. (1751–72; Elmsford, N. Y.: Pergamon, n.d.), XII:828.

109 Cited in Couvreur, *Jean-Baptiste Lully*, 343.

110 Quinault, *Livrets d'opéra*, II:154, I:112.

111 Thomas Corneille, *Médée* (Paris: Christophe Ballard, 1693), 3.

112 Ibid., 8.

113 Ovid, *Fasti: Roman Holidays*, trans. Betty Rose Nagle (Bloomington and Indianapolis: Indiana University Press, 1995), 111.

114 Jacques Truchet, ed., *Recherches de thématique théâtrale* (Tübingen: Gunter Narr Verlag, 1981), 167.

115 Quinault, *Atys*, 35. In act 1, scene 3, of Pierre Corneille's *Suréna*, the hero refers to the illusory desire of perpetuating one's own existence through that of one's descendants: "Et le moindre moment d'un bonheur souhaité / Vaux mieux qu'une si froide, et vaine éternité" [And the slightest moment of a desired happiness / Is better than such a cold, vain eternity] (Pierre Corneille, *Oeuvres complètes*, ed. Georges Couton, 3 vols. [Paris: Gallimard, 1980–87], III:1254). Serge Doubrovsky has called this endpoint "the death of the hero" (*Corneille et la dialectique du héros* [Paris: Gallimard, 1963], 429).

116 Quinault, *Atys*, 43.

117 La Rochefoucauld, *Maximes*, ed. Jacques Truchet (Paris: Garnier Frères, 1967), 8.

118 Quinault, *Atys*, 43.

119 Catherine Kintzler calls this relation an "inverse parallelism" (*Poétique de l'opéra français*, 243).

120 Quinault, *Livrets d'opéra*, II:97–98.

121 Pierre Corneille, "Discours de l'utilité et des parties du poème dramatique," *Oeuvres complètes*, III:129. Corneille refers here specifically to his Cléopâtre from the tragedy, *Rodogune* (1645).

122 Quinault, *Livrets d'opéra*, II:117, II:123.

123 Ibid., II:132.

124 Ibid., II:108

125 See, for example, René Descartes, *Les Passions de l'âme* (Paris: Gallimard, 1988), 186; and Blaise Pascal, *Pensées* (Paris: Garnier, 1964), 200.

126 Quinault, *Livrets d'opéra*, I:12–13. The topic of Apollo's victory over Python was also allegorized in early Italian courtly *intermedi*. See Rosand, *Opera in Seventeenth-Century Venice*, 10n3.

127 Quinault, *Livrets d'opéra*, II:155.

128 Louis XIV, *Mémoires pour l'instruction du dauphin*, 2 vols. (Paris: Didier, 1860), II:314–15.

129 Jean-Marie Apostolidès, *Le Prince sacrifié: théâtre et politique au temps de Louis XIV* (Paris: Minuit, 1985), 181.

130 Apostolidès, *Le Roi-machine*, 64, 141.

131 Ibid., 131.

132 Néraudau, *L'Olympe du roi-soleil*, 257.

133 Ibid., 145.

134 Chapelain, *Lettres*, II:275, II:275n4.

135 Charles Louis de Secondat, baron de la Brède et de Montesquieu, *Oeuvres complètes*, ed. Roger Caillois, 2 vols. (Paris: Gallimard, 1949–51), II:378; my emphasis. The passage in question discusses the correct observance of the right to wage war.

3 THE ASCENDANCE OF MUSIC AND THE DISINTEGRATION OF THE HERO IN *ARMIDE*

1 Pascal Quignard, *Rhétorique spéculative* (Paris: Calmann-Lévy, 1995), 38.

2 See James R. Anthony, "The Musical Structure of Lully's Operatic Airs," in Jérôme de La Gorce and Herbert Schneider, eds., *Jean-Baptiste Lully:*

Actes du colloque Saint-Germain-en-Laye–Heidelberg 1987 (Laaber:
Laaber-Verlag, 1990), 65–76. As Anthony has pointed out, "the basic
problem . . . in French opera is to separate air from recitative" (66). Lois
Rosow remarks that "the virtual lack of contrasting structural elements
in Quinault's poetry lends itself to the absence of strong differentiation
between song and declamation in this style" and notes further that this
ambiguity "involves dramatic function as well" ("The Articulation of
Lully's Dramatic Dialogue," in John Hajdu Heyer, ed., *Lully Studies*
[Cambridge: Cambridge University Press, 2000], 92–93).

3 Catherine Kintzler, "L'opéra français, hyper-théâtre et hypo-théâtre," *Les
Papiers du Collège International de Philosophie* 16 (1992), 24. See Burgess's
critique of Kintzler's position (Burgess, "Ritual in the *tragédie en musique*,"
481–82). Burgess notes that Kintzler cannot account for the ways in which
certain kinds of violence were "relegated to the wings": for example, "in
the entire repertoire [1673–1749], only one murder is actually committed
in public view" (ibid., 487).

4 Le Cerf de la Viéville, *Comparaison*, 1:9.

5 Alison A. Stonehouse, "The Attitude of the French Towards Metastasio
as Poet and Dramatist in the Second Half of the Eighteenth Century"
(Ph.D. dissertation, University of Western Ontario, 1997), 3, 16.

6 Fumaroli, *Héros et orateurs*, 493.

7 D'Aubignac, *La Pratique du théâtre*, 67. D'Aubignac reasons after Aristotle's
Poetics (1452a), as does Pierre Corneille when he makes the distinction
between ordinary and extraordinary verisimilitude in his "Discours
de la tragédie et des moyens de la traiter selon le vraisemblable
ou le nécessaire" (*Oeuvres complètes*, III:168–69). See also Rapin, *Les
Réflexions sur la poétique de ce temps*, 39. For more on the poetics of
le merveilleux, see Kintzler, *Poétique de l'opéra français*, 172–78, 217–21,
291–97.

8 Jean de La Bruyère, *Oeuvres complètes* (Paris: Gallimard, 1951), 79.

9 On the mechanism of this final scene, see Jérôme de La Gorce, *Berain:
dessinateur du roi soleil* (Paris: Herscher, 1986), 88. For an overview on the
physical characteristics of the theaters and the use of machines, see
Barbara Coeyman, "Theatres for opera and ballet during the reigns of
Louis XIV and Louis XV," *Early Music* 18.1 (1990): 22–37. For more on the
debate surrounding the use of machines in actual performances of these
operas, see Brooks, "Lully and Quinault at Court and on the Public

Stage"; and William Brooks, "Further Remarks on Lully and Quinault at Court," *Seventeenth-Century French Studies* 11 (1989), 147–50.

10 Theodor Adorno suggested that cinema took the place of opera in bourgeois culture, since both forms make a similar appeal to spectacular effects and to romance (*Quasi una fantasia*, trans. Rodney Livingstone [London: Verso, 1992], 42). Catherine Kintzler has remarked on the striking similarity between the position of early opera and early cinema within their respective cultural contexts (*Poétique de l'opéra français*, 245). Seventeenth-century dramatic theorists, however, gave epic poetry much greater latitude than theater in the representation of *le merveilleux*. Tasso's *Gerusalemme liberata* went much further in this direction than any stage medium possibly could. See, for example, the episode in which Godfrey's soldiers are transformed into fish: Torquato Tasso, *Jerusalem Delivered*, trans. Edward Fairfax (New York: Capricorn Books, [1963]), canto 10, stanzas 66–67, p. 218.

11 See Tasso's *Jerusalem Delivered*, where the metaphor of the female sorceress is expressed even more directly: "To all deceit she could her beauty frame, / False, fair, and young, a virgin and a witch" (canto 4, stanza 23, p. 67). On the complexity of the figure of the enchantress, see Perry Gethner, "La Magicienne à l'opéra, source de subversion."

12 Kintzler, *Poétique de l'opéra français*, 283.

13 Quinault, *Livrets d'opéra*, II:255. Subsequent references will be included parenthetically in the text, referring to act, scene, and page numbers in this volume. For references to the prologue, only the page numbers will be cited. I have also consulted the first edition of the libretto and of the score (*Armide: tragédie en musique* [Paris: Ballard, 1686]), but have used the modernized version of the text found in Buford Norman's edition of the libretti.

14 Le Cerf de la Viéville praises this scene above all others in French opera (*Comparaison*, 1:80). The *Querelle des bouffons* was also launched by an attack on this scene by Rousseau in his *Lettre sur la musique française*: see Jean-Jacques Rousseau, *Oeuvres complètes*, ed. Bernard Gagnebin and Marcel Raymond, 5 vols. (Paris: Gallimard, 1959–95), v:322–28; and Jean-Philippe Rameau's response to Rousseau's critique in his *Observations sur notre instinct pour la musique*: see Jean-Philippe Rameau, *Complete Theoretical Writings*, ed. Erwin R. Jacobi, 6 vols. (n.p.: American Institute of Musicology, 1967–72), III:301–29. For recent analyses of these

two texts, see Charles Dill, "Rameau reading Lully: Meaning and system in Rameau's recitative tradition," *Cambridge Opera Journal* 6.1 (1994): 1–17; and Cynthia Verba, "The Development of Rameau's Thoughts on Modulation and Chromatics," *Journal of the American Musicological Society* 26.1 (1973): 69–91. See also Cynthia Verba, *Music and the French Enlightenment: Reconstruction of a Dialogue: 1750–1764* (Oxford: Clarendon Press, 1993), 23–30.

15 Rousseau, *Oeuvres complètes*, v:322.

16 Rameau notes Lully's masterful setting of the first two verses (Rameau, *Observations*, 74–75). On Rameau's concept of modulation, see Dill, "Rameau reading Lully," 2–4.

17 In Monteverdi's *L'incoronazione di Poppea* (1642), Amore intervenes in a similar way to save Poppea from her jealous lover, Ottone.

18 See Cuthbert Girdlestone, *La Tragédie en Musique (1673–1750) considérée comme genre littéraire* (Geneva: Droz, 1972). Girdlestone is off the mark when he asserts that the sorceress does not see her own predicament (114). The tragedy, as always, centers around the combination of blinding self-awareness and willful misrecognition.

19 Given this view of *Armide*, I disagree with William Brooks's claim – a common one – that the visual is present in opera at the expense of the drama: "[opera] has little of the internalized drama we expect of classical theatre, but rather, visual action, movement, noise (La Fontaine condemns the sheer numbers of participants on stage), and it luxuriates in the process of scene-setting, a deliberate and emphasized exposition of the visual, of the static at the expense of the narrative" (Brooks, "Lully and Quinault at Court and on the Public Stage," 105). In *Armide*, dramatic moments and spectacular effects feed off of one another.

20 Herbert Blau, *The Audience* (Baltimore: The Johns Hopkins University Press, 1990), 61.

21 Ibid., 52.

22 The claim that opera was all show and no substance was quite common. Adrien Baillet suggested that Quinault's and Lully's *Alceste* had ruined Euripides's tragedy. He agreed with Furetière that lack of substance was a serious problem in theater based solely on "l'Action ou la Représentation" [Action or Representation] (*Jugemens des sçavans*, vol. IV, pt. 5, pp. 323–24). See also my discussion of the matter in chapter 1.

23 On the dream in seventeenth-century tragedy, see Jacques Morel, *Agréables mensonges: essais sur le théâtre français du XVIIe siècle* (Paris:

Klincksieck, 1991), 35–44. Morel notes that Hardy and his contemporaries placed apparitions on stage, but that this practice declines with the generation of Tristan L'Hermite, in whose plays the vision itself is replaced by a sleeping or just awakened hero. In the *pièces à machines*, the dream entirely loses its earlier violence. In the introduction to his edition of Quinault's *Atys*, Stéphane Bassinet remarks that "the dream is common in seventeenth-century theater. But in tragedy it is recounted (that of Athalia, for example), and in the *pastorale*, the author most often limits himself to having another character describe the sleeper, watching him as he lies on the stage before him. In opera, the dream – practically a required moment after *Atys* – is almost always represented" (Quinault, *Atys*, 32).

24 Jean-Marie Villégier, *"Atys*, une tragédie sans extérieur," *Les Papiers du Collège International de Philosophie* 16 (1992), 18. Villégier remarks that in stage plays, such as those of Racine, the characters escape to spaces away from the outside world, away from the pressing crowds; however, in lyric tragedy, there is no escape, no space that is not already staged.

25 See Jean Laplanche and J.-B. Pontalis, *The Language of Psycho-Analysis*, trans. Donald Nicholson-Smith (New York: W. W. Norton, 1973). The definition given by Laplanche and Pontalis is that of an "imaginary scene [*scénario*] in which the subject is a protagonist, representing the fulfilment of a wish (in the last analysis, an unconscious wish) in a manner that is distorted to a greater or lesser extent by defensive processes" (314). For Freud, fantasy occurs most often as a daydream and consists in "scripts [*scénarios*] of organised scenes which are capable of dramatisation – usually in visual form" (318).

26 Ibid., 318.

27 For Lacan, *jouissance* is understood to be correlative to castration because it is predicated on a desire for an impossible object. See Jacques Lacan, *Le Séminaire XX: Encore* (Paris: Seuil, 1975), 12–13.

28 Immanuel Kant, *Critique of Judgment*, trans. Werner S. Pluhar (Indianapolis: Hackett, 1987), 106.

29 Ibid., 129, 117; Edmund Burke, *A Philosophical Enquiry into the Origin of our Ideas of the Sublime and Beautiful*, ed. J. T. Boulton (London: Routledge and Kegan Paul, 1958), 124. Burke opposes the admiration and astonishment that are the effects of the sublime and the attachment and pleasure associated with beauty: "the sublime . . . always dwells on great objects, and terrible; the latter [love] on small ones, and pleasing; we submit to

what we admire, but we love what submits to us; in one case we are forced, in the other we are flattered into compliance" (113). Though there are many differences in the accounts Burke and Kant give of the sublime, a review of them would be neither pertinent to, nor within the scope of, this essay.

30 Barbara Claire Freeman, *The Feminine Sublime: Gender and Excess in Women's Fiction* (Berkeley: University of California Press, 1995), 3.

31 Kant, *Critique of Judgment*, 129.

32 Freeman, *The Feminine Sublime*, 22.

33 Tom Furniss, *Edmund Burke's Aesthetic Ideology: Language, Gender, and Political Economy in Revolution* (Cambridge: Cambridge University Press, 1993), 37. See also Burke, *A Philosophical Enquiry*, 113–14, 149–50.

34 Furniss, *Edmund Burke's Aesthetic Ideology*, 27.

35 See Jean de La Fontaine, *Oeuvres diverses*, ed. Pierre Clarac (Paris: Gallimard, 1958). In La Fontaine's "Le Comte de Fiesque au Roi," the god of gods himself takes lessons from Louis XIV: "Vous savez conquérir les États et les hommes; / Jupiter prend de vous des leçons de grandeur" [You know how to conquer Nations and men; / Jupiter takes lessons in grandeur from you] (620). Also of note in this context is the emphasis on the power of the eyes in royal panegyrics: see Marc Fumaroli, "Microcosme comique et macrocosme solaire: Molière, Louis XIV, et *L'Impromptu de Versailles*," *Revue des sciences humaines* 37.145 (1972), 104.

36 Tellingly, the sublime is a preferred mode of discourse *on* opera in the late seventeenth century, serving to associate the unprecedented spectacle of the *tragédie en musique* with the unfathomable grandeur and military feats of Louis XIV. See for example, Robinet and Laurent, *Le théâtre et l'opéra vus par les gazetiers Robinet et Laurent*, 143–44. See also the account of the production of *Persée* at Versailles in the *Mercure galant* (July 1684).

37 Le Cerf de la Viéville, *Comparaison*, 2:16.

38 Claude Jamain, "L'Imaginaire de la musique au siècle des Lumières" (Ph.D. dissertation, Université François Rabelais, Tours, 1996), 54–55. Jamain sees in this conclusion a double and contradictory royal image. Antoine-Louis LeBrun is one of the few contemporaries to place more weight on the victory of Renaud in his comments on the opera: "if Armide in love moves your soul, the courageous Renaud teaches you how to overcome love, which is unworthy of a Hero who must triumph over himself" (*Théâtre lyrique*, 22).

39 Françoise Karro, "Le prologue d'*Armide*," in Jean-Paul Capdevielle and Peter-Eckhard Knabe, eds., *Les Écrivains français et l'opéra* (Cologne: dme-Verlag, 1986), 40.

40 Ibid., 43–44.

41 Frances Ferguson, *Solitude and the Sublime* (New York: Routledge, 1992), 68.

42 For Freud and Lacan, the Oedipus "problem" turns on appropriation and identification. On psychoanalysis' preference for object-desire (appropriation) over identification, see Mikkel Borch-Jacobsen, "The Oedipus Problem in Freud and Lacan," *Critical Inquiry* 20 (1994): 267–82.

43 Longinus, *On the Sublime*, trans. W. Hamilton Fyfe (1927; Cambridge, Mass.: Harvard University Press, 1982), 139. In his translation of Longinus, Boileau explained that the ultimate effect of the sublime was one of loss and dispossession – "that extraordinary and marvellous quality that strikes one in discourse and that causes a work to captivate, to ravish, to transport" (Boileau, *Oeuvres complètes*, III:442).

44 Louis Marin, "Le Sublime dans les années 1670: un je ne sais quoi?," in Selma A. Zebouni, ed., *Actes de Baton Rouge, Papers in French Seventeenth-Century Literature* 25 (1986), 188.

45 Louis de Cahusac saw in Armide's passion the principal interest of the opera (*Épitre sur les dangers de la poésie suivie de La Danse ancienne et moderne*, 4 vols. [1739–54; Geneva: Slatkine, 1971], III:87–88). In his account of *Armide*, Jean-Marie Clément lingers on the sorceress and his own enthusiastic reaction to act 2, scene 5, describing the passionate rendering of Armide's predicament. Later, however, he seems to feel guilty about his pleasures and expresses some reservation, noting that Quinault makes too much of Armide's charms and too little of Renaud's valor (Jean-Marie Clément [et l'abbé de la Porte], *Anecdotes dramatiques*, 3 vols. [Paris: Veuve Duchesne, 1775], I:113). Modern critic Philippe Beaussant blithely goes along with this line of reasoning, chiding Quinault for making Renaud "a bit pale" in comparison to Armide (Philippe Beaussant, *Lully ou le musicien du soleil* [Paris: Gallimard, 1992], 692).

46 "Do you know anything in any of our operas that is more able to *seize* and to move everyone?" (Le Cerf de la Viéville, *Comparaison*, I:80; my emphasis).

47 Ibid., I:170.

48 Rameau, *Observations*, 102–3. The question of music and possession is
treated in the anthropological work of Gilbert Rouget, who has
suggested that "opera . . . can be seen, in some ways, as the last avatar of
the ceremonies of possession" (*La Musique et la transe* [1980; Paris:
Gallimard, 1990], 434).

49 Gabriel Bonnot, abbé de Mably, *Lettres à Madame la Marquise de P . . . sur
l'opéra* (Paris: Didot, 1741), 22.

50 Ibid., 83.

51 Ibid., 65–66.

52 Rousseau, *Oeuvres complètes*, v:378.

53 See Bruce McIntyre, "*Armide* ou le monologue féminin," *Australian
Journal of French Studies* 36.2 (1999), 168, 170.

54 Like the sublime as Longinus describes it, opera always runs the risk of
falling into ludicrousness, as Catherine Clément has remarked in *Opera,
or the Undoing of Women*, trans. Betsy Wing (Minneapolis: University of
Minnesota Press, 1988). She writes: "[T]here is nothing sillier than seeing
a love story sung on stage. Opera is grotesque when one takes the
slightest distance on it and sublime when one goes along with
identification" (9). See Longinus's discussion of the faults of poets who,
"through trying to be uncommon and exquisite, and above all to
please . . . founder instead upon the tinsel reefs of affectation" (*On the
Sublime*, 131). *Tragédie en musique* is at some level always, in Catherine
Kintzler's words, "a cardboard world" ("L'opéra français, hyper-théâtre
et hypo-théâtre," 26).

55 "Weight, grandeur, and energy in writing are very largely produced,
dear pupil, by the use of 'images' . . . inspired by strong emotion, you
seem to see what you describe and bring it vividly before the eyes of
your audience" (Longinus, *On the Sublime*, 171). See also the new French
translation of Longinus: Longin, *Du Sublime*, trans. Jackie Pigeaud (Paris:
Rivages, 1991). Pigeaud renders φαντ αδίαι as "apparitions" (79).

56 Marin, "Le Sublime dans les années 1670," 188.

57 Michel Poizat, *The Angel's Cry: Beyond the Pleasure Principle in Opera*,
trans. Arthur Denner (Ithaca: Cornell University Press, 1992), 103.

58 Rapin, *Les Réflexions sur la poétique de ce temps*, 104. As I argued in the
previous chapter, already in *Atys*, the characters are caught in a world
where the recovery of *gloire* is impossible from the outset. In a general
comment about *tragédie en musique*, Catherine Kintzler, too, remarks

that "allusions to a bygone or disappearing theater are numerous. I am thinking in particular of those very repetitive, stereotyped, almost mechanical scenes borrowed from the dramatic *pastorale* of the beginning of the century" ("L'opéra français, hyper-théâtre et hypo-théâtre," 26).

59 Apostolidès, *Le Prince sacrifié*, 181. Taking the political aesthetic of the period as his point of departure, Apostolidès does convincingly remark on the opera prologues as a petrification of the image of the monarch (ibid., 135–47). See also his earlier study, *Le Roi-machine*, which raises the issue of dispossession, reflecting on the passivity of Louis XIV's courtiers who are "dispossessed" after the disappearance of the *ballet de cour* and the emergence of opera (*Le Roi-machine*, 64). The dispossession of courtiers, however, does not necessarily imply that the representation of the king becomes unequivocal or unproblematic.

60 Richard Taruskin, "Of Kings and Divas: Opera, Politics, and the French Boom," *The New Republic* 209.24 (December 13, 1993), 39.

61 McIntyre, "*Armide* ou le monologue féminin," 168.

62 Clément, *Opera, or the Undoing of Women*, 5. Burgess remarks the very different dynamic that is set in motion when men sing laments: "most French operatic heroes appropriate [lament] grounds at precisely the moments where they assert their command over loss and thereby affirm their heroism and masculinity" (Burgess, "Ritual in the *tragédie en musique*," 213).

63 Linda Hutcheon and Michael Hutcheon, "'Here's Lookin'at You, Kid': The Empowering Gaze in *Salome*," *Profession* (1998), 16. Tassie Gwilliam notes that "masculine investment in – and identification with – feminine wiles emerges repeatedly" in eighteenth-century men's accounts of female behavior (*Samuel Richardson's Fictions of Gender* [Stanford: Stanford University Press, 1993], 23).

64 Wayne Koestenbaum, *The Queen's Throat: Opera, Homosexuality, and the Mystery of Desire* (New York: Poseidon, 1993), 235.

65 Blau, *The Audience*, 132.

66 Philippe Lacoue-Labarthe has remarked that the association between music and dispossession, which he defines in relation to the notion of the proper, "seems very much to be the first and last word on music in Western philosophy" (*Musica Ficta (Figures of Wagner)*, trans. Felicia McCarren [Stanford: Stanford University Press, 1994], 111). In Lacoue-Labarthe's analysis, Heidegger comes very late, yet continues

the same old discourse on music, seeing in Wagner's music enervation, weakness, torpor, and submission.

4 THE DISRUPTION OF POETICS I: *MÉDÉE*'S EXCESSIVE VOICE

1 Wagner to August Röckel, January 25–26, 1854, *Selected Letters of Richard Wagner*, trans. and ed. Stewart Spencer and Barry Millington (London and Melbourne: J. M. Dent & Sons, 1987), 308. See also William E. McDonald, "What Does Wotan Know? Autobiography and Moral Vision in Wagner's *Ring*," *19th-Century Music* 15.1 (1991), 36–51.

2 Edward T. Cone, *The Composer's Voice* (Berkeley, Los Angeles, London: University of California Press, 1974), 80.

3 Among the many works to treat the politics of opera in late seventeenth-century France, see Couvreur, *Jean-Baptiste Lully*; Robert Isherwood, *Music in the Service of the King* (Ithaca and London: Cornell University Press, 1973); James R. Anthony, *French Baroque Music from Beaujoyeulx to Rameau* (New York: W. W. Norton, 1974); and Beaussant, *Lully ou le musicien du soleil*.

4 Mitchell Greenberg, *Subjectivity and Subjugation in Seventeenth-Century Drama and Prose* (Cambridge: Cambridge University Press, 1992), 56–57.

5 Boileau, *Oeuvres complètes*, II:399, II:64.

6 Euripides, *Cyclops, Alcestis, Medea*, ed. and trans. David Kovacs (Cambridge, Mass.: Harvard University Press, 1994), 395.

7 Pierre Corneille, "A Monsieur P. T. N. G.," *Médée*, ed. André de Leyssac (Geneva: Droz, 1978), 87. Subsequent references in the text will refer to act, scene, and page numbers in this edition.

8 See Kintzler, *Poétique de l'opéra français*, 283. Kintzler notes that this progression from natural to supernatural is determined by the implicit poetics of *tragédie en musique*. However, that this progression constitutes a law of the genre does not diminish the particular significance of the contrast I want to establish between Medea's conduct in Thomas's version and Pierre's representation of her.

9 Marc-Antoine Charpentier, *Médée* (1694; Farnborough: Gregg Press, 1968), 205. Subsequent references in the text will refer to act, scene, and page numbers in this facsimile edition.

10 Jacques Lacan, *Écrits: a Selection*, trans. Alan Sheridan (New York: Norton, 1977), 86.

11 Seneca, *Medea*, trans. Moses Hadas, in *Roman Drama* (Indianapolis: Bobbs-Merrill, 1965), 391.

12 François and Claude Parfaict, *Histoire de l'Académie Royale de Musique*, 1:80.

13 Serré de Rieux, *La Musique* (1714; The Hague: Abraham Henry, 1737), 18.

14 Le Cerf de la Viéville, *Comparaison*, 2:347. The *Journal de Trévoux* (November, 1704) uses the same term but in a different light: "Lully is not the only composer with which we can confront Italy. Charpentier, as learned as the Italians, possessed to the highest degree the art of joining words to the most appropriate tones. We are referring to his Church music" (1895–96).

15 Charpentier made this connection quite openly in a secular, cantata-like work from the late 1690s, the *Epitaphium Carpentarij*, in which the composer's ghost returns to earth to announce that "musica mihi parvus honos / sed magnum onus fuit" (music became a small honor / and a heavy burden). The ghost derides the music of Charpentier's predecessor at the Sainte-Chapelle du Palais, François Chaperon. See Charpentier, *Vocal Chamber Music*, ed. John S. Powell (Madison: A-R Editions, 1986), x, xx.

16 Gustave Reynier, *Thomas Corneille, sa vie et son théâtre* (1892; Geneva: Slatkine, 1970), 268. An exception to this view is found in Volker Kapp, "Thomas Corneille librettiste," in Jean-Paul Capdevielle and Peter-Eckhard Knabe, eds., *Les Écrivains français et l'opéra* (Cologne: dme-Verlag, 1986), 54.

17 Catherine Cessac, *Marc-Antoine Charpentier*, trans. E. Thomas Glasow (Portland, Oreg.: Amadeus Press, 1995), 344.

18 Judith Butler, *Bodies that Matter* (New York and London: Routledge, 1993), 95.

19 Wiley Hitchcock, *Marc-Antoine Charpentier* (Oxford: Oxford University Press, 1990), 109.

20 Carolyn Abbate, *Unsung Voices* (Princeton: Princeton University Press, 1991), 10.

21 The other reference to Italian musical culture in *Médée* is in an entirely different, playful register, and is separated from the main story. Act 2, scene 7 consists of a *divertissement* (both diegetic and extradiegetic) in which Oronte, who has come to Corinth to assist Jason in its defense and to take Créuse as bride for his trouble, stages a little *divertissement* to express his love for her. At its center, one of Cupid's captives (the female

one) sings in Italian and the chorus responds, also in Italian, echoing the refrain "O non vuol gioire, / O cuore non hà" (2.7.134). Catherine Cessac notes that this moment plays musically on Italian and French styles, the flowery virtuosity of "non hà" standing in opposition to the conventional melisma on "gioire" (Cessac, *Marc-Antoine Charpentier*, 353).

22 Burgess, "Ritual in the *tragédie en musique*," 370. See Burgess's comprehensive examination of the Medea character in five early French operas (ibid., 359–466).

23 This is the condition upon which Admète can return from the dead. In act 2, scene 9, Apollo announces the following exchange: "Le Destin me promet de te rendre à la vie, / Si quelque autre pour toi veut s'offrir à la mort" [Fate has promised me to give you back to the living, / If someone will offer himself to death in your place] (Quinault, *Livrets d'opéra*, 1:84).

24 See Cessac, *Marc-Antoine Charpentier*, 355. On the theory of dissonance and *supposition*, see Thomas Christensen, *Rameau and Musical Thought in the Enlightenment* (Cambridge: Cambridge University Press, 1993), 123–29; and Albert Cohen, "*La Supposition* or the Changing Concepts of Dissonance in Baroque Theory," *Journal of the American Musicological Society* 24 (1971): 63–85.

25 See, for example, Serré de Rieux, *La Musique*, 31.

26 On the concept of modulation, see Dill, "Rameau reading Lully."

27 See Cessac, *Marc-Antoine Charpentier*, 346.

28 Stanley Cavell, *A Pitch of Philosophy* (Cambridge, Mass.: Harvard University Press, 1994), 137.

29 Jean Duron, "Commentaire littéraire et musical," *L'Avant-scène Opéra* 68 (1984; 1993): 77. Duron's remarks were directed specifically at act 2, scene 2, but could be applied to several other passages as well.

30 Euripides, *Cyclops, Alcestis, Medea*, 325.

31 Seneca, *Medea*, 375.

32 Cavell, *A Pitch of Philosophy*, 136.

33 Marc-Antoine Charpentier, *Médée*, ed. Edmond Lemaître (Paris: Editions du Centre National de la Recherche Scientifique, 1987), 590. This description comes from a variant copy of the score, which does not appear in the facsimile edition cited throughout this chapter.

34 Though *Thésée* was based on a separate mythological episode, the two plots nonetheless bear some resemblance to each other: in Quinault's and Lully's work, the jealous Medea combats an entire kingdom disputing

her rival, Aegle, for the hand of Theseus. However, the similarity stops there. In addition to the opera's conclusion, Medea's monologues, however striking, do not yield the same harmonic complexity as those of Charpentier's Medea; nor do they fit into the same narrative of difference.

35 Burgess, "Ritual in the *tragédie en musique*," 346.

36 Catherine Clément, "Au-delà des roches couleur de nuit," *L'Avant-scène Opéra* 68 (1984; 1993), 34.

37 Michal Grover-Friedlander, "Voicing Death in Opera," *Common Knowledge* 5.2 (Fall, 1996), 139–40.

38 Poetry, he writes, describes "equally good and bad actions," and seeks to affect the spectator "by their ugliness which it seeks to represent to us accurately" (Pierre Corneille, *Médée*, 88).

39 "What is virtue? Seen in any light, it is a sacrifice of oneself. The imagined sacrifice of oneself prepares one for self-sacrifice in reality" (Denis Diderot, *Éloge de Richardson*, *Oeuvres complètes*, ed. Jean Varloot, 25 vols. [Paris: Hermann, 1975–86], xiii:194).

40 Quoted in Pierre Corneille, *Oeuvres*, 12 vols. (Paris: Antoine-Augustin Renouard, 1817), xii:72.

41 Grover-Friedlander, "Voicing Death in Opera," 142.

42 Catherine Clément, "Au-delà des roches couleur de nuit," 34.

43 Koestenbaum, *The Queen's Throat*, 44.

5 THE DISRUPTION OF POETICS II: *HIPPOLYTE ET ARICIE* AND THE REINVENTION OF TRAGEDY

1 Pascal Quignard, *La Haine de la musique* (Paris: Calmann-Lévy, 1996), 239.

2 Fumaroli, *Héros et orateurs*, 508.

3 Olivier Pot, "Phèdre ou le suicide de la tragédie," *Travaux de littérature* 6 (1993), 162–63, 159.

4 Fumaroli, *Héros et orateurs*, 516.

5 Racine, *Théâtre complet*, 542–46; Racine, *Phaedra*, trans. Richard Wilbur (San Diego, New York, London: Harcourt Brace Jovanovich, 1986), 39. Subsequent citations are given in the text of this chapter with act, scene, and page numbers from the French original, followed by the page numbers from the English verse translation.

6 Fumaroli, *Héros et orateurs*, 517.

7 Racine, *Théâtre complet*, 510.

8 See Sylvie Bouissou, "La première version d'*Hippolyte et Aricie*; un retour aux sources," in *Hippolyte et Aricie*, opera program (Paris: Opéra National de Paris, 1996), 51–55.

9 Claude-François de Ménestrier, "Préface," *Des représentations en musique anciennes et modernes* (Paris: René Guignard, 1681), n.p.

10 Terrasson, *Dissertation critique*, 1:208, 1:209.

11 Jean Léonor le Gallois Grimarest, *Traité du récitatif* (1760; New York: AMS Press, 1978), 121.

12 Antoine Houdar de la Motte, *Reflexions sur la critique* (Paris: G. Dupuis, 1716), 243.

13 Anne Dacier, *Causes de la corruption du goust* (Paris: Rigaud, 1714), 30.

14 Pierre-Charles Roy, *Lettre sur l'opéra*, in Élie Catherine Fréron, *Lettres sur quelques écrits de ce temps*, 2 vols. (1752; Geneva: Slatkine, 1966), letter 1 (September 8, 1749), II:8–9.

15 Qtd. in Graham Sadler, "Un Débutant timide?," in *Hippolyte et Aricie*, opera program (Paris: Opéra National de Paris, 1996), 34. Unfortunately, the standard view of French operatic history continues to portray the period between Lully and Rameau as an operatic wasteland. Leslie Ellen Brown has attempted to nuance such criticisms. "It is incorrect," she notes, "to attribute any weaknesses in the préramiste works to a subordination of the dramatic to the decorative components. On the contrary, dramatic continuity and convincing character expressions were realised through an expansive repertoire of devices that Lully himself did not utilize" ("Departures from Lullian Convention in the *Tragédie Lyrique* of the *Préramiste* Era," *Recherches sur la musique française classique* 22 [1984], 76). On the evolution of the lyric theater in the late seventeenth and early eighteenth centuries, see also Paolo Russo, "'L' Isola di Alcina: Funzioni drammaturgiche del 'divertissement' nella 'tragédie lyrique' (1699–1735)," *Nuova rivista musicale italiana* 21.1 (1987): 1–16.

16 Jean-Philippe Rameau, *Oeuvres complètes*, ed. C. Saint-Saëns et al., 18 vols. (1895–1924; New York: Broude Bros., [1968]), VI:xxxix.

17 Ibid.

18 Ibid.

19 Catherine Kintzler, "La Préface d'*Hippolyte et Aricie* ou la critique de *Phèdre*," in *Hippolyte et Aricie*, opera program (Paris: Opéra National de Paris, 1996), 69.

20 Buford Norman, "Remaking a Cultural Icon: *Phèdre* and the Operatic Stage," *Cambridge Opera Journal* 10.3 (1998), 238.

21 Rameau, *Oeuvres complètes*, VI:17.

22 Paul-Marie Masson, *L'Opéra de Rameau* (Paris: Henri Laurens, 1930), 219, 551.

23 *Mercure de France* (October, 1733), 2249.

24 François et Claude Parfaict, "Histoire de l'Académie Royale de Musique," II:67.

25 I owe a great deal of this analysis to Charles Dill's insightful comments in his *Monstrous Opera: Rameau and the Tragic Tradition* (Princeton: Princeton University Press, 1998), 31–35. Dill's study examines Rameau's lyric tragedies in their successive variants, exploring the composer's complex and sometimes contradictory reception history and his response to it.

26 "*Hippolyte*, that treasure of modern Music, without intrigues, without patronage, without *prophecies*, created in 1733 this great revolution in French Music . . ." (*L'Année littéraire* [March 16, 1757], 24). "This was the time of the revolution that occurred in music and of its newfound progress in France. Mr. Rameau must be, and surely will always be, considered as its creator and principal cause. The part of the public which judges and decides only by impression was at first surprised by music that was much denser and richer in images than the music we were used to hearing in the theater. This new genre was nonetheless appreciated, and the public applauded it in the end" ("Essai d'Eloge historique de feu M. Rameau," *Mercure de France* [October, 1764], 187–88).

27 Quoted in Masson, *L'Opéra de Rameau*, 43.

28 Voltaire, *Les Oeuvres Complètes/The Complete Works*, ed. Theodore Besterman, vol. LXXXVI, *Correspondence*, vol. II (Geneva: Institut et Musée Voltaire; Toronto: University of Toronto Press, 1968–), 403.

29 Ibid., 430, 451.

30 *Mercure de France* (October, 1733), 2249.

31 See Cuthbert Girdlestone, *Jean-Philippe Rameau* (1957; New York: Dover, 1969), 191.

32 Dill, *Monstrous Opera*, 35.

33 Rameau, *Oeuvres complètes*, VI:180–92. In order to allow for the inclusion of this extensive example, I have eliminated the orchestral accompaniment, which is represented in the figured bass.

34 Rameau, *Complete Theoretical Writings*, III:91.

35 See Christensen, *Rameau and Musical Thought in the Enlightenment*, 199–207.

36 See Graham Sadler, "Rameau, Pellegrin and the Opera: the revisions of
    Hippolyte et Aricie during its first season," *Musical Times* 124. 1687 (1983), 533.
37 Burgess, "Ritual in the *tragédie en musique*," 382.
38 *L'Année littéraire* (March 16, 1757), 31.
39 Rameau, *Complete Theoretical Writings*, III:92.
40 Rameau, *Oeuvres complètes*, VI:xxxix.
41 Ibid., VI:xxxix–xl.
42 Ibid., VI:xxxix.
43 Rameau, *Complete Theoretical Writings*, IV:208.
44 H.-J. Pilet de La Mesnardière, *La Poëtique* (1640; Geneva: Slatkine, 1972),
    22–27. See John Lyons's informative discussion of this distinction in his
    essay, "The Barbarous Ancients," 1143–45; and his detailed reading of La
    Mesnardière, "The Decorum of Horror: A Reading of La Mesnardière's
    Poëtique," in Sylvie Romanowski and Monique Bilezikian, eds., *Homage
    to Paul Bénichou* (Birmingham, Ala.: Summa, 1994), 27–41.
45 Lyons, "The Decorum of Horror," 27.
46 Ibid., 34.
47 *Encyclopédie ou dictionnaire raisonné des arts et des métiers*, XVI:184, VIII:312.
48 Pierre Louis d' Aquin de Chateaulyon, *Siècle littéraire de Louis XV, ou
    Lettres sur les hommes célèbres*, 2 vols. (Amsterdam and Paris: Duschesne,
    1752), I:70–71.
49 Rameau, *Complete Theoretical Writings*, III:91.
50 Dubos, *Réflexions critiques*, 150.
51 Ibid., 151.
52 Rameau, *Complete Theoretical Writings*, II:50–51.
53 Dill, "Rameau reading Lully," 10. Cynthia Verba has examined the
    dramatic dimensions of Rameau' s harmonic practice, arguing for a
    position somewhere in between those of Dill and Masson on the matter
    of how airs are differentiated from recitatives: see her "What Recitatives
    Owe to the Airs: a Look at the Dialogue Scene, Act I scene 2 of Rameau's
    Hippolyte et Aricie – Version with Airs," *Cambridge Opera Journal* 11.2 (1999):
    103–34.
54 Ibid., 13.
55 Rameau, *Complete Theoretical Writings*, III:213.
56 Masson, *L'Opéra de Rameau*, 522. In *Zoroastre*, Rameau also used clarinets
    for the first time at the Opéra (Girdlestone, *Jean-Philippe Rameau*, 294;
    Masson, *L'Opéra de Rameau*, 523–26).

57 Rameau, *Oeuvres complètes*, VI:337.

58 Ibid., VI:340.

59 *Mercure de France* (October, 1733), 2247.

60 Ibid. (September, 1742), 2077–78.

61 See Geoffrey Burgess, "'Le théâtre ne change qu'à la troisième scène': the hand of the author and the unity of place in Act V of *Hippolyte et Aricie*," *Cambridge Opera Journal* 10.3 (1998): 275–87.

62 Pierre François Guyot Desfontaines, *Observations sur les écrits modernes*, 4 vols. (Geneva: Slatkine, 1967), IV:678.

63 *L'Année littéraire* (March 16, 1757), 35.

64 Bernard le Bovier de Fontenelle, "Discours sur la nature de l'églogue," *Oeuvres complètes*, 3 vols. (1818; Geneva: Slatkine, 1968), III.57.

65 Terrasson, *Dissertation critique*, I:214. Burgess sees in Rameau the final "aestheticization" of *tragédie en musique* (Burgess, "Ritual in the *tragédie en musique*," 355).

66 Jean-Marie Villégier, "Musicien dans un paysage de ruines," in *Hippolyte et Aricie*, opera program (Paris: Opéra National de Paris, 1996), 81.

67 Ibid., 82.

68 Rameau, *Oeuvres complètes*, VI:239–41.

69 Pot, "Phèdre ou le suicide de la tragédie," 170.

6 HEART STRINGS

1 Quignard, *La Haine de la musique*, 72–73.

2 Lacoue-Labarthe, *Musica Ficta (Figures of Wagner)*, 111. On lyricism and possession, see Susan Stewart, "Lyric Possession," *Critical Inquiry* 22.1 (Autumn 1995): 34–63.

3 Theodor W. Adorno, "Bourgeois Opera," in David J. Levin, ed., *Opera Through Other Eyes* (Stanford: Stanford University Press, 1994), 36.

4 Longinus, *On the Sublime*, 131.

5 "I wonder sometimes where the obsession [*folie*] comes from that I have for that nonsense; it is hard to understand . . . therefore I think that it is dreadful [Calprenède's style] and yet I let myself get stuck in it like in glue" (Sévigné, *Correspondance*, I:294).

6 See his *Monteverdi and the End of the Renaissance* (Berkeley: University of California Press, 1987); *Music in Renaissance Magic*; and *Metaphysical Song: An Essay on Opera* (Princeton: Princeton University Press, 1999).

7 Cited in Claude V. Palisca, *Humanism in Italian Renaissance Musical Thought* (New Haven and London: Yale University Press, 1985), 102–03.

8 Marsilio Ficino, *Three Books on Life*, ed. and trans. Carol V. Kaske and John R. Clark (Binghamton, N.Y.: Medieval & Renaissance Texts & Studies, 1989), 358–59.

9 Louis Le Caron, *Dialogues*, ed. Joan A. Buhlmann and Donald Gilman (Geneva: Droz, 1986), 254. See also 278–86.

10 Ibid., 255. I reproduce the translation provided by Timothy J. Reiss (*Knowledge, Discovery and Imagination in Early Modern Europe* [Cambridge: Cambridge University Press, 1997], 177).

11 Pontus de Tyard, *Solitaire premier*, ed. Silvio Baridon (Geneva: Droz, 1950), 16–17.

12 Pontus de Tyard, *Solitaire second*, ed. Cathy M. Yandell (Geneva: Droz, 1980), 70.

13 Ibid., 71.

14 Reiss, *Knowledge, Discovery and Imagination*, 168.

15 Michel Foucault, *The Order of Things: An Archaeology of the Human Sciences* (New York: Pantheon, 1970), 55.

16 Dubos, *Réflexions critiques*, 151–52. I have translated *récit* as "song" following the first edition of the *Dictionnaire de l'Académie française* which defines the word as "ce qui est chanté par une voix seule" [that which is sung by a solo voice] (*Dictionnaire de l'Académie française* [book on line] [Paris: chez la veuve de Jean Baptiste Coignard, 1694, accessed May 25, 2001], s. v. "récit"; available from http://www.lib.uchicago.edu/efts/ARTFL/projects/dicos/ACADEMIE/PREMIERE/premiere.html).

17 Denis Ballière de Laisemont, *Théorie de la musique* (Paris: Didot le jeune, 1764), 44.

18 Marin Mersenne, "Livre de l'utilité de l'harmonie," *Traité des instruments à chordes, Harmonie universelle*, ed. François Lesure, 3 vols. (1636; Paris: Éditions du Centre National de la Recherche Scientifique, 1963), III:47.

19 Mersenne, "Des chants," *Traité de la voix, et des chants*, ibid., II:99.

20 René Descartes, *Abrégé de musique / Compendium musicae*, ed. and trans. Frédéric de Buzon (Paris: Presses universitaires de France, 1987), 63.

21 Nicolas Bergier, *La Musique speculative* (Cologne Arno Volk, 1970), 186. For a discussion of the effects of rhythm, meter, and instrumental temperaments on the passions, see Downing A. Thomas, *Music and the*

Origins of Language: Theories from the French Enlightenment (Cambridge: Cambridge University Press, 1995), 29–30.

22 Reiss, *Knowledge, Discovery and Imagination*, 179.

23 Ibid., 189–90. See also Penelope Gouk, "Music, Melancholy, and Medical Spirits in Early Modern Thought," in Peregrine Horden, ed., *Music as Medicine: The History of Music Therapy since Antiquity* (Aldershot: Ashgate, 2000), 173–94.

24 Tomlinson, *Monteverdi and the End of the Renaissance*, 215–18.

25 Ibid., 259. Italian opera depreciated during the seventeenth and eighteenth centuries for many reasons, Tomlinson argues: there was "the codification of discrete, reproducible musical gesture for the depiction of various passions" in *opera seria*; and "the growing reliance on virtuosity instead of the projection of emotion to maintain musical vitality; the continuing decay of the ideal of close syntactic linkage of text and music typical of early recitative; and the increasing emphasis on standardized musical forms" (ibid., 258–59).

26 Tyard, *Solitaire second*, 75.

27 John Neubauer, *The Emancipation of Music from Language: Departure from Mimesis in Eighteenth-Century Aesthetics* (New Haven and London: Yale University Press, 1986), 7–8.

28 Bourdelot and Bonnet, *Histoire de la musique et de ses effets*, 74.

29 Ibid., 70–71.

30 Ibid., 73–74.

31 Franchino Gaffurio, *Practica musicae*, ed. and trans. Irwin Young (Madison, Milwaukee, and London: University of Wisconsin Press, 1969), 11.

32 Jacques Bonnet, *Histoire générale de la danse sacrée et prophane* (Paris: D'Houry fils, 1723), 100.

33 Ibid., 183, 184.

34 Ibid., 193.

35 For a detailed account of the eighteenth-century rise of sensibility in medical discourse, see Vila, *Enlightenment and Pathology*, 13–107. See also Elizabeth A. Williams, *The Physical and the Moral: Anthropology, Physiology, and Philosophical Medicine in France, 1750–1850* (Cambridge: Cambridge University Press, 1994). Williams's study traces eighteenth-century medicine from Montpellier vitalism to the decline of "reciprocally flowing physical-moral *rapports* in the nineteenth

century" (19). On the early history of emotion and *sensibilité*, and on the
close relationship between fiction and medical discourse on sensibility,
see DeJean, *Ancients Against Moderns*, 78–94.

36 Claude-Nicolas Le Cat, *Traité de l'existance, de la nature et des propriétés du
fluide des nerfs, et principalement de son action dans le mouvement musculaire*
(Berlin: n. p., 1765), 305.

37 Ibid., 308.

38 Claude-Nicolas Le Cat, *Traité des sens* (Amsterdam: J. Wetstein, 1744), 2.

39 Ibid., 38.

40 Ibid., 47.

41 Ibid., 63.

42 Ibid., 64.

43 Ibid., 65.

44 Ibid.

45 Ibid., 65–66.

46 Ibid., 66–67. The ability of music to cure those bitten by the tarantula
was perhaps the most discussed example of musical medicine in the
eighteenth century. See also the chevalier de Jaucourt's description of
this process in his article, "Tarentule," in the *Encyclopédie*. See Alain
Cernuschi's discussion of the subject in his *Penser la musique dans
l'Encyclopédie: étude sur les enjeux de la musicographie des Lumières et sur ses
liens avec l'encyclopédisme* (Paris: Honoré Champion, 2000), 193–220.
Peregrine Horden devotes an entire section to tarantism in her anthology
of essays on *Music as Medicine*, 249–312.

47 Joseph-Louis Roger, *Traité des effets de la musique sur le corps humain*,
trans. and ed. Etienne Sainte-Marie (Paris: Brunot; Lyon: Reymann and
J. Roger, an XI [1803]), xvj, xxij. Subsequent citations will be given in the
text.

48 In his *Essai sur le beau*, originally published in 1741, Yves-Marie André
claimed, similarly, that "the structure of the human body is entirely
harmonic" (*Essai sur le beau* [Amsterdam: Schneider, 1759], 145).

49 Francis Hutcheson, *An Inquiry Concerning Beauty, Order, Harmony, Design*,
ed. Peter Kivy (The Hague: Martinus Nijhoff, 1973), 76, 81.

50 Gottfried Wilhelm Leibniz, *Philosophical Papers and Letters*, ed. and trans.
Leroy E. Loemker, 2 vols. (Chicago: University of Chicago Press, 1956),
II:698.

51 Daniel Webb, *Observations on the Correspondence Between Poetry and Music* (1769; New York: Garland, 1970), 6–8.
52 Ibid., 7n.
53 Jean-Baptiste-Joseph Lallemant, *Essai sur le méchanisme des passions en général* (Paris: Le Prieur, 1751), 14. For a discussion of Lallemant's argument, see Thomas, *Music and the Origins of Language*, 154–56.
54 Lallemant, *Essai sur le méchanisme des passions en général*, 18.
55 Ibid., 119–20.
56 Ibid., 6.
57 Le Cat, *Traité de l'existance, de la nature et des propriétés du fluide des nerfs*, 33.
58 Ibid., 17.
59 Ibid., 18 20.
60 Ibid., 20.
61 Kivy, *Osmin's Rage*, 15.
62 Ibid., 108.
63 Ibid., 118, 120. Kivy does recognize the inseparability of "the 'pure'and the 'emotional' parts" of music for these writers, yet he insists on projecting their essential difference – a modern distinction – back onto the eighteenth-century discussion (120). In the relationship that Kivy establishes between philosophy and music, Handel is to Cartesianism as Mozart's *opera buffa* is to associationism (188). The da capo aria form reproduces static, Cartesian passions, whereas sonata form reveals a complexity that leads to multiform expression (222). In the finest "drama-made-music," which he identifies with Mozart's finales, form (music) and content (emotion) coincide perfectly (232).
64 Michel Paul Guy de Chabanon, *De la musique considérée en elle-même et dans ses rapports avec la parole, les langues, la poésie et le théâtre* (1785; Geneva: Slatkine, 1969), 101.
65 Ibid., 107.
66 Ibid., 108.
67 Ibid., 105.

7 MUSIC, SYMPATHY, AND IDENTIFICATION AT THE OPÉRA-COMIQUE

1 Claudine-Alexandrine Guérin de Tencin, *Mémoires du comte de Comminge* ([Paris]: Mercure de France, 1996), 37.

2 Pierre Jean Baptiste Nougaret, *De l'art du théâtre*, 2 vols. (Paris: Cailleau, 1769), II:166. See Marian Hobson's discussion of this work in *The Object of Art* (Cambridge: Cambridge University Press, 1982), 157–58.

3 Nougaret, *De l'art du théâtre*, II:168–69.

4 D'Aquin de Chateaulyon, *Siècle littéraire de Louis XV*, I:17.

5 Ibid., 24.

6 Ibid., 25.

7 Though quoted sources differ, for clarity and consistency in my own text I have followed the practice of distinguishing between the genre, *opéra comique*, and the institution, the Opéra-Comique.

8 Charles Batteux, *Les Beaux-Arts réduits à un même principe*, ed. Jean-Rémy Mantion (Paris: Aux Amateurs de livres, [1989]), 235.

9 Diderot, *Oeuvres complètes*, ed. Jean Varloot, XXIII:25; Diderot, *Jacques the Fatalist and His Master*, trans. J. Robert Loy (New York: New York University Press, 1959), 5. I have modified the translations in some instances for style and clarity.

10 Diderot, *Oeuvres complètes*, ed. Varloot, XXIII:38–39; Diderot, *Jacques the Fatalist*, 17.

11 Jean Starobinski, "Diderot et l'art de la démonstration," *Recherches sur Diderot et sur l'Encyclopédie* 18–19 (1995), 179–80.

12 Étienne de Condillac, *De l'art de raisonner*, *Oeuvres complètes*, 16 vols. (1821–22; Geneva: Slatkine, 1970), VI:6. Condillac distinguishes evidence deriving from fact, evidence deriving from sentiment, and evidence deriving from reason. Analogy, which reveals to us the *sensibilité* of others, is the supplement of evidence (184–86).

13 Adam Smith, *The Theory of Moral Sentiments*, ed. D. D. Raphael and A. L. Macfie (1976; Indianapolis: Liberty Fund, 1984), 9.

14 On conceptions of sociability in eighteenth-century France, see Daniel Gordon, *Citizens Without Sovereignty: Equality and Sociability in French Thought, 1670–1789* (Princeton: Princeton University Press, 1994), 42–85. See also Dena Goodman, *The Republic of Letters: a Cultural History of the French Enlightenment* (Ithaca and London: Cornell University Press, 1994).

15 Pierre Force, "Self-Love, Identification, and the Origin of Political Economy," *Yale French Studies* 92 (1997), 46.

16 Rousseau, *Basic Political Writings*, trans. Donald A. Cress (Indianapolis: Hackett, 1987), 54.

17 Force, "Self-Love," 47.

18 Helvétius, *De l'esprit* (Verviers, Belgium: Gérard, 1973), 74.

19 Force, "Self-Love," 54.

20 Smith, *Theory of Moral Sentiments*, 21.

21 Elena Russo, "The Self, Real and Imaginary: Social Sentiment in Marivaux and Hume," *Yale French Studies* 92 (1997), 138.

22 Anne C. Vila, "Beyond Sympathy: Vapors, Melancholia, and the Pathologies of Sensibility in Tissot and Rousseau," *Yale French Studies* 92 (1997), 89. Sympathy, however, was also a double-edged sword in the eyes of medical specialists. Vila notes that "medical specialists from the 1750s onward seemed convinced that an epidemic of nervous maladies was fast overtaking Europe's cities – the very places where moral sympathy seemed most crucial because of the complexity and sophistication of the social interactions that took place there" (90).

23 Frances Ferguson, "A Reply to Tzvetan Todorov's 'Living Alone Together,'" *New Literary History* 27 (1996), 25. See also Tzvetan Todorov, "Living Alone Together," *New Literary History* 27 (1996): 1–14.

24 Karin Pendle, "L'Opéra-comique à Paris de 1762 à 1789," in Philippe Vendrix, ed., *L'Opéra-comique en France au XVIIIe siècle* (Liège: Mardaga, 1992), 80.

25 Diderot, *Oeuvres complètes*, ed. Varloot, x:337.

26 Ibid., x:129–31.

27 Ibid., x:332.

28 Ibid., x:100.

29 Ibid., x:335.

30 Ibid., x:144. Marion Hobson has remarked that "it was not in the 'straight' theatre but at the *Opéra comique* that 'conditions' were first used as theatrical material" (*The Object of Art*, 156).

31 David Marshall, *The Surprising Effects of Sympathy* (Chicago: University of Chicago Press, 1988), 130–31.

32 Smith, *Theory of Moral Sentiments*, 24.

33 Diderot, *Oeuvres complètes*, ed. Varloot, x:368.

34 Jay Caplan, *Framed Narratives: Diderot's Genealogy of the Beholder* (Minneapolis: University of Minnesota Press, 1985), 19. In his pioneering *Absorption and Theatricality: Painting and Beholder in the Age of Diderot* (Berkeley: University of California Press, 1980), Michael Fried argues that by placing absorbed figures in their compositions painters sought to produce a homogeneous space thereby appearing to exclude the viewer

from the scene; the paradoxical effect of this strategy of exclusion, however, is that it entices the viewer into the fiction.

35 David Bromwich, "The Sublime Before Aesthetics and Politics," *Raritan* 16.4 (Spring 1997), 36.

36 Caplan, *Framed Narratives*, 22.

37 Diderot, *Oeuvres complètes*, ed. Varloot, x:335.

38 Even if Freud turned away from these notions, aspects of them remained in his practice, since some form of disappearance of self (hypnosis, trance) remains in the psychoanalytic transference, based as it is in the narrative of the analysand.

39 Sigmund Freud, *The Standard Edition of the Complete Psychological Works*, ed. and trans. James Strachey, 24 vols. (London: The Hogarth Press, 1953–74), XVIII:105.

40 Ibid., XVIII:106.

41 Diana Fuss, *Identification Papers* (New York and London: Routledge, 1995), 45. For a view of these issues that is perhaps closer and more sympathetic to psychoanalysis, see Julia Kristeva, *Histoires d'amour* (Paris: Denoël, 1983), 36–45.

42 Butler, *Bodies that Matter*, 99. In his book on opera and gay desire, *The Queen's Throat*, Wayne Koestenbaum plays on the double-take of desire and identification described by Butler: "Am I in love with Julie Andrews, or do I think I *am* Julie Andrews?" (18).

43 Fuss, *Identification Papers*, 10.

44 Mikkel Borch-Jacobsen, *The Emotional Tie: Psychoanalysis, Mimesis, and Affect* (Stanford: Stanford University Press, 1992), 42. Borch-Jacobsen goes on to argue for the continued presence of trance-like phenomena in the transference: "If the transference tends to dominate the whole analytical situation, and if the analyst's silence, rather than keeping the transference at bay [as it should, since maintaining the transference would mean maintaining the harmful attachment that the analysis is supposed to free the patient from in the first place], actually provokes it, then one can no longer oppose, as Freud has done earlier, the pure interpretative listening of the analyst to the direct suggestion of the hypnotist, or the interventionism of the hypnotist to the abstentionism of the analyst" (54).

45 Ibid., 100.

46 Diderot, *Oeuvres complètes*, ed. Varloot, x:150.

47 Ibid., x:150–51.

48 On Diderot and *opéra comique*, see Maria Majno Golub, "Diderot et l'opéra-comique: absolution du burlesque, réussite du pathétique," in *Diderot: les beaux-arts et la musique* (Aix: Université de Provence, 1986), 261–75; and Jean-Christophe Rebejkow, "Diderot et l'opéra-comique: de la farce au pathétique," *Romanische Forschungen* 107.1–2 (1995): 145–56.

49 See the recent critical edition: Jean-Jacques Rousseau, *Le Devin du village*, ed. Charlotte Kaufman (Madison: A-R Editions, 1998).

50 Maurice Barthélemy reviews some of these distant origins: see his "L'opéra-comique des origines à la Querelle des Bouffons," in Philippe Vendrix, ed., *L'Opéra-comique en France au XVIIIe siècle* (Liège: Mardaga, 1992), 12–16; see also Georges Cucuel, *Les Créateurs de l'Opéra-Comique français* (Paris: Félix Alcan, 1914), 3–12. Robert M. Isherwood mentions as precedents "the obscene farces of the late Middle Ages, the comedies of Molière, and commedia dell'arte" (Robert M. Isherwood, *Farce and Fantasy: Popular Entertainment in Eighteenth-Century Paris* [New York and Oxford: Oxford University Press, 1986], 60). Manuel Couvreur and Vendrix argue, however, that *comédie-ballet* does not truly have any direct descendants in the eighteenth century ("Les Enjeux théoriques de l'Opéra-Comique," in Vendrix, ed., *L'Opéra-comique en France au XVIIIe siècle*, 219). Martine de Rougemont places the origins of *opéra comique* at the beginning of the century in the fair theaters: see Martine de Rougemont, *La Vie théâtrale en France au XVIIIe siècle* (Paris and Geneva: Champion-Slatkine, 1988), 43–46. For an extended history of the fair theaters and the development of *opéra comique*, see Barthélemy, "L'opéra-comique des origines à la Querelle des bouffons," 29–71.

51 See *Le Mercure galant* (July, 1715), 282.

52 Michel Noiray, "*Hippolyte* et *Castor* travestis: Rameau à l' opéra-comique," in Jérôme de La Gorce, ed., *Jean-Philippe Rameau: Colloque international* (Paris and Geneva: Champion-Slatkine, 1987), 109. For details on the competition between the Parisian theaters, see Henri Lagrave, *Le Théâtre et son public à Paris de 1715 à 1750* (Paris: Klincksiek, 1972), 361–413.

53 Bruce Alan Brown, "Editions anciennes et modernes d'opéras-comiques: problèmes et méthodologies," in Philippe Vendrix, ed., *Grétry et l'Europe de l'opéra-comique* (Liège: Mardaga, 1992), 357.

54 See Alain René Le Sage and d' Orneval, *Le Théâtre de la foire ou l'Opéra comique*, 10 tomes in 2 vols. (1737; Geneva: Slatkine, 1968).

55 Michael F. Robinson makes this point in *"Opera buffa* into *opéra comique,*
1771–90,"* in Malcolm Boyd, ed., *Music and the French Revolution*
(Cambridge: Cambridge University Press, 1992), 37. There is no significant
formal difference between those lyric interventions termed "airs" and
those called "ariettes." In the article, *"Ariette,"* from his *Eléments de*
littérature, Jean-François Marmontel wrote: "We realized, whatever
Rousseau may have said about it, that our language was susceptible of
the true beauties of Italian music. It was therefore necessary to
distinguish, from that point on, the *ariette* which was only scintillating,
from the expressive and passionate air. But the general custom was to call
ariettes all of the airs of an *opéra comique"* (Jean-François Marmontel,
Oeuvres complètes, 8 vols. [Paris: A. Belin, 1819], IV:146–47). David Charlton
clarifies that "the word 'ariette' in the context of the early years of the
new opéra-comique did not – oddly enough – mean 'aria' (let alone
'little aria') but 'newly composed pieces of any sort.' Thus Vadé calls the
final quartet in *Les Troqueurs* 'Ariette en quatuor' just as Sedaine would
call the first number of *Blaise le savetier* 'Ariette en duo' " (David Charlton,
French Opera 1730–1830: Meaning and Media [Aldershot: Ashgate, 2000],
2:19–20).

56 Friedrich Melchior Freiherr von Grimm, *Correspondance littéraire,*
philosophique et critique, 16 vols. (Paris: Garnier Frères, 1877–82), VI:187.

57 Clément and Laporte, *Anecdotes dramatiques,* II:248–49.

58 The *Journal de musique théorique, pratique, dramatique et instrumentale*
(May, 1770) commented that following *Le Maréchal ferrant,* "les Auteurs
adoptèrent ce nouveau genre, qui n'était point celui de l'Italie" (13).

59 Nougaret, *De l'art du théâtre,* I:58–59.

60 These developments are usefully summarized in Charlton, *French Opera*
1730–1830, 2:15–16.

61 Nicolas Bricaire de la Dixmérie, *Les Deux âges du goût et du génie français*
sous Louis XIV et sous Louis XV (1769; Geneva: Slatkine, 1970), 248.

62 Sedaine claimed that the success of his *On ne s'avise jamais de tout,* with
music by Pierre-Alexandre Monsigny, "became the cause of the union
of the Opéra-Comique and the Comédie-Italienne," in René Charles
G. de Pixérécourt, *Théâtre choisi,* 4 vols. (Paris: Tresse, 1841–43), IV:506.

63 Karin Pendle, "L'Opéra-comique à Paris de 1762 à 1789," 79.

64 See M. Elizabeth C. Bartlet's brief summary in *The New Grove Dictionary*
of Opera, s.v. "Opéra comique."

65 Nicolas Bricaire de La Dixmérie, *Lettres sur l'état présent de nos spectacles* (Amsterdam et se trouve à Paris: Duchesne, 1765), 4–8.

66 Grimm, *Correspondance littéraire*, VIII:331.

67 *Les Spectacles de Paris, ou Calendrier Historique & Chronologique des théâtres* (Paris: Veuve Duchesne, 1782), III–12.

68 Isherwood, *Farce and Fantasy*, 251, 80.

69 Barthélemy, "L'opéra-comique des origines à la Querelle des Bouffons," 74.

70 Ibid., 60. Though Martine de Rougemont does describe an ideological recuperation of *opéra comique* away from the "dangerous" productions of the fair theaters, she nonetheless recognizes that *"opéra comique* testifies to an extraordinary vitality and suppleness" (*La Vie théâtrale*, 46). Rougemont remarks that "it has been too quickly assumed that eighteenth-century *opéra comique* was a frivolous thing" (46).

71 Couvreur and Vendrix, "Les Enjeux théoriques de l'Opéra-Comique," 231.

72 Cited in ibid., 233.

73 On the ambivalence of Marmontel's theorization of the *opéra comique*, see Couvreur and Vendrix, "Les Enjeux théoriques de l'Opéra-Comique," 218–19.

74 Grimm, *Correspondance littéraire*, VI:190.

75 Ibid., VII:137.

76 Charles Collé, *Journal et mémoires*, 3 vols. (Paris: Firmin Didot Frères, 1868), III:140.

77 Bricaire de la Dixmérie, *Les Deux âges*, 249.

78 Chabanon, *De la musique considérée en elle-même*, 337.

79 Ibid.

80 Ibid., 340.

81 Grimm, *Correspondance littéraire*, VIII:318–20.

82 Barnabé Farmian de Rozoi, *Dissertation sur le drame lyrique* (The Hague and Paris: Veuve Duchesne, 1775), 46.

83 Nougaret, *De l'art du théâtre*, II:14.

84 Laurent Garcin, *Traité du mélo-drame, ou réflexions sur la musique dramatique* (Paris: Vallat-la-Chapelle, 1772), 189.

85 Contant d'Orville, *Histoire de l'opéra bouffon*, 2 tomes in 1 vol. (1768; Geneva: Slatkine, 1970), II:108.

86 Marmontel, *Oeuvres complètes*, IV:781.

87 Garcin, *Traité du mélo-drame*, 120.

88 *Journal de musique théorique, pratique, dramatique et instrumentale* (September, 1770), 8–9. Regarding the focus on sentiment, Marmontel made it clear that there was a connection between the aims of his prose fiction and those of his *opéras comiques*: see Marmontel, *Mémoires*, ed. John Renwick, 2 vols. (Clermont-Ferrand: G. de Bussac, 1972), 1:261.

89 Jean Laurent de Béthisy, *Effets de l'air sur le corps humain, considérés dans le son; ou Discours sur la nature du chant* (Amsterdam and Paris: Lambert and Duchesne, 1760), 9. Subsequent references to this work are included in the text.

90 The sole criticism of *opéra comique* that he ventures is of its complex quartets and trios which, he argues, are too distracting (37–38n).

91 Rozoi, *Dissertation*, 9.

92 Ibid., 16.

93 Ibid., 15.

94 Ibid., 16.

95 Ibid., 17.

96 Chabanon, *De la musique considérée en elle-même*, 313.

97 "Sur le genre larmoyant dans les Drames en Musique," *Journal de musique théorique, pratique, dramatique et instrumentale* (September, 1770), 5.

98 Rozoi, *Dissertation*, 11.

99 Manuel Couvreur and Philippe Vendrix, "Les Enjeux théoriques de l'Opéra-Comique," 223–24.

100 Jean-François Marmontel, *Poétique françoise*, 2 vols. (Paris: Lesclapart, 1763), II:133.

101 Ibid., II:404.

102 Ibid., II:146.

103 Marmontel, *Oeuvres complètes*, 4:74.

104 Ibid., 4:74–75.

105 Marmontel, *Poétique françoise*, II:146–47. Though he recognized the increasing popularity of *opéras comiques*, Nougaret ironically stated his preference for the more stately productions of the Opéra: whereas "a man of letters toils to make Alexander, Brutus, and our most august kings live again," he remarked, the authors of the Opéra-Comique "pride themselves on showing us a yokel, a simple fisherman, a baker" (Nougaret, *De l'art du théâtre*, 1:77). Though Charles Collé also noted that his preferences were not those of the public, he judged the moral

tone of *Les Moissonneurs* by Favart and Duni unpalatable. He found abhorrent "the antithetical, moral, and sermonizing style of all the characters." Collé identified at least one spectator who shared his views: "a noblewoman said a few days ago upon leaving this edifying rhapsody: 'I thought I was going to the theater, and I found myself at one of Father Elizée's sermons. One does not expect that at the *Italiens*; it is a trap" (Collé, *Journal et mémoires*, III:184).

106 Samuel Weber, "Family Scenes: Some Preliminary Remarks on Domesticity and Theatricality," *South Atlantic Quarterly* 98:3 (Summer 1999), 361.

107 Mary Hunter, *The Culture of Opera Buffa in Mozart's Vienna: A Poetics of Entertainment* (Princeton: Princeton University Press, 1999), 45–46.

108 Ibid., 88–91.

109 Ibid., 91.

110 Ibid., 154–55.

111 "Never has a flop been more spectacular" (Grimm, *Correspondance littéraire*, VI:218–19). Grimm relates a joke based on a pun on Poinsinet's name that was made at his expense on the stage of the fair theaters following the performance of *Tom Jones*. An ass was brought on stage and praised for its cleanliness. When its excrement appeared, there were cries of "point si net! point si net!" [not so clean! not so clean!] (ibid., VI:219).

112 See ibid., VI:491.

113 François-André Danican Philidor and Antoine Alexandre Henri Poinsinet, *Tom Jones, comédie lyrique en trois actes* (Paris: chez M. de la Chevardiere, [1766]), 26. In the first version of this scene, Honora tells Sophie of seeing Jones, on his knees, admiring Sophie's portrait. In a re-enactment of this scene, Honora places Sophie in the place of the portrait and sings, as Jones, of his love for her in the *ariette*, "Image tendrement chérie." Note that the second version maintains a focus on the performance of the song, rather than on the image. See the first edition of the libretto: Poinsinet, *Tom Jones* (Paris: Duchesne, 1765).

114 Weber, "Family Scenes," 357.

115 See Stefano Castelvecchi, "From *Nina* to *Nina*: Psychodrama, Absorption and Sentiment in the 1780s," *Cambridge Opera Journal* 8.2 (1996), 95, 111.

116 Philidor and Poinsinet, *Tom Jones* (Paris: chez M. de la Chevardiere, 1766), 27. One cannot help regretting the first version of the *opéra comique* in which Mme. Western makes her entrance with an *ariette* in which she comments on current events taken from the gazette she is reading. See Poinsinet, *Tom Jones* (Paris: Duchesne, 1765), 12.

117 Philidor and Poinsinet, *Tom Jones* (Paris: chez M. de la Chevardiere, 1766), 63.

118 Ibid., 51. The contrast is even more in evidence in the early version. As Blifil begins an elaborately polite response following M. Western's offer of his daughter's hand in marriage, M. Western reveals his no-nonsense approach to life: "oh! Point de grands mots, touche-là, & la rends heureuse" [oh! forget the big words, let's shake on it, and make her happy]. He remarks that he could live in London if he wished, "mais je me plais encore mieux ici entouré de mes paysans qu'au milieu de nos Beaux d'Angleterre, de nos Lords, avec leurs broderies & les cordons" [but I enjoy myself more here surrounded by my countryfolk than among our English nobles, among our lords with their fancywork and ribbons] (Poinsinet, *Tom Jones* [Paris: Duchesne, 1765], 55, 44).

119 Philidor and Poinsinet, *Tom Jones* (Paris: chez M. de la Chevardiere, 1766), 91–92.

120 Tom McCall, "Liquid Politics: Towards a Theorization of 'Bourgeois' Tragic Drama," *The South Atlantic Quarterly* 98.3 (Summer 1999), 605.

121 Garcin, *Traité du mélo-drame*, 221.

122 Ibid., 225–26.

123 Philidor and Poinsinet, *Tom Jones* (Paris: chez M. de la Chevardiere, 1766), 142–44.

124 Poinsinet, *Tom Jones* (Paris: chez la veuve Duchesne, 1771), 49–50.

125 Garcin, *Traité du mélo-drame*, 301–02.

126 Philidor and Poinsinet, *Tom Jones* (Paris: chez M. de la Chevardiere, 1766), 167–69.

127 Hunter, *The Culture of Opera Buffa in Mozart's Vienna*, 157.

128 Cited in Couvreur and Vendrix, "Les Enjeux théoriques de l'Opéra-Comique," 242.

129 "Sur le genre larmoyant dans les Drames en Musique," *Journal de musique théorique, pratique, dramatique et instrumentale* (September, 1770), 8.

130 Charlton, *French Opera 1730–1830*, 2:16. Vaudevilles, as Robert Darnton has argued, were often used as a means of conveying information about

current events. Referring specifically to a song about Mme de Pompadour, "Qu'une bâtarde de catin" [A Bastard Strumpet], Darnton remarks that "the song functioned like a tabloid newspaper set to music" (Robert Darnton, "Paris: the Early Internet," *The New York Review of Books* 47.11 [June 29, 2000], 45). A performance of the song can be found in the internet version of Darnton's article: http://www.indiana.edu/ahr/darnton/songs/

131 Charlton, *French Opera 1730–1830*, 2:2.

132 Ibid., 2:6. Elsewhere, I have discussed the continued importance of the verbal paradigm for eighteenth-century music: see Thomas, *Music and the Origins of Language*, 12–33.

133 Chabanon, *De la musique considérée en elle-même*, 346.

134 Bernard Germain Etienne Médard de la Ville-sur-Illon, comte de Lacépède, *La Poétique de la musique*, 2 vols. (Paris: l'imprimerie de Monsieur, 1785), II:287.

135 Charlton, *French Opera 1730–1830*, 2:42.

136 André-Ernest-Modeste Grétry and Thomas d'Hèle, *L'Amant jaloux, comédie en trois actes* (Paris: M. Houbaut, [1779]), 53–54.

137 Garcin, *Traité du mélo-drame*, 95–96. See Charlton's discussion of Garcin: *French Opera 1730–1830*, 2:27–29.

138 Garcin, *Traité du mélo-drame*, 122.

139 Ibid., 229–30.

140 Ibid., 131.

141 Diderot, "Observations sur un ouvrage intitulé Traité du mélodrame ou Réflexions sur la musique dramatique," *Oeuvres complètes*, ed. Roger Lewinter, 15 vols. (Paris: Club Français du Livre, 1969–73), IX:939–40.

142 Ibid., IX:940.

143 "Neither act 3 of Sedaine and Grétry's *Richard Coeur-de-lion* (1784), nor act 3 of Bouilly and Cherubini's *Les deux journées* (1800) contains a single individual solo number, that is, a solo uncomplicated by chorus or other technical intervention. The reason for this state of affairs, notionally inexplicable within the Dahlhaus model, must be that opéra-comique had already attained a complex of narrative modes in music way beyond just 'a drama of affects'" (Charlton, *French Opera 1730–1830*, 2:34).

144 *La Fausse magie* was extremely popular, marking 169 performances from 1775 to 1794. It was seen every year until 1823, with the sole exceptions of 1810 and 1819 (David Charlton, *Grétry and the growth of opéra-comique*

[Cambridge: Cambridge University Press, 1986], 138). Karin Pendle suggests that *La Fausse magie* "represents a high point in Grétry's writing" ("The Opéras Comiques of Grétry and Marmontel," *The Musical Quarterly* 62.5 [1976]: 431).

145 André-Ernest-Modeste Grétry and Jean-François Marmontel, *La Fausse magie, comédie en un acte* (Paris: M. Houbaut, [1775]), 46. *La Fausse magie* was revised in 1776. The differences between this two-act version and the original one-act play are discussed by Charlton (*Grétry*, 137–38). Subsequent citations in the text are to the one-act version. Minor modifications in punctuation have been made for clarification.

146 Charlton provides this summary (*Grétry*, 131–32). He notes that *oison* [gosling] also means dupe or dope (*Grétry*, 132n3).

147 "The quartet is a masterpiece where the character traits, the truth [of the situations], the contrasts, the variety, the various tempos, the picturesque expressions of the music form a ravishing whole" (*Mercure de France* [March, 1775], 171).

148 Charlton, *Grétry*, 135–36.

149 Ibid., 132.

150 *Mercure de France*, (March, 1775), 171. Grétry, too, later remarked on the way in which the orchestra produced meaning in the work: see André-Ernest-Modeste Grétry, *Mémoires ou essais sur la musique*, 2 vols. (1797; New York: Da Capo, 1971), 1:260. Charlton remarks that "Grétry, like Mozart, strove to capture action in music" (*Grétry*, 10).

151 Michel-Jean Sedaine, *Richard Coeur de Lion* (Paris: Chez Brunet, 1786), 35, 52.

152 Grétry and d'Hèle, *L'Amant jaloux*, 109.

153 Grimm criticized this device, which disappeared in the two-act version (*Correspondance littéraire*, XI:221).

154 Charlton, *Grétry*, 108. Grimm, who always preferred Sedaine to Marmontel, expressed his disapproval of the librettist: "M. Marmontel is cold: he has no feeling; he doesn't understand the theater" (Grimm, *Correspondance littéraire*, IX:437). Charlton remarks on Marmontel's sources: "the substance of the story is taken from *La belle et la bête* by Jeanne Marie Le Prince de Beaumont, and the names and the setting from *Amour pour amour*, a verse play by P. C. Nivelle de La Chaussée (1742). The precedent of a long *opéra comique* using the supernatural and dances can be found in Duni and Favart's *La fée Urgèle*" (*The New*

Grove Dictionary of Opera, s. v. "*Zémire et Azor*"). Charlton also notes that Mozart owned a copy of Grétry's score (ibid.).

155 Grimm, *Correspondance littéraire*, IX:442.

156 André-Ernest-Modeste Grétry and Jean-François Marmontel, *Zémire et Azor, comédie-ballet en vers et en quatre actes* (Paris: Chez Houbaut, [1772]), 47–48.

157 "Emotional wealth ... is raw capital, carrying a tremendous potential for conversion to actual material wealth" (McCall, "Liquid Politics," 605). It is interesting to note in this context that *Les Fausses apparences* revolves around a rich widow, Léonore, whose father, Lopez, is writing a letter to his business partner as act 1 opens, assuring him that he will do everything in his power to prevent Léonore from remarrying so that her late husband's fortune – one hundred thousand piastres – will remain invested in their business venture (Grétry and d'Hèle, *L'Amant jaloux*, 13). When a French officer, Florival (who is in love with Isabelle, believing her to be Léonore), arrives on the pretext of borrowing money, he extolls Lopez's "wealth," referring between the lines to his daughter as well as to his fortune. Florival remarks: "Riche! Vous possédez un trésor" [Rich! You possess a treasure]. Lopez replies, thinking he is referring to his money: "Pas absolument un trésor, mais je suis à mon aise" [Not exactly a treasure, but I am comfortable] (ibid., 85).

158 Grimm, *Correspondance littéraire*, IX:440.

159 Charlton has identified a melodic figure that repeatedly accompanies demonstrations of virtue at several different points in the work (*Grétry*, 107). Virtue is therefore a musically coherent presence in *Zémire et Azor*, presented with the intention of being identified as such by the listener.

160 McCall, "Liquid Politics," 595, 601.

161 Marmontel, *Mémoires*, 1:268. An added dimension to the effect of the *opéra comique* in its first performances was the fact that Clairval, playing Azor, was a remarkably attractive actor. Grétry remarked that "he knew how to draw everyone's heart to him," and added that "I always believed that the charming looks of this actor, already appreciated by the spectators, had contributed to the illusion that he created in this role" (Grétry, *Mémoires*, 1:227).

162 Marmontel, *Mémoires*, 1:268–69.

163 Charlton, *Grétry*, 103. Grétry recalled the genesis of the trio: "I had written this number twice, when Diderot came to my home." Diderot

immediately declaimed his own version of the line: "I substituted musical sounds for the declaimed sounds of the beginning, and the rest of the piece immediately came together" (Grétry, *Mémoires*, 1:225).

164 Charlton, *Grétry*, 103.
165 Grimm, *Correspondance littéraire*, IX:441.
166 *Mercure de France* (January, 1772), 163.
167 Hunter, *The Culture of Opera Buffa in Mozart's Vienna*, 91.
168 Rozoi, *Dissertation*, 7–8.
169 Charlton, *French Opera 1730–1830*, 2:38.
170 Pierre Augustin Caron de Beaumarchais, "Essai sur le genre dramatique serieux," *Théâtre complet* (Paris: Gallimard, 1957), 10.
171 Scott S. Bryson, *The Chastised Stage: Bourgeois Drama and the Exercise of Power* (Saratoga, California: Anma Libri, 1991), 38.
172 Jay Caplan, *In the King's Wake: Post-Absolutist Culture in France* (Chicago and London: University of Chicago Press, 1999), 2.

8 ARCHITECTURAL VISIONS OF LYRIC THEATER AND SPECTATORSHIP

1 Jean-Marie Pérouse de Montclos, *Histoire de l'architecture française* (n.p.: Mengès, 1989), 408. For a discussion of the relationship between the opera house and the repertory during Lully's time, see Barbara Coeyman, "Walking Through Lully's Opera Theatre in the Palais Royal," in John Hajdu Heyer, ed., *Lully Studies* (Cambridge: Cambridge University Press, 2000), 216–42.
2 Jeffrey S. Ravel has read the debates on the elimination of the *parterre* in eighteenth-century French theaters in light of Jürgen Habermas's theory of the public sphere. See Jeffrey S. Ravel, "Seating the Public: Spheres and Loathing in the Paris Theaters, 1777–1788," *French Historical Studies* 18 (Spring 1993), 174–175. Ravel incorporates this analysis into his discussion of the *parterre* and French national identity in *The Contested Parterre: Public Theater and French Political Culture, 1680–1791* (Ithaca and London: Cornell University Press, 1999), 191–224. See also James H. Johnson, *Listening in Paris: A Cultural History* (Berkeley, Los Angeles, London: University of California Press, 1995), 9–34, 53–70. Johnson discusses the development of a musical public in the late eighteenth century through changing ideas of, and responses to, the lyric theater.

3 Anthony Vidler, *Claude-Nicolas Ledoux: Architecture and Social Reform at the End of the Ancien Régime* (Cambridge, Mass.: MIT Press, 1990), 165. In his review of Cochin's *Voyage en Italie*, Diderot's comments point to the importance of the Italian models: "a critic [*juge*] everywhere else, Cochin was a student in Rome" (Diderot, "Sur le *Voyage en Italie* par Cochin," *Oeuvres complètes*, ed. Lewinter, III:225).

4 Charles-Nicolas Cochin, *Lettres sur l'opéra* (Paris: L. Cellot, 1781), 61; hereafter cited in the text.

5 Reviews of the 1761 production of Lully's *Armide* note the modifications that were made to bring seventeenth-century opera up to date, notably the expansion of the *divertissements* and the lack of machine effects. See Lois Rosow, "How eighteenth-century Parisians heard Lully's operas: the case of *Armide*'s fourth act," in John Hajdu Heyer, ed., *Jean-Baptiste Lully and the Music of the French Baroque: Essays in Honor of James R. Anthony* (Cambridge: Cambridge University Press, 1989), 233.

6 Diderot, *Oeuvres complètes*, ed. Varloot, X:150–51.

7 Until it moved to the Tuileries (1770–81) and then to the Odéon (1782), the Comédie-Française was located in a theater built by d'Orbay in 1689 in the rue des Fossés-Saint-Germain, now rue de l'Ancienne-Comédie. For a general overview of the history of theater architecture, see Pierre Pougnaud, *Théâtres: 4 siècles d'architectures et d'histoire* (Paris: Éditions du Moniteur, 1980).

8 Pierre Patte, *Essai sur l'architecture théâtrale* (Paris: Moutard, 1782), 16.

9 Chevalier de Chaumont, *Véritable construction d'un théâtre d'opéra à l'usage de la France* (Paris: De Lormel, 1766), 17.

10 Cited by Bryson, *The Chastised Stage*, 53. Diderot adopts the same metaphor in *De la poésie dramatique* (*Oeuvres complètes*, ed. Varloot, X:337).

11 Claude-Nicolas Ledoux, *L'Architecture considérée sous le rapport de l'art, des moeurs et de la législation*, 2 vols. (Paris: chez l'auteur, 1804), I:230, I:229.

12 Cited in Tom Lawrenson, "The Ideal Theatre in the Eighteenth Century: Paris and Venice," in *Drama and Mimesis* (Cambridge: Cambridge University Press, 1980), 59.

13 André Roubo, *Traité de la construction des théâtres et des machines théâtrales* (Paris: Cellot & Jombert fils jeune, 1777), 24.

14 Patte, *Essai sur l'architecture théâtrale*, 165.

15 Howarth, *French Theatre in the Neo-classical Era, 1550–1789*, 535.

16 Although the role architects and theorists allotted to women is not the subject of this chapter, it is a topic that would merit further attention. In the projects I have examined, women have three roles as spectators and objects of male spectatorship in the theater: first, they served to ornament the *salle*, as both Cochin and Patte noted; second, as Ledoux remarked, women acted as attractors, generating the energy required for public gathering and spirit; third, projects for the reform of the parterre claimed that women had a moral influence on men because the presence of women would incite gallantry and thus calm the violent and destructive male passions that reigned there.

17 Lagrave, *Le Théâtre et le public à Paris de 1715 à 1750*, 417.

18 The proscenium arch was also called *frontispice*. In Dumont's *Parallèle de plans des plus belles salles de spectacle*, a "Projet d'une salle de spectacle pour la ville de Brest" is introduced by a conventional *frontispice* that plays with the two meanings of the word and with the border between the two spaces defined by the frame. On the title page, a frame encloses the title of the project. Above the title shines a sun which is part of the decorative proscenium frame but whose rays extend beyond the frame itself, giving an impression of depth and inviting comparison with the effect of a theatrical machine. Below, an urn smokes which, like the sun above, is placed both within the frame and on the fictional stage beyond. See Gabriel Pierre Martin Dumont, *Parallèle de plans des plus belles salles de spectacle d'Italie et de France* (Paris: rue des Arcis, 1774).

19 Patte, *Essai sur l'architecture théâtrale*, 184–85. Henri Lagrave writes that there were spectators on stage at the Comédie-Française, the Comédie-Italienne, at the fair theaters, but not at the Opéra, at least since 1697 when "the King forbid Mr. Francine to let anyone be seated on the stage of the Opera . . . " (Lagrave, *Le Théâtre et le public*, 110n19). However, some theaters apparently were still equipped with loges built into the proscenium. See also Howarth, *French Theatre in the Neo-Classical Era*, 368, 371.

20 Diderot, *Oeuvres complètes*, ed. Varloot, x:341.

21 Patte, *Essai sur l'architecture théâtrale*, 183.

22 Vidler, *Claude-Nicolas Ledoux*, 177. See also Anthony Vidler, *The Writing of the Walls* (Princeton: Princeton Architectural Press, 1987), 39–40.

23 Vidler notes that Ledoux also adopted a triple scene, "following De Wailly's first project for the Comédie-Française, and like Cochin in

1765 undoubtedly referring to Palladian precedent" (*Claude-Nicolas Ledoux*, 183).

24 Etienne Haeringer, *L'Esthétique de l'opéra en France au temps de Jean-Philippe Rameau* (Oxford: Voltaire Foundation, 1990), 113. In his entry on "Theater Architecture," Edward A. Langhans notes that "by 1711 the designer Ferdinando Galli-Bibiena recommended a vanishing point 30 metres behind the scenic area" (*The New Grove Dictionary of Opera*, 4:712).

25 Diderot, *Oeuvres complètes*, ed. Varloot, x:334–35.

26 Ferguson, *Solitude and the Sublime*, 31.

27 Nicolas Edme Rétif de la Bretonne, *La Mimographe, ou Idées d'une honnête femme pour la réformation du théâtre national* (Amsterdam. Changuion/La Haie: Gosse & Pinet, 1770), 53.

28 Diderot, *Oeuvres complètes*, ed. Varloot, xx:99, xx:128.

29 Grimm, *Correspondance littéraire*, vi:170–71.

30 See Jürgen Habermas, *The Structural Transformation of the Public Sphere*, trans. Thomas Burger (Cambridge, Mass.: MIT Press, 1989), 27–30.

31 Ibid., 50–51. In a more recent text, Habermas criticizes Richard Sennett for making "certain features of representative publicness an integral part of the classical bourgeois public sphere . . . staging the presentation of oneself behind a mask that removes private emotions and everything subjective from sight should properly be considered part of the highly stylized framework of a representative publicness whose conventions had already crumbled in the eighteenth century, when bourgeois private people formed themselves into a public and therewith became the carriers of a new type of public sphere" (Jürgen Habermas, "Further Reflections on the Public Sphere," in Craig Calhoun, ed., *Habermas and the Public Sphere* [Cambridge, Mass.: MIT Press, 1992], 426–27). One might argue, however, that it is an oversimplification to assume that stylized representation and performance somehow disappear in the face of liberal communication.

32 Ravel has nuanced Habermas's model within the specific context of the theater ("Seating the Public," 177). See also Keith Michael Baker, "Defining the Public Sphere in Eighteenth-Century France: Variations on a Theme by Habermas," in Calhoun, ed., *Habermas and the Public Sphere*, 181–211.

33 Patte, *Essai sur l'architecture théâtrale*, 170.

34 Jacques François Blondel, *Cours d'architecture*, 6 vols. (Paris: Desaint, 1771–77), I:53, I:75.

35 Diderot, *Oeuvres complètes*, ed. Varloot, XIV:384.

36 Marvin Carlson, "The Theatre as Civic Monument," *Theatre Journal* 40.1 (1988), 18.

37 Voltaire, *Les Oeuvres Complètes/The Complete Works*, XXXIB:213–14. See also Carlson, "The Theatre as Civic Monument," 20.

38 This was the effect that Rousseau contested in his *Lettre à d'Alembert* on spectacles, arguing that the spectator is alienated because he will "forget his friends, his neighbors, his loved ones" and thus becomes more concerned with the false theatricality of the stage than with social relations and civic responsibilities (*Oeuvres complètes*, V:16). See also David Marshall's reading of Rousseau's view of theatricality in *The Surprising Effects of Sympathy* (Chicago: University of Chicago Press, 1988), 135–77.

39 Jean Starobinski, *1789: les emblèmes de la raison* (Paris: Flammarion, 1973), 65.

40 Voltaire, *Oeuvres Complètes*, XXIII:297.

41 Carlson, "The Theatre as Civic Monument," 18.

42 Ledoux, *L'Architecture*, I:223.

43 Louis-Étienne Boullée, *Treatise on Architecture*, ed. Helen Rosenau (London: Alec Tiranti, 1953), 55. Subsequent references are given in the text.

44 Marvin Carlson, *Places of Performance* (Ithaca: Cornell University Press, 1989), 92.

45 Rétif de la Bretonne, *La Mimographe*, 14.

46 Charles de Wailly, "Plan d'aménagement de la place du théâtre français, transformée en aire de rassemblement public, avec gradins et tribune d'orateur," and "Vue perspective de la place de l'Odéon, des gradins et du velum," project from l'an II [1794]. Bibliothèque-Musée de la Comédie Française, Paris. In their introduction to a volume of essays on Paris theaters during the Revolution, Giuseppe Radicchio and Michèle Sajous D'Oria cite an anecdote that could be used as an example of the extension of the theater into the urban landscape during the Revolution. The actors of the Opéra, which had been transferred to the Boulevard Saint-Martin after the second fire in the Palais-Royal, decided to honor Marat and Lepelletier with an open-air spectacle: "the facade of the Opéra . . . became a mountain which advanced all the way to the middle

of the boulevard and on which rose the Temple of the Arts and of
Liberty; a chariot stopped at the foot of the mountain and two divinities,
Liberty and Equality, descended from it in order to reach the Temple;
young girls, dressed in white tunics tied with tricolor scarves, draped
garlands on the busts of the two heroes" (Radicchio and D'Oria, *Les
Théâtres de Paris pendant la Révolution*, trans. Laura Casati and Françoise
Lenoir [Paris: Bibliothèque Historique de la Ville de Paris, 1990], 28).

47 Ravel, *The Contested Parterre*, 220.

48 Alexandre-Balthazar-Laurent Grimod de la Reynière, *Le Censeur
dramatique, ou Journal des principaux théâtres de Paris et des départements*,
4 vols. (1797–98; Geneva: Minkoff, 1973), 1:13.

49 Ibid., 1.14.

9 OPERA AND COMMON SENSE: LACÉPÈDE'S *POÉTIQUE DE LA MUSIQUE*

1 Lawrence Kramer, *Classical Music and Postmodern Knowledge* (Berkeley
and Los Angeles: University of California Press, 1995), 67.

2 Ora Frishberg Saloman, "La Cépède's *La poétique de la musique* and Le
Sueur," *Acta Musicologica* 47.1 (1975), 146.

3 Lacépède, *La Poétique de la musique*, 1:v; hereafter cited in the text.

4 The *querelle* lasted a few years, spurred by a rivalry that opposed Gluck's
Armide, which had its premiere in September, 1777, and Piccinni's *Roland*
which was performed the following January. Fueling the dispute, each
composer set an *Iphigénie en Tauride*, given in 1779 and 1781 respectively.
Though Lacépède' s work is in no way a polemical text, Lacépède clearly
favored Gluck's dramatic aesthetic to the Italian predilection for
"virtuoso showpieces" which, for Lacépède, showed the singer's vocal
ability but represented nothing (ibid., 1:315).

5 Paul Alpers, *What is Pastoral?* (Chicago and London: University of
Chicago Press, 1996), 22.

6 Buffon's man first experiences the uncoordinated sensations of sight,
smell, and taste. See Georges-Louis Leclerc, Comte de Buffon, *Histoire
naturelle*, ed. Jean Varloot (Paris: Gallimard, 1984), 117.

7 Both Rousseau and Lacépède divided the world into southern climates
favorable to the natural development of music and culture, and northern
climates whose harsh conditions stunted human feeling and social

development. However, whereas Rousseau saw the unison as the only natural harmony, the same unison for Lacépède reflected the retarded development of the brutish northern peoples (1:35–36).

8 Alpers, *What is Pastoral?*, 81.

9 Polygenetic theories, though espoused by some (such as Hume and Voltaire), were not the most prevalent ones in the eighteenth century, as they would be in the nineteenth. Rather, the essential unity of humanity is asserted, however divided it may be by cultural and historical factors, such as form of government, or geographical factors such as climate. See Ann Thomson, "Sauvages, barbares, civilisés: l'histoire des sociétés au XVIIIe siècle," in Jean-Louis Chevalier, Mariella Colin and Ann Thomson, eds., *Barbares & sauvages: images et reflets dans la culture occidentale* (Caen: Presses universitaires de Caen, 1993), 79–89.

10 Michel de Certeau, "Vocal Utopias: Glossolalias," trans. Daniel Rosenberg, *Representations* 56 (Fall 1996), 30.

11 Ibid., 37.

12 For a recent overview of the topic, see John C. O'Neal, *The Authority of Experience: Sensationist Theory in the French Enlightenment* (University Park, Pa.: The Pennsylvania State University Press, 1996). On the medical and philosophical concepts and their literary and cultural inscription, see Frank Baasner, *Der Begriff 'sensibilité' im 18. Jahrhundert* (Heidelberg: Carl Winter Universitätsverlag, 1988), 235–394.

13 John W. Yolton, *Thinking Matter: Materialism in Eighteenth-Century Britain* (Minneapolis: University of Minnesota Press, 1983), 153.

14 Ann Jessie Van Sant, *Eighteenth-Century Sensibility and the Novel* (Cambridge: Cambridge University Press, 1993), 8.

15 Van Sant notes that this placement may also reveal an echo of Aristotle for whom the heart was also the center of sensation (ibid., 9).

16 Laurence Sterne, *The Sermons of Mr. Yorick*, ed. and introd. Wilbur Cross, 2 vols. (New York: J. F. Taylor & Co., 1904), 1:45.

17 See Hubert L. Dreyfus, *Being-in-the-World* (Cambridge, Mass.: MIT Press, 1991), 169–74.

18 Van Sant, *Eighteenth-Century Sensibility and the Novel*, 11.

19 Vila, *Enlightenment and Pathology*, 166–81.

20 Castelvecchi, "From *Nina* to *Nina*," 91.

21 Kramer, *Classical Music and Postmodern Knowledge*, 21–22.

22 See my references to the work of Michael Fried and Jay Caplan on the exclusion of the beholder in chapter 7.

23 Castelvecchi, "From *Nina* to *Nina*," 102–03.
24 Michel de Certeau, "Vocal Utopias: Glossolalias," 32.
25 Pietro Metastasio, *Opere drammatiche*, 4 vols. (Venice: G. Bettinelli, 1733–37), IV:46–47. Lacépède knew *Ciro riconosciuto* by way of a French opera, *Cyrus*, based on Metastasio, by Pierre Paganel. According to Lacépède, the French opera "has not yet been published" (1:134n). Pierre Paganel, an acquaintance of Lacépède, was later a deputy at the Convention Nationale of 1792. I have found no trace of his opera. Lacépède may also have referred to the French translation of Metastasio's *Tragédies-opera*, trans. César Pierre Richelet, 5 vols. (Vienna: n.p., 1751). For my translation of the original Italian, I have referred to Richelet's translation and to John Hoole's eighteenth-century translation/adaptation, *Cyrus: A Tragedy* (London: T. Davies, 1768).
26 Hoole, *Cyrus: A Tragedy*, 34.
27 Elena Sala Di Felice, *Metastasio: Ideologia, drammaturgia, spettacolo* (Milan: Franco Angeli, 1983), 107.
28 Diderot, *Oeuvres complètes*, ed. Varloot, x:84.
29 Castelvecchi, "From *Nina* to *Nina*," 101.
30 Alice Brin Renken, "Marin Marais's *Alcione*: An Edition with Commentary," PhD dissertation, Washington University, 1981, xxi, ix.
31 Christoph Willibald Gluck, *Sämtliche Werke*, series I, vol. 9, *Iphigénie en Tauride*, ed. Gerhard Croll (Kassel: Bärenreiter, 1973), 204.
32 Ibid., 217 18.
33 Anne Vincent-Buffault, *The History of Tears: Sensibility and Sentimentality in France*, trans. Teresa Bridgeman (New York: St. Martin's Press, 1991), 243, 45.
34 Chris Jones notes that in Smith's view, however, "we more readily sympathize with the rich and powerful," a position that ultimately upholds the status quo of social distinctions and class hierarchies (*Radical Sensibility: Literature and Ideas in the 1790s* [London and New York: Routledge, 1993], 31.

CONCLUSIONS

1 J. M. Bernstein, *The Fate of Art: Aesthetic Alienation from Kant to Derrida and Adorno* (University Park, Pa.: The Pennsylvania State University Press, 1992), 3.

2 Genette discusses the fragility of Kant's description: "everyone judges beautiful that which pleases him (and ugly that which displeases him) disinterestedly, and claims universal assent in the name, first of all, of the inner certainty of this disinterestedness and, secondly, of the reassuring hypothesis of a shared taste [*une identité de goût*] among men" (Gérard Genette, *L'Oeuvre de l'art*, vol. II, *La Relation esthétique* [Paris: Seuil, 1997], 84).

3 Steven Knapp, *Literary Interest: the Limits of Anti-Formalism* (Cambridge, Mass.: Harvard University Press, 1993), 50.

4 Bernstein, *The Fate of Art*, 3.

5 G. W. Hegel, *Lectures on Fine Art*, trans. T. M. Knox (Oxford: Clarendon Press, 1975), 155.

6 Jean-Luc Nancy, *The Muses*, trans. Peggy Kamuf (Stanford: Stanford University Press, 1996), 89.

7 Christopher Norris, *Paul de Man* (New York: Routledge, 1988), 149.

8 Jean-Joseph Goux, "The Eclipse of Art?," *Thesis Eleven* 44 (1996), 60.

9 See Philippe Lacoue-Labarthe, *Musica ficta (figures de Wagner)* (Paris: Christian Bourgois, 1991), 77; and Thomas Pavel, "L'Esthétique, le Romantisme et la démocratie," *Littérature* 89 (1993): 98–112.

10 Nancy, *The Muses*, 4.

11 Renato Barilli, *A Course on Aesthetics*, trans. Karen E. Pinkus (Minneapolis, London: University of Minnesota Press, 1993), 6.

12 Ibid., 8.

13 Luc Ferry makes the mistaken assumption that taste, from the beginning of aesthetics in 1750, operates exclusively within the bounds of intimate subjectivity, and is a strictly "immediate" response (Luc Ferry, *Homo aestheticus: l'invention du goût à l'âge démocratique* [Paris: Grasset, 1990], 33, 27).

Abbate, Carolyn. *Unsung Voices*. Princeton: Princeton University Press, 1991.

Adam, Antoine. *Histoire de la littérature française au XVIIe siècle*. 4 vols. Paris: Éditions Domat, 1954.

Adam, Antoine, Georges Lerminier, Édouard Morot-Sir et al. *Littérature française*. 2 vols. Paris: Larousse, 1967.

Adorno, Theodor. *Quasi una fantasia*. Trans. Rodney Livingstone. London: Verso, 1992.

"Bourgeois Opera." In David J. Levin, ed., *Opera Through Other Eyes*. Stanford: Stanford University Press, 1994.

Alpers, Paul. *What is Pastoral?* Chicago and London: University of Chicago Press, 1996.

André, Yves-Marie. *Essai sur le beau*. Amsterdam: Schneider, 1759.

L'Année littéraire.

Anthony, James R. *French Baroque Music from Beaujoyeulx to Rameau*. New York: W. W. Norton, 1974.

"The Musical Structure of Lully's Operatic Airs." In Jérôme de La Gorce and Herbert Schneider, eds., *Jean-Baptiste Lully: Actes du Colloque Saint-Germain-en-Laye–Heidelberg 1987*. Laaber: Laaber-Verlag, 1990. 65–75.

Apostolidès, Jean-Marie. *Le Roi-machine: spectacle et politique au temps de Louis XIV*. Paris: Minuit, 1981.

Le Prince sacrifié: théâtre et politique au temps de Louis XIV. Paris: Minuit, 1985.

Aquin de Chateaulyon, Pierre Louis d'. *Siècle littéraire de Louis XV, ou Lettres sur les hommes célèbres*. 2 vols. Amsterdam and Paris: Duschesne, 1752.

Arnauld, Antoine. *Lettres*. 9 vols. Nancy: Joseph Nicolai, 1727.

Aubignac, François Hedelin, abbé d'. *La Pratique du théâtre*. Amsterdam: Jean Frederic Bernard, 1715.

Baasner, Frank. *Der Begriff 'sensibilité' im 18. Jahrhundert*. Heidelberg: Carl Winter Universitätsverlag, 1988.

Baillet, Adrien. *Jugemens des sçavans sur les principaux ouvrages des auteurs*. 4 tomes in 9 vols. Paris: Antoine Dezallier, 1686.

Baker, Keith Michael. "Defining the Public Sphere in Eighteenth-Century France: Variations on a Theme by Habermas." In Craig Calhoun, ed., *Habermas and the Public Sphere*. Cambridge, Mass.: MIT Press, 1992. 181–211.

Barilli, Renato. *A Course on Aesthetics*. Trans. Karen E. Pinkus. Minneapolis, London: University of Minnesota Press, 1993.

Barthélemy, Maurice. "L'opéra-comique des origines à la Querelle des Bouffons." In Philippe Vendrix, ed., *L'Opéra-comique en France au XVIIIe siècle*. Liège: Mardaga, 1992. 9–78.

Batteux, Charles. *Les Beaux-Arts réduits à un même principe*. Ed. Jean-Rémy Mantion. Paris: Aux Amateurs de livres, [1989].

Beaumarchais, Pierre Augustin Caron de. *Théâtre complet*. Paris: Gallimard, 1957.

Beaussant, Philippe. *Lully ou le musicien du soleil*. Paris: Gallimard, 1992.

Beauvais, Lydia and Jean-François Méajanès. *Le Brun à Versailles*. Paris: Musée du Louvre, [1985].

Benjamin, Walter. *The Origin of German Tragic Drama*. Trans. John Osborne. London: NLB, 1977.

Bergier, Nicolas. *La Musique speculative*. Cologne: Arno Volk, 1970.

Bernstein, J. M. *The Fate of Art: Aesthetic Alienation from Kant to Derrida and Adorno*. University Park, Pa.: The Pennsylvania State University Press, 1992.

Béthisy, Jean Laurent de [marquis de Mézières]. *Effets de l'air sur le corps humain, considérés dans le son; ou Discours sur la nature du chant*. Amsterdam and Paris: Lambert and Duchesne, 1760.

Beugnot, Bernard. "Pour une poétique de l'allégorie classique." In Marc Fumaroli, ed., *Critique et création littéraires en France au XVIIe siècle*. Paris: Éditions du Centre National de la Recherche Scientifique, 1977. 409–19.

Blau, Herbert. *The Audience*. Baltimore: The Johns Hopkins University Press, 1990.

Blondel, Jacques François. *Cours d'architecture*. 6 vols. Paris: Desaint, 1771–77.

Bluche, François. *Louis XIV*. Paris: Fayard, 1986.

Boileau, Nicolas. *Oeuvres complètes*. 4 vols. Paris: Garnier Frères, 1870–73.

Bonnet, Jacques. *Histoire générale de la danse sacrée et prophane*. Paris: D'Houry fils, 1723.

Borch-Jacobsen, Mikkel. *The Emotional Tie: Psychoanalysis, Mimesis, and Affect*. Stanford: Stanford University Press, 1992.

"The Oedipus Problem in Freud and Lacan." *Critical Inquiry* 20 (1994): 267–82.

Bouissou, Sylvie. "La première version d'*Hippolyte et Aricie*; un retour aux sources." In *Hippolyte et Aricie*, opera program. Paris: Opéra National de Paris, 1996. 51–55.

Boullée, Louis-Étienne. *Treatise on Architecture.* Ed. Helen Rosenau. London: Alec Tiranti, 1953.

Bourdelot, Pierre and Jacques Bonnet. *Histoire de la musique et de ses effets.* Paris: Cochart, 1715.

Bricaire de la Dixmérie, Nicolas. *Lettres sur l'état présent de nos spectacles.* Amsterdam et se trouve à Paris: Duchesne, 1765.

Les Deux âges du goût et du génie français sous Louis XIV et sous Louis XV. 1769. Geneva: Slatkine, 1970.

Bromwich, David. "The Sublime Before Aesthetics and Politics." *Raritan* 16.4 (Spring 1997): 30–51.

Brooks, William. "Lully and Quinault at Court and on the Public Stage, 1673–86." *Seventeenth-Century French Studies* 10 (1988): 101–21.

"Further Remarks on Lully and Quinault at Court." *Seventeenth-Century French Studies* 11 (1989): 147–50.

Brown, Bruce Alan. "Editions anciennes et modernes d'opéras-comiques: problèmes et methodologies." In Philippe Vendrix, ed., *Grétry et l'Europe de l'opéra-comique.* Liège: Mardaga, 1992. 355–65.

Brown, Leslie Ellen. "Departures from Lullian Convention in the Tragédie Lyrique of the Préramiste Era." *Recherches sur la musique française classique* 22 (1984): 59–77.

Bryson, Norman. *Word and Image: French Painting of the Ancien Régime.* Cambridge: Cambridge University Press, 1981.

Bryson, Scott S. *The Chastised Stage: Bourgeois Drama and the Exercise of Power.* Saratoga, Calif.: Anma Libri, 1991.

Buffon, Georges Louis Leclerc, comte de. *Histoire naturelle.* Ed. Jean Varloot. Paris: Gallimard, 1984.

Burgess, Geoffrey Vernon. "Ritual in the *tragédie en musique* from Lully's *Cadmus et Hermione* [1673] to Rameau's *Zoroastre* [1749]." Ph.D. dissertation, Cornell University, 1998.

"'Le théâtre ne change qu'à la troisième scène': the hand of the author and the unity of place in Act V of *Hippolyte et Aricie*." *Cambridge Opera Journal* 10.3 (1998): 275–87.

Burke, Edmund. *A Philosophical Enquiry into the Origin of our Ideas of the Sublime and Beautiful.* Ed. J. T. Boulton. London: Routledge and Kegan Paul, 1958.

Burke, Peter. *The Fabrication of Louis XIV.* New Haven: Yale University Press, 1992.

Butler, Judith. *Bodies that Matter.* New York and London: Routledge, 1993.

Cahusac, Louis de. *Épitre sur les dangers de la poésie suivie de La Danse ancienne et moderne.* 4 vols. 1739–54. Geneva: Slatkine, 1971.

Caplan, Jay. *Framed Narratives: Diderot's Genealogy of the Beholder.* Minneapolis: University of Minnesota Press, 1985.

  In the King's Wake: Post-Absolutist Culture in France. Chicago and London: University of Chicago Press, 1999.

Carlson, Marvin. "The Theatre as Civic Monument." *Theatre Journal* 40.1 (1988): 12–32.

  Places of Performance. Ithaca: Cornell University Press, 1989.

Castelvecchi, Stefano. "From *Nina* to *Nina*: Psychodrama, Absorption and Sentiment in the 1780s." *Cambridge Opera Journal* 8.2 (1996): 91–112.

Cavell, Stanley. *A Pitch of Philosophy.* Cambridge, Mass.: Harvard University Press, 1994.

Cernuschi, Alain. *Penser la musique dans l'Encyclopédie: étude sur les enjeux de la musicographie des Lumières et sur ses liens avec l'encyclopédisme.* Paris: Honoré Champion, 2000.

Certeau, Michel de. "Vocal Utopias: Glossolalias." Trans. Daniel Rosenberg. *Representations* 56 (Fall 1996): 29–47.

Cessac, Catherine. *Marc-Antoine Charpentier.* Trans. E. Thomas Glasow. Portland, Oreg.: Amadeus Press, 1995.

Chabanon, Michel Paul Guy de. *De la musique considérée en elle-même et dans ses rapports avec la parole, les langues, la poésie et le théâtre.* 1785. Geneva: Slatkine, 1969.

Chapelain, Jean. *Lettres.* 2 vols. Paris: Imprimerie Nationale, 1883.

Chappuzeau, Samuel. *Le Théâtre françois.* Lyon: Michel Mayer, 1674.

Charlton, David. *Grétry and the growth of opéra-comique.* Cambridge: Cambridge University Press, 1986.

  French Opera 1730–1830: Meaning and Media. Chapters individually paginated. Aldershot: Ashgate, 2000.

Charpentier, Marc-Antoine. *Médée.* 1694. Farnborough: Gregg Press, 1968.

  Vocal Chamber Music. Ed. John S. Powell. Madison: A-R Editions, 1986.

Médée. Ed. Edmond Lemaître. Paris: Editions du Centre National de la Recherche Scientifique, 1987.

Châteauneuf, François de. *Dialogue sur la musique des anciens*. Paris: Noël Pissot, 1725.

Chaumont, Chevalier de. *Véritable construction d'un théâtre d'opéra à l'usage de la France*. Paris: De Lormel, 1766.

Christensen, Thomas. *Rameau and Musical Thought in the Enlightenment*. Cambridge: Cambridge University Press, 1993.

Christout, Marie-Françoise. *Le Ballet de cour de Louis XIV: 1643–1672*. Paris: A. et J. Picard, 1967.

Clément, Catherine. "Au-delà des roches couleur de nuit." *L'Avant-scène Opéra* 68 (1984; 1993): 34–38.

Opera, or the Undoing of Women. Trans. Betsy Wing. Minneapolis: University of Minnesota Press, 1988.

Clément, Jean Marie Bernard, and Joseph de Laporte. *Anecdotes dramatiques*. 3 vols. Paris: Veuve Duchesne, 1775.

Cochin, Charles-Nicolas. *Lettres sur l'opéra*. Paris: L. Cellot, 1781.

Coeyman, Barbara. "Theatres for opera and ballet during the reigns of Louis XIV and Louis XV." *Early Music* 18.1 (1990): 22–37.

"Walking Through Lully's Opera Theatre in the Palais Royal." In John Hajdu Heyer, ed., *Lully Studies*. Cambridge: Cambridge University Press, 2000. 216–42.

Cohen, Albert. "*La Supposition* or the Changing Concepts of Dissonance in Baroque Theory." *Journal of the American Musicological Society* 24 (1971): 63–85.

Cohen, Sarah R. *Art, Dance, and the Body in French Culture of the Ancien Régime*. Cambridge: Cambridge University Press, 2000.

Colbert: 1619–1683. Paris: [Hôtel de la Monnaie], 1983.

Collé, Charles. *Journal et mémoires*. 3 vols. Paris: Firmin Didot Frères, 1868.

Condillac, Étienne de. *Oeuvres complètes*. 16 vols. 1821–22. Geneva: Slatkine, 1970.

Cone, Edward T. *The Composer's Voice*. Berkeley, Los Angeles, London: University of California Press, 1974.

Corneille, Pierre. *Oeuvres*. 12 vols. Paris: Antoine-Augustin Renouard, 1817.

Médée. Ed. André de Leyssac. Geneva: Droz, 1978.

Oeuvres complètes. Ed. Georges Couton. 3 vols. Paris: Gallimard, 1980–87.

Corneille, Thomas. *Médée*. Paris: Christophe Ballard, 1693.

Cornette, Joël. *Le Roi de guerre: essai sur la souveraineté dans la France du Grand Siècle.* Paris: Payot, 1993.

Cotin, Charles. *Réflexions sur la conduite du roy.* Paris: Pierre Le Petit, 1663.

Couvreur, Manuel. *Jean-Baptiste Lully: musique et dramaturgie au service du prince.* [Brussels]: Marc Vokar, 1992.

Couvreur, Manuel and Philippe Vendrix. "Les Enjeux théoriques de l'Opéra-Comique." In Philippe Vendrix, ed., *L'Opéra-Comique en France au XVIIIe siècle.* Liège: Mardaga, 1992. 213–81.

Coypeau d'Assoucy, Charles. *Poësies et lettres.* Paris: Jean Baptiste Loyson, 1653.

Cucuel, Georges. *Les Créateurs de l'Opéra-Comique français.* Paris: Félix Alcan, 1914.

Dacier, André. *La Poëtique d'Aristote.* Paris: Claude Barbin, 1692.

Dacier, Anne. *Causes de la corruption du goust.* Paris: Rigaud, 1714.

Darnton, Robert. "Paris: the Early Internet." *The New York Review of Books* 47.11 (June 29, 2000): 42–47.

DeJean, Joan. *Tender Geographies: Women and the Origins of the Novel in France.* New York: Columbia University Press, 1991.

Ancients Against Moderns: Culture Wars and the Making of a Fin de Siècle. Chicago: University of Chicago Press, 1997.

Descartes, René. *Abrégé de musique / Compendium musicae.* Ed. and trans. Frédéric de Buzon. Paris: Presses universitaires de France, 1987.

Les Passions de l'âme. Paris: Gallimard, 1988.

Desfontaines, Pierre François Guyot. *Observations sur les écrits modernes.* 4 vols. Geneva: Slatkine, 1967.

Dictionnaire de l'Académie française. Book on line Paris: chez la veuve de Jean Baptiste Coignard, 1694. Accessed May 25, 2001. http://www.lib.uchicago.edu/efts/ARTFL/projects/dicos/ACADEMIE/PREMIERE/premiere.html

Diderot, Denis. *Jacques the Fatalist and His Master.* Trans. J. Robert Loy. New York: New York University Press, 1959.

Oeuvres complètes. Ed. Roger Lewinter. 15 vols. Paris: Club Français du Livre, 1969–73.

Oeuvres complètes. Ed Jean Varloot. 25 vols. Paris: Hermann, 1975–86.

Dill, Charles. "Rameau reading Lully: Meaning and system in Rameau's recitative tradition." *Cambridge Opera Journal* 6.1 (1994): 1–17.

Monstrous Opera: Rameau and the Tragic Tradition. Princeton: Princeton University Press, 1998.

Doubrovsky, Serge. *Corneille et la dialectique du héros.* Paris: Gallimard, 1963.

Dreyfus, Hubert L. *Being-in-the-World.* Cambridge, Mass.: MIT Press, 1991.

Dubos, Jean-Baptiste. *Réflexions critiques sur la poésie et sur la peinture.* Paris: École nationale supérieure des Beaux-Arts, 1993.

Dumont, Gabriel Pierre Martin. *Parallèle de plans des plus belles salles de spectacle d'Italie et de France.* Paris: rue des Arcis, 1774.

Duro, Paul. *The Academy and the Limits of Painting in Seventeenth-Century France.* Cambridge: Cambridge University Press, 1997.

Duron, Jean. "Commentaire littéraire et musical." *L'Avant-scène Opéra* 68 (1984; 1993): 59–97.

"Atys, 'opéra du Roi.'" *L'Avant-scène opéra* 94 (1987): 20–21.

"Commentaire musical et littéraire." *L'Avant-scène Opéra* 94 (1987): 32–80.

Encyclopédie ou dictionnaire raisonné des arts et des métiers. Ed. Denis Diderot and Jean le Rond d'Alembert. 28 vols. 1751–72. Elmsford, N.Y.: Pergamon, n.d.

Euripides. *Cyclops, Alcestis, Medea.* Ed. and trans. David Kovacs. Cambridge, Mass.: Harvard University Press, 1994.

Félibien, André. *Les Fêtes de Versailles: chroniques de 1668 & 1674.* Paris: Dédale, 1994.

Ferguson, Frances. *Solitude and the Sublime.* New York: Routledge, 1992.

"A Reply to Tzvetan Todorov's 'Living Alone Together.'" *New Literary History* 27 (1996): 25–34.

Ferrier-Caverivière, Nicole. *L'Image de Louis XIV dans la littérature française de 1660 à 1715.* Paris: Presses universitaires de France, 1981.

Ferry, Luc. *Homo aestheticus: l'invention du goût à l'âge démocratique.* Paris: Grasset, 1990.

Ficino, Marsilio. *Three Books on Life.* Ed. and trans. Carol V. Kaske and John R. Clark. Binghamton, N.Y.: Medieval & Renaissance Texts & Studies, 1989.

Fontenelle, Bernard le Bovier de. *Entretiens sur la pluralité des mondes.* Paris: M. Guerout, 1687.

Oeuvres complètes. 3 vols. 1818. Geneva: Slatkine, 1968.

Force, Pierre. "Self-Love, Identification, and the Origin of Political Economy." *Yale French Studies* 92 (1997): 46–64.

Foucault, Michel. *The Order of Things: An Archaeology of the Human Sciences*. New York: Pantheon, 1970.

Franko, Mark. *Dance as Text: Ideologies of the Baroque Body*. Cambridge: Cambridge University Press, 1993.

Freeman, Barbara Claire. *The Feminine Sublime: Gender and Excess in Women's Fiction*. Berkeley: University of California Press, 1995.

Freud, Sigmund. *The Standard Edition of the Complete Psychological Works*. Ed. and trans. James Strachey. 24 vols. London: The Hogarth Press, 1953–74.

Fried, Michael. *Absorption and Theatricality: Painting and Beholder in the Age of Diderot*. Berkeley: University of California Press, 1980.

Fulcher, Jane F. *The Nation's Image: French Grand Opera as Politics and Politicized Art*. Cambridge: Cambridge University Press, 1987.

Fumaroli, Marc. "Microcosme comique et macrocosme solaire: Molière, Louis XIV, et *L'Impromptu de Versailles*." *Revue des sciences humaines*, 37.145 (1972): 95–114.

Héros et orateurs. Geneva: Droz, 1990.

Furetière, Antoine. *Recueil des factums*. 2 vols. Paris: Poulet-Malassic et De Broise, 1859.

Furniss, Tom. *Edmund Burke's Aesthetic Ideology: Language, Gender, and Political Economy in Revolution*. Cambridge: Cambridge University Press, 1993.

Fuss, Diana. *Identification Papers*. New York and London: Routledge, 1995.

Gaffurio, Franchino. *Practica musicae*. Ed. and trans. Irwin Young. Madison, Milwaukee, and London: University of Wisconsin Press, 1969.

Garcin, Laurent. *Traité du mélo-drame, ou réflexions sur la musique dramatique*. Paris: Vallat-la-Chapelle, 1772.

Gareau, Michel. *Charles Le Brun: First Painter to King Louis XIV*. New York: Harry N. Abrams, 1992.

Genette, Gérard. *L'Oeuvre de l'art*. Vol. ii, *La relation esthétique*. Paris: Seuil, 1997.

Gethner, Perry. "La 'Morale Lubrique' dans les opéras de Quinault." In *Les Visages de l'amour au XVIIe siècle*. Toulouse: Université de Toulouse-Le Mirail, 1984. 145–54.

"On the Use of Music and Dance in the Machine Tragedies." *Papers on French Seventeenth-Century Literature* 15.29 (1988): 463–76.

"Staging and Spectacle in the Machine Tragedies." In David Trott and Nicole Boursier, eds., *L'Age du théâtre en France / The Age of Theatre in France*. Edmonton: Academic Printing & Publishing, 1988. 231–246.

"Comedy-Ballet and Court Festivities: Three Extreme Scenarios." *Cahiers du dix-septième* 3.1 (1989): 207–23.

"La Magicienne à l'opéra, source de subversion." In Roger Duchêne and Pierre Ronzeaud, eds., *Ordre et contestation au temps des classiques*. *Papers on French Seventeenth-Century Literature* 73 (1992): 301–07.

"La Mémoire agent de consécration et génératrice du spectacle." In Volker Kapp, ed., *Les Lieux de mémoire et la fabrique de l'oeuvre*. *Papers on French Seventeenth-Century Literature* 80 (1993): 297–305.

Girdlestone, Cuthbert. *Jean-Philippe Rameau*. 1957. New York: Dover, 1969.

La Tragédie en Musique (1673–1750) considérée comme genre littéraire. Geneva: Droz, 1972.

Gluck, Christoph Willibald. *Sämtliche Werke*. Ed. Rudolf Gerber. Kassel: Bärenreiter, 1951–   .

Sämtliche Werke. Series I, vol. IX, *Iphigénie en Tauride*. Ed. Gerhard Croll. Kassel: Bärenreiter, 1973.

Golub, Maria Majno. "Diderot et l'opéra-comique: absolution du burlesque, réussite du pathétique." In *Diderot: les beaux-arts et la musique*. Aix: Université de Provence, 1986. 261–75.

Goodman, Dena. *The Republic of Letters: a Cultural History of the French Enlightenment*. Ithaca and London: Cornell University Press, 1994.

Gordon, Daniel. *Citizens Without Sovereignty: Equality and Sociability in French Thought, 1670–1789*. Princeton: Princeton University Press, 1994.

Gouk, Penelope. "Music, Melancholy, and Medical Spirits in Early Modern Thought." In Peregrine Horden, ed., *Music as Medicine: The History of Music Therapy since Antiquity*. Aldershot: Ashgate, 2000. 173–94.

Goux, Jean-Joseph. "The Eclipse of Art?" *Thesis Eleven* 44 (1996): 57–68.

Greenberg, Mitchell. *Subjectivity and Subjugation in Seventeenth-Century Drama and Prose*. Cambridge: Cambridge University Press, 1992.

Grétry, André-Ernest-Modeste. *Mémoires ou essais sur la musique*. 2 vols. 1797. New York: Da Capo, 1971.

Grétry, André-Ernest-Modeste and Thomas d'Hèle. *L'Amant jaloux, comédie en trois actes*. Paris: M. Houbaut, 1779.

Grétry, André-Ernest-Modeste and Jean-François Marmontel. *Zémire et Azor, comédie-ballet en vers et en quatre actes*. Paris: Chez Houbaut, 1772.

La Fausse magie, comédie en un acte. Paris: M. Houbaut, 1775.

Grimarest, Jean Léonor le Gallois. *Traité du récitatif*. 1760. New York: AMS Press, 1978.

Grimm, Friedrich Melchior Freiherr von. *Correspondance littéraire, philoso-phique et critique*. 16 vols. Paris: Garnier Frères, 1877–82.

Grimod de la Reyniére, Alexandre-Balthazar-Laurent. *Le Censeur dramatique, ou Journal des principaux théâtres de Paris et des départements*. 4 vols. 1797–98. Geneva: Minkoff, 1973.

Gros, Etienne. *Philippe Quinault: sa vie et son oeuvre*. Paris: Champion, 1926.

Grover-Friedlander, Michal. "Voicing Death in Opera." *Common Knowledge* 5.2 (Fall, 1996): 136–144.

Gwilliam, Tassie. *Samuel Richardson's Fictions of Gender*. Stanford: Stanford University Press, 1993.

Habermas, Jürgen. *The Structural Transformation of the Public Sphere*. Trans. Thomas Burger. Cambridge, Mass.: MIT Press, 1989.

   "Further Reflections on the Public Sphere." In Craig Calhoun, ed., *Habermas and the Public Sphere*. Cambridge, Mass.: MIT Press, 1992. 421–61.

Haeringer, Etienne. *L'Esthétique de l'opéra en France au temps de Jean-Philippe Rameau*. Oxford: Voltaire Foundation, 1990.

Hanning, Barbara Russano. *Of Poetry and Music's Power: Humanism and the Creation of Opera*. 1969. Ann Arbor: UMI Research Press, 1980.

Hegel, G. W. *Lectures on Fine Art*. Trans. T. M. Knox. Oxford: Clarendon Press, 1975.

Helvétius. *De l'esprit*. Verviers, Belgium: Gérard, 1973.

Herzel, Roger W. "Racine, Laurent, and the *Palais à Volonté*." *PMLA* 108.5 (1993): 1064–82.

Himelfarb, Hélène. "Un domaine méconnu de l'empire lullyste: le Trianon de Louis XIV, ses tableaux et les livrets d'opéras (1687–1714)." In Jérôme de La Gorce and Herbert Schneider, eds., *Jean-Baptiste Lully: Actes du colloque Saint-Germain-en-Laye–Heidelberg 1987*. Laaber: Laaber-Verlag, 1990. 287–306.

Himmelsbach, Siegbert. *L'épopée ou la 'case vide': La réflexion poétologique sur l'épopée nationale en France*. Tübingen: Max Niemeyer, 1988.

Hitchcock, Wiley. *Marc-Antoine Charpentier*. Oxford: Oxford University Press, 1990.

Hobson, Marian. *The Object of Art*. Cambridge: Cambridge University Press, 1982.

Hoole, John. *Cyrus: A Tragedy*. London: T. Davies, 1768.

Horden, Peregrine, ed. *Music as Medicine: The History of Music Therapy since Antiquity*. Aldershot: Ashgate, 2000.

Houdar de la Motte, Antoine. *Reflexions sur la Critique*. Paris: G. Dupuis, 1716.

Howard, Patricia. "The Positioning of Woman in Quinault's World Picture." In Jérôme de La Gorce and Herbert Schneider, eds., *Jean-Baptiste Lully: Actes du colloque Saint-Germain-en-Laye–Heidelberg 1987*. Laaber: Laaber-Verlag, 1990. 193–99.

Howarth, William D., ed. *French Theatre in the Neo-Classical Era, 1550–1789*. Cambridge: Cambridge University Press, 1997.

Hunter, Mary. *The Culture of Opera Buffa in Mozart's Vienna: A Poetics of Entertainment*. Princeton: Princeton University Press, 1999.

Hutcheon, Linda and Michael Hutcheon. "'Here's Lookin'at You, Kid': The Empowering Gaze in *Salome*," *Profession* (1998): 11–22.

Hutcheson, Francis. *An Inquiry Concerning Beauty, Order, Harmony, Design*. Ed. Peter Kivy. The Hague: Martinus Nijhoff, 1973.

Isherwood, Robert. *Music in the Service of the King*. Ithaca and London: Cornell University Press, 1973.

 Farce and Fantasy: Popular Entertainment in Eighteenth-Century Paris. New York and Oxford: Oxford University Press, 1986.

Jamain, Claude. "L'Imaginaire de la musique au siècle des Lumières." Ph.D. dissertation, Université François Rabelais, Tours, 1996.

Johnson, James H. *Listening in Paris: A Cultural History*. Berkeley, Los Angeles, London: University of California Press, 1995.

Jones, Chris. *Radical Sensibility: Literature and Ideas in the 1790s*. London and New York: Routledge, 1993.

Journal de musique théorique, pratique, dramatique ct instrumentale.

Journal de Trévoux.

Kant, Immanuel. *Critique of Judgment*. Trans. Werner S. Pluhar. Indianapolis: Hackett, 1987.

Kantorowicz, Ernst H. *The King's Two Bodies: A Study in Mediaeval Political Theology*. Princeton: Princeton University Press, 1957.

Kapp, Volker. "Thomas Corneille librettiste." In Jean-Paul Capdevielle and Peter-Eckhard Knabe, eds., *Les Écrivains français et l'opéra*. Cologne: dme-Verlag, 1986. 49–59.

Karro, Françoise. "Le prologue d'*Armide*." In Jean-Paul Capdevielle and Peter-Eckhard Knabe, eds., *Les Écrivains français et l'opéra*. Cologne: dme-Verlag, 1986. 39–47.

Kavanagh, Thomas. *The Esthetics of the Moment*. Philadelphia: University of Pennsylvania Press, 1996.

Kintzler, Catherine. *Poétique de l'opéra français de Corneille à Rousseau*. Paris: Minèrve, 1991.

"L'opéra français, hyper-théâtre et hypo-théâtre." *Les Papiers du Collège International de Philosophie* 16 (1992): 21–28.

"La Préface d'*Hippolyte et Aricie* ou la critique de *Phèdre*." In *Hippolyte et Aricie*, opera program. Paris: Opéra National de Paris, 1996. 67–73.

Kivy, Peter. *Osmin's Rage: Philosophical Reflections on Opera, Drama, and Text*. Princeton: Princeton University Press, 1988.

Knapp, Steven. *Literary Interest: the Limits of Anti-Formalism*. Cambridge, Mass.: Harvard University Press, 1993.

Koestenbaum, Wayne. *The Queen's Throat: Opera, Homosexuality, and the Mystery of Desire*. New York: Poseidon, 1993.

Kramer, Lawrence. *Classical Music and Postmodern Knowledge*. Berkeley and Los Angeles: University of California Press, 1995.

Kristeva, Julia. *Histoires d'amour*. Paris: Denoël, 1983.

La Bruyère, Jean de. *Oeuvres complètes*. Paris: Gallimard, 1951.

Lacan, Jacques. *Le Séminaire XX: Encore*. Paris: Seuil, 1975.

Écrits: a Selection. Trans. Alan Sheridan. New York: Norton, 1977.

Lacépède, Bernard Germain Etienne Médard de la Ville-sur-Illon, comte de. *La Poétique de la musique*. 2 vols. Paris: l'imprimerie de Monsieur, 1785.

Lacoue-Labarthe, Philippe. *Le Sujet de la philosophie*. Paris: Aubier-Flammarion, 1979.

Musica ficta (figures de Wagner). Paris: Christian Bourgois, 1991.

Musica Ficta (Figures of Wagner). Trans. Felicia McCarren. Stanford: Stanford University Press, 1994.

La Fontaine, Jean de. *Oeuvres complètes*. Ed. René Groos, Jacques Schiffrin and Pierre Clarac. 2 vols. Paris: Gallimard, 1954–58.

Oeuvres diverses. Ed. Pierre Clarac. Paris: Gallimard, 1958.

La Gorce, Jérôme de. *Berain: dessinateur du roi soleil*. Paris: Herscher, 1986.

Lagrave, Henri. *Le Théâtre et son public à Paris de 1715 à 1750*. Paris: Klincksiek, 1972.

La Harpe, Jean-François. *Lycée, ou cours de littérature ancienne et moderne*. 16 tomes in 19 vols. Paris: H. Agasse, 1799–1805.

Laisemont, Denis Ballière de. *Théorie de la musique*. Paris: Didot le jeune, 1764.

Lallemant, Jean-Baptiste-Joseph. *Essai sur le méchanisme des passions en général*. Paris: Le Prieur, 1751.

La Mesnardière, H.-J. Pilet de. *La Poëtique*. 1640. Geneva: Slatkine, 1972.

Lanson, Gustave. "Notice." In Jean Racine, *Théâtre choisi*. Paris: Hachette, 1896.
    Histoire de la littérature française. 2 vols. Paris: Hachette, 1951.

Laplanche, Jean and J.-B. Pontalis. *The Language of Psycho-Analysis*. Trans.
    Donald Nicholson-Smith. New York: W. W. Norton, 1973.

La Rochefoucauld, François VI, duc de. *Maximes*. Ed. Jacques Truchet. Paris:
    Garnier Frères, 1967.

Lawrenson, Tom. "The Ideal Theatre in the Eighteenth Century: Paris and
    Venice." In *Drama and Mimesis*. Cambridge: Cambridge University Press,
    1980.

LeBrun, Antoine-Louis. *Théâtre lyrique*. Paris: Pierre Ribou, 1712.

Le Caron, Louis. *Dialogues*. Ed. Joan A. Buhlmann and Donald Gilman.
    Geneva: Droz, 1986.

Le Cat, Claude-Nicolas. *Traité des sens*. Amsterdam: J. Wetstein, 1744.
    *Traité de l'existence, de la nature et des propriétés du fluide des nerfs, et princi-
    palement de son action dans le mouvement musculaire*. Berlin: n.p., 1765.

Le Cerf de la Viéville, Jean Laurent, sieur de Freneuse. *Comparaison de la
    musique italienne et de la musique françoise*. 2nd ed., 3 tomes in 1 vol. Brussels:
    François Foppens, 1705.

Ledoux, Claude-Nicolas. *L'Architecture considérée sous le rapport de l'art, des
    moeurs et de la legislation*. 2 vols. Paris: chez l'auteur, 1804.

Leibniz, Gottfried Wilhelm. *Philosophical Papers and Letters*. Ed. and trans.
    Leroy E. Loemker. 2 vols. Chicago: University of Chicago Press,
    1956.

Léoni, Sylviane. *Le Poison et le remède: théâtre, morale et rhétorique en France et
    en Italie, 1694–1758*. Oxford: Voltaire Foundation, 1998.

Léris, Antoine de. *Dictionnaire portatif historique et littéraire des théâtres*. 2nd ed.
    Paris: C. A. Jombert, 1763.

Le Sage, Alain René and d'Orneval. *Le Théâtre de la foire ou l'Opéra comique*.
    10 tomes in 2 vols. 1737. Geneva: Slatkine, 1968.

Lippman, Edward. *A History of Western Musical Aesthetics*. Lincoln, Nebr. and
    London: University of Nebraska Press, 1992.

Longinus. *Du Sublime*. Trans. Jackie Pigeaud. Paris: Rivages, 1991.
    On the Sublime. Trans. W. Hamilton Fyfe. 1927. Cambridge, Mass.: Harvard
    University Press, 1982.

Louis XIV. *Mémoires pour l'instruction du dauphin*. 2 vols. Paris: Didier, 1860.

Lully, Jean-Baptiste and Philippe Quinault. *Armide: tragédie en musique*. Paris:
    Ballard, 1686.

Lyons, John D. "The Decorum of Horror: A Reading of La Mesnardière's *Poëtique*." In Sylvie Romanowski and Monique Bilezikian, eds., *Homage to Paul Bénichou*. Birmingham, Ala.: Summa, 1994. 27–41.

"The Barbarous Ancients: French Classical Poetics and the Attack on Ancient Tragedy." *MLN* 110.5 (1995): 1135–47.

Mably, Gabriel Bonnot, abbé de. *Lettres à Madame la Marquise de P . . . sur l'opéra*. Paris: Didot, 1741.

Marin, Louis. "Le Sublime dans les années 1670: un je ne sais quoi?" In Selma A. Zebouni, ed., *Actes de Baton Rouge. Papers in French Seventeenth-Century Literature* 25 (1986): 185–201.

Portrait of the King. Trans. Martha Houle. Minneapolis: University of Minnesota Press, 1988.

Marmontel, Jean-François. *Poétique françoise*. 2 vols. Paris: Lesclapart, 1763.

Oeuvres complètes. 8 vols. Paris: A. Belin, 1819.

Mémoires. Ed. John Renwick. 2 vols. Clermont-Ferrand: G. de Bussac, 1972.

Marshall, David. *The Surprising Effects of Sympathy*. Chicago: University of Chicago Press, 1988.

Massé, Jean-Baptiste. *La Grande galerie de Versailles, et les deux salons qui l'accompagnent*. Paris: chez la Veuve Amaulry, 1753.

Masson, Paul-Marie. *L'Opéra de Rameau*. Paris: Henri Laurens, 1930.

Maynard, François. *Les Oeuvres de Maynard*. Paris: Augustin Courbe, 1646.

Mazouer, Charles. *Molière et ses comédies-ballets*. Paris: Klincksieck, 1993.

McCall, Tom. "Liquid Politics: Towards a Theorization of 'Bourgeois' Tragic Drama." *The South Atlantic Quarterly* 98.3 (Summer 1999): 593–622.

McDonald, William E. "What Does Wotan Know? Autobiography and Moral Vision in Wagner's *Ring*." *19th-Century Music* 15.1 (1991): 36–51.

McGowan, Margaret. *L'Art du ballet de cour en France, 1581–1643*. Paris: Centre National de la Recherche Scientifique, 1963.

McIntyre, Bruce. "*Armide* ou le monologue féminin." *Australian Journal of French Studies* 36.2 (1999): 157–72.

Ménestrier, Claude-François de. *Des représentations en musique anciennes et modernes*. Paris: René Guignard, 1681.

Mercure de France.

Le Mercure galant.

Mérot, Alain. *French Painting in the Seventeenth Century*. Trans. Caroline Beamish. New Haven: Yale University Press, 1995.

Mersenne, Marin. *Harmonie universelle*. Ed. François Lesure. 3 vols. 1636. Paris: Éditions du Centre National de la Recherche Scientifique, 1963.

Metastasio, Pietro. *Opere drammatiche*. 4 vols. Venice: G. Bettinelli, 1733–37. *Tragédies-opéra*. Trans. César Pierre Richelet. 5 vols. Vienna: n.p., 1751.

Meyer, Daniel. *L'Histoire du Roy*. Paris: Éditions de la Réunion des Musées Nationaux, 1980.

Molière. *Oeuvres complètes*. Ed. Georges Couton. 2 vols. Paris: Gallimard, 1971.

Montagu, Jennifer. *The Expression of the Passions: the Origin and Influence of Charles Le Brun's Conférence sur l'expression générale et particulière*. New Haven: Yale University Press, 1994.

Montclos, Jean-Marie Pérouse de. *Histoire de l'architecture française*. N.p.: Mengès, 1989.

Montesquieu, Charles Louis de Secondat, baron de la Brède et de. *Oeuvres complètes*. Ed. Roger Caillois. 2 vols. Paris: Gallimard, 1949–51.

Morel, Jacques. *Agréables mensonges: essais sur le théâtre français du XVIIe siècle*. Paris: Klincksieck, 1991.

Nancy, Jean-Luc. *The Muses*. Trans. Peggy Kamuf. Stanford: Stanford University Press, 1996.

Néraudau, Jean-Pierre. *L'Olympe du roi-soleil: mythologie et idéologie royale au Grand Siècle*. Paris: Les Belles Lettres, 1986.

"Du Christ à Apollon: les chemins d'une mythologie de la cour." In *La Tragédie lyrique*. Paris: Cicero, 1991. 5–21.

Neubauer, John. *The Emancipation of Music from Language: Departure from Mimesis in Eighteenth-Century Aesthetics*. New Haven and London: Yale University Press, 1986.

Noiray, Michel. "*Hippolyte* et *Castor* travestis: Rameau à l'opéra-comique." In Jérôme de La Gorce, ed., *Jean-Philippe Rameau: Colloque international*. Paris and Geneva: Champion-Slatkine, 1987.

Norman, Buford. "Le Héros contestataire dans les livrets de Quinault: politique ou esthétique." In Roger Duchêne et Pierre Ronzeaud, eds., *Ordre et contestation au temps des classiques*. *Papers on French Seventeenth-Century Literature* 73 (1992): 289–300.

"'Le Théâtre est un grand monument': l'évocation du passé et des passions dans l'*Alceste* de Quinault." In Volker Kapp, ed., *Les lieux de mémoire et la fabrique de l'oeuvre*. *Papers on French Seventeenth-Century Literature* 80 (1993): 321–29.

"Remaking a Cultural Icon: *Phédre* and the Operatic Stage." *Cambridge Opera Journal* 10.3 (1998): 225–45.

Norris, Christopher. *Paul de Man*. New York: Routledge, 1988.

Nougaret, Pierre Jean Baptiste. *De l'art du théâtre*. 2 vols. Paris: Chez Cailleau, 1769.

O'Neal, John C. *The Authority of Experience: Sensationist Theory in the French Enlightenment*. University Park, Pa.: The Pennsylvania State University Press, 1996.

Orville, Contant d'. *Histoire de l'opéra bouffon*. 2 tomes in 1 vol. 1768. Geneva: Slatkine, 1970.

Ovid. *Fasti: Roman Holidays*. Trans. Betty Rose Nagle. Bloomington and Indianapolis: Indiana University Press, 1995.

Palisca, Claude V. *Humanism in Italian Renaissance Musical Thought*. New Haven and London: Yale University Press, 1985.

Parfaict, François and Claude Parfaict. "Histoire de l'Académie Royale de Musique depuis son établissement jusqu'au present." 2 vols. Nouv. Acq. Fr. 6532, Bibliothèque Nationale de France, Paris.

Pascal, Blaise. *Pensées*. Paris: Garnier, 1964.

Patte, Pierre. *Essai sur l'architecture théâtrale*. Paris: Moutard, 1782.

Pavel, Thomas. "L'Esthétique, le Romantisme et la démocratie." *Littérature* 89 (1993): 98–112.

Pellisson-Fontanier, Paul. *Oeuvres diverses*. 3 tomes in 1 vol. 1735. Geneva: Slatkine, 1971.

Pendle, Karin. "The Opéras Comiques of Grétry and Marmontel." *The Musical Quarterly* 62.5 (1976): 409–34.

"L'Opéra-comique à Paris de 1762 à 1789." In Philippe Vendrix, ed., *L'Opéra-comique en France au XVIIIe siècle*. Liège: Mardaga, 1992. 79–177.

Perrault, Charles. *Critique de l'opéra*. Paris: Louis Billaine, 1674.

Parallèle des anciens et des modernes en ce qui regarde les arts et les sciences. 4 tomes in 1 vol. 1688–97. Munich: Eidos Verlag, 1964.

Philidor, François-André Danican and Antoine Alexandre Henri Poinsinet. *Tom Jones, comédie lyrique en trois actes*. Paris: chez M. de la Chevardiere, 1766.

Picard, Raymond. *La carrière de Jean Racine*. Paris: Gallimard, 1961.

Pixérécourt, René Charles G. *Théâtre choisi*. 4 vols. Paris: Tresse, 1841–43.

Poinsinet, Antoine Alexandre Henri. *Tom Jones*. Paris: Duchesne, 1765.

Tom Jones. Paris: chez la veuve Duchesne, 1771.

Poizat, Michel. *The Angel's Cry: Beyond the Pleasure Principle in Opera.* Trans. Arthur Denner. Ithaca: Cornell University Press, 1992.

Pot, Olivier. "Phèdre ou le suicide de la tragédie." *Travaux de littérature* 6 (1993): 159–72.

Pougnaud, Pierre. *Théâtres: 4 siècles d'architectures et d'histoire.* Paris: Éditions du Moniteur, 1980.

Prunières, Henry. *L'Opéra italien en France avant Lulli.* Paris: Champion, 1913.

Quignard, Pascal. *Rhétorique speculative.* Paris: Calmann-Lévy, 1995.

La Haine de la musique. Paris: Calmann-Lévy, 1996.

Quinault, Philippe. *Théâtre contenant ses tragédies, comédies et opéra.* 5 tomes in 1 vol. 1778. Geneva: Slatkine, 1970.

Atys. Ed. Stéphane Bassinet. Geneva: Droz, 1992.

Alceste. Ed. William Brooks, Buford Norman and Jeanne Morgan Zarucchi. Geneva: Droz, 1994.

Livrets d'opéra. Ed. Buford Norman. 2 vols. Toulouse: Société de littératures classiques, 1999.

Racine, Jean. *Oeuvres complètes.* 2 vols. Ed. Raymond Picard. Paris: Gallimard, 1950–52.

Phaedra. Trans. Richard Wilbur. San Diego, New York, London: Harcourt Brace Jovanovich, 1986.

Théâtre complet. Ed. Jacques Morel and Alain Viala. Paris: Dunod, 1995.

Radicchio, Giuseppe and Michèle Sajous D'Oria. *Les Théâtres de Paris pendant la Révolution.* Trans. Laura Casati and Françoise Lenoir. Paris: Bibliothèque Historique de la Ville de Paris, 1990.

Rameau, Jean-Philippe. *Oeuvres complètes.* Ed. C. Saint-Saëns et al. 18 vols. 1895–1924. New York: Broude Bros., [1968].

Complete Theoretical Writings. Ed. Erwin R. Jacobi. 6 vols. N.p.: American Institute of Musicology, 1967–72.

Rapin, René. *Les Réflexions sur la poétique de ce temps et sur les ouvrages des poètes anciens et modernes.* Ed. E. T. Dubois. Geneva: Droz, 1970.

Ravel, Jeffrey S. "Seating the Public: Spheres and Loathing in the Paris Theaters, 1777–1788." *French Historical Studies* 18 (Spring 1993): 173–210.

The Contested Parterre: Public Theater and French Political Culture, 1680–1791. Ithaca and London: Cornell University Press, 1999.

Rebejkow, Jean-Christophe. "Diderot et l'opéra-comique: de la farce au pathétique." *Romanische Forschungen* 107.1–2 (1995): 145–56.

Reiss, Timothy J. *Knowledge, Discovery and Imagination in Early Modern Europe.* Cambridge: Cambridge University Press, 1997.

[Renaudot, Théophraste.] *Gazette.* L'Impression de Lyon.

Renken, Alice Brin. "Marin Marais's *Alcione*: An Edition with Commentary." Ph.D. dissertation, Washington University, 1981.

Rétif de la Bretonne, Nicolas Edme. *La Mimographe, ou Idées d'une honnête-femme pour la réformation du théâtre national.* Amsterdam: Changuion/ The Hague: Gosse & Pinet, 1770.

Reynier, Gustave. *Thomas Corneille, sa vie et son théâtre.* 1892. Geneva: Slatkine, 1970.

Rieux, Serré de. *La Musique.* 1714. The Hague: Abraham Henry, 1737.

Robinet, Charles and Jacques Laurent. *Le Théâtre et l'opéra vus par les gazetiers Robinet et Laurent.* Ed. William Brooks. *Papers on French Seventeenth-Century Literature* 78 (1993).

Robinson, Michael F. "*Opera buffa* into *opéra comique*, 1771–90." In Malcolm Boyd, ed., *Music and the French Revolution.* Cambridge: Cambridge University Press, 1992. 37–56.

Roger, Joseph-Louis. *Traité des effets de la musique sur le corps humain.* Ed. and trans. Etienne Sainte-Marie. Paris: Brunot; Lyon: Reymann and J. Roger, an XI [1803].

Rosand, Ellen. *Opera in Seventeenth-Century Venice.* Berkeley and Los Angeles: University of California Press, 1991.

Rosow, Lois. "How eighteenth-century Parisians heard Lully's operas: the case of *Armide*'s fourth act." In John Hajdu Heyer, ed., *Jean-Baptiste Lully and the Music of the French Baroque: Essays in Honor of James R. Anthony.* Cambridge: Cambridge University Press, 1989. 213–37.

"The Articulation of Lully's Dramatic Dialogue." In John Hajdu Heyer, ed., *Lully Studies.* Cambridge: Cambridge University Press, 2000. 72–99.

Rossi, Luigi. *Orfeo.* Ed. Clifford Bartlett. 3 vols. Redcroft, Bank's End, Wyton, Huntingdon: King's Music, [1997].

Roubo, André. *Traité de la construction des théâtres et des machines théâtrales.* Paris: Cellot & Jombert fils jeune, 1777.

Rougemont, Martine de. *La Vie théâtrale en France au XVIIIe siècle.* Paris and Geneva: Champion-Slatkine, 1988.

Rouget, Gilbert. *La Musique et la transe.* 1980. Paris: Gallimard, 1990.

Rousseau, Jean-Jacques. *Oeuvres complètes.* Ed. Bernard Gagnebin and Marcel Raymond. 5 vols. Paris: Gallimard, 1959–95.

Basic Political Writings. Trans. Donald A. Cress. Indianapolis: Hackett, 1987.

Le Devin du village. Ed. Charlotte Kaufman. Madison: A-R Editions, 1998.

Roy, Pierre-Charles. *Lettre sur l'opéra*. In Élie Catherine Fréron, *Lettres sur quelques écrits de ce temps*. 2 vols. 1752. Geneva: Slatkine, 1966.

Rozoi, Barnabé Farmian de. *Dissertation sur le drame lyrique*. The Hague and Paris: Veuve Duchesne, 1775.

Russo, Elena. "The Self, Real and Imaginary: Social Sentiment in Marivaux and Hume." *Yale French Studies* 92 (1997): 126–48.

Russo, Paolo. "'L'Isola di Alcina: Funzioni drammaturgiche del 'divertisse-ment' nella 'tragédie lyrique' (1699–1735)." *Nuova rivista musicale italiana* 21.1 (1987): 1–16.

Sadie, Stanley, ed. *The New Grove Dictionary of Opera*. 1992. London: Macmillan, 1997.

Sadler, Graham. "Rameau, Pellegrin and the Opera: the revisions of *Hippolyte et Aricie* during its first season." *Musical Times* 124.1687 (1983): 533–37.

"Un Débutant timide?" In *Hippolyte et Aricie*, opera program. Paris: Opéra National de Paris, 1996. 33–36.

Saint-Évremond, Charles de Marguetel de Saint-Denis, seigneur de. *Les Opéra*. Geneva: Droz, 1979.

"Sur les opera." In François Lesure, ed., *Textes sur Lully et l'opéra français*. Geneva: Minkoff, 1987. 77–119.

Saint-Mard, Rémond de. *Réflexions sur l'opéra*. 1741. Geneva: Minkoff, 1972.

Sala Di Felice, Elena. *Metastasio: Ideologia, drammaturgia, spettacolo*. Milan: Franco Angeli, 1983.

Saloman, Ora Frishberg. "La Cépède's *La poètique de la musique* and Le Sueur." *Acta Musicologica* 47.1 (1975): 144–54.

Sedaine, Michel-Jean. *Richard Coeur de Lion*. Paris: Chez Brunet, 1786.

Seneca. *Medea*. Trans. Moses Hadas. In *Roman Drama*. Indianapolis: Bobbs-Merrill, 1965.

Sévigné, Marie de Rabutin-Chantal, marquise de. *Correspondance*. Ed. Roger Duchêne. 3 vols. Paris: Gallimard, 1972–78.

Silin, Charles I. *Benserade and his Ballets de Cour*. The Johns Hopkins Studies in Romance Literatures and Languages, extra volume xv. Baltimore: The Johns Hopkins University Press, 1940.

Smith, Adam. *The Theory of Moral Sentiments*. Ed. D. D. Raphael and A. L. Macfie. 1976. Indianapolis: Liberty Fund, 1984.

Les Spectacles de Paris, ou Calendrier Historique & Chronologique des théâtres. Paris: Veuve Duchesne, 1782.

Starobinski, Jean. *1789: les emblèmes de la raison*. Paris: Flammarion, 1973.

"Diderot et l'art de la demonstration." *Recherches sur Diderot et sur l'Encyclopédie* 18–19 (1995): 171–90.

Staton, Henry. *Eros in Mourning*. Baltimore: The Johns Hopkins University Press, 1995.

Sterne, Laurence. *The Sermons of Mr. Yorick*. Ed. Wilbur Cross. 2 vols. New York: J. F. Taylor & Co., 1904.

Stewart, Susan. "Lyric Possession." *Critical Inquiry* 22.1 (Autumn 1995): 34–63.

Stonehouse, Alison A. "The Attitude of the French Towards Metastasio as Poet and Dramatist in the Second Half of the Eighteenth Century." Ph.D. dissertation, University of Western Ontario, 1997.

Taruskin, Richard. "Of Kings and Divas: Opera, Politics, and the French Boom." *The New Republic* 209.24 (December 13, 1993): 31–44.

Tasso, Torquato. *Jerusalem Delivered*. Trans. Edward Fairfax. New York: Capricorn Books, [1963].

Tencin, Claudine-Alexandrine Guérin de. *Mémoires du comte de Comminge*. [Paris]: Mercure de France, 1996.

Terrasson, Jean. *Dissertation critique sur l'Iliade d'Homere, où à l'occasion de ce Poëme on cherche les regles d'une Poëtique fondée sur la raison, & sur les exemples des Anciens & des Modernes*. 2 vols. 1715. Geneva: Slatkine, 1971.

Thomas, Downing A. *Music and the Origins of Language: Theories from the French Enlightenment*. Cambridge: Cambridge University Press, 1995.

Thomson, Ann. "Sauvages, barbares, civilisés: L'histoire des sociétés au XVIIIe siècle." In Jean-Louis Chevalier, Mariella Colin and Ann Thomson, eds., *Barbares & sauvages: images et reflets dans la culture occidentale*. Caen: Presses universitaires de Caen, 1993. 79–89.

Todorov, Tzvetan. "Living Alone Together." *New Literary History* 27 (1996): 1–14.

Tomlinson, Gary. *Monteverdi and the End of the Renaissance*. Berkeley: University of California Press, 1987.

  Music in Renaissance Magic: Toward a Historiography of Others. Chicago and London: University of Chicago Press, 1993.

  Metaphysical Song: An Essay on Opera. Princeton: Princeton University Press, 1999.

Truchet, Jacques, ed. *Recherches de thématique théâtrale*. Tübingen: Gunter Narr Verlag, 1981.

Tyard, Pontus de. *Solitaire premier*. Ed. Silvio Baridon. Geneva: Droz, 1950.

  Solitaire second. Ed. Cathy M. Yandell. Geneva: Droz, 1980.

Van Sant, Ann Jessie. *Eighteenth-Century Sensibility and the Novel*. Cambridge: Cambridge University Press, 1993.

Verba, Cynthia. "The Development of Rameau's Thoughts on Modulation and Chromatics." *Journal of the American Musicological Society* 26.1 (1973): 69–91.

——— *Music and the French Enlightenment: Reconstruction of a Dialogue: 1750–1764*. Oxford: Clarendon Press, 1993.

——— "What Recitatives Owe to the Airs: a Look at the Dialogue Scene, Act I scene 2 of Rameau's *Hippolyte et Aricie* – Version with Airs." *Cambridge Opera Journal* 11.2 (1999): 103–34.

Vertron, Claude-Charles Guyonnet de. *Paralèlle de Louis le Grand avec les princes qui ont esté surnommez Grands*. Paris: Le Febvre, 1685.

Vidler, Anthony. *The Writing of the Walls*. Princeton: Princeton Architectural Press, 1987.

——— *Claude-Nicolas Ledoux: Architecture and Social Reform at the End of the Ancien Régime*. Cambridge, Mass.: MIT Press, 1990.

Vila, Anne C. "Beyond Sympathy: Vapors, Melancholia, and the Pathologies of Sensibility in Tissot and Rousseau." *Yale French Studies* 92 (1997): 88–101.

——— *Enlightenment and Pathology: Sensibility in the Literature and Medicine of Eighteenth-Century France*. Baltimore and London: The Johns Hopkins University Press, 1998.

Villégier, Jean-Marie. "*Atys*, une tragédie sans extérieur." *Les Papiers du Collège International de Philosophie* 16 (1992): 17–20.

——— "Musicien dans un paysage de ruines." In *Hippolyte et Aricie*, opera program. Paris: Opéra National de Paris, 1996. 75–82.

Villiers, Pierre de. *Poëmes et autres poësies*. Paris: Jacques Collombat, 1712.

Vincent-Buffault, Anne. *The History of Tears: Sensibility and Sentimentality in France*. Trans. Teresa Bridgeman. New York: St. Martin's Press, 1991.

Vitruvius. *Les Dix livres d'architecture de Vitruve*. Paris: Jean Baptiste Coignard, 1684.

Voltaire. *Les Oeuvres Complètes / The Complete Works*. Ed. Theodore Besterman. Geneva: Institut et Musée Voltaire; Toronto: University of Toronto Press, 1968– .

Wagner, Richard. *Selected Letters of Richard Wagner*. Ed. and trans. Stewart Spencer and Barry Millington. London and Melbourne: J. M. Dent & Sons, 1987.

Wailly, Charles de. "Plan d'aménagement de la place du théâtre français, transformée en aire de rassemblement public, avec gradins et tribune d'orateur" and "Vue perspective de la place de l'Odéon, des gradins et du velum." Project from l'an II [1794]. Bibliothèque-Musée de la Comédie Française, Paris.

Webb, Daniel. *Observations on the Correspondence Between Poetry and Music*. 1769. New York: Garland, 1970.

Weber, Samuel. "Family Scenes: Some Preliminary Remarks on Domesticity and Theatricality." *South Atlantic Quarterly* 98:3 (Summer 1999): 355–66.

Williams, Elizabeth A. *The Physical and the Moral: Anthropology, Physiology, and Philosophical Medicine in France, 1750–1850*. Cambridge: Cambridge University Press, 1994.

Yolton, John W. *Thinking Matter: Materialism in Eighteenth-Century Britain*. Minneapolis: University of Minnesota Press, 1983.

Zanger, Abby E. "The Spectacular Gift: Rewriting the Royal Scenario in Molière's *Les Amants Magnifiques*." *Romanic Review* 81.2 (1990): 173–188.

Zaslaw, Neal. "The first opera in Paris: a study in the politics of art." In John Hajdu Heyer, ed., *Jean-Baptiste Lully and the Music of the French Baroque*. Cambridge: Cambridge University Press, 1989. 7–23.

INDEX